Development, Education and Learning in Sri Lanka

Development, Education and Learning in Sri Lanka

An international research journey

Angela W. Little

First published in 2024 by
UCL Press
University College London
Gower Street
London WC1E 6BT

Available to download free: www.uclpress.co.uk

Text © Author, 2024
Images © Author and copyright holders named in captions, 2024

The author has asserted her right under the Copyright, Designs and Patents Act 1988 to be identified as the author of this work.

A CIP catalogue record for this book is available from The British Library.

Any third-party material in this book is not covered by the book's Creative Commons licence. Details of the copyright ownership and permitted use of third-party material is given in the image (or extract) credit lines. If you would like to reuse any third-party material not covered by the book's Creative Commons licence, you will need to obtain permission directly from the copyright owner.

This book is published under a Creative Commons Attribution-Non-Commercial 4.0 International licence (CC BY-NC 4.0), https://creativecommons.org/licenses/by-nc/4.0/. This licence allows you to share and adapt the work for non-commercial use providing attribution is made to the author and publisher (but not in any way that suggests that they endorse you or your use of the work) and any changes are indicated. Attribution should include the following information:

Little, A. W., 2024. *Development, Education and Learning in Sri Lanka: An international research journey*. London: UCL Press. https://doi.org/10.14324/111.9781800081550

Further details about Creative Commons licences are available at https://creativecommons.org/licenses/

ISBN: 978–1–80008–157–4 (Hbk)
ISBN: 978–1–80008–156–7 (Pbk)
ISBN: 978–1–80008–155–0 (PDF)
ISBN: 978–1–80008–158–1 (epub)
DOI: https://doi.org/10.14324/111.9781800081550

Contents

List of figures, tables and boxes	vii
List of abbreviations and acronyms	ix
Acknowledgements	xi
Introduction	1

Part I: Mapping the journey

Preface to Part I	9
1 Sri Lanka past and present	11
2 Development and education: the international discourse	27
3 Learning from developing countries	53

Part II: Modernisation, human capital and dependency

Preface to Part II	75
4 School examination reforms in the 1970s: modernisation or dependent underdevelopment?	77
5 Human capital, education and development	103
6 The diploma disease	119

Part III: Basic needs and education for all

Preface to Part III	139
7 Education for all, welfare and basic needs: 1931–91	141
8 The 1997 education reforms: origins, political will and implementation	161
9 Behind the scenes: the technical work of planning for 'education for all'	183

Part IV: Globalisation, education and social disparities

Preface to Part IV	205
10 The export-led plantation economy and educational opportunity: 1840–2020	209

11	Late twentieth-century globalisation, education and social disparities	231
12	Globalisation, education and skills: comparing Sri Lanka with elsewhere	255

Part V: Sustainable development and learning

Preface to Part V — 273

13	The teaching of English in the early twenty-first century	277
14	Multi-level teaching in Sri Lanka and elsewhere	289
15	Assessment for sustainable learning and development	309
16	Lessons and reflections	327

References — 349
Index — 367

List of figures, tables and boxes

Figures

3.1	Attributions for success and failure classified by locus, stability and controllability.	56
3.2	Patterns of relationship between assessment-orientation, interest-orientation and significant other-orientation.	64
9.1	The Primary Education Planning Project (PEPP): goal, purpose and activities.	186
14.1	Zones of inclusion in and exclusion from learning.	293

Tables

1.1	Government schools, teachers, students, student-teacher ratio, student-school ratio, adult literacy rate, population: 1950–2021.	26
2.1	Stages of development of primary education.	37
13.1	Hierarchy of on-task and off-task teaching and learning activities, time percentages.	284
14.1	Comparing findings from teaching and learning behaviours, by schools and training of teachers.	301
15.1	Student assessment surveys – international, regional and foundational skills.	313

Boxes

15.1	Example of an error diagnosis.	323
15.2	Example of remediation plan.	324

List of abbreviations and acronyms

ABL	activity-based learning
ASER	Annual Status of Education Report (India)
BNA	basic needs approach
CAS	Ceylon Administrative Service
CCS	Ceylon Civil Service
CWC	Ceylon Workers' Congress
DSD	Divisional Schools Development
EFA	education for all
EGMA	Early Grade Mathematics Assessment
EGRA	Early Grade Reading Assessment
EN	Escuela Nueva (Colombian education programme)
ERIU	Education Reforms Implementation Unit
GCE A	General Certificate of Education Advanced level
GCE O	General Certificate of Education Ordinary level
GDP	Gross Domestic Product
GNP	Gross National Product
HC	human capital
HCA	human capabilities approach
HCI	Human Capital Index
HCM	human capital and modernisation (approach)
HDI	Human Development Index
HNCE	Higher National Certificate of Education
HPAE	High Performing Asian Economy
ICT	information and communications technology
ILO	International Labour Organization
ISD	Improvement of Schools by Division
ISI	import substitution industrialisation
JVP	Janatha Vimukthi Peramuna (People's Liberation Front)
LLECE	Laboratorio Latinamericano de Evaluatión de la Calidad de la Educatión
MDGs	Millennium Development Goals
MGML	multi-grade multi-level (teaching approach)
ML	multi-level (teaching approach)
MOE	Ministry of Education
MPPE	Master Plan for Primary Education

NALO	national assessment of learning outcomes
NAM	Non-Aligned Movement
NATO	North American Treaty Organization
NCGE	National Certificate of General Education
NEC	National Education Commission
NER	net enrolment rate
NEREC	National Educational Research and Evaluation Centre
NIE	National Institute of Education
NMD	neo-Marxist and dependency (theory)
OECD	Organisation for Economic Co-operation and Development
PASEC	Programme for the Analysis of Education Systems
PEPP	Primary Education Planning Project
PISA	Programme for International Student Assessment
PPT	provincial planning team
PTF	Presidential Task Force
RIVER	Rishi Valley Institute for Educational Resources
SACMEQ	Southern and Eastern Africa Consortium for Monitoring Educational Quality
SDGs	Sustainable Development Goals
SLFP	Sri Lanka Freedom Party
TEVT	technical education and vocational training
TIMSS	Trends in International Mathematics and Science Study
UN	United Nations
UNDP	United Nations Development Programme
UNESCO	United Nations Educational, Scientific and Cultural Organization
UNICEF	United Nations Children's Fund
UNP	United National Party
USAID	United States Agency for International Development
UWEZO	Education Programme of Twaweza East Africa (Swahili word: capability)
VNEN	Vietnam Escuela Nueva Programme

Acknowledgements

I would like to thank the many people who have accompanied me on my international research journey through *Development, Education and Learning in Sri Lanka*.

They have contributed to my knowledge about Sri Lanka in so many ways – through joint fieldwork, analysis and writing, through assisting me in meeting policymakers, politicians and practitioners at every level of the education system, arranging access to myriad schools, classrooms, homes, communities and offices, and through the sharing of their research and knowledge. They have also provided opportunities to share my research with a wide range of people – from academics to policymakers and implementors, education officers, teachers, religious leaders, trade union staff, politicians, and those who work in international cooperation agencies. Throughout, I have been offered friendship, hospitality and advice that smoothed the journey and of a kind I have been unable to reciprocate fully.

They include, but are not limited to, the following: Felicia Adihetty, Pat Alailima, Harsha Aturupane, Buchand Baidya, Jayantha Balasooriya, Daela Bandara, Sunil Bastian, John Bowles, Andy Brock, Nigel Brooke, Priya Cabraal, Paul Casperz, Jonas Cels, Tara Coomaraswamy, Tara de Mel, Ariya de Silva, Eric de Silva, Priyan Dias, Ronald Dore, Cyril Edirisighe, Jane Evans, Nishara Fernando, George Gnanamuttu, Andy Green, Vince Greaney, Chandra Gunawardene, G. B. Gunawardene, Lalitha Gunawardene, Eve Hadshar, Ray Harris, David Hayes, Kamal Herath, Siri Hettige, Upul Indika, Daya Jayasinghe, J. E. Jayasuriya, S. Jayatilleke, Swarna Jayaweera, Kumari Jayewardene, James Jennings, Sangeeta Kamat, Sunderi Kariyawasam, Charles Kemp, Elsie Kotalawala, Peter Kutnick, Keith Lewin, John Lowe, Sugath Mallawaarachchi, P. P. Manikam, Emma Mba, Byron T. Mook, Mick Moore, R. Murugesu, Mahen Muttiah, G. L. S. Nanayakkara, C. Navaratne, Liz Nissan, Moses Oketch, John Oxenham, Gowry Palaniappan, Wimela Palihakkara, Asoka Pandithasekere, Kamala Peiris, Rohanti Perera, Stirling Perera, Wilfred Perera, M. D. D. Pieris, Sirome Rajaratnam, Vijayanandan Ramanathan, Caine Rolleston, Gunilla Rosengart, Tiziana Rossetto, S. Rupasinghe, Ricardo Sabates, V. K. Samaranayake, S. Sandarasegaram, Jouko Sarvi, Jorgen Schønning, Priyanthi Sepalika, Marie Shojo, Mohamed Sibli,

Muthu Sivagnanam, R. Sivasithambaram, Upul Sonnadara, Jock Stirrat, Edward Vickers, Thilini Vithanachchi, Manjula Vithanapathirana, Dilly Weerarathne, Madura Wehella, Clive Whitehead, E. L. Wijemanne, Subarshinie Wijesundara, and Swarna Wijetunge.

I am grateful for financial support from various sources, including the Nuffield Foundation, the Leverhulme Foundation, the UK Government Overseas Development Administration and Department for International Development, the UK Global Challenges Research Fund, the Swedish International Development Authority, Deutsche Gesellschaft für Technische Zusammenarbeit, UNICEF and the World Bank. I am also very grateful for the time afforded by my home institutions to undertake this research – the Institute of Development Studies at the University of Sussex and the UCL Institute of Education, London.

This book would not have been completed without exemplary support from the entire UCL Press team. Thank you for your patience and meticulous work.

Sources

Chapters 1, 2, 12, 14 and 16 are newly written for this book. Chapter 3 is an edited version of my inaugural professorial lecture (Little, 1988). Chapter 4 is based on new material and edited sections of an Institute of Development Studies discussion paper co-authored with Keith M. Lewin (Lewin & Little, 1984). Chapter 5 is based on new material and edited sections of a previously published article (Little, 1980), and on research undertaken jointly with Jasbir Sarjit Singh (Little & Singh, 1992). It is also derived in part from an article published in *Compare: A Journal of Comparative and International Education* © 2003 Taylor & Francis Ltd (available online: https://www.tandfonline.com/doi/10.1080/0969594970040105, reprinted with permission). Chapter 6 is based on new material and is derived in part from an article published in *Assessment in Education: Principles, Policy & Practice* © 1997 Taylor & Francis Ltd (available online: https://www.tandfonline.com/doi/10.1080/0969594970040105, reprinted with permission). Chapters 7 and 8 are based on new material and edited sections of a monograph produced within the work of the Consortium for Research on Educational Access, Transitions and Equity (Little, 2010, 2011). Chapter 9 is based on an edited section of Little 2003b. Chapter 10 is based on new material and edited sections of Little 1987b and 1999b. Chapter 11 is based on new material and edited sections of research co-authored with Siri Hettige

(Little & Hettige, 2013), reproduced by permission of Taylor & Francis Group and published under a CC-BY-NC-ND Creative Commons License. Chapter 13 is based on new material and edited sections of a paper co-authored with Mari Shojo, Upul Sonnadara and Harsha Aturupane published in *Language, Culture and Curriculum* © 2018 Taylor & Francis Ltd (available online: https://www.tandfonline.com/doi/10.1080/07908318.2018.1532437, reprinted with permission). Chapter 15 is based on new material and edited sections of Little 2018.

Permissions from co-authors and publishers for re-use of material are gratefully acknowledged. No part of this book has been created through Artificial Intelligence software.

Introduction

I suspect that my career, like that of many of yours, has been punctuated by a series of identities developed across several contexts. From being a school student on the small independent Isle of Man in the middle of the Irish sea, I 'crossed the water' in 1968 to England, to become a university student of the social sciences. From England I journeyed to Nigeria as a volunteer teacher of mathematics and science, returning to my island slowly via North Africa and Europe, and wondering where my next journey would lead. After a short spell working as a volunteer in the Isle of Man's only school for children with 'physical and mental handicaps', I landed somewhat serendipitously at the Institute of Development Studies at the University of Sussex on a short-term research contract. I then trained as a primary school teacher in England, before returning to the Institute to work on a long-term research programme on 'Labour market backwash and the quality of education in developing countries'.

During this time, I made my first of many journeys to Sri Lanka for what would become a lifetime of work. In 1987 I moved to the established Chair of Education ('with special reference to Developing Countries', as it was named at that time) at the Institute of Education, University of London. This position enabled me to establish formal relations with research institutions, researchers and students, including Sri Lankans, many of which continue, albeit more informally, to the present day. This book provides glimpses of my Sri Lankan research undertaken between 1975 and 2020, a period during which much has changed in Sri Lanka, in the 'international development community', in the world at large, and in the field of study of development and education.

Formerly known as Ceylon, Sri Lanka became well known among the international development community for her performance in education, literacy, health, and other indicators of human development.

This book is about development, education and learning in Sri Lanka. It comprises a collection of new and edited writings compiled over almost fifty years of engagement with the Sri Lankan research community. It discusses ideas, policies and practices in Sri Lanka in relation to those that have circulated in the international development discourse over the past eighty years. Some ideas, policies and practices have been inspired by that international discourse, while others have inspired it. Still others have remained firmly rooted in Sri Lankan soil.

The book explores changing fortunes and inequalities in education. It delineates the distinctive and changing features of the Sri Lankan education system through comparisons with systems elsewhere, through an understanding of national political, economic and social conditions, crises and upheavals, through changes in education policy and through shifting patterns of opportunity among diverse social groups. Empirical analyses are framed by concepts and theories from the international development discourse, ranging from modernisation to basic needs to globalisation and sustainable development and post-colonialism.

Three broad questions run through the book. Which ideas, policies and practices in Sri Lanka have been influenced by the international development discourse? Conversely, which ideas, policies and practices in the international discourse have been influenced by Sri Lankan ideas, policies and practices? And to what extent have ideas drawn from the international discourse been tested empirically in the Sri Lankan context?

The book is organised in five parts. Part I – Mapping the journey – offers the reader a set of sketch maps to assist with an orientation to Sri Lanka, to concepts and theories of development and education, and to my own position in and aspirations for the field of study of development and education, as expressed in the mid-1980s. Chapter 1 – Sri Lanka past and present – introduces the reader to the Sri Lankan education system and its distinctiveness. It describes the cultural and linguistic diversity of the peoples of Sri Lanka and their longstanding traditions in education, and outlines a series of policies and achievements in education from the colonial period, through the transition to independence in 1948, and on to more recent times. Chapter 2 – Development and education: the international discourse – offers a stroll through the major concepts and theories of development and education, with a focus on the post-Second World War period. It addresses the meanings of 'development' and 'underdevelopment' through ideas, policies and practices clustered around the themes of modernisation, human capital, dependency, basic needs, education for all, neo-liberalism and structural adjustment, globalisation, sustainable development and post-colonialism. It offers some clues to the answer to the first broad question above: Which ideas, policies and practices in Sri Lanka have been influenced by the international development discourse? Chapter 3 – Learning from developing countries – is the text of my inaugural professorial lecture delivered in 1988. Based on empirical research conducted up to that time, it calls for refinements to Western education theory to reflect the grounded realities of 'developing countries', offers a model for collaborative education research, and suggests that 'developed' countries may have something to learn from the ideas, policies and practices of education in 'developing' countries.

Part II – Modernisation, human capital and dependency – applies concepts from human capital, modernisation and dependency to Sri Lankan education policies and employment practices from the 1970s to the 1990s. It addresses aspects of the third broad question above: To what extent have ideas drawn from the international discourse been tested empirically in the Sri Lankan context? Chapter 4 – School examination reforms in the 1970s – assesses the adequacy of perspectives from human capital and modernisation theory on the one hand, and neo-Marxist and dependency theory on the other, to explain two major school examination reforms, the first in 1972 and the second in 1977. Chapter 5 – Human capital, education and development – applies human capital ideas about education, productivity and earnings to workplaces in the Sri Lankan public and private sectors during the 1970s, and explores whether and when the concept of human capital appeared in Sri Lanka's policy research discourse. Chapter 6 – The diploma disease – employs the concept of 'late development' to build a critique of human capital and offers an alternative thesis, inspired by the Sri Lankan context of the early 1970s, known as 'the diploma disease'. Five propositions of this thesis are examined through an analysis of education in Sri Lanka from the 1970s to the 1990s.

Part III – Basic needs and education for all – employs a different approach. Rather than applying concepts to the Sri Lankan context, the chapters in this part explore the history of education policy development in Sri Lanka from the 1930s through to the early 2000s, and provide some answers to the second question above: Which ideas, policies and practices in the international discourse have been influenced by Sri Lankan ideas, policies and practices? Chapter 7 – Education for all, welfare and basic needs: 1931–91 – describes the course of Sri Lankan politics from the 1930s and the design of policies created to promote the principle of 'equality of educational opportunity'. By the 1980s, Sri Lanka's impressive performance in literacy and enrolment was being mentioned frequently by international development economists who promoted development strategies of basic needs, redistribution with growth and human development. Chapter 8 – The 1997 education reforms: origins, political will and implementation – demonstrates the political underpinnings of education policy reform. In contrast with the reforms of the 1940s, which were mainly driven by the politics of independence, the reforms of the 1990s arose in response to the political turmoil, insurrections and civil war of the 1980s. Both sets of reforms underlined the role of 'political will' in creating and implementing policy reforms. Chapter 9 is more practice oriented. It invites the reader to look 'behind the scenes' at activities that go hand in hand with the political cut and thrust of policy debate and formulation – the nuts-and-bolts work of education 'planning'. While often thought of as a purely technical exercise, this account of the educational planning work that followed the formulation of Sri Lanka's 1997 education reforms will illustrate the influence of politics on planners.

Part IV – Globalisation, education and social disparities – explores direct and indirect links between globalisation, education and social disparities. Chapter 10 – The export-led plantation economy and educational opportunity: 1840–2020 – begins its story in the nineteenth century, when globalisation was expressed in colonial ideas, policies and practices of export-led coffee, tea and rubber plantations. While the influence of the plantation economy on the educational opportunities of the majority of those who worked within the plantations was limited, the revenues they generated enabled the colonial and early post-colonial governments to fund educational opportunities for those who lived beyond the plantations to a greater extent than was found within. Chapter 11 – Late twentieth-century globalisation, education and social disparities – explores the links between twentieth-century globalisation, education and social equality through shifts in economic and education policies, labour markets, skill requirements, education, training and qualification provision, and public, private and 'internationalised' education, training and qualification provision. Chapter 12 – Globalisation, education and skills: comparing Sri Lanka with elsewhere – offers an analysis of economic, political and educational developments among countries in the Asia region whose development successes in the late twentieth and early twenty-first centuries have far outstripped those of Sri Lanka – the country that in the mid-twentieth century had offered a development model worthy of emulation.

Part V – Sustainable development and learning – invites the reader to consider the concept of sustainable development, which pervades much of the contemporary international development discourse in the countries of the 'North' as well as those of the 'South'. Three recent pieces of research – on the learning of English (Chapter 13), the grouping of learners for learning (Chapter 14), and the summative and formative assessment of learning (Chapter 15) – focus on the learners who lie at the heart of 'sustainable development', and a consideration of what they are learning, how they are learning, whether they are learning, and whether they are likely to sustain their learning into the future. I suggest that sustainable development is as much about sustainable personal development and sustainable learning as it is about environment, society and economy. Finally, in Chapter 16, I reflect on what I have learned from development and education in Sri Lanka, revisit the efficacy of some of Sri Lanka's exceptionalisms in education, revisit international development and education concepts in the light of Sri Lankan experience, and comment on recent proposals for education reform. Chapters are self-contained and may be read in any order. The order presented in the book reflects broad shifts in the international discourse on development and education.

The book's overriding messages are the need to understand education and development in a country's own terms, and the need to place learning at the heart of education policy, situating it within broader conceptions of the purpose, values and means of development.

Part I
Mapping the journey

Preface to Part I

The chapters in the first part of this book offer the reader a set of maps to help them follow my international research journey. These maps orient the reader to Sri Lankan education and its peoples, to concepts and theories of development and education, and to my own position and aspirations for the field of study of development and education, as expressed in the mid-1980s. Chapter 1 offers a snapshot of the education system of today, along with a brief survey of pre-colonial, colonial and post-colonial education traditions. The distinctiveness of the system is described through seven 'exceptionalisms', comprising historically strong performance, gender parity, mother tongue education from kindergarten to university, fee-free government provision from kindergarten to university, a very small private education sector, a long span of non-selective education, and a small proportion of government expenditure on education. Alongside education the reader is introduced to the country, its peoples, its changing political, societal and economic conditions and relations with the rest of the world, and the main changes in and drivers of education policy from the nineteenth century to the present day.

Chapter 2 surveys the international literature on development and education, the changing meanings of 'development', the theoretical relations between development and education, and the rapidly changing and politically sensitive terms used to describe the development status of a country or groups of countries. It offers a survey of the main international development and education approaches adopted by the international development community since the end of the Second World War. These approaches include 'development' as economic growth, as modernisation, as the fulfilment of basic needs, as human development and as sustainable development, most of which development ends are achieved, in part, through the means of education and the development of human capital. Alongside these approaches are those that focus on 'underdevelopment', defined as economic underdevelopment, dependency, cultural alienation and neo/post-colonialism. In these approaches, education curricula, language policies and inequities in access to high-quality schooling are implicated in the reproduction of underdevelopment.

Chapter 3 is my inaugural professorial lecture – 'Learning from developing countries' – delivered at the Institute of Education, University of London in March 1988, a few months after I took up my professorship. In it I take stock of development and education at that time, including some of my own research up to that point. I employ concepts of learning, educating and pedagogy to reflect on the broader processes then current of knowledge transfer between 'developed' and 'developing' countries. I call for greater voice to be given to researchers and educators well-grounded in the societal, cultural and economic context of specific countries and for more equal knowledge creation and exchange on the North-South knowledge superhighway.

1
Sri Lanka past and present

Throughout the 1980s many members of the international development community regarded Sri Lanka as a 'development model'. Here was a low-income country that appeared to have achieved much in education, health and 'human development'. Ceylon, as Sri Lanka was known until 1972, was regarded as the 'senior colony of the Empire' and a constitutional pioneer – one of the first colonies to have a jury system, to grant universal franchise and to establish a Western-style democracy (D. L. Jayasuriya, 2001).

Following a visit in the 1950s, Lee Kwan Yew, shortly to become Singapore's first prime minister, was of the opinion that Sri Lanka was Britain's model Commonwealth country and a developing country worthy of emulation (Yew, 2000). In 1960 the literacy rate in Singapore was 57 per cent and in Sri Lanka 72 per cent. By the turn of the millennium fortunes had changed, the relative positions of Sri Lanka and Singapore on a range of development indices had reversed, and Sri Lanka was now looking to Singapore and other countries in the Asia region for strategies for successful development.

Today's system of education

Today's system of education in Sri Lanka bears similarities with the characteristics of education systems worldwide. The general education system comprises 13 grade levels which students enter at age 5+. The 13 grades are divided into four stages: primary (Grades 1–5), junior secondary (Grades 6–9), senior secondary (Grades 10–11) and collegiate (Grades 12–13). In 2020, around 4.4 million students, taught by almost 250,000 teachers, were enrolled in 11,091 government schools (91.5 per cent), pirivenas (monastic colleges) (7.4 per cent), government-approved private schools (0.8 per cent) and special schools (0.27 per cent). The majority of government-funded schools are managed at the provincial level. A minority (3.7 per cent) are managed centrally and are known as national schools or, more colloquially, 'popular' schools.

A further 395 schools, with an estimated total enrolment of 143,000 students, are described as 'international schools': private schools that fall beyond the purview of the Ministry of Education (NEC, 2022). In addition, madrasa schools registered with the Department of Muslim Religious and Cultural Affairs offer supplementary classes in religious education to students, most of whom also attend a government school during the daytime. Supplementary classes in a range of subjects are offered through an extensive array of unregulated private tuition arrangements for students of all ages (Aturupane & Little, 2020).

There are three academic selection points and public examinations. The first is the Grade 5 exam, which children sit at the end of their primary education to seek admission to the national or 'popular' schools. The second is the General Certificate of Education (GCE) Ordinary level (O level) subject exams at the end of Grade 11, the results of which influence decisions about GCE Advanced Level (A level) course enrolment, vocational course enrolment and employment. The third is GCE A level subject exams at Grade 13, which determine access to diverse types of higher education and employment.

School curricula, textbooks and exams are controlled and created by the National Institute of Education, the Department of Educational Publications and the Department of Examinations, respectively. Teachers are trained through a variety of programmes offered by the universities, colleges of education, the National Institute of Education and teacher training colleges. Training is offered face-to-face and through a 'blend' of face-to-face/online/paper-based media.

Approximately half of all children aged 3–4 years access early childhood education programmes. As in other countries, this provision is offered mainly by the private sector. At the opposite end of the system, tertiary education is offered by the universities, degree-awarding institutions, professional education institutions, and vocational and technical training. There are currently 17 universities under the authority of the University Grants Commission. Six other universities operate under other ministries. A further 25 institutes and colleges, mostly private, have degree-awarding powers. The Organisation of Professional Associations of Sri Lanka comprises 51 member associations and 32 fields of professional practice. Many of these offer professional education and certification, some of which are linked directly with foreign education and certification bodies. Technical and vocational education caters mainly to male and female youth aged 15–29 years, among whom are school leavers, workers with experience, returnees from overseas work and those seeking to upgrade their skills. In any one year, approximately 140,000 young people are enrolled in public training institutions and 50,000 enrol in registered private institutions (NEC, 2018). A National Vocational Qualification System provides the framework for seven levels of qualification, including degree-level education and qualifications at universities and degree-awarding institutes.

Sri Lanka's exceptionalisms in education

While several of the characteristics of Sri Lanka's education system described above bear similarities to those of many systems around the world, the Sri Lankan system is distinct in several respects. The first is historically high performance in literacy and other measures of human development. At the time of political independence in 1948 the literacy rate was already 58 per cent, while that in her nearest neighbour, India, was just 19 per cent in 1950. As early as 1901 the literacy rate was estimated to be 26 per cent. Sri Lanka's post-independence record of increasing rates of literacy and declining infant mortality was one of the reasons why the international community came to regard Sri Lanka as a 'poster child' for development – a 'development darling'. Following the granting of universal suffrage as early as 1931 and its exercise during elections in 1931 and 1936, a welfare state emerged to protect the poor through, *inter alia*, 'equality of education opportunity' designed, in principle, to promote upward social mobility in an otherwise class-, ethnic- and caste-stratified society (Alailima, 1991).

A second exceptionalism is Sri Lanka's record on gender and education. At independence in 1948 the gender gap in adult literacy rates was marked: 70 per cent for males and 44 per cent for females. By 2001 the gap had closed to 93 per cent for males and 90 per cent for females – a gap reduction that can be traced to steady improvements in female school enrolment ratios. Already by the early 1960s there was gender parity in primary school level enrolments, and by the 1980s parity had been achieved at secondary level too. Nowadays, girls in Sri Lanka outnumber boys in junior and senior secondary education and in all university-level subjects, bar engineering.

A third exceptionalism is the language of instruction and the availability of education in the mother tongue from kindergarten to university. Prior to independence, an English-medium education was the privilege of the upper and middle classes, who could afford to pay fees. Following independence, the fee-paying and largely English-medium denominational schools were nationalised, and all students were educated from Grade 1 to university in either Sinhala, the language of the majority, or Tamil, the language of the minority. Few countries in the Asia region offer minority-group children the opportunity to study from kindergarten to university in their mother tongue.

A fourth exceptionalism is fee-free provision of primary, secondary and university education in government institutions. During the British colonial period, no fees were charged in the vernacular schools and school fees in the fee-charging government schools were abolished in the 1940s. At the primary and secondary levels there are additional financial subsidies, including free provision of textbooks, uniforms, subsidised travel and meals.

A fifth exceptionalism is the small size of the private sector. The majority of students attend fee-free government schools, with only a small minority enrolled in private fee-paying institutions (estimated to be 3 per cent in government-approved private schools and 3.2 per cent in international schools). Several of the most prestigious schools are the fee-free government schools. In recent years, private provision has expanded in the tertiary sector, in part through arrangements with foreign universities, but Sri Lankan universities remain nationally funded and fee-free.

A sixth exceptionalism is the open-access nature of the system. Although there is a public exam at the end of Grade 5 (primary stage of education), this serves only, though no less importantly, to select students for the 'popular' or prestigious national schools. All students proceed to Grade 6 and enjoy open, fee-free access to Grade 11. In its most recent five-year plan for education 2021–5, the government reaffirmed its commitment to guarantee and enforce fee-free access to 13 years of formal education. A phased implementation of this plan began in 2016 (Ministry of Education, 2020).

These achievements in literacy, enrolment, mother-tongue education and fee-free provision are all the more remarkable in light of the seventh exceptionalism: a declining level of public investment in education over time. Public expenditure on education as a proportion of GDP has been declining since independence. It averaged 3.1 per cent during the 1950s, 4.2 per cent in the 1960s, 3.5 per cent in the 1970s and

3 per cent in the 1980s. By 2010 the figure was around 2.0 per cent. This was the lowest percentage out of 42 countries in East Asia and the Pacific, bar Myanmar (Little, Aturupane & Shojo, 2013). South Korea, Vietnam, Malaysia and Thailand were spending between 5.0 and 6.6 per cent on education (UNESCO, 2011). Public expenditure on education as a proportion of all public expenditure is also exceedingly low – around 10 per cent compared with an average of 17.3 per cent across all low- and middle-income countries (Dundar et al., 2017).

As we shall see in subsequent chapters, Sri Lanka's exceptional achievements in education have occurred through the introduction and implementation of a series of policies within a populist political agenda of social egalitarianism and the emergence of the post-independence state. But first, let us step back in time to understand something of the diversity of the country's people and history.

An island's people

It is customary for authors writing for a global audience to introduce Sri Lanka as an island nation located in South Asia with a population of around 22 million (2020), lying in the Indian Ocean and separated from her nearest neighbour, India, by the Gulf of Mannar and the narrow Palk Strait. 'Island nations' are sometimes thought of as places disconnected from elsewhere and their peoples independent and self-sufficient. Sri Lanka is by no means an 'island nation' in this sense. The country has been at a 'crossroads' of peoples, of trade, of cultures, of ideas and of knowledge systems since time immemorial (Bandaranayake, 1990; Hayhoe & Pan, 2001; Little, 2003a; Biedermann & Strathern, 2017).

Sri Lanka's connections with the rest of the world were not simply vested in the exchange of goods. They were vested in movements of people, language and religion in ways that have rendered the Sri Lanka of today ethnically, linguistically and culturally diverse. The vast majority of Sri Lanka's people – Sinhalese and Tamils – migrated to and settled the island by land and sea thousands of years ago, at a time when a small and now-almost-extinct group, the Veddas, formed the indigenous population. The precise history of these settler waves is contested – but they are certainly of long standing. The majority of today's population, the Sinhalese, trace their roots in Sri Lanka to the semi-legendary king, Prince Vijaya, who is said to have landed on the island with his followers around the fifth century BCE. The Sri Lanka Tamils (also known as Ceylon Tamils and Eelam Tamils), who form a significant minority, trace their settlement roots to at least the second or third centuries BCE. The Sinhalese and Sri Lankan Tamil populations currently stand at 74.7 per cent and 11.2 per cent respectively of the total population of almost 22 million (Department of Census and Statistics, 2021).

The geographical origin of the first Sinhalese settlers is contested. Some claim that they arrived from the present-day Indian states of Odisha, Jharkhand, Northern Andhra Pradesh, Bengal or Bihar, while others trace their origins to Malaya or even Singapore. The geographical origin of the Tamil settlers is generally agreed to lie in the south-east of India, mainly in the present-day Indian state of Tamil Nadu. The languages and scripts of the Sinhalese and Tamil people reflect these different origins. Sinhala is an Indo-Aryan language influenced by Pali and Sanskrit, and Tamil is a Dravidian language. The formal written forms of both languages date back to the second to fifth centuries BCE. The predominant religions of the Sinhalese and Tamils are Buddhism and Hinduism respectively, with significant numbers of Christians in both groups.

The third most populous group are the Sri Lankan Moors, who comprise 9.2 per cent of the population. The ancestry of the Moors is diverse. Some trace their roots to intermarriage between Arab or Indian traders with Sinhalese or Tamil women stretching back nine hundred years; another group, sometimes referred to as Indian Moors, arrived from India during the British colonial period in search of business opportunities. Tamil is usually their first language, and many speak Sinhala as a second language. The majority follow the religion of Islam.

A much later wave of migration from Tamil Nadu occurred in the nineteenth century, during British rule. The Indian Tamils were brought to work originally in the coffee (and subsequently tea and rubber) plantations. Like the Sri Lanka Tamils, they trace their roots to the present-day state of Tamil Nadu, they speak Tamil and are mainly Hindus. Their inherited caste status was and is generally lower than that of the Sri Lanka Tamils. They currently comprise 4.2 per cent of the population – a significant decline from 11 per cent at the time of independence. The reason for this decline and the story of educational growth among this population will be addressed in Chapter 10.

Smaller population groups include the Sri Lanka Malays (0.2 per cent), who arrived in successive waves of migration. A first wave is claimed to have settled around 200 BCE. During a second wave, Malay speakers from Indonesia were brought to the island by the Dutch and from Malaya by the British. The Burgher people comprise a small Eurasian group, descended from intermarriages between Portuguese,

Dutch or British men and Sri Lankan women. The percentage of Burghers in the population declined over the years and many migrated to Australia and Canada.

The island's maritime trade

For the people who live near Sri Lanka's coast, the sea has provided sustenance over centuries. Sri Lanka's maritime location and deep natural harbours have rendered her of great strategic importance to traders from beyond her shores – an importance that endures to the present day. Lying almost in the centre of the Indian Ocean, she was a key port of call on the ancient navigational and maritime trading routes that connected East Africa, the Middle East, South-East Asia and China.

Trade became entwined with foreign political domination during the first wave of European colonisation. The Portuguese were the first to control trade through political domination (1505–1658), followed by the Dutch (1658–1796). Both colonised the littoral (coastal) areas. The British displaced the Dutch in the coastal areas from 1798 and extended their control over the entire island, known then as Ceylon, from 1815. Trincomalee, on the east coast, provided the home port of the Eastern Fleet of the British Royal Navy and for submarines and flying boats of the Dutch Navy.

Maritime trade was further strengthened from the 1830s through the British colonial government's 'export-led' economic strategy. Coffee plantations, followed by tea and rubber plantations, were established to grow and export agricultural products to Britain and the rest of the world. This was an example of a 'classic commodity export strategy' which integrated sections of the economy in an emerging global capitalist system. A 'modern' sector comprised plantations, transport and communications, external trade and public administration; and a 'traditional' sector comprised peasant agriculture, small-scale fishing, cottage industries and a range of informal service activities. Flows of labour to work on the plantations came from the south of India and flows of finance capital came from Britain (Snodgrass, 1966). Coffee, tea and rubber were the 'engines' of economic growth. The plantation sector rode out the world economic depression of the 1930s. With its trade to GDP ratio of over 70 per cent, the economy was, at independence in 1948, well integrated in a global trading system, in contrast to neighbouring India where the ratio was just 15 per cent (S. Jayasuriya, 2005). Godfrey Gunatilleke, one of Sri Lanka's foremost economists, explains how, with a strong 'balance of payments' and government surplus, Sri Lanka was able to maintain expenditure on social welfare, including education and health, enabling her people to enjoy a standard of living among the highest in the South and South-East Asian countries (Gunatilleke, 1974, 2018).

A national political movement, starting in the early twentieth century, resulted in independence from British rule in 1948 and the creation of Ceylon as a dominion within the British Commonwealth. The dominion became a Republic in 1972, was renamed Sri Lanka, and remained within the Commonwealth. Sri Lanka's geographical position has continued to be strategic, with successive trade and political alliances swinging between the West, the North, the South and the East. The new twenty-first-century silk route – otherwise known as the 'Belt and Road' initiative of the Chinese – has cemented Chinese trade with Sri Lanka. China today is also a major player in the political economy of the island. The operations of the port of Hambantota, strategically positioned on the south coast, are now controlled by the Chinese government on a long lease (the Chinese having foreclosed on massive loans to the Sri Lankan government, which had defaulted on its loan repayments).

Settler and colonial roots of education

Trade, migrations and invasions lead to the circulation of ideas, language, religion and education. The circulation of ideas does not guarantee their absorption into 'local' culture, however. They may be rejected, adopted, adapted or completely transformed (Steiner-Khamsi, 2004; Biedermann & Strathern, 2017). In this section I outline some of these 'borrowings' and fusions in relation to education.

Early settlers

Formal education has a long history in Sri Lanka. Temple and village schools within the Buddhist and Hindu traditions, and maktabs and madrasas in the Islamic tradition, were established by the early settlers, long before the arrival of the European colonisers. For centuries, the purpose of Buddhist, Hindu and Muslim educational provision was religious. It was designed to inculcate values and 'civilised' behaviour – a mission common to most education systems found around the world. A superior layer of education produced future religious leaders for the temples and mosques, while an inferior layer provided for the common man.

In the superior schools, secular subjects were also studied (Rahula, 1956; Gunawardana, 1979; J. E. Jayasuriya, 1969). Examinations formed an integral part of these early systems of education. For example, in the Buddhist temple schools, student progress was managed through learning assessments conducted by superiors. Three levels of attainment (*nissaya*) – *samucchanaka, parisupathapaka* and *bhikkunovalaka* – were based on the successful memorisation of Buddhist texts (Rahula, 1956). Monks specialising in studies of the canon were rewarded materially, with particularly high reward being given to those who studied the texts on the *Abhidharma*. Knowledgeable monks could gain promotion within the social hierarchy of the monastery over more senior but less sagacious colleagues. King Uddaya (797–801) awarded bronze bowls to monks who studied meritoriously. Laymen who successfully followed courses in Buddhism gained paid employment in temples and monasteries (Gunawardana, 1979).

European settlers

The European colonisers brought Christianity and their 'civilising mission' with them. These religions included the Catholicism of the Portuguese, the Protestantism of the Dutch Reformed Church, and the Anglicanism, Methodism, Baptist and other Protestant religions of the British. The civilising of the population through conversion to Christianity was the major rationale for the establishment of schools.

During a first wave of European colonisation, the Portuguese established an extensive network of parish schools linked with the Catholic churches in the coastal areas. The schools were, in principle, open to all children, who were taught in the language of Sinhala or Tamil. The Jesuits and Franciscans established and ran a superior layer of secondary schools and colleges for a small minority. The language of instruction was Sinhala or Tamil, and Portuguese and Latin were taught as language subjects (Ruberu, 1962). Buddhist, Hindu and Islamic schools were officially discouraged during this period, but some survived.

The Dutch displaced the Portuguese in 1658 and continued the Portuguese tradition of promoting religious conversion through education. Determined to destroy the 'influence of Popery' and maintain the safety of the Dutch themselves, a new network of Protestant Dutch Reformed churches with associated parish schools was established (J. E. Jayasuriya, 1979; Ruberu, 1962). Like the Portuguese schools before them, the medium of instruction was either Sinhala or Tamil. A parish teacher was required to profess the Protestant faith. His role was extensive and included registering births and marriages and transacting property rights. School attendance was compulsory up to the age of 15, enforced through a system of fines. The study of Dutch, Latin, Greek and Hebrew was undertaken at the Colombo seminary for those destined to become teachers and preachers. The Dutch relied on 'native officials' for local administration and perpetuated the system of social status amongst the population based on caste (Wickremaratne, 1973, p. 165).

If the role of education in determining social status was relatively weak during the Dutch period, it would become much stronger during the period of British rule (1796–1948). The early years of British rule were confined, like the Portuguese and Dutch periods, to coastal areas. Political stability and the subsequent establishment of an export economy was the major concern. The British were less concerned with the promotion of social welfare through education – a lack of concern that reflected the laissez-faire approach to education in England at that time.

British colonial education policy

In a detailed account of British colonial education policy, J. E. Jayasuriya (1979) explores myriad policy changes over time, each subject to pressures from different social groups. During the early British colonial period, and as a result of pressure from parish schoolmasters employed by the Dutch, the government rehabilitated the parish schools. This was a time when government funding for education was not the norm back in England. Roman Catholics were permitted to start or restart schools that had been banned by the Dutch. In the parish schools the medium of instruction was the vernacular (Sinhala or Tamil), and English was not taught as a subject. The Colombo Academy and preparatory 'feeder' schools were established to promote the Anglican religion and prepare young men – usually of high-caste Sinhalese, Tamil and Dutch Burgher background – for colonial government service and positions in the Anglican church. These young men were taught through the medium of English, and English was also a subject of study.

In 1812 Governor Brownrigg, a religious conversion enthusiast, encouraged the Protestant missions and their schools. By 1830 there were five layers of educational provision: (i) government schools, comprising the Colombo Academy, associated preparatory schools and parish schools; (ii) mission schools (Baptist, Wesleyan, American and Anglican); (iii) private schools; (iv) Roman Catholic schools; and (v) indigenous schools. The government schools enrolled relatively few children – an estimated 1,900 were enrolled in 97 parish schools.

The mission schools enrolled almost 10,000, the private schools 8,400 and the Roman Catholic 1,400. Estimates of enrolments in Hindu and Muslim schools are not available from this time – but more than 1,000 Buddhist schools attracted an estimated enrolment of 6,000. While the Dutch had tried to implement compulsory education for girls as well as boys, the early British colonial government did not; enrolment of girls fell far behind that of boys (Little, 1999b, p. 77).

British colonial education policy changed significantly in the 1830s following the Colebrooke-Cameron Commission's recommendations for administrative, judicial, financial, economic and educational reform. A major recommendation, borne of financial and political expediency, was the recruitment of Sri Lankans to the lower ranks of the civil service. English would become the medium of instruction in government schools from which these Sri Lankans would be recruited. Government-funded vernacular-medium parish schools, where the teachers were generally not competent in English, were 'destroyed almost overnight' (J. E. Jayasuriya, 1979, p. 196). Henceforth, vernacular education was left in the hands of the missionary and other non-government schools.

The next major change in colonial education policy arose from the Morgan Committee of 1867 and its recommendation that the 'grant-in-aid' system of financing non-government schools be extended. This system, similar to one introduced in England in the late 1850s, was designed to increase the number of schools and student enrolments. Between 1869 and 1900 the number of government-aided schools grew from 229 to 1,328. A few Buddhist and Hindu schools (some of which are amongst the most popular schools today) succeeded in gaining grants-in-aid, though not without opposition from Protestant groups (J. E. Jayasuriya, 1979, pp. 270–3). By 1920, 64 per cent of government-aided schools were Christian, 25 per cent were Buddhist, 10.5 per cent were Hindu and 5 per cent were Muslim (Russell, 1982, p. 276).

During the early part of the twentieth century, local pressure grew for compulsory elementary education, a more relevant secondary education, better recognition of the place of the national languages in English-medium schools, and the establishment of a university. But despite the pressures there was little tangible change. Social class divisions continued between those enrolled in vernacular-medium elementary schools and those in the 'fully organised secondary schools' providing an English-medium education linked with Cambridge University and London University school examinations. The denominational schools, supported by grants-in-aid, continued to thrive. During the period 1900–20 the number of government schools grew by 419 and the grant-in-aid schools grew by 794 (J. E. Jayasuriya, 1979).

Buddhist, Hindu and Islamic schools were discouraged by the Portuguese, the Dutch and the British. However, the communities that supported them were resilient; their provision never disappeared completely and, as noted above, there was a significant revival of Buddhist and Hindu schools during the later part of the nineteenth century. Today these traditions survive through the teaching of religion in government schools, in Buddhist pirivena day schools, and in after-school madrasas and classes connected with Buddhist and Hindu temples.

Building a unified system of education

The building of the unified system of education that is recognisable today began in 1920. It was a slow process, and one in which the vested interests of the denominational schools exerted a significant brake. The education ordinance of 1920 gave the central Department of Education the power to fund elementary education in government schools, relieving local government bodies of this obligation.

The Donoughmore Commission recommended universal suffrage and limited self-rule, both of which were introduced in 1931, and set in motion 'welfarist' policies in education, health and labour welfare. The period from 1931 to the granting of full independence in 1948 is referred to by D. L. Jayasuriya (2001) as the 'late colonial period'. In 1931 the control of education was placed in the hands of a popularly elected minister of education, Dr C. W. W. Kannangara, who held that office until 1947. Universal suffrage boosted popular demands for education, and it was Dr Kannangara who would deliver them. A nationalist politician committed to egalitarian principles who steered through radical change in education, he was the person who would make education in Sri Lanka 'unique in the South Asian region' (Jayaweera, 1989, p. 1).

By 1939, the mainstream education 'system' was marked by 'dualities', described succinctly by J. E. Jayasuriya (1979). These included duality of management (government vs denominational bodies and private individuals), language medium (English vs the vernacular, or *Swabasha*), location (urban vs rural), career destinations (high status vs low status) and school fees (fee-charging vs fee-free). It was these dualities and divisions that Dr Kannangara sought to remove in order to create a unified system of education.

Early transitions: anti-colonial and egalitarian

Already by the early years of the post-independence period, the country was edging away from a dual system of education and towards a unitary system. In 1956 the left-wing Mahajana Eksath Peramuna, a coalition of the Sri Lanka Freedom Party and various left-leaning smaller parties, came to power, representing the interests of the rural masses, rural teachers, ayurveda doctors, Buddhist priests and peasants. The takeover of the denominational schools, with their superior facilities and access to university education, was hotly debated in the lead-up to the general election of 1960, which was won narrowly by the Sri Lanka Freedom Party. Despite considerable resistance from the Christians and the Catholics, the takeover of denominational schools was legislated for in the same year. English as a medium of instruction for the privileged few was replaced by vernacular-language instruction for all students attending government schools, and school fees were removed.

By 1960, major colonial changes had been reversed. Language and religion ceased, in principle, to be a barrier to educational opportunity. The education system was unified, with only 63 out of over 9,000 schools functioning as private schools. The national languages were the media of instruction in secondary schools, with an English stream for Muslim and Burgher students (Jayaweera, 1986, p. 10). Further legislation in 1961 prohibited the establishment of new private schools – a law that remains in force today, and which singles out Sri Lanka as a country with an extremely small percentage of its students in private education.

Political and economic changes and crises

From the late 1950s and during the 1960s a number of significant political and economic changes occurred. Briefly, they included a change in political regime from the conservative United National Party to a socialist-oriented coalition led by S. W. R. D. Bandaranaike in 1956, a change of direction for economic policy that advocated greater state intervention, and the creation of a 10-year development plan from 1959 with an emphasis on poverty reduction (National Planning Council, 1959). English was replaced as the official language of public administration with the language of the majority population, Sinhala. This policy, which became known as the 'Sinhala only' Act, enraged the Tamil-speaking minority and created conditions for subsequent unrest.

By the 1960s, welfare measures introduced from the early 1930s had become a welfare tradition. Free education, free health, improved nutrition, subsidised food, low cost of living and fair distribution of income became the articles of faith in the political credos of all parties (Gunatilleke, 1974, p. 17). D. L. Jayasuriya (2001) refers to the period from formal independence in 1948 to 1970 as the period of the welfare state and a transition from a colonial to a post-colonial state. Health improvements led to a steady increase in population, and student enrolments in general education grew by more than 60 per cent between 1950 and 1960. These students were moving through the system and seeking jobs. But economic growth had slowed and there were insufficient jobs available to meet the expectations of these newly qualified youth. Unemployment increased.

As youth unemployment increased, so too did political unrest and crisis. A Sinhala youth insurrection of April 1971 led to changes in education policy designed to provide a better match between employment and education. Despite subsequent changes in political regime and economic policy, there were further waves of unrest and violence. Education-related grievances of the Tamil minority voiced through the 1970s led to increasing calls for an independent state of Tamil Eelam, armed combat in 1983 and, by 1987, full-scale ethnic conflict and a civil war that concluded only in 2009. Between 1987 and 1989 education and employment grievances amongst rural Sinhalese youth erupted into violence once again, with the eventual creation of the 1997 education reforms. The most recent crisis in 2022 led to urban political unrest that transcended ethnic groups and resulted in the removal of the prime minister and president. The implications of these economic and political shifts will be explored in subsequent chapters of this book.

Growth in educational opportunity 1950–2021

In the seven and a half decades since independence, access to education has expanded greatly. Access to formal education continues to be perceived as the main channel of social mobility and as a primary means of poverty reduction. Table 1.1 shows the growth in the number of government schools, students and teachers in government schools, student-teacher ratios and adult literacy rates over the period since independence to the present day. Following nationalisation of the denominational and private schools in 1960–1, the number of government schools increased dramatically. From the 1980s there has been an increase in the number of teachers employed, resulting in a reduction in the teacher-student ratio to a level rarely seen in school systems worldwide. There has also been a steady increase in the adult literacy rate.

Moving forward

The subsequent chapters of this book offer insights into how and why these distinctive characteristics of Sri Lankan education have arisen, why and how policies and practices in education have shifted over time, introducing new distinctions on the way, and the extent to which Sri Lankan education policies have been consistent with Sri Lankan and international 'development' policies. Chapter 2 provides a historical overview of the broader international discourse on development and education and the position of Sri Lanka within that. It identifies ideas that have influenced Sri Lanka and ideas from Sri Lanka that have influenced it. This is followed by my inaugural professorial lecture, 'Learning from developing countries', delivered at the University of London's Institute of Education in 1988.

The remaining 13 chapters, organised into four parts, reflect the course of development and education discourses: education as human capital, modernisation and dependency; basic needs and 'education for all'; globalisation and education; and learning for sustainable development. They also reflect the chronology of my Sri Lankan research journey undertaken alongside a host of travelling companions.

Table 1.1 Government schools, teachers, students, student-teacher ratio, student-school ratio, adult literacy rate, population: 1950–2021. Source: figures for 1950–2021 based on Department of Census and Statistics (2021); Ministry of Education School Census (2008, 2019); Central Bank of Sri Lanka (2003, 2005, 2018, 2019). Literacy rates are for census years 1953, 1963, 1971, 1981, 2001, 2011 and 2021. The literacy rate for 1991 is estimated from the Household Survey.

	1950	1960	1971	1981	1991	2002	2011	2021
Government schools	3,188	4,394	8,585	9,521	9,998	9,826	9,732	10,146
Students in government schools	1,349,345	2,192,379	2,828,070	3,451,358	4,258,698	4,027,075	3,973,909	4,048,937
Teachers in government schools	38,086	69,658	94,858	135,869	177,231	191,812	219,766	241,054
Students per teacher in government schools	35	31	30	25	24	21	18	17
Students per government school	423	499	329	362	426	410	408	399
Adult literacy rate (%)	65	72	79	87	87	91	91	92
Population (millions)	7.95	9.90	12.74	15.27	17.53	19.06	20.4	22.16

2
Development and education: the international discourse

Introduction

As we saw in Chapter 1, Sri Lanka has developed a distinct society, economy and education system over centuries, driven by endogenous and exogenous conditions, ideas, policies and practices. Sri Lanka is also but one of more than 200 countries in the world that has grappled with a wide range of policy ideas about the meaning and goals of development, the means to their achievement and the relationship of education to them.

Since time immemorial, 'travellers' have visited Sri Lanka (Serendib in earlier times) and exchanged ideas about society and education. Those travellers increased greatly in number during the Portuguese, Dutch and British colonial periods, when ideas were more likely to have been imposed rather than exchanged.

The majority of the British population left Sri Lanka in the late 1940s/early 1950s in the years following Sri Lanka's political independence. This was a time when United Nations specialist organisations were being established and the Colombo Plan for Cooperative Economic and Social Development in Asia and the Pacific was launched. The Colombo Plan was a regional intergovernmental organisation for the economic and social advancement of the peoples of South and South-East Asia and was based around the concepts of self and mutual help in the development process.

Working within and around those international and regional organisations were researchers and policymakers from many countries, including a number of Sri Lankans appointed to senior positions. A rapidly expanding 'international' literature on development and education began to emerge, driven by the search for examples of 'successful development' ideas, policies and practices, and for prescriptions for other countries to emulate (Jolly, Emmerij & Weiss, 2009). Notwithstanding the fact that these prescriptions were often rooted in specific contexts of time and space, some were projected by international and regional organisations as having global relevance and application.

The purpose of this chapter is to provide the reader with a rapid overview of the international literature on development and education, introducing widely employed terms, concepts and theories. In so doing it builds from numerous texts and provides a general 'framing' for subsequent chapters of this book.

The meaning of 'development'

'Development' has several meanings. In everyday terms, it refers to a process that leads to progress, positive growth or positive change. It can also refer to an emerging, unfolding or maturing of potential. The process, or the verb, 'to develop' can be transitive (for example, 'the International Development Association loan programme developed the country'; 'those who designed and passed the Sri Lankan Free Education Act through parliament developed the country's educational provision'); or it may be intransitive (for example, 'the country's education system developed'). In turn, the subject of the transitive verb may be exogenous (external – for example, the International Development Association loan programme) or endogenous (internal – for example, those who designed and passed the Sri Lankan Free Education Act through parliament). In a broad literature which draws on several of the social sciences, many terms are used interchangeably with 'development', such as social change, growth, evolution, progress, advancement and modernisation.

We also talk about 'development' at several levels of analysis: regional development, country development, national economic development, societal development, cultural development, education system development, school development, human development and personal development. In the education sphere, the term 'human development' is used so loosely that 'important distinctions are obscured between "individual development", "social progress" and "economic growth"' (Serpell, 1999). The term 'human development' has been a central concept in human psychology since the late nineteenth century. In branches of economics, by contrast, its usage and meaning date only from the late twentieth century.

The concept of development is often clouded with political and ideological overtones and a future agenda; that is, an agenda of what development should consist of and how should it come about, rather than an analysis of what development has consisted of and how it came about.

However, development does not always lead to positive outcomes, or outcomes that benefit all social groups. One strand of the literature focusses on the negative aspects of so-called 'development'. The term 'underdevelopment' is often used to describe a process that leads to regression, stagnation, negative growth, breakdown or negative change. We may speak of economic stagnation or decline, of the decline of the rural communities, or of the stagnation or decline of an education system.

At a different level of analysis – that of the individual – we speak of the development of an individual's learning through time, or its underdevelopment or loss. We may speak of an individual's development of 'freedoms' or his/her 'denial of freedoms'.

For parents and teachers and those who work in 'child development', it is the development and growth of children's learning in all its respects (physical, cognitive, socio-emotional) that is the main focus of interest. For economists, by contrast, it is usually the economic growth of a country and the contribution that micro-individual economic decisions make to it that provide the main foci of interest. For policymakers and politicians, national development, sovereignty and political survival interest them most.

For much of the past seventy years, theories of 'development' have focussed mainly on the economic dimension of national development. This continues a tradition of writing that dates back to well before the twentieth century – for example Adam Smith writing about the wealth of nations in 1776, or Marx and Engels' writings on the growth of capitalism in the mid-nineteenth century. While much of this work focussed on European countries and the United States, a new branch of economics – 'development economics' – emerged from the 1940s. Development economics focussed on the conditions and challenges faced by the poorer countries of the world, especially those countries in transition from colonial rule to political independence, or those that remained under colonial rule. Those who wrote about 'development' were based mainly in institutions and universities in the US and Britain, many of them émigrés from Russia, Ukraine, Germany, Hungary and Austria. Others were based in Latin America and India. All were influenced by the circumstances and first-hand experiences of the times and places in which they wrote, and from which they had emigrated (Harris, 2014).

Terminology

The terms employed to describe individual countries and groups of countries have changed considerably over time. Nineteenth-century social scientists referred to 'advanced' and 'primitive' institutions and societies. At the beginning of the Cold War, the French demographer Alfred Sauvy coined the term 'Tiers Monde' ('Third World') to describe countries, many of them former colonies, that aligned politically with neither the First World (largely the industrialised capitalist economies and members of the North Atlantic Treaty Organization (NATO)) nor the Second World (the communist/socialist countries and members of the Warsaw Pact). Sauvy spoke of 'Three Worlds, One Planet' (Wolf-Phillips, 1979).

In 1961, many 'Third World' countries grouped together to form the Non-Aligned Movement (NAM). Some years later, the term 'Fourth World' was coined by George Manuel, Chief of the National Indian Brotherhood (now the Assembly of First Nations), to refer largely to indigenous, self-sufficient (albeit economically poor), non-sovereign communities without political ties (Manuel & Posluns, 1974). In the 1960s and 1970s the terms 'less developed', 'underdeveloped' and 'undeveloped' were commonly used by economists, while many sociologists classified countries, and areas within countries, as 'modern' or 'traditional'. The terms 'the North' and 'the South' are of different origin. Gramsci originally used the term 'South' to refer to the colonisation by capitalists in Northern Italy of the peasants in the South in 1926 (Gramsci, 2005). Economists Prebisch and Singer introduced the terms 'core' and 'periphery' to describe the differential economic power of countries within the world trade system (Toye & Toye, 2003). Later, the sociologist and historian Immanuel Wallerstein (1976) wrote of the modern 'world system of economic relations' and the ways in which transnational structures constrain both national and local development.

More recently, the terms 'Global North' and 'Global South' have emerged to describe groups of countries that enjoy differential degrees of geopolitical power. By pointing to social and political movements in the South that have emerged to challenge the political and economic dominance of the countries of the North, some have suggested that these terms challenge the notion that the increasing economic globalisation of the 1990s led to a growing homogenisation of cultures and societies (Dados & Connell, 2012).

Meanwhile, international organisations were creating ever finer classifications of countries across a range of economic and social dimensions, measures and indices: low income, lower middle income, upper middle income, high income countries (World Bank, 2023); the Human Development Index, based on education, life expectancy and per capita income (United Nations, 1990); and the Human Capital Index, based on survival and stunting rates, years of schooling and quality of schooling (World Bank, 2021). A country's educational performance is ranked against goals and targets in myriad ways, such as Universal Primary Education (Fredriksen, 1978), Education for All (Inter-Agency Commission, 1990), the Millennium Development Goal for Education (United Nations, 2000) and the Sustainable Development Goal for Education (United Nations, 2015a).

Many of these terms will be employed in the rest of this book. Terminology has changed over time. Some terms, for example 'Third World' and 'modern vs traditional', attracted widespread usage in their day, but are seldom heard today. Where I have used these earlier terms in my own writings, stretching back up to fifty years, I retain them. I also retain them if they have been employed in the writings of others from which I quote.

The United Nations – country, regional and world goals for education

The end of the Second World War ushered in the creation of institutions and the declaration and circulation of ideas designed to prevent a Third World War. The United Nations was created

> to save succeeding generations from the scourge of war … to reaffirm faith in fundamental human rights, in the dignity and worth of the human person, in the equal rights of men and women and of nations large and small, and to establish conditions under which justice and respect for the obligations arising from treaties and other sources of international law can be maintained, and to promote social progress and better standards of life in larger freedom … (United Nations, 1945)

Countries ravaged by the war needed support in their reconstruction, and the very poorest countries needed support to improve the lives of their peoples. The International Monetary Fund and the World Bank, often referred to as the Bretton Woods institutions, were created to establish an efficient system of foreign exchange, prevent competitive exchange devaluations, promote international economic growth, lend money, and offer policy advice for development. From their inception, the international organisations pursued a view of development consistent with economic growth and social and political modernisation.

For over seventy years the work of the United Nations has been undertaken by specialised agencies across different sectors (Jolly, Emmerij & Weiss, 2009). The constitution of the United Nations Educational, Scientific and Cultural Organization (UNESCO) was adopted in London in 1945. Its remit was to build peace through the 'intellectual and moral solidarity of mankind'. In 1948, the United Nations Universal Declaration of Human Rights was proclaimed, Article 26 of which declared that everyone has the right to education, and that education in the elementary stage and compulsory stages shall be fee-free. Education shall be directed to the full development of the human personality, to the strengthening of respect for human rights and fundamental freedoms, to understanding, tolerance and friendship among all nations, racial and religious groups, and to support the United Nations in the maintenance of world peace (United Nations, 1948).

In 1959 and 1960, UNESCO organised regional conferences in Addis Ababa, Santiago, Karachi and Tripoli to promote universal primary education. At the Asian conference, held in Karachi, the impressive achievements in universal access to primary education in Sri Lanka and Japan were recognised (Pires, 1960). The first UN-sponsored education conference held on a world scale was the *World Conference on Education for All: Meeting basic learning needs*. Held in Jomtien, Thailand in 1990, it led to the declaration of six 'education for all' goals. A decade later, the World Education Forum modified the goals a little and produced the *Dakar Framework for Action: Education for all*. The Jomtien and Dakar conferences were landmarks in international efforts to promote and support education for all and were driven by the powerful intergovernmental organisations of the UN system, including UNESCO (Little & Miller, 2000; Little, 2003b). The declarations that arose from both conferences emphasised the need for improvements in learning outcomes and quality of education.

While the Jomtien and Dakar declarations had focussed specifically on goals within the education sector, the United Nations Millennium Summit, held in New York in 2000, declared eight Millennium Development Goals (MDGs) across *all* development sectors. The MDG education goal was defined as the achievement of universal primary education with the target of ensuring that, by 2015, children everywhere, boys and girls alike, should achieve a full course of schooling. Three indicators were attached to this target: the net enrolment ratio (NER) in primary education, the proportion of pupils starting Grade 1 who reach the last grade of primary education, and the literacy rate of 15–24-year-olds, both women and men (Lewin, 2006).

On a world scale, much of the news on educational progress was positive. The NER, defined as the number of pupils in the country-defined age group for primary education who are enrolled in either primary or secondary education, compared with the population of children in that age group, had increased from 80 per cent in 1991 to 88 per cent in 2006. And the percentage of girls' enrolment in primary education relative to that of boys had increased from 87 to 94 per cent across all developing countries over the same period. At the same time, the NERs disguised wide variations across countries, across the individual grades of primary education, and within countries, by income group, gender and other social characteristics. Moreover, in some contexts, enrolment meant little more than having one's name recorded in an enrolment register. Attending school is different from participating in learning opportunities. And participation in learning is different from achieving learning outcomes that are useful, relevant and enduring.

At the UN General Assembly in 2015 the MDGs were superseded by the 2030 Agenda for 'Sustainable Development' with its 17 Goals (SDGs), 169 targets and 304 indicators. Within this broad agenda education has several roles to play. On the one hand, there is the achievement of the Goal itself – the goal for educational expansion and improved quality, as measured by learning outcomes. At the same time, the education goal is a means to the ends of the other SDGs, such as health and environmental sustainability.

How does development come about?

In 1962 the United Nations asserted:

> … development concerns not only man's material needs, but also the improvement of the social conditions of his life and his broad human aspirations. Development is not just economic growth, it is growth plus change. (United Nations, 1962)

But if the definition of development, whether as economic growth, or the satisfaction of material needs, or improvements in the social conditions of life, or the satisfaction of human aspirations, has attained a broad consensus among policymakers around the world, the policies, strategies and methods through which these aims have been or can be achieved have not.

This is where development theory comes in. Among the questions addressed by development theorists are: through what means, historically, has development come about? What have been the goals of that development? Are there stages of development through which all countries must pass? Can countries compress or leapfrog the stages of development? Is there an end point of development?

From the outset, economists positioned economic growth and its antecedents, especially technical change and industrialisation, as the main goal of development. The intellectual debates about economic development – and the policies that flowed from them – revolved largely around the respective roles of 'states' and 'markets' as the drivers of economic growth. Structuralist theories stressed the role of the state in driving forward economic growth, while liberal and neo-liberal theories placed more emphasis on markets (Harris, 2014; Colclough & Manor, 1991).

Economic growth through import substitution

In the early years following the end of the Second World War, the Bretton Woods institutions recommended that the best means of achieving economic growth was through 'import substitution industrialisation' (ISI). This strategy encouraged nations to achieve economic self-sufficiency by nationalising domestic industries and protecting domestically produced goods from competition from imports. The general objective was to reduce the economic dependency of developing countries on developed countries and the former colonial powers. ISI involved a high degree of state intervention and the implementation of tariffs, import quotas and subsidised government loans. ISI strategies had already shown promise in Latin American countries, and the experiences of Brazil and Argentina were shared widely elsewhere in the 'developing world'. In Sri Lanka ISI was adopted from 1956.

Some countries, notably in East Asia, eschewed the strategy, adopting instead a strategy of export-led development, based on manufactured goods.

Development as modernisation

Economic ideas about 'development' soon attracted other social science disciplines, including sociology and political science, both of which had their modern roots in the nineteenth century. During the 1950s and 1960s, 'modernisation theory' became the 'dominant sociological theory of development' (Kiely, 2006). The path to an end state of 'development' required countries to proceed through stages. The process of development involved a transition from 'tradition' to 'modernity' – a shift away from a past where social roles were ascribed from birth to a future based on the meritocratic achievement of social roles and status, as well as the creation of wealth and its reinvestment. The concept of 'development' became construed as 'modernisation and economic growth'.

Modernisation provided an optimistic agenda for political and social change, as well as for economic growth. Political scientists focussed on nation-building, how nation states achieve legitimacy, the basis for power, and power sharing and national identity. Sociologists focussed on the social differentiation effects of technology-driven economic growth and on the development of 'modern values'. Demographers focussed on patterns of urban settlement and changes in the size, growth and densities of population. New schools and universities, as well as factories, were viewed as institutions in which the modern values required for modern behaviours, modern society and economic development could be fashioned. The school was presented as a 'context for modernisation' (Inkeles, 1973). Schools provided one means of developing a 'need for achievement' and the establishment of meritocracies that would replace ascriptive status systems found in 'traditional' societies.

Within this view, the main goal of 'development' was the achievement of 'modernity' driven by economic development. It was assumed that a rising tide of affluence would benefit all. There was an optimism about the role of newly formed states and of national elites to drive national development forward (Humphrey, 2007).

Stages of development

In 1960 Rostow posited five stages of development through which all countries needed to pass on the road to 'maturity' and 'development': (i) 'traditional society' (subsistence agriculture, low savings and investment); (ii) 'preconditions for take-off' (mechanisation of agriculture, emergence of surpluses, savings begin to grow to about 5 per cent of GDP); (iii) 'take-off' (manufacturing grows, political institutions develop, savings rates increase to 10–15 per cent of GDP); (iv) 'drive to maturity' (savings steady at 10–20 per cent, growth spreads to other sectors, technological improvement, increasing diversity); and (v) the 'age of mass consumption' (output driven by consumption, beginning of shift to tertiary sector) (Rostow, 1960).

Rostow envisaged that it could take between forty and sixty years for economies to move from take-off to maturity. Notwithstanding its attractiveness as a blueprint for economic development and policy, the 'stages' approach came to be criticised for its 'one size fits all' approach, the assumptions made about the desirable character of the end stage of development, and the focus on national economy and society to the exclusion of international trade and competition.

Perhaps inspired by the 'stages of development' idea, Clarence Beeby, Director of Education in New Zealand with additional responsibilities for education in Samoa and Pacific Island dependencies, offered four stages in the development of a primary school education system in 1966 (Table 2.1).

Beeby described the first stage as the 'dame school', where teachers were described as ill-educated and untrained, schooling was 'unorganised, involving relatively meaningless symbols and narrow subject content', standards were low, and there was a strong emphasis on memorisation. Successive stages become more formalised, with teachers gradually better educated and better trained. In the final stage the curriculum and teaching methods employed were more varied, individual differences catered for, and activity-methods, problem-solving and creativity encouraged (Beeby, 1966).

In the mid-1960s Beeby (1966) judged that the majority of developing country education systems were at stage 2, while the primary school systems in developed countries lay between stages 3 and 4. Progression from the beginning of the stage of 'formalism' to the end of the stage of 'meaning' would occur largely through the better education and training of teachers. While changes in teacher education would be a necessary driver of change, other factors would also be necessary, especially materials and finance.

Human capital

In one of the most influential writings on the role of education in economic growth, American economist Theodore W. Schultz

Table 2.1 Stages of development of primary education (adapted from Beeby, 1966).

Stage	Teachers	Characteristics
I. Dame school	Ill-educated, untrained	Unorganised, relatively meaningless symbols, very narrow subject content – three Rs; very low standards; memorisation all important
II. Formalism	Ill-educated, trained	Highly organised; symbols with limited meaning; rigid syllabus; emphasis on 3 Rs; rigid methods – 'one best way'; one textbook; external examinations; inspection stressed; discipline tight and external memorisation heavily stressed; emotional life largely ignored
III. Transition	Better-educated, trained	Roughly same goals as stage II, but more efficiently achieved; more emphasis on meaning, but still rather 'thin' and formal; syllabus and textbooks less restrictive, but teachers hesitate to use greater freedom; final leaving examination often restricts experimentation; little in classroom to cater for emotional and creative life of the child
IV. Meaning	Well-educated, well-trained	Meaning and understanding stressed; somewhat wider curricula, variety of content and methods; individual differences catered for; activity methods, problem solving and creativity; internal tests; relaxed and positive discipline; emotional and aesthetic life, as well as intellectual; closer relations with community; better buildings and equipment essential

advanced the idea that the skills and knowledge created through education should be construed as investment in the future rather than consumption in the present. Schultz termed this skill and knowledge 'human capital' and viewed it as key to economic production alongside the classical factors of land, labour and capital (Schultz, 1961). The 'human investment revolution in economic thought' (Bowman, 1966) influenced thinking about the meaning of development and the role of education within it.

Analysis of the relative contribution of the classical factors of production – land, labour and capital – in the explanation of growth in Gross National Product between 1909 and 1959 in the United

States showed that there was a large 'residual' of unexplained variance (Denison, 1962). This was attributed to changes in technology and economies of scale, and to the quality of labour, measured in terms of levels of education (that is, human capital). The concept of human capital began to circulate around the world and trickle into the policy statements of presidents, policymakers and education planners.

Beyond human capital

While human capital was a dominant focus of early writers on the relationship between education and economic development, other writers addressed the contribution of education to development objectives that went beyond the economic to include the political, social and personal. (For examples see Anderson & Bowman, 1965; Mayer & Rubinson, 1975; Lewin, Little & Colclough, 1983a, b; Fagerlind & Saha, 1989; Lewin, 1991; Mebrahtu, 1991; Leach & Little, 1999; Yates & Little, 2005; Harber, 2014; McGrath & Gu, 2016; McCowan & Unterhalter, 2021.)

Underdevelopment

Dependency and cultural alienation

Through the late 1960s and 1970s, the optimistic models of the modernisation and human capital theorists were being challenged. Marxist ideas on the exploitation of the proletariat by the bourgeoisie and Lenin's writings on imperialism were combined to create a theory of dependency (Frank, 1967; Galtung, 1971). Notwithstanding their formal political independence, 'dependency' addressed the extent to which peripheral poor countries continued to be economically dependent on their former colonial powers. These writers did not challenge the idea of development as economic growth; rather they were concerned to explain why economic growth was not happening at the rate expected. They focussed on economic 'underdevelopment' rather than 'development', and on the maintenance of economic relations of dependency rather than independence. Many on the political Left focussed their attention on 'underdevelopment' rather than 'development' (for example classical theories of imperialism, neo-Marxist theory, dependency theory, world systems theory), suggesting that it was 'the West' that posed the main obstacle to development (Schmitz, 2007). Central to the maintenance of these economic relations of dependency were indigenous elites, firmly wedded to the international capitalist system, rewarded handsomely by it, and with no interest in giving up their rewards (Cardoso, 1972; Dos Santos, 1973).

Dependency ideas were associated with the idea of 'cultural alienation'. The structure of dependent economic relations, it was asserted, created a 'cultural dependency' or 'cultural alienation', in which values, norms, technology, concepts and art forms were inspired exogenously rather than endogenously. Education was implicated in the process through which cultural alienation occurred. The dependency perspective drew attention to, *inter alia*, continuing economic and cultural relations between newly independent countries and their former colonisers, constraints on development, increasing disparities of income between and within countries, the increasing presence of 'multinational' interests in national economies, the formation of 'transnational elites', and the creation of 'underclass' countries.

Writing mainly from a South Asian and Sri Lankan perspective, Goonatilake (1982) expressed the idea of cultural alienation in terms of 'crippled minds'. While he did not write specifically about the role played by colonial education in the production of such, his concern was with the processes through which European expansion from the fifteenth century threw 'a near complete cultural blanket over almost all the world … [which] suppressed local culture, local arts, local systems of valid and relevant science' (Goonatilake, 1982, p. vi). In an earlier article in which he reflected on development models and theories extant in the 1970s, Goonatilake asserted that they too were a form of 'cultural neo-colonialism' (Goonatilake, 1975; for a reply see Lipton, 1975). In some respects, his writings foreshadowed some of the ideas of subsequent post-colonial theory, to which I will return later in this chapter.

With their focus on underdevelopment rather than development, ideas about cultural alienation presented a pessimistic view of the future and underlined the ways in which education impedes rather than promotes development. Schooling in the 'Third World' fed into the maintenance of dependent economic relations (Carnoy, 1974). Despite political independence from former colonial powers, education systems continued to be dependent on them in matters of curriculum, textbooks and exams (for examples see Mazrui, 1975; Carnoy, 1974; Altbach & Kelly, 1978). Alongside these observations was the Marxist idea that in all societies education was largely reproductive of its broader social and economic class divisions. Schools socialised young people for their position in society in line with that of their parents (see for example Bowles & Gintis, 1976).

A key idea in dependency theory is the role played by comprador or transnational elites in the perpetuation of dependent economic relations – that is, the elites within a country or who move between countries who are grounded in globalised circulations of trade, accumulation and ideas.

Dependency ideas were consistent with the principles of the NAM, which, as noted above, was established in 1961 following the Korean War and during the period of the Cold War in which the two major powers of the time – America and Russia – attempted to draw the rest of the world into their respective orbits of power through membership of NATO and the Warsaw Pact respectively. The NAM's fundamental principles stressed national independence and sovereignty, territorial integrity and peaceful coexistence. The movement was part of the struggle against imperialism, colonialism and neo-colonialism, occupation and domination by hegemonic countries. The major players in its establishment in 1961 were the presidents and prime ministers of Yugoslavia, India, Egypt, Ghana and Indonesia. The NAM is now a forum of 120 countries not formally aligned with or against any major power bloc. It is the second largest grouping of states worldwide, the United Nations being the largest.

The diploma disease

Following worldwide optimism about economic growth in the post-war years, a degree of disillusionment was setting in by the early 1970s and was being expressed through the ideas of dependency and economic underdevelopment. Disillusionment also set in around the optimistic discourse of modernisation and human capital and the ability of education to contribute to economic growth. In the Sri Lankan case, it was becoming clear that investment in education did not lead automatically to productive employment and economic growth. Sri Lanka's first National Development Plan (1958–68) focussed on unemployment, the need for an expansion of employment opportunities, and the need for education to meet the requirements of employment and economic growth. While education held the promise of 'good' modern sector jobs for many, it could not create them per se and certainly not for everybody. Education could increase the number of young people qualified to enter those jobs. However, if the economy did not expand, then many young qualified people would become underemployed or underemployed (ILO, 1971a).

'Qualification-seeking' in the context of the slow growth economy that characterised Sri Lanka in the late 1960s inspired the concept of

the 'diploma disease' and the publication of a book of the same name –
The diploma disease: Education, qualification and development, written
by sociologist Ronald Dore of the Institute of Development Studies,
Sussex (Dore, 1976). The ideas for the book 'took root during visits
to Sri Lanka's schools at the time of the "youth insurrection" of 1971'
(Dore, 1976). Dore was critical of many economists' assumptions about
human capital theory. He was also influenced by Gerschenkron's (1952)
notion of 'late development': countries that develop early (that is,
industrialise early) transform the external conditions in which countries
that develop later begin their drive towards industrialisation (Dore,
1972, 1997b). The 'diploma disease' explored the relations between
education, qualifications and development in 'early', 'late', 'later' and
'much later' developing countries. The mismatch between economic
and educational growth led to an intense pursuit of qualifications – a
pursuit which undermined the process of learning itself, with 'deplorable
consequences' for development, not only in Sri Lanka but also for other
'late developing' societies. The overriding thesis was that education was
'underdeveloping' the potential abilities and skills of young people.

The beginnings of my own research journey in Sri Lanka are rooted
in this period and in Dore's ideas, which inspired and challenged me in
equal measure. In Chapter 6 I test out some of the propositions of the
diploma disease thesis.

Neo-liberalism and structural adjustment

From the early 1970s, economic growth in much of the 'developed', industrialised world had slowed. The oil crisis of 1973 and the energy crisis of 1979 underlined the interdependence and vulnerability of countries heavily dependent on oil imports. This affected social sector expenditure in rich and poor countries alike. Between 1970 and 1977/8, mean public expenditure on education in industrialised countries declined from 14.3 to 13.1 per cent of total government expenditure, and in developing countries from 16.1 to 15.1 per cent (Lewin, Little & Colclough, 1982). In the UK and the US, governments shifted from the Left to the Right and introduced monetarist policies designed to increase economic growth – policies which came to be known as Thatcherism and Reaganomics. The Mexican debt crisis of 1982 led the International Monetary Fund and the World Bank, amongst others, to impose new conditionalities on lending to 'developing countries'. 'Developing countries' needed to stabilise and 'structurally adjust' their economies and ensure the implementation of liberal economic policies. The measures to achieve this involved, *inter alia*, tax reductions, privatisation of state-owned companies, trade liberalisation, reductions in public expenditure and competitive exchange rates. Policy advice on reductions in public expenditure and privatisation was reflected in many countries through an increase in research and policy recommendations on private education, although this was not the case in Sri Lanka.

Basic needs and redistribution with growth

The shortcomings of policies of previous decades inform new thinking, approaches and policies. The basic needs approach (BNA) to development arose in response to the realisation that in many countries state-driven import substitution economic policies were not generating benefits for all. Neither poverty nor inequality was reducing, and the 'basic needs' of large numbers remained unfulfilled (Stewart, 2006). In a landmark paper, *The meaning of development*, Seers (1969) suggested that the main index of economic development – Gross National Product – needed to be replaced by a notion of development as a reduction or elimination of poverty, inequality and unemployment. These ideas infused the analysis and recommendations of a series of International Labour Organization (ILO) 'Employment Missions', including the mission to Sri Lanka titled *Matching employment opportunities and expectations* (ILO, 1971a, b; Jolly, 1976; Emmerij, 2010). This work was accompanied by the idea that approaches to growth needed to be – and could be – accompanied by redistributing its outcomes and benefits to the poorest (Jolly, 1974; Chenery et al., 1974). People, especially the poorest, required access not only to money but also to the basic goods and services that would enable them to increase their incomes. This included education, health services, jobs, access to clean water and sanitation, and food. Access to education was both a constituent part of the definition of development and a means to increased incomes. Poverty reduction lay at the heart of Sri Lanka's first 10-year development plan (1959–68) (National Planning Council, 1959). Compared with the development plans of other countries at the time, this emphasis was unusual and far ahead of the international discourse on poverty reduction.

As BNA ideas circulated, the experience of Sri Lanka was often cited, alongside that of China, Cuba and the state of Kerala in India, as an example of a country that, despite low economic growth, had successfully achieved poverty reduction through good access to education and health services (for examples see Gunatilleke, 1974; Sen, 1981, 1999; Isenman, 1980; Ruttan, 1984; Anand & Kanbur, 1991; Kelegama, 2000; D. L. Jayasuriya, 2001). If these low-income countries could achieve the fulfilment of basic needs, then why not others?

In the late 1970s and 1980s, basic needs missions were undertaken under the auspices of the ILO's Jobs and Skills Programme for Africa. I was privileged to be invited to join one of the earliest, in Nigeria in 1979, led by Dudley Seers. In a discussion of the 'needs of the Nigerian people' it was recognised that the concept of basic human needs was not a new subject, its identification and measurement having preoccupied social scientists for decades. However, the practice of 'inserting basic needs as specific objectives in development strategies' was novel (ILO/JASPA, 1981). In my chapter on the basic need for education in Nigeria I persuaded the editors that it should be titled 'learning' rather than 'education'.

> We are concerned with education, not as an end in itself, but as an instrument, and would judge types of education by their relative success in promoting learning relevant to life and to other basic needs. This is in line with the thinking of the mission, that provision of services as such is not to be confused with the satisfaction of needs. (ILO/JASPA, 1981, ch. 6)

Running alongside the concept of 'basic needs' was that of 'integrated rural development'. Integrated rural development programmes required simultaneous and coordinated programme investment across all sectors of rural economies and societies as a means to achieve poverty reduction. There were several examples of integrated rural development programmes involving cross-sector investment in Sri Lanka, including in education (Little, 1995a).

Stewart (2006) describes how, over time, the BNA discourse lost support because it was misunderstood to imply that economic growth was no longer important for development. Moreover, there was an arbitrariness in the choice of and targets for basic needs goods and services, the approach lacked theoretical elegance, and it appeared to be advocated by developed countries for developing countries but not for themselves. Significantly, the BNA development discourse was overtaken by world events – the debt crisis, the 'lost decade of the 1980s' and the 'obsession with stabilisation' and structural adjustment (Stewart, 2006, p. 17; Emmerij, 2010), described above.

Development as 'human development' and human capability

Despite concerns about poor economic growth and the promotion of policies designed to stabilise economies, development ideas about basic needs and the more equal sharing of the benefits of growth did not disappear. Rather, they re-emerged in an invigorated discourse focussed on 'human development' (Jolly, 2010). The authors of the United Nations Development Programme's first Human Development Report drew together the early work on BNA with that of one of its authors – Amartya Sen – and his concept of 'human capabilities' (United Nations, 1990). With its focus on the fulfilment of people's basic needs, the human capability approach (HCA) resonated with BNA. BNA and HCA identify a similar range of basic needs or basic capabilities, including education. In contrast with BNA, HCA was underpinned by a 'more elegant philosophical foundation' (Stewart, 2006), by a definition of development focussed on individuals more than groups, and by an extension of needs beyond 'basic' capabilities. Sen (1999) wrote of 'development as freedom':

> Expansion of freedom is … both the primary end and … the principal means of development. Development consists of the removal of various types of unfreedoms that leave people with little choice and little opportunity of exercising their reasoned agency. The removal of substantial unfreedoms … is constitutive of development … (Sen, 1999, pp. xi–xii)

The notion of 'development as freedom' recognises the 'deep complementarity' between individual agency and social arrangements. It recognises the instrumentality of other freedoms to meet this 'main object of development' – for example economic opportunities, political freedoms, social facilities (including education) and protective security. In turn these are influenced by societal arrangements and institutions including states, markets, the legal system, political parties, the media, public interest groups and public discussion forums (Sen, 1999, pp. xii–xiii). Sen singles out Sri Lanka as the country in South Asia that had, by 1991, achieved life expectancy at birth above 60 years, despite a low level of GDP per capita. He contrasts this experience with that of South Africa and Brazil where, despite higher levels of GDP per capita, life expectancy was lower (Sen, 1999, pp. 47, 99).

The concept of human development came to be defined as an increase in the capabilities and the freedom of choice of men and women in the spheres of work, in politics, in family decision-making and in leisure (Fukuda-Parr, 2003). Along with its strong focus on individuals, it was Sen's intention that it should be applied to people in rich as well as poor countries and should focus attention more on the special needs of particular groups such as the 'disabled' (Stewart, 2006). Overall, it sought to position economic growth as a means to the end of human development rather than as a development end in itself (Little, 1992). This was an important shift in development thinking for many social scientists, including some, but not all, economists.

Sen's ideas in relation to education have been explored comprehensively by Robeyns (2005). These ideas have a strong normative character – that is, they assert what, in value terms, development should be about, and how education freedoms should be viewed as both a constituent part of and a means to development. However, in the discussion of 'means' they overlook the possibility that some socio-economic groups of individuals might increase their capabilities and freedoms in education at the expense of others. As we shall see in Chapter 10, it was the labours and revenues of the plantation community that provided the financial means to expand free education of children beyond the plantations, while the children in the plantations did not enjoy the same freedoms. In other words, the unfreedoms of one social group created the means for the freedoms of another.

Globalisation

While this strand of thinking and policy development was being advanced, the term 'globalisation' was entering the development and education lexicon. From the early 1980s the manifestations of globalisation were largely economic – growth of global trade, increased volumes of international finance capital and the domination of international technology flows by transnational corporations (see for example Wood, 1995; Stewart, 1996). There were also political, social and cultural manifestations. These included, *inter alia*, an increasing tendency for national and local politics to be played out on a world stage (see for example Ohmae, 1990; Giddens, 1999), the increased distribution and dissemination of cultural images, information and values worldwide, and convergences in lifestyles and cultural aspirations (see for example Waters, 1995). Andy Green and I would go on to define the manifestations of globalisation simply as 'the accelerated movement of goods, services, capital and people and ideas across national borders' (Little & Green, 2009).

The manifestations of globalisation are different from its underlying drivers. Sklair (2006) identifies four clusters of approach to the question of who or what is driving globalisation. The first is the 'world systems' approach based on the distinction between core, semi-peripheral and peripheral countries in terms of their changing roles in the international division of labour dominated by the capitalist world system. The second starts with the globalisation of culture rather than economy. The driver of globalisation is a homogenising mass media-based culture which undermines national and/or local cultures and identities. The third focusses on the emergence of global polity and society, the receding power of the nation state and the increasing significance of supra-national, transnational and global institutions and belief systems, driven in part by the rise of global public opinion, globalising social movements and international non-governmental organisations. The fourth focusses on the capitalist economy and the role played by transnational corporations, the transnationalist capitalist class and the culture-ideology of consumerism as the drivers of a global capitalist project.

The processes of economic globalisation began long before it became a focus of research in Development Studies. Historians point to the maritime trade routes of long ago, to the triangular trade routes during periods of slavery, and to the classic export commodity trade routes promoted by colonial regimes. In the immediate post-Second World War period, most trade occurred between North America and Europe. 'Developing' countries were linked with either North America or Europe, but less with each other. From the 1970s regional blocs in America, Europe and East and South-East Asia became important for trade between countries within these respective blocs. China embarked on her post-Cultural Revolution drive to transform her economy from a socialist 'planned economy' to a socialist 'commodity' economy, and from a self-reliant national economy to one that traded within the international economy. By the early 2000s, other large economies were growing rapidly and the term 'BRICS' was coined to describe five emerging, fast-growing economies – Brazil, Russia, India, China and South Africa – predicted to dominate the global economy by 2050.

Millennium Development Goals

By the end of the century, the goal of gender equality through women's rights and empowerment, which had emerged in the UN development decade of the 1960s and was central to the 1995 Beijing Declaration and Platform for Action, had assumed greater importance in the international development discourse than hitherto. The earlier BNA and HCA approaches gained new impetus at the United Nations Millennium Summit, held in New York in 2000, where eight MDGs and 18 targets, including targets for education and gender equality, were declared. I alluded earlier to the MDG goal and targets for education. The goal of gender equality was closely aligned with MDG2. Its sole target was 'to eliminate gender disparity in primary and secondary education by 2005, and in all levels of education by 2015'. By 2000, Sri Lanka was already well on the way to achieving these international targets at all three levels of education. While the ideas of basic needs and human development resonated with the content of the MDGs, the idea that the goals should be accompanied by performance 'targets' arose from the International Development Targets formally adopted by the Development Assistance Committee in Paris in 1996.

Development as 'sustainable development'

The idea of development as 'sustainable development' was also moving centre stage. The roots of this idea may be traced to the 1972 United Nations Conference on the Human Environment, beginning the dialogue between countries on the links between economic growth, air and water pollution and human well-being (United Nations, 1972). In 1987 the Brundtland Commission defined the concept of 'sustainable development' as development 'that meets the needs of the present without compromising the ability of future generations to meet their own needs' (World Commission on Education and Development, 1987).

In 1992 the world's governments adopted Agenda 21 at the Earth Summit, held in Rio de Janeiro. The agenda introduced the idea of 'sustainable consumption' and called for people in rich countries to change their consumption patterns so that sustainable development might be achieved (United Nations, 1992). At this conference the Sri Lankan physicist, engineer and economist Mohan Munasinghe introduced the *Sustainomics* framework with its three spheres of activity – environment (including water and waste), society (including employment, human rights, gender equity, peace and human security) and economy (including poverty reduction, corporate responsibility and accountability) (M. Munasinghe, 1992, 2019b). A second World Summit on Sustainable Development, convened in Johannesburg in 2002, recognised the vital role of education in the future realisation of a 'vision of sustainability that links economic well-being with respect for cultural diversity, the Earth and its resources'. UNESCO declared the Decade of Education for Sustainable Development, which would run from 2005–14, its overall goal being to 'integrate values, activities and principles that are inherently linked to sustainable development into all forms of education and learning' (UNESCO, 2007, pp. 5–6).

In 2015 the United Nations advanced 17 global goals for sustainable development. They came to be known as the Sustainable Development Goals and replaced the previous eight Millennium Development Goals. Sustainable development recognises that the eradication of poverty, the combating of inequality within and among countries, the preservation of the planet, and the creation of sustainable economic growth and social inclusion are interdependent (United Nations, 2015b). Education is positioned as Goal 4 within its ambitious list of 17 goals.

The challenges faced at the global, national and local scales in reconciling the goals of economic growth, environmental protection and social development and in reaching international agreements for global action are brought into sharp focus at the climate summits held around the world each year. Not only is the development of 'clean' energy technology central to the global environmental challenge, so too is a reliable supply of that energy for the world's population.

Post-development and post-colonial perspectives

By the end of the twentieth century the optimistic views of modernisation theorists in the 1960s had been substantially modified. Western modernity was questioned as the main development goal for all countries, optimism had been replaced by pessimism, and 'states' were now perceived to be part of the problem rather than the solution to development problems. The nation state was no longer the main or only unit of analysis for an understanding of development policy and practice. Now the efficacy of the nation state needed to be analysed in relation to the influences of global flows of goods, services and capital (resonating with similar calls from the dependency theorists in the 1970s) and regionalisation on the one hand, and sub-national economic strategies and inequalities on the other (Humphrey, 2007). The rise of several of the East Asian economies in the 1980s (to be explored in Chapter 12), and of China in particular, were challenging the assumption that 'Western' models and ideals of 'development' were always best (Schmitz, 2007).

The early optimism of the modernisation theorists, combined with the pessimism of the dependency theorists, led to an impasse in development thinking and to a range of writings carrying the label of 'post-'. Drawing on 'post-structuralism' and 'post-modernism', 'post-development' and 'post-colonial' perspectives entered the development discourse.

'Post-development' refers to the 'deconstruction' of development ideas, whether they be capitalist, socialist and/or Western, and the creation of a 'post-development era' in which 'development' does not take place solely under a Western gaze and in which vernacular cultures needed to be revalorised. These ideas constitute less of an explanation of development and more a call for a reconsideration of how the idea of development might be conceived of in the future, and by whom. This future would place greater value on ordinary people's definitions of development, especially those that embrace humane, culturally and environmentally sustainable worlds, and greater value on the power of social movements and grassroots mobilisation to bring those worlds into being (see for example Rahnema & Bawtree, 1997; Escobar, 2011).

'Post-colonial theory' embraces a very wide range of approaches focussed on the cultural, political and economic legacies of colonialism (usually Western). For some, the term 'post-colonial' has a temporal connotation and refers simply to developments in a country during the period following formal political independence. For others, post-colonial theory is about exploring the power relations between and within countries that sustain colonialism in the present. Some explore how colonisers generated knowledge and language (categories) about the culture of the people they colonised and how the colonised, the 'subalterns', viewed the process of colonisation (for example Spivak, 1988). The challenge ahead is to 'decolonise'. Others challenge the notion of decolonisation itself and suggest that to deny agency to those who live in and govern former colonies is condescending and overlooks the benefits of retaining and adapting some institutions (though by no means all) introduced by former colonial regimes (for example Taiwo, 2022).

Aspects of these post-colonial writings resonate with the writings of those who were developing economic and cultural dependency perspectives fifty years ago, outlined earlier, and with the anti-colonial writers who went on to inspire independence movements and, in some cases, lead their countries in the early years of independence (for example Fanon, 1961; Nyerere, 1967).

Applications of 'post-colonial' and 'post-development' ideas to education have been largely ones of critique – of revealing hidden assumptions about 'the other' and 'veiled disparagement' of indigenous cultures (McCowan, 2021, p. 50). The writings explore the effects of Western cultures on non-Western cultures in colonised societies, as well as current education arrangements that arise from the experience of European colonialism. They include, *inter alia*, colonial education curricula and the challenges faced by 'post-colonial' governments in trying to create alternatives; attempts to fuse indigenous with colonial traditions in education; the choice and role of language-media in former colonial systems of education; and the challenges faced by policymakers caught between colonial legacies and the demands of the contemporary wave of 'globalisation' (for examples see Crossley & Tickly, 2004; Tikly & Bond, 2013; Del Monte & Posholi, 2021). While many of these writings are today 'framed' by post-colonial theory, many of the same issues have been examined in the past without the need to employ a post-colonial or decolonial lens explicitly (for examples see Fasheh, 1999; Aikman, 1999; Teasdale & Teasdale, 1999; Helu-Thaman, 1999).

Both post-development and post-colonial approaches place a stronger emphasis on the normative (what should be) than on the non-normative (what has been). They have been criticised for, *inter alia*, their ideological and dogmatic status and their lack of positive policies for the future (Unterhalter, 2007). They also underplay the *changes* – as well as the continuities – apparent in education policy and practice during both the colonial and post-colonial periods. That colonial legacies live on in present-day education curricula and systems is an important proposition. However, critical to this discussion is an understanding of the conditions in which actors and circumstances have combined to challenge and overturn such legacies and have succeeded in creating new models of education more relevant to the present day. Tracing these legacies involves examining not only the colonial legacies which endure and those which have disappeared, but also the post-colonial or post-independence legacies which have endured and those which have disappeared. Some of these in Sri Lanka will be explored in Chapters 4, 6, 7, 8, 10 and 13.

Locating Sri Lankan ideas, policies and practices on an international map

This chapter has provided a sketch map of a vast literature on development and education – a literature that has been heavily dominated by development goals that are economic in character and that has, over many years, come to be regarded by many academics, policymakers and practitioners as an 'international', if not a 'global', discourse.

So where does Sri Lanka sit on this international/global map of ideas, policies and practices? Sri Lanka has participated in the creation of this discourse in myriad ways. It was a signatory to the constitution of UNESCO in 1945 and the Declaration of Human Rights in 1948, a founder member of the Colombo Plan for regional cooperation and development in 1950, a founder member of the Non-Aligned Movement in 1961 and the host of its fifth summit in 1976 held at the Bandaranaike Memorial International Conference Hall, gifted by the Chinese, and named after the country's fourth prime minister, S. W. R. D. Bandaranaike.

Sri Lanka has sent delegations to almost all of the major UN-sponsored conferences and summits since the 1950s, and several experienced Sri Lankan economists, policymakers and educationalists have been appointed to senior positions in international and regional organisations and foreign universities. Many delegations sent by multi-lateral and bilateral organisations and 'aid' agencies have interacted with Sri Lankan policymakers and practitioners in almost every field of endeavour. These organisational, institutional, social and personal interactions have created a dense, intricate network of channels through which the exchange of ideas, policies and practices flows.

As we will see in future chapters, much policy research in Sri Lanka, especially in the social sciences, has been framed by concepts flowing from the international map of ideas about development and education. Conversely, some concepts grounded in the Sri Lankan context have framed research elsewhere. Some international ideas and policies have influenced development and education policies in Sri Lanka. Conversely, some Sri Lankan ideas and policies have influenced the thinking of the international development community.

3
Learning from developing countries

This public inaugural professorial lecture was delivered at the Institute of Education, University of London on 15 March 1988, during a conference organised by the Department of International and Comparative Education marking 60 years of the Institute's engagement with education in the Caribbean, Africa, Asia, Oceania and Latin America. The lecture was chaired by the Institute's director, Professor Denis Lawton.

I am sure that most of us have at one time or another eaten spaghetti in an Italian restaurant. But I wonder how recently it was that we learned that spaghetti originates not from Italy, but from China? Or that the roots of Eric Clapton's musical inspiration are to be found not in suburban London but in West Africa? And how long ago did we forget that the monitorial system, which was to form part of the bedrock of mass elementary schooling in England in the early part of the nineteenth century, was an educational innovation of its day which originated not in England, but in India? Or that ethnography, on which so many contemporary British educational studies are based, is an analytic approach and set of research techniques grounded not in London, Liverpool, Manchester or Milton Keynes, but in the Trobriand islands in Melanesia and elsewhere in those areas of the world now classified as developing countries?

Developing countries are regarded as those which are economically poor, where substantial proportions of the population are employed in agriculture and where the social conditions of the mass of the population are depressed. The majority of countries in Latin America, the Caribbean, Africa, Asia and Oceania fall into this general category, though the variations between countries on these and many other economic, social and political dimensions of development are enormous.[1]

I explore my theme, Learning from Developing Countries, in three ways. First, I shall describe and comment on a recent advance in Western educational theory which cries out for refinement and elaboration by researchers in and from developing countries if it is to justify itself as a theory having international status; second, I shall discuss recent work on learning orientation which was developed in collaboration with educators and researchers from developing countries and which offers one model for the creation of international knowledge about education; and third, I shall identify some policies and practices in developing countries which have relevance for our thinking about contemporary problems and issues in education in Britain.

The examples which I shall use to illustrate these three aspects of learning *from* developing countries[2] draw on work on student achievement, assessment and motivation.

Attribution theory

Let us start, then, with a fairly well-known theory of achievement and motivation – attribution theory, associated with several American social psychologists, including Harold Kelley (1972) and Bernard Weiner (1979). The theory was elaborated in the early 1970s and has received empirical development over the past decade, when it also began to filter into educational circles. For those of you who are unfamiliar with this theory, may I first offer a little background?

The theory is predicated on the notion that an adequate understanding of human social behaviour must rest on a description of how human beings perceive and report their social world. It is assumed that all people want to predict and control their social environment, a desire which leads the individual to perceive events as being caused, or, to use the words of the attribution theorist, to assign attributions to events.

---

[1] As we saw in Chapter 2, the terms 'developing countries' and 'developed countries' were in general use in the 1980s and have since been superseded.
[2] The use of the preposition 'from' is not intended to be interpreted as 'extractive' – that is, as learning that is for the benefit of developed countries. It refers to the need for staff working in institutions such as the Institute of Education to learn about a wide range of models and practices of education available in the countries from which their students flow, and to include these in their work with students.

Moreover, and this is the critical point, the individual's attribution of causes is assumed to have a significant impact on future achievement behaviour. We do not have to read the theory, however, to know that students and their teachers and parents are seeking out explanations for academic success and failure daily. A teacher's diary (Marshall, 1976) records dialogue between himself and the father of one of his Ugandan students.

Father: Teachers at Malobe school are lazy.
Teacher: That's not quite true you know.
Father: But your results are bad.
Teacher: You mean the students' results.
Father: No, not the students' results, students only do as the teachers tell them. When the teachers tell them the wrong thing, they get bad results.
Teacher (perplexed): But surely the students have something to do with it. Some are cleverer than others …
Father: At Budo students always get good results because the teachers are good. At Malobe they get bad results because the teachers are bad.

English principals and students also have notions about the causes of success and failure. In the 1930s, a nine-year-old girl won first prize for reciting a poem in a drama festival. When the girl returned triumphant to Huntingdon Road Elementary School, the headmistress remarked, 'You were lucky'. 'I wasn't lucky,' she replied, 'I deserved it.' This sentiment was echoed at her victory press conference in 1975, when a reporter asked her, 'Why do you think you won?' 'Merit,' replied Margaret Thatcher briskly!

Cleverness, laziness, good luck and merit are perceived by different people at various times as causes of, or attributions for, academic success and failure. But how do these attributions for success and failure form, how do they develop, and what implications do they have for learning experience in the classroom and, as the last illustration suggested, for future experience in the world outside? Here the attribution theorists have been highly active in their experimental designs. As with most American social psychology, the empirical development of the work has been experimental, rigorous, logical and controlled. We have learned, for example, that people who attribute success to ability have a greater expectation of future success than those who attribute success to effort or luck. We have also learned that American men tend to attribute their own success to ability and their failure to lack of effort or bad luck and have high expectations of success in the future; whereas American women tend to attribute their success to effort and good luck and their failure to lack of ability, and have lower expectations of success in the future. Men, incidentally, while attributing *men's* success to ability, tend to attribute *women's success* to effort and good luck.

Attribution theory explains such findings in terms of the dimensions of controllability, locus and stability (Figure 3.1). Attribution theorists classify ability as internal to the individual, stable over time and uncontrollable. Luck, on the other hand, is classified as external, unstable and uncontrollable. Effort is usually classified as internal, unstable and controllable. The dimension of stability is considered to be critical for future expectations of success and failure, while the dimensions of controllability and locus are crucial for other outcomes concerning affect, esteem and interpersonal judgement.

The socio-economic context that gave rise to attribution theory and its main experimental base is Western, industrialised, American and, until quite recently, adult. Cross-cultural interest in the theory has grown rapidly in the last few years and many of the American experiments have been replicated. But the process of replication side-steps sociological and anthropological studies which have documented cultural variations in beliefs about personal causation. And as well as cultural differences, how well would attribution theory account for the attributions of schoolchildren in diverse cultures making daily sense of academic success and failure in the *classroom* rather than in the experimental laboratory? After all, the matrix of attributions was derived from the personal introspection of the attribution theorists themselves, and it was a good ten years after experimental research had started in earnest that Kelley and

	LOCUS			
	Internal		External	
CONTROLLABILITY	Stable	Unstable	Stable	Unstable
Uncontrollable	ability	mood	task ease	luck
Controllable	typical effort	immediate effort	teacher bias	unusual help from others

Figure 3.1 Attributions for success and failure classified by locus, stability and controllability (Weiner, 1979).

Michela (1980) suggested that the irony of the research was the lack of enquiry into the causal distinctions made by ordinary people. How much more ironic, then, that attribution researchers should apply this ungrounded matrix first to American children and second to children in other cultures.

In the mid-1970s, I examined attributions among schoolchildren in England and Sri Lanka (Little, 1985, 1987a). Although Sri Lanka is a poor country with a low level of income per capita, it has a literacy rate of 86 per cent and a long record of high social demand for education. In both countries educational success and failure are key determinants and legitimators of access to positions of power and status.

The present education system in Sri Lanka is centrally controlled and financed, textbooks are free, and students follow a national curriculum in most subjects and sit national examinations. But it is a system wedded to a socio-cultural context that is, though not exclusively, Sinhala Buddhist, a culture whose characteristics are well described by Sri Lankan anthropologists such as Gananath Obeyesekere (1979).

Sinhala-Buddhism provides a lay ethical code and a set of beliefs which help people to explain their daily existence. Among the beliefs which make up Sinhala-Buddhism is Karma, or 'the law of moral causation' and the associated belief in rebirth. Honourable deeds bear good fruit, either in this life or in a future rebirth, and bad deeds bear bad fruit. The present is the fruit of the past and the seed of the future.

In my own attribution study, schoolchildren aged five to fourteen years in Sri Lanka and England were presented with stories describing familiar events from their own classrooms. They were encouraged through interviews to explain freely why they thought the events had occurred. Why, for example, did children obtain different marks in a maths test, or why did children who started reading a book at the same time finish at various times? The data from the English and Sri Lankan children were analysed at the same time, thus avoiding the temptation so common in cross-cultural studies to examine the way in which the data from the second culture (usually the developing country) approximate the data from the first culture (usually the industrialised country). The analysis sought to identify categories which were common and uncommon across the two cultures. It confirmed the salience of categories used conventionally within attribution research but went further. Children in both cultures produced attributional responses not normally considered by conventional models – for example, good classroom behaviour and bad classroom behaviour, expressed as, 'He mucks about in class, that's why he's not doing very well', or age, 'She's older, that's why she's doing better'. Attributions were also seen to emerge developmentally in both cultures, especially those of ability and effort.

One of the most intriguing findings was the Sri Lankan children's elaboration of Karma. Forty-nine of the 11- and 14-year-olds were asked directly whether Karma could affect the learning of a child in school. Just over half said it could – but how? A few children did not explain any further, but the majority did. Some perceived a direct connection between good and bad deeds in a past life and high and low achievement in this life, for example, 'He must have given some books to another boy in his past life, that's why he is doing well now'. Others perceived the link between Karma and achievement to be mediated by economic circumstance. In these explanations good or bad deeds in the past life were perceived to determine the wealth or poverty respectively of the family into which one is born in this life. The economic condition then determined how well one learned in school.

The problem for attribution theory is how to classify an attribution like Karma. Remember that the concern of the theory is with the *lay* person's understanding of the social world and with the consequences of this understanding for future action.

One's first inclination as a Western observer is to relate it to the work on locus of control by Rotter, Seeman and Liverant (1962), on mystical and ascetic religion by Weber (1963), or on the characteristics of Inkeles and Smith's 'modern man' (1974). Following these writers Karma would end up classified as external, uncontrollable and stable. But Karma appears in forms which defy easy classification. Karma, remember, is a causal force that is thought to link past life with present and future life. At any one time a person is influenced both by his or her past Karma and by present Karma. Present Karma is equivalent in meaning to present deeds and action, including (and this is the difficult bit) present effort. Since life is a continuum, present Karma, which includes present effort, becomes past Karma for the next life, just as one's current Karma reflects earlier effort. Effort and Karma are compatible explanations, mutually reinforcing. Moreover, a bad Karma from the past life can usually be overcome by present effort. Only a belief in an extremely strong past Karma leads to feelings of resignation and uncontrollability.

Since it is the dimensions of attributions which are considered crucial for future action, it is important that attributions are not misclassified within the taxonomy. For example, Karma, like effort, may be viewed as internal, stable and controllable. This possibility also raises the question of whether the dimensions of lay people's theories should be *elicited from* the subject, rather than *imposed by* the researcher. One would think that this question is important enough for intra-cultural studies. For cross-cultural studies it is crucial.

This excursion into a branch of current education theory and examination of part of one small study highlights the importance of examining processes and outcomes of education and schooling in the context of their broader society and culture. The blind or blinkered export of attribution models by Western scholars and their blind or blinkered import by scholars in countries such as China, India or Nigeria would no doubt lead to a proliferation of replication studies and hundreds of PhDs. Through these we should learn a great deal about the extent to which Indian, Chinese and Nigerian children and adults approximated Western attribution models, but we should never know – and, more importantly, Indians, Chinese and Nigerians would never know – whether the most important attributions or dimensions had been identified and elaborated *ab initio*, or whether the most important concepts of social and interpersonal causality had been examined.

Attribution theory is based on the Aristotelian concept of 'efficient causality', but other concepts of causality are used by children and adults alike in trying to understand and act on the world around them.

If cross-cultural attribution studies follow this replication and reproduction route over the next few years, they will not be the first to have done so. In the 1950s and 1960s, studies of children's intelligence and achievement conducted in a number of African countries were based on Western theories and tests of intelligence. In the 1960s and 1970s, 'need for achievement' tests and the International Association for the Evaluation of Educational Achievement's tests of school achievement swept through much of the developing world; so too did Piaget's tests of 'conservation', designed to examine the speed and sequence of transition from pre-operational to concrete stages of thought among primary-school-age children. The view of economic, social and cognitive development implicit in these studies is linear. Development proceeds along a continuous line or up a ladder of stages. The important results are the comparisons of the economic, social, educational or psychological indicators with 'international' criteria set by outsiders. Internally designed criteria are less important, may not be considered, and are often unavailable.

Those who may be in a position to lead the development of internally designed criteria have often been trained in the West, following curricula designed for students from the West, and their professional reference groups may well be Western or, more accurately these days, cosmopolitan. The rarity of locally set research questions in developing countries, embodied in local or national intellectual, social and cultural values, concerns some of us who work with students from developing countries. It sometimes gives rise to the feeling that we may not always be contributing optimally, together with local universities and colleges, to the creation of a critical mass of people who have the professional self-confidence and the intellectual tools to research new fields of study which are socially and culturally attuned to their own circumstances and are relevant for the *mass* of their country's populations, rather than for the urban, middle-class minorities. Such a contribution by Western institutions is of course a very tall order. Let us think about it for a moment in reverse.

Imagine that a British teacher decides to follow postgraduate education studies in a Chinese university. Before leaving England, she struggles for two years learning *pu tong hua*. All the lectures are on the Chinese education system, on Chinese curriculum and assessment issues, on Chinese political economy. She reads books on pedagogy by Liu Fonian and on educational psychology by Pan Shu.

Few of the sociologically oriented studies she reads focus on social class and its implications for educational achievement and occupational selection. She visits Chinese schools and learns of the key role of moral and political education, and observes how class peers are invited to assess publicly each other's class performance and provide social and peer group reinforcement for academic success and failure. She also observes how children perform eye muscle exercises to music each morning to reduce eye strain and the chances of scoring a poor mark on the eyesight test which will prevent access to a key high school. In the library she finds Chinese translations of Russian texts and just a handful of books in English written by American and British authors, many published in the nineteenth century. She may be lucky and be able to enrol on a course on comparative education where she will read books by Professor Wang Cheng Xu, one of China's foremost scholars on comparative education in general, and on British education in particular. If she visits the library at Beijing Normal University she will be lucky indeed: not only will she find books by Watts, Peel and Lauwerys, and recent handbooks on international education written by colleagues from my own department, but she will also find no fewer than four books by Professor Lawton! At the end of her period of studies she returns home to Britain, where she is promoted to a very senior education post in a county education authority.

An unlikely scenario, you may say. Yes indeed, but in reverse this scenario happens regularly, perhaps not so noticeably with Chinese students since their numbers are still relatively few, but with many students from elsewhere in Asia and Africa, who are often promoted to extremely senior positions on their return home after completing postgraduate studies.

The learning experience of a developing country student in educational institutions in an industrialised country like Britain is less problematic when the student is a member of a group where British students are not in the majority. When the formal and hidden curriculum is genuinely international, where the student is exposed to a variety of educational models and to a wide range of education policy and practice, including that from his or her own country, then the process of evaluating *and valuing* one's own country's experience can begin. Yet the situation is still far from ideal, the most striking shortcoming being that the theoretical perspectives on education and development which subtend discussions of policy and practice are still offered disproportionately by Western scholars.

Collective creation of knowledge about education

I turn now to the second aspect of Learning from Developing Countries, in which I shall describe a learning exercise involving researchers and educators from industrialised and developing countries, and which offers the beginnings of a model of working practice for the creation of knowledge with international relevance.

The Student Learning Orientations Group, better known by its acronym SLOG, is a network of educational researchers based in India, Sri Lanka, Nigeria, Malaysia, Japan and England. SLOG is interested in students' definitions of why they learn (Little, 1987c). Though related indirectly to the attribution theory research described earlier, this work focusses on students' definitions of learning motivation, rather than on their explanations for learning success and failure. The work arises out of Ronald Dore's well-known, if controversial, thesis of the 'diploma disease' and subsequent research on labour markets, qualifications, assessment and the quality of learning in Mexico, Ghana, Sri Lanka, Malaysia and China, conducted at the Institute of Development Studies, Sussex in the 1970s (Dore, 1976; Oxenham, 1984). The SLOG group is concerned with the extent to which assessment goals are perceived to motivate learning in the classroom and, by comparing the assessment motive with other motives for learning, the extent to which assessment goals dominate other motives for learning.

Students vary in their perceptions of the purposes of and motives for learning. One student in an English comprehensive school expressed it in this way:

> I don't think anyone would come to school if there were no exams – most people associate exams with working hard and getting something out of working. So, if you are going to come to school and stay on for an extra two years and then get nothing for it, you think, 'God, what a waste of time'.

Another student in the same class, however, put it like this:

> I love learning – I do enjoy school and I don't want it to end. Some of our subjects are really interesting, so interesting that even after the exams are finished, I'll go on learning.

Our research is not confined to the classroom, however, for we are concerned with the transfer of this hidden curriculum of the affective learning environment from school to work. Is there any link between what students learn to believe motivates them to learn at school and what adults learn to believe motivates them at work? More particularly, and this is the controversial suggestion embodied in the 'diploma disease' thesis, does the headlong rush for assessment and qualifications inhibit the long-term motivation for sustained learning, challenge, innovation and creativity? We have not completed our quest – do we ever? – but I will share a few of our findings with you now.

As a starting point for our empirical work, we emphasised the importance of developing new measures of students' perceptions of motivation which had *intra*-cultural relevance as their primary aim and *inter*-cultural relevance as their secondary aim. Consequently, we have produced related but different sets of measures for the six countries.

Our insistence on grounding our empirical work in classrooms in six countries and the development of research measures *simultaneously* in these six countries meant that concepts and measures which would have been *excluded* had the entire conceptual framework been defined in the West, and then applied cross-culturally, were now *included*. For example, Asian colleagues insisted on the inclusion of what came to be known as 'significant others', especially parents, as a perception of learning motivation among secondary school students. In the questionnaires which we developed out of interview material, items such as the Japanese translation of 'When I do not do well in examinations my mother gets quite upset' became a key part of the Japanese definition of the concept of parental pressure, but did not survive as an important measurement of the concept of parental orientation in the English research. In Malaysia the item in Bahasa translation which read 'I am learning now in order to enter a prestigious university' was a key element in what the Malaysian researchers labelled extrinsic job orientation. It was important also for the Japanese, but not for the English.

When we moved from our intra-cultural measures to our inter-cultural measures, we found that the overall structure of learning orientation varied between cultures. At the inter-cultural level, we were able to distinguish between three learning orientations – assessment, task interest, and others – and examined patterns of relationship between them (Figure 3.2).

The Sri Lankan and Nigerian patterns were similar to each other. There appeared to be a high degree of interrelationship between an orientation to assessment, to task interest and to others, especially parents. A student who expressed the importance of one was likely to express the importance of the other. But the Malaysian pattern was different. There appeared to be a degree of differentiation in the structure. Whereas an orientation to others was strongly related to assessment, an orientation to learning interest was weakly related to both assessment and others. What this means is that a student highly oriented to assessment would tend also to be highly oriented towards others but less oriented towards task interest. The Japanese pattern approximated the Malaysian, though the relation between interest and others was even weaker than the Malaysian, and the relationship between others and assessment stronger, reflecting what both Japanese and Western researchers have written about the social definition of achievement in Japan.

The English pattern approximated none of the other patterns. Here assessment and interest were moderately related, but an orientation to others was hardly related to either assessment or interest, reflecting the more individual and personal definition of the meaning and purpose of assessment and achievement.

None of these findings has enabled us yet to refute or confirm the general propositions about assessment orientation, but that is less important at the moment than the knowledge about our own and each other's education system and the methods through which we have sought that knowledge. Our Asian colleagues' insistence on the inclusion of the concept and measurement of significant others, especially parents,

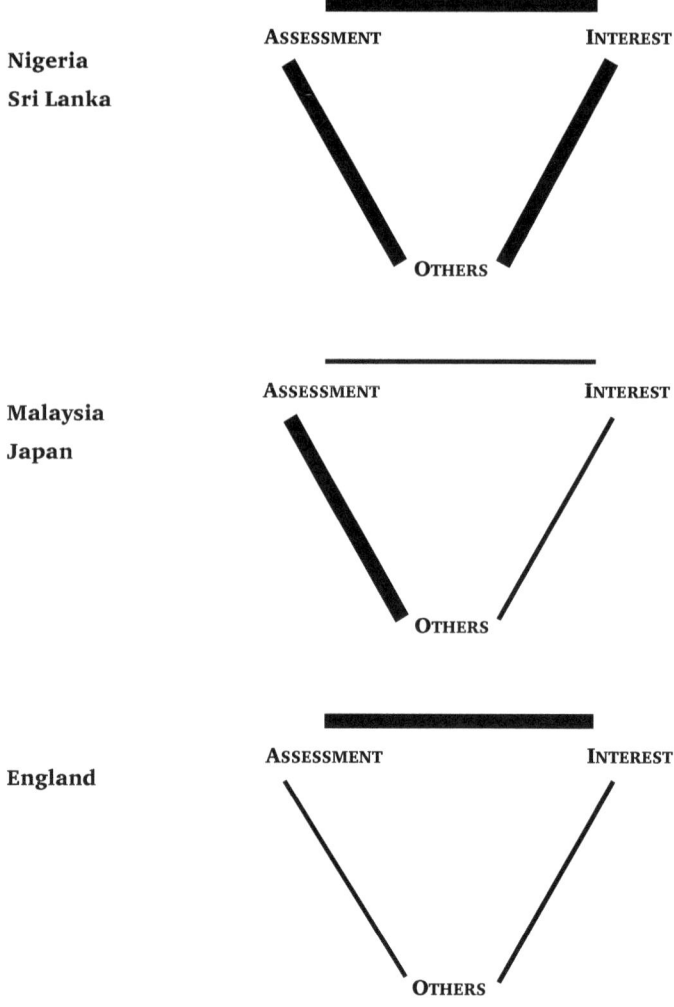

Figure 3.2 Patterns of relationship between assessment-orientation, interest-orientation and significant other-orientation. Source: Author.

broadened the conceptual framework, which, had it been left to the British researcher, would probably have focussed on assessment and interest motivation. This is not to suggest that parental motivation is not perceived to be important at all by English students, but, given what English students expressed in free response interviews, the overall framework of the research (the link between learning motivation and innovation and creativity at work) and the need to focus the research progressively, this more restricted framework would probably have emerged.

Our insistence that empirical work be conducted simultaneously, and that the empirical data had to be analysed against intra-cultural standards first, and against so-called international standards only second, allowed us to develop item banks and measures which could be useful for other colleagues working primarily in a national rather than international setting. It also freed our thinking about levels of analysis and allowed us to seek out dimensions appropriate at one level (for example the national) and less appropriate at another (for example the international). For example, an orientation common within one culture will not, by definition, emerge as something which differentiates students in that culture. But commonality within one culture can be apprehended at the international level of analysis, where it might then differentiate between one national population and another. Though we could see the possibilities we were less able to translate them into practice, hampered as we were by funding restrictions, and had to resort to a number of analyses which are still less than ideal.

Another weakness of our study which we hope others involved in international and comparative work will see their way to overcome is that, while we encouraged empirical specificity and differences between countries, we worked within a common conceptual framework. One of the challenges for international and comparative work in the future is the building of conceptual and theoretical models which take national conceptual models as their priority reference point. Only from such a firm base can truly international conceptual models be created.

* * *

Education borrowing and lending

I turn now to the third aspect of Learning from Developing Countries, and here I change my role slightly. While my main professional commitment is to the expansion and qualitative improvement of education in developing countries, there will be in the audience this evening educators whose main professional commitment is to education in Britain and who may be most interested in exploring whether Britain herself has anything to learn from the experience of education in developing countries. And there may be others who consider the very notion that Britain has something to learn *from* developing countries just a little obtuse.

Let us think for a moment about the concept of social and economic development. Most conceptions of development still place countries with high levels of Gross National Product per capita at the top end of the development ladder. Countries at the top end of the ladder have either reached their destination or are assumed to be moving even higher. Countries at the bottom end only have to look ever upwards to see where they are going. As Marx wrote in the preface to *Das Kapital*, 'The country that is more developed industrially only shows to the less developed the image of its own future'.

In *Development in a divided world*, Dudley Seers and Leonard Joy (1971) challenged this linear and evolutionary thinking and drew attention to the interaction between the stage of development and the nature of the international economic and political environment in which development takes place. In his elaboration of a similar idea, Dore, drawing on Gerschenkron's concept of 'late development', distinguished between early developing countries, late developing countries and later developing countries (1972). Early developers such as England began their drive towards industrialisation at a time when the international economic and political environment was quite different from that facing a later developer such as Japan in the latter part of the nineteenth century. And the international conditions facing Japan were different again from those facing countries as diverse as Tanzania, Sri Lanka and China today. The developmental patterns of each of these will be conditioned, to different degrees, by the contemporary realities of international debt, economic dependence and political struggle, and the interactions between each of these and respective national economic, social and political structures and histories.

The futures of developing countries are not necessarily pre-set to follow the image of the more industrialised countries. As Trotsky commented when writing his *History of the Russian Revolution*: 'England in her day revealed the future of France, considerably less of Germany, but not in the least of Russia and not of India.'

Thought of in this way, development patterns and policies of an industrialised country like Britain are unlikely to be reproduced anywhere in the developing world. Indeed, there may be a sense in which development images are offered in a reverse direction. Later developing countries tend to borrow from elsewhere models of education and employment which are current internationally when their industrialisation begins. Under some conditions the subsequent development of these models may be more rapid than their rate of development in their country of origin. Japan was a hesitant pioneer of job certification and manpower training practices which were borrowed selectively from elsewhere, but which developed in the Japanese context very rapidly and are now being taken for granted worldwide. Education selection systems based on exam achievement were a late addition to the British education systems and were exported widely to developing countries at a time when their Western-oriented systems of education were in their infancy. The subsequent development of these selection systems may have been more rapid than in Britain, where selection based on achievement overlays selection traditions based on ascriptive criteria such as social class.

Let me illustrate the idea that industrialised countries may identify images of their own future with an example from Tanzania. In 1974, the Tanzanian Ministry of Education introduced nationally controlled continuous assessment as part of the O and A level examination system. Continuous assessment was part of a package of reforms adopted by the ruling party, TANU, known as the 'Musoma Resolution', designed to redefine and extend the policy of education for self-reliance. An excerpt gives the flavour of the policy:

> We have to get rid of the ambush type of examination ... the excessive emphasis placed on written examinations must be reduced and students' progress in the classroom, plus his performance of other functions and the work which he will do as part of his education, must all be continuously assessed and the combined result is what should constitute his success or failure.

How similar much of this sounds to policy documents currently being produced by the Secondary Examinations Council in Britain today [1988] in connection with the introduction of GCSE.

The integration of Tanzania's national system of continuous assessment with more formal assessment began in 1976. Continuous assessment contributed 50 per cent of the marks in every subject examined and was broken down further into 25 marks for exercises, 20 for tests and 5 for projects. In addition, what is known as 'character assessment' was conducted as part of the continuous assessment. In Britain we would translate this term as a pupil profile, focussing on personal and social skills. In Tanzania, the profile included items such as 'attends classes punctually', 'works well with others regardless of their status or rank', 'assumes responsibilities when given leadership', 'accepts reasonable demands even though disliking them', 'inspires others to follow'. One example from Britain, from the county of Dorset where profiling has mushroomed over the last four years, includes a similar range: 'punctuality', 'works well in a team', 'leadership', 'working with those in authority'. Unlike Tanzania's Examinations Council however, the Secondary Examinations Council in this country has not issued a single profile to be used country-wide – not yet anyway!

Teachers and educators from abroad are often struck, if not to say a little mystified, by the decentralised system of education in this country. Centralised curricula and examinations are the rule, not the exception, in most developing countries in Africa and Asia, though less so in Latin America.

Last year in April, I accompanied a group of African and Asian curriculum developers and examiners on a visit to the School Curriculum Development Committee and the Secondary Examinations Council over in Newcombe House in Notting Hill Gate. During our meeting with Sir Wilfred Cockcroft, my Tanzanian colleague, Dr Agnes Njabili, suggested during discussion that Britain might think seriously about introducing a national curriculum and a national examination system. From her Tanzanian point of view, it seemed one way forward for Britain. Sir Wilfred smiled. As we left Newcombe House just after 4 o'clock that afternoon we were handed a press release: 'The Government has today announced plans for a national curriculum ...'

I do not propose to say anything more about the national curriculum – that is Professor Lawton's task tomorrow evening in this Institute.[3] But I would like to draw out one or two points from the Tanzanian example. I am not implying that the British Conservative Government has in any way borrowed an educational model from Socialist Tanzania – not consciously at least! Nor am I implying that Britain *should* borrow or emulate models from Tanzania, or from Germany, Japan or the United States of America for that matter. How could I argue that when I was stressing earlier the importance of endogenous models of education and development and was urging against the importation of inappropriate external models?

What I am saying is that educational innovation does not always start in industrialised countries trickling down to developing countries. There is and always has been considerable educational innovation in developing countries, innovation which faces problems to be sure – but where is the educational innovation anywhere in the world which does not? But industrialised countries are less good at recognising innovation in developing countries than are developing countries at recognising innovations in industrialised countries.

---

[3] Professor Denis Lawton, Director of the Institute of Education, gave a lecture entitled 'The national curriculum' on 16 March 1988 as part of a series on the Education Reform Bill.

I chose to illustrate my point about images of Britain's future through just one example from Tanzania. I might have selected educational experiences from any number of developing countries, examples which, while not offering themselves as models for import, nonetheless provide contrasting experiences which help throw into relief the problems and possibilities at home. Were Desmond Nuttall in the audience this evening, he would be able to describe how and why a new form of moderation currently in use by the Caribbean Examinations Council may well be a forerunner of things to come in England and Wales.

Others in the audience this evening could offer developing countries experience of education for pluralism, the vocationalisation of the curriculum, or full employment schemes, all of which resonate in discussions in Britain today. I would also suggest that questions of computer literacy and computer illiteracy may well find illumination from the work on literate and pre-literate societies, a literature which is already international, benefiting from experience from both industrialised and developing countries. If we look beyond our shores at all for ideas and experience of educational relevance for Britain, then we usually look no further than across the Atlantic, the North Sea and the English Channel. I am suggesting that it might be worth looking just a little further.

Lessons

Let me draw to a close by focussing on the implications of what I have been saying for work on international education in this Institute. First, theory and research. Ten years ago, when the Department of Education in Developing Countries was celebrating its 50th anniversary, rather than its 60th which we celebrate today, C. E. Beeby, writing about teachers, teacher educators and research, commented, 'the educational theorists for the most part have stayed cosily in their rich countries without risking their theories in the rough and tumble of the poor ones ...'. To the extent that we are interested in developing educational theory which generalises across national boundaries then we need to be able to understand the context of the subject of our theory. At one level of analysis – the individual child at school, for example – this may mean understanding much more than now about the development of and interaction between attitudes, aspirations, cognition and the quality of learning environment among children, living in a very wide range of social and economic settings, the most typical of which bear little resemblance to those we find in this country.

The schools attended by the children of the rich in many developing countries provide computerised learning environments not dissimilar to those found in the best British schools. But these are not typical. More typical are those whose teachers are struggling to provide a minimum quality of learning against a background of diminishing resources, a rural economy and, often still, a pre-literate population. It is all too easy for us to forget that nine hundred million of the world's population aged 15 and over are illiterate, 98 per cent of whom live in developing countries, half of them in China and India. Although most developing countries have made impressive strides in combating illiteracy especially among younger school-age populations, population growth rates and declining resources available for education may conspire and ensure that innumeracy and illiteracy will persist and worsen well into the twenty-first century. Even in my own department the dominant focus of our current work is on children and young people *in* the formal education system rather than those *outside*.

At another level of analysis, we need to understand much more than now about the interrelations between education and ethnicity, caste, language, religion, gender, tribal group and economic class. Our understanding of the process of development and the role of education in that process enjoyed a significant advance in the 1970s when the then dominant theories of modernisation were challenged by the dependency theorists from Latin America. We learned to appreciate the significance of relations between a dependent economy and its *metropole*, to focus on the reproductive role of education in the legitimation of local elite status, and to understand the role of education in the incorporation of elites into a transnational economy.

But dependency theory, like most others, is partial, relying as it does on a restrictive definition of class and its almost exclusive focus on the reproductive role of education. Ten years ago, Ali Mazrui (1978), in his *Political values and the educated class in Africa*, argued that the Marxian concept of class be reconceptualised for an understanding of social and political formation in Africa. Social formation, he argued, emerges from the question 'Who knows what?' rather than 'Who owns what?', thus emphasising education's active role in social formation rather than the more passive, reproductive and legitimating role to which dependency theory consigns it. I look forward to the integration of Mazrui's views into improved international theory on education and development.

The second implication of what I have been saying concerns consultancy. The emphasis on better understanding and theory should encourage the development of better advice, on those occasions when we are still asked. A better understanding usually implies a more complex understanding which, because it takes time, will slow down the headlong rush to provide the 'quick fix' panaceas of which there are precious few in quality learning and education. In saying this, I realise that I am speaking a little against the economic tide which is pulling British universities further towards the national and international marketplace. That international marketplace certainly has a stall which we should rent, but we should respond to the opportunities which this market presents with a degree of caution. Only when prepared to spend the time doing our homework to learn and understand more about the situation on which advice is sought, and only when prepared to share responsibility when things go wrong, should we erect our 'for sale' signs. International consultancy work is difficult, and time and energy consuming, if it is to be done well.

My third implication concerns the learning environment in which to collaborate with colleagues and students from developing countries. Those of us involved in teaching students from developing countries must continue to keep abreast of their literature, to recognise their intrinsic merit and to help students to evaluate them in relation to literatures from elsewhere. We also need to be aware that the dominant flow of traffic of theory and empirical standards in education on the North-South motorway is changing in shape and is beginning to filter into some side-street routes to improved knowledge and understanding.

National educational research associations in developing countries are growing in strength, as are national educational research institutes, funded frequently by international agencies. Regional networks for information-exchange and research between developing countries are enriching the already elaborate networks of economic, cultural and social exchange and are reinforcing regional identities. But the pool of educational experience in developing countries is not yet fully integrated into the realms of international knowledge. To achieve this, we need constantly to expand our library resources and explore more ways of bringing scholars from developing countries to collaborate with members of the department and with our students over periods of time.

Our aim is to help students from developing countries to value their own country's experience and further the development of endogenous and national models of education. The existence and recognition of endogenous models in turn provide the conditions necessary for the collective *creation* of knowledge and models of education that have international application.

Part II
Modernisation, human capital and dependency

Preface to Part II

The chapters in this part of the book address the following broad questions: To what extent have ideas about education and development found in the international discourse been tested empirically in the Sri Lankan context? And did any of these originate in the Sri Lankan context?

My early research on development and education was undertaken as a member of a multi-country team exploring the relationships between education quality, learning outcomes, labour market supply and, ultimately, economic growth and development. Success in public exams provides access to positions of power, prestige and income in domestic and international labour markets and is a central feature of modernising societies in which achievement criteria replace ascriptive criteria in the allocation of social and economic roles.

Chapter 4 examines two sets of reforms in the school examination system that took place between 1972 and 1977, their underlying drivers, their implementation, their contradictions and their further reform. The analysis addresses the relative power of analytical frameworks dominant in the international development discourse during the 1960s and 1970s – human capital and modernisation (HCM) theory on the one hand, and neo-Marxist and dependency (NMD) theory on the other. While both perspectives assert that change arises from conflict between the education system and the wider socio-economic system, they differ in the degree to which conflict is understood as a dominant or deviant characteristic of society; the relative strength of group vs individual interests; the certificating vs legitimating role of exams; the role of historical context in understanding current education and economic processes; and the role of social and political elites as 'modernisers' vs 'conspiratorial hegemonists'.

Chapter 5 explores some of the tenets of human capital theory and questions, through comparative studies conducted in Sri Lanka, Ghana and Mexico, whether education levels are necessarily related to job performance and whether earnings are a reliable proxy for 'productivity'. Through detailed interviews with Sri Lankan job supervisors, I suggest that the ingredients of job performance go beyond cognitive skills and abilities to include a wide range of social and personal abilities/orientations. I suggest a range of perceived motivations for both learning and working that go beyond anticipated financial return, the staple 'return' of economists. While human capital was a dominant concept in much of the early work of development agencies, until quite recently it featured relatively little in the education research and policy discourse in Sri Lanka. It would be much later, in the second decade of the twenty-first century, that the World Bank, in its dialogue with the Sri Lankan government and the Ministry of Education, would frame its education sector analysis around this concept (World Bank, 2021) and it would begin to appear in national policy statements.

Chapter 6 offers a partial critique of both modernisation and human capital theory, through a consideration of Ronald Dore's 'diploma disease' thesis (Dore, 1976, 1997b; Dore and Little, 1982; Open University, 1997). The thesis was inspired by Dore's personal experience of Sri Lanka's youth insurgency in 1971 and near collapse of the government of the day. It is an example of a development and education idea that was grounded in the Sri Lankan context and which subsequently entered the development and education discourse. The thesis links the quality of education with the timing of a country's drive towards modernisation, imbalances between school enrolments and modern sector jobs, and employers' uses of educational qualifications. Not only do public exams mediate between labour market allocation and the education and learning process; they also come to dominate that process. So important are the results of exams that the examination system itself is under constant scrutiny and attracts much social and political debate. The thesis is based on a comparative history of England, presented as an 'early developer', Japan as a 'late developer', Sri Lanka as a 'later developer' and Kenya as a 'much later developer'. In Chapter 6 I present the thesis and explore empirically the validity of some of its key propositions.

4
School examination reforms in the 1970s: modernisation or dependent underdevelopment?

Introduction

In 1972, 24 years after independence, far-reaching changes were introduced into Sri Lanka's education system. For the first time since the nineteenth century a system of public examining, disconnected from English norms, was introduced in secondary schools with the specific purpose of breaking finally with colonially inherited patterns of schooling. Although the Ceylon General Certificate of Education Ordinary (GCE O) level and Advanced (GCE A) level exams were, at this time, set and marked locally, they had maintained a degree of equivalence with the GCE O and A level exams in England. In 1972 they were replaced by National and Higher National Certificates of Education (NCGE and HNCE). These were designed to assess attainment in subjects whose syllabi and curriculum content were designed locally and derived from locally defined education priorities. In contrast to the GCE O and A level exams, which had been sat on completion of 10 or 12 years of education, respectively, the NCGE and HNCE exams were sat after 9 and 11 years, respectively. In 1977 NCGEs and HNCEs were abandoned in favour of a return to GCE O and A level-type examining and an emphasis on the international comparability of public-school exams.

This chapter outlines reforms in school examinations during the nineteenth and twentieth centuries. This forms a backdrop to a consideration of why the 1972 and 1977 examination reforms occurred. It analyses the origins and implementation of these reforms through a detailed analysis of documentary sources and through the application of concepts from competing perspectives on 'development' that were current at that time.

A focus on examination reform requires a brief elaboration. Centralised examination systems have played a key role in the development of education systems around the world (Dore, 1976; Eckstein & Noah, 1993). Not only do they define educational standards and educational aims, but they also legitimate access to further educational and occupational futures in modern sector economies. The more restricted the educational and occupational opportunities available in a society, and the more unequal the benefits associated with them, the greater the likelihood that examination 'backwash' becomes a determining characteristic of the quality of school achievement. The education systems of most 'developing countries' are strongly influenced by the content and timing of selection examinations. Sri Lanka is no exception (Government of Ceylon, 1972).

Against a long history of exams shaped by norms in England, the sharp break from them in 1972 is particularly interesting since it appeared, in principle, to remove an overriding constraint on educational development oriented towards nationally defined goals. The return of GCE O and A level examining after 1977, a superficially retrograde step, also merits considered analysis since it was a movement against the emerging orthodoxy of much general development theory at that time which stressed the importance of breaking colonially inherited links – an emerging orthodoxy that was simultaneously at odds with the values of many among the post-colonial power elites.

This chapter is organised into five sections. In the first, concepts from neo-classical economics and modernisation theory on the one hand and neo-Marxist and dependency theory on the other are described briefly and provide the reader with ways of thinking about the purposes of exams and education and examination reform. The second offers a historical overview of the use of exams in selecting young people for jobs and for further education between 1833 and 1970. The third focusses specifically on the economic and political conditions that led to examination reform in 1972. The fourth explores the course of the 1972 examination reform and its replacement through further reforms in 1977. The final section returns to the theoretical concepts and discusses their adequacy in our understanding of the 1972 and 1977 reforms.

Theoretical perspectives

As we saw in Chapter 2, two broad theoretical frameworks dominated 'development' thinking in the West between the 1950s and 1970s.

The first broad perspective combines the focus of development economists on Gross National Product (GNP), labour supply and human capital with the focus of sociologists on industrialisation and modern societies. I refer to it in shorthand as human capital and modernisation (HCM). During this period, development economists moved from an almost obsessional concern with incremental capital output ratios and rates of growth in GNP towards a more eclectic appreciation of the importance of the finer structure of the economy and qualitative aspects of manpower supply (Nurske, 1957; Schultz, 1961; Denison, 1964). As noted in Chapter 2, Seers (1969) suggested that the main index of economic development – GNP – needed to be replaced by a notion of development as a reduction or elimination of poverty, inequality and unemployment.

Human capital theory (Becker, 1964) moved centre stage in educational planning, and the technological functionalism on which it was based provided clear links with the functionalist tradition of sociological analysis most clearly exemplified by K. Davis and Moore (1945). Modernisation theory emerged in the 1960s, partly in response to the frustration of planners impatient with the disappointing record of the United Nations' First Development Decade, such failure being thought to originate within the structure of society and the 'culture' of poor countries. Thus, the 'solution' to the 'problem' of development became linked to the need to create 'modern man', characterised as universalistic, future oriented, educated, achievement oriented and rationally minded (Inkeles & Smith, 1974; McClelland, 1961). Education would be accorded a key role in the development of human capital and the socialisation of 'modern man'.

The second broad perspective combines the focus of neo-Marxist and dependency economists with the focus of sociologists on the formation of indigenous elites, cultural alienation and education's role in their creation. I refer to these concerns in shorthand as neo-Marxist and dependency (NMD). This provides a competing theoretical framework for the discussion of development. As described in Chapter 2, a 'dependency' perspective focusses on 'underdevelopment' rather than 'development'. Underdevelopment is posited as an outcome of systematic exploitation and manipulation of the periphery by the centre. Poor countries are conditioned by their economic relationships with rich economies to occupy a subordinate and dependent role (for example Frank, 1967; Cardoso, 1972; Dos Santos, 1973; Foster Carter, 1974; Leys, 1975). This subordination inhibits their development through the expropriation by others of investible surpluses.

Indigenous (or endogenous) elites, firmly wedded to the international capitalist system and rewarded handsomely by it, are motivated to be dependent, while simultaneously possessing the power to prevent other sectors of their society from becoming less so. The underlying drivers of development are a combination of current national structures, historical conditions and the international system of 'global exploitation' managed by developed capitalist countries. Dependency also produced, through education, cultural alienation (Carnoy, 1974) and 'crippled minds' (Goonatilake, 1982; Wurgaft, 1985).

Theoretical analyses depend in part on the interests and locus of those who offer them, and in part on the economic-political-social nexus of the contexts which gave rise to them. As we saw in Chapter 2, most formal analyses of general relationships between development and education have been generated from contexts beyond those to which they are applied subsequently. This is not to imply that such analyses are necessarily irrelevant for contexts beyond those that generate them. The strength of abstract concepts resides in their transferable nature. But some concepts are likely to be more context-bound than others (Little, 1999a). In the rest of this chapter, I explore the relevance of concepts drawn from HCM and NMD in their application to the question of examination reform.

Educational change and conflict

The HCM and NMD perspectives on the relationship between the education system of a country and its wider economic and social context are similar. Both HCM and NMD view the content and processes of education as reflecting extant patterns of social organisation and production. Emile Durkheim, a founding father of the sociology of education and 'social functionalism', from which the HCM perspective descends, suggested that 'educational transformations are always the result and the symptom of the social transformation in terms of which they are to be explained' (Durkheim & Bierstedt, 1969). Similarly, Bowles and Gintis (1976), writing from the NMD perspective, advanced a principle of 'correspondence' – schooling reflects and replicates the social relations of production in the economy; educational change occurs in response to changes in those relations. Neither perspective denies the possibility of a more autonomous, less reproductive role for education. While the HCM perspective advances the notion that education is an 'engine of growth', the NMD perspective acknowledges that schooling has a degree of autonomy and can produce individuals who become agents of educational change within a dependent system (Carnoy, 1974).

In both perspectives, educational *change* arises through conflicts between the education system and the wider socio-economic context, followed by adjustments. It is in *the reasons for such conflict* and the means of their resolution that substantial differences between the HCM and NMD approaches appear. These are addressed below.

Consensus or conflict? Norm or deviation?

The first difference is that the HCM perspective adopts the functionalist assumption that societies enjoy a high degree of normative consensus, and that conflict is a pathological deviation from that consensus (Paulston, 1976). Thus, changes which do not clearly arise from 'societal needs' are treated as 'dysfunctional'. By contrast, the NMD perspective posits conflict as a necessary consequence of competition between groups for power and control, rather than a pathology. For HCM, societal consensus is the norm; conflict is a pathological deviation from it. For NMD, conflict is the norm; consensus is a pathological deviation from it.

Group or individual interests?

The two approaches place a different stress on the relative importance of socio-economic class group and individual interests in generating conflict and consensus and in generating change. In the HCM perspective, normative consensus is primarily an expression of the convergence of individual interests. Consensus, conflict, competition and reward are all viewed as individual-level phenomena. Within the NMD perspective, by contrast, class interests define the nature of social and economic interaction. Consensus, conflict, competition and reward are primarily group-level phenomena.

The certification of competency or legitimation of economic inequality?

A third difference is the legitimacy accorded to public exams in the allocation of economic roles in society. HCM perspectives generally stress the necessity and fairness of selection through meritocratic examination competition. Examinations certify achievements, abilities and effort and provide access to differential rewards in the economy.

Such rewards are distributed in accordance with the supply and demand for particular skills and reflect the value of the individual's contribution to the productive process. Sorting and selection are inevitable, and schools and exams are the institutions which perform this function (Clark, 1962). Within the NMD perspective, the social function of selection is interpreted differently. The competition is far from fair because meritocratic and promotion standards favour the economically advantaged. Selection through exams serves primarily to reproduce social class divisions (Bowles, Gintis & Simmons, 1976).

Historical context: endogenous or exogenous conditions?

A fourth difference lies in the nature of historical conditions considered to be important for economic development. As we saw in Chapter 2, HCM approaches include 'stage' theories of development (for example Rostow, 1960) which highlight the longstanding role of endogenous conditions, such as feudal and 'traditional' institutions and rural oligarchies which inhibit 'development'. By contrast, the NMD perspective emphasises historical exogenous as well as endogenous factors and the relations between them. A specific country's historical development process must be analysed in relation to the evolution of capitalism around the world and its local manifestations:

> The establishment of colonies, the struggle against the colonisers, decolonisation … transfers of foreign institutions and culture generally – these all play a central role in the historical evolution of every underdeveloped country. (Sunkel, 1979)

National elites – beneficent modernisers or conspiratorial hegemonists?

A fifth difference lies in the nature and the role of national elites. Both perspectives regard the formation, attitudes and behaviour of national elites as important determinants of social change. The HCM perspective generally treats national elites as beneficent modernisers whose interests coincide with those of the mass of their peoples. 'Modernising' elites tend to be guided by Western models of education, career development, job allocation and patterns of consumption. The expansion of Western-style secondary and tertiary education is seen as a good thing as far as it extends opportunity to the mass of the population and acts as a vehicle to enhance 'modernisation' of the entire population.

By contrast, the NMD perspective uses the language of class stratification and conflict to describe national elites as 'comprador classes' and 'bourgeois elites' who act within a 'transnational' convergence of interests. They enjoy a coincidence of interests with internationally dominant classes and are challenged by local class groups (Cardoso & Faletto, 1979).

School examinations during the British colonial period

A brief overview of education and assessment in pre-colonial and European colonial times was presented in Chapter 1. It was not until the period of British colonial rule that examinations began to play an important part in selection for colonial government employment. A small number of preparatory schools were established with the express purpose that they be 'for the education of children of Burghers and of those of the natives whose families are eligible to dignities and charges given by government to the native servants' (J. E. Jayasuriya, 1979).

The curricula in these schools were oriented to Christianity and the learning of English, and were offered to a tiny elite. Those who graduated from the preparatory schools and a single post-preparatory school (known initially as the Academy and subsequently as the Royal College) gained low- and middle-grade government positions and worked mainly as translators and interpreters.

The Ceylon Civil Service (CCS) was established in 1802; initially all of its 'administrative' positions were reserved for Europeans. The Ceylonese had access only to less prestigious government service jobs. The Colebrooke Commission of 1833 recognised the inequities that this created, and in 1844 the first Ceylonese was admitted, following a competitive exam, to the lower grades of the CCS. From 1870 Ceylonese began to be admitted to the senior grades, through a competitive exam. Over time, access to the CCS for Ceylonese improved and the 'meritocratic' link between government jobs and exam achievement permeated the whole of the government service, from the CCS down to junior-grade clerks. It was also during this period that aspiring Ceylonese began to emulate on a large scale the colonial rulers they eventually replaced. The values, habits, dress and organisational behaviour gleaned from the British became part of the culture of the elite in a more general sense than had previously been the case.

As early as 1862, a 'local' eighth-grade school exam was introduced to certify attainment and to provide access to further education and jobs. The exam was 'a copy of what was going on at the time in England' and was set and marked locally by the Department of Public Instruction in Sri Lanka (Government of Ceylon, 1972). This exam survived for 18 years, when it was replaced by the exams of the Examinations Syndicate of the University of Cambridge. Cambridge Senior Local and Junior Local examinations were held for the first time in 1880. Soon after, the Matriculation, Intermediate in Arts and Intermediate in Laws examinations of the University of London were introduced from 1882. During this time, Sinhala- and Tamil-speaking students from a few missionary schools sat the examinations of the Universities of Calcutta and Madras, but this arrangement would be abandoned in due course.

The abandonment in 1880 of 'local' in favour of the London and Cambridge examinations has been interpreted by some Sri Lankans as a blessing and by others as a curse. On the one hand, J. E. Jayasuriya maintains that foreign exams provided all Ceylonese with a new confidence in their abilities and removed 'from the minds of the people the feeling of inferiority that came from being a subject race' (J. E. Jayasuriya, 1979, p. 303). On the other hand, the select committee appointed to inquire into public examinations at secondary school level in 1972 deplored the failure to build a local system of examining from those early beginnings (Government of Ceylon, 1972).

By the latter part of the nineteenth century, the correspondence between educational levels and government jobs was well established. Access to the highest of these levels was concentrated amongst groups who were socially ascendant for reasons of caste, ethnicity, sex, religion, language, gender and geographical location. The English-speaking elite enjoyed preferential access to government jobs. The concentration of missionary activity in the maritime provinces had given low-country Sinhalese access to English-medium schools and contact with English culture, ahead of up-country Sinhalese. Similarly intensive missionary activity in the north around Jaffna gave some Tamils educational advantages which persisted through the twentieth century. The growth of vernacular-medium schools in the twentieth century did little to redress imbalances of access to high-quality education, for this growth occurred within a dual system in which English-medium schools were superior. And it was during this period that a new 'colonial elite', later to become the national elite, began to displace the status of traditional elites in rural areas (R. Pieris, 1976).

In the years leading up to independence there was further growth in the number of both foreign and local examinations. The Cambridge Senior and Junior 'School Certificate' replaced the Cambridge Senior and Junior Local examinations in 1916 and the subjects of Sinhala and

Tamil were introduced for the first time in 1919. In addition to the London examinations introduced from 1882, the University of London had, by 1920, added Bachelor of Arts, Intermediate in Science, Bachelor of Science, Bachelor of Laws and Bachelor of Medicine and Surgery. All of these examinations were set and marked in England.

A new local school English-medium examination, the Elementary School Leaving Certificate, was introduced in 1914 for those English-medium schools that chose not to enter their students for the Cambridge Junior School Certificate. In 1917 a Vernacular School Leaving Certificate examination was introduced for students completing the eighth grade in Sinhala- or Tamil-medium schools. Those successful in this exam were given special consideration for appointment to jobs such as headman or registrar. In 1902 the Department of Public Instruction appointed a Committee on Oriental Studies to introduce Preliminary, Intermediate and Final examinations in subjects including Sanskrit, Pali, Sinhalese, and the History and Archaeology of Ceylon.

Between 1920 and 1948 there was a gradual move to greater independence in the setting and marking of school and university exams. The Cambridge Junior and Senior School Certificates were abandoned in 1936 and 1942, respectively. The locally run School Leaving Certificates in three languages – English, Tamil and Sinhala – were renamed Junior School Certificates from 1933 and were abandoned from 1944. A preliminary exam for teachers was introduced in 1926 and was renamed the Senior School Certificate Examination in 1941. An Advanced School Certificate was established in 1943.

The move to greater independence in the setting and marking of exams was spurred on by the Second World War, during which time the safe transport of exam papers to Colombo and scripts back to London became uncertain. From 1941 London Matriculation papers, albeit based on University of London syllabi, were set and marked in Colombo. The London Matriculation exam was abandoned in 1948. The Ceylon GCE O level was established in 1952, followed by the Ceylon GCE A level in 1964. Despite their titles, these exams were not linked formally to the English school exams bearing the same names.

Increased participation in school examinations in the post-independence period

By the late 1960s, high levels of educational provision, local oversupply of high-level manpower, low levels of remuneration and internationally recognised qualifications provided the conditions for the export of qualified manpower, or 'brain drain', on a substantial scale. By the 1970s, exam success was a precondition for all non-manual jobs in the modern sector and was increasingly used to select for manual wage employment (Deraniyagala, Dore & Little, 1978). Growth in educational enrolment, particularly at the secondary and tertiary levels, outstripped the economic demand for educated manpower, with the predictable consequences of large-scale 'educated unemployment' and 'qualification escalation' (ILO, 1971a). In an increasingly bureaucratised modern sector labour market, the only option open to most students for gaining wage and salary jobs was to remain in the fee-free education system and increase their competitive advantage over school leavers at lower levels. With high levels of unemployment, the opportunity costs were low or negligible and employers were explicitly using educational qualifications as a convenient 'filter' to limit the number of applicants for jobs rather than select those thought to have special skills or talents (Deraniyagala, Dore & Little, 1978).

The practice of children attending extra private tuition classes after school and during the weekends to prepare for exams became widespread. A survey of successful entrants to physical science courses at the University of Colombo revealed that 70 per cent had received private tuition in one or more subjects (Samaranayake, 1978). Press advertisements for tuition providers usurped familiar names from elsewhere – the Brighton Institute, the Oxonia Institute, Aquinas. Belief that personal effort is the major determinant of success or failure in academic pursuits was widespread amongst parents and students (Little, 1982) and echoed the earlier concerns of the British Victorian middle classes for meritocratic selection based on achievement. This 'modern' belief in the efficacy of personal effort (Inkeles & Smith, 1974) interacted with more traditional beliefs and behaviours. Young people and their families – Buddhists and Hindus alike – implored the gods of knowledge and wisdom for exam success. Young people and their families made pilgrimages to Kataragama and Anuradhapura to fulfil vows after exam success (Little, 1982). These practices continue to this day.

The interrelationships between power, prestige, educational qualifications, jobs, class and caste were perhaps best captured in the operation of the marriage market as expressed through the English- and vernacular-language national papers. One example from the English-language *Sunday Observer* on 23 March 1980 makes the point:

> Respectable Govigama Buddhist parents seek Doctor, Engineer, Chartered Accountant, Varsity Lecturer, CAS for slim fair daughter

29, Visakhian Science Teacher 65" [5ft 5in]. Dowry over five lakhs, cash one lakh, two bungalows, coconut land, etc. Horoscope essential.

The desirable attributes are clear – *govigama* is the highest Sinhalese caste; CAS is the Ceylon Administrative Service (the successor to the CCS); 'fair' means light skinned; *Visakha* is a premier girls' school with more exam distinctions at A level than any other Colombo school in 1980; one lakh is one hundred thousand rupees – a not insubstantial amount of money in 1980.

The 1972 school examination reforms

Precursors and proposals

The Sri Lankan economy of the 1970s remained largely agricultural, with around 50 per cent of the labour force directly involved in food production for local consumption and the production of cash crops for export. Only about 10 per cent of the working-age population and 16 per cent of the total labour force were employed in wage and salary employment in the modern sector (Deraniyagala, Dore & Little, 1978). Growth rates in the modern sector were low, rising little above 1.5 per cent per annum between 1953 and 1971.

In May 1970, the Sri Lanka Freedom Party (SLFP) was returned to office in a coalition government that included Trotskyist and Communist factions. In its 1970 election manifesto the SLFP committed itself to improving equality of access to education and ameliorating the worsening problems of unemployment facing school-leavers. The ideological complexion of the coalition favoured a weakening of those links between Sri Lanka and other countries that encouraged economic dependence and loss of national autonomy. The development strategy that emerged focussed on the development of indigenous resources (Ministry of Planning and Employment, 1971). This was reflected in education policy:

> The present type of education has also placed a premium on examinations and diplomas rather than the development of skills so necessary for economic development. Thus today in nearly all sectors, there is a tendency to depend on foreign technical skills and resources and the foreign expert, and foreign aid has become a substitute for the development of indigenous skills

and resources ... The present divorce of education from the world of work has uprooted an entire generation from the type of production which can readily be developed in the country and has pushed the person who would normally have gone into some productive activity into a fruitless search for white collar employment, the expansion of which can no longer be supported by the country's productive sectors. (Ministry of Planning and Employment, 1971)

An Education Review Committee established in late 1970 reported on the restructuring of the education system in line with the new government aims and a new vision of 'development'. The first public suggestion that this would involve abolishing the Ceylon GCE O and A levels emerged in the *Ceylon Daily News* of 28 February 1971. The need to shift the education system away from its dominant obsession with academic schooling was part of the rationale for their abolition and was consistent with the government's policy objective of vocationalising the curriculum (Ministry of Planning and Employment, 1971).

The proposal attracted strident criticism in the press. It was claimed that such a change would interrupt the education of pupils and that it would be change for the sake of change. The cry that there should be 'no more guinea pigs please' (*Ceylon Daily News*, 28 February 1971) from the main teachers' union, the Jathika Sangamaya, echoed a general reluctance to depart from the existing system. It was hardly unexpected that groups who saw their children's chances threatened by changes that would require them to adjust to new courses and examinations should react in this way. Indeed, their opposition might have been decisive in ensuring a still birth for the proposal had the youth insurrection of 1971 not intervened.

For a few days in April 1971, the SLFP government was close to collapse as a result of a widespread insurrection. The insurrection was apparently organised by disaffected youths frustrated at the slow pace of the election promises to reduce unemployment and improve equity. According to one commentator, 85 per cent of those ultimately detained had GCE O level qualifications (Wilson, 1972). A subsequent and probably more realistic analysis suggests that 75 per cent of all suspected insurgents had received secondary education to Grades 5–8 or to GCE O level. Only 19 per cent had received only primary education or none at all, and the remaining 6 per cent were A level and university students (Obeyesekere, 1974). The insurgents were viewed as:

> a deprived group but not a depressed group like a *lumpen proletariat* ... many of them would simply not be able to enter university either due to lack of vacancies there, or financial difficulties. Even if they did complete a university degree there was no guarantee of employment. Thus, if they were not already aware of the bleak future that awaited them they could easily be made conscious of it. Their youth and idealism could then be tapped for a new movement that held promise for the future. (Obeyesekere, 1974)

The insurgency focussed attention on the education system as a fomenter of insurrection and muted those who had previously opposed reform. Public debate on the causes of the insurrection centred on educational structure in general and examination patterns in particular. As the then minister of education put it:

> In an education system that was little more than assembly line or academic factory, in the socially irrelevant context of education and in the chronic maladjustment between the educational process and the national economy, any person of discernment could see the source of tension and the ever-widening ripples of discontent sweeping the surface of our society. (*Ceylon Daily News*, 1 June 1971)

Once civil order had been re-established, the embryonic proposals of the Education Review Committee were revitalised. They resulted in a restructuring of the education system that was more far-reaching than it would have been had the insurrection not occurred (Wijemanne, 1978). Those who argued that the time had come to abandon the colonially inherited pattern of education and exams were in the ascendancy. Two new national exams – the National Certificate of General Education (NCGE) and the Higher National Certificate of Education (HNCE) – replaced the GCE O and A level examinations, dating from 1952 and 1964, respectively. From 1975, the NCGE was sat as the first selection point in the education system, at the culmination of nine, rather than ten, years of a general education curriculum with a 'pre-vocational' bias. The HNCE was held after two more years of schooling, partly as a university qualifying exam and partly as a school leaving certificate for those who could not enter higher education. Both exams were intended to shift the emphasis in achievement away from the recall of information towards the application of knowledge, problem-solving and skills of direct employment benefit.

It was argued that new exams would open the door for curriculum change of a kind that could not take place within the existing examining structure. The school entry age was raised to 6 years, the length of pre-university schooling was reduced from 12 to 11 years, early selection for the former GCE O level streams in schools was abolished in favour of a common curriculum up to Grade 9, and new curricula were designed to reduce academic content in favour of locally relevant job skills. The spirit in which these reforms were introduced appears to have indicated a genuine and novel commitment to improve the education of the majority of students who did not progress to the end of the system at a time when only about 10 per cent of each age cohort reached upper secondary school and no more than 1 to 2 per cent reached university.

A strong and consistent theme surrounding the discussion of the proposals was that the new structure would serve 'the causes of intellectual de-colonisation' (Curriculum Development Centre, 1975). The scale and scope of the 1972 reform proposals were unprecedented. Moreover, they arose more from an attempt to resolve internal political conflicts than from any overt influence from external agencies. Although the 1971 International Labour Organization mission to Sri Lanka (ILO, 1971a) did see some of its recommendations on education incorporated into the 1972 government policy, there is no evidence to suggest that the Sri Lankan government was under any direct pressure to do so. As for more subtle psychological dependence on the wisdom of advice from outsiders, the then secretary of the Ministry of Education was clearly well immunised:

> Of all the great deficiencies created in our societies by colonial rule nothing is so pervading as a lack of moral courage and strength to think beyond the intellectualism imposed on us by the imperial powers ... The pre-occupation of us all with what occurs in developed societies has stifled our intellectuals, thinkers and innovators in education. (Curriculum Development Centre, 1975)

Nonetheless, the government felt it necessary subsequently to justify changes through international comparison. The raising of the school entry age to 6 years was defended by reference to a UNESCO study of 109 countries which indicated that only seven countries started schooling at 5 years and 55 started at 6 years (Ministry of Education, 1973).

Implementation of the 1972 reforms

The initial development work for the NCGE examinations was undertaken by Curriculum Development Centre staff. The reforms aimed to improve the traditional exam to better promote the aims of the curriculum. Trial exams were designed not so much for the pupils but to encourage teachers to realise more fully the intentions behind the programmes. Attempts were made to involve teachers directly in the design of assessment items, and teachers in each district of the country were invited to contribute questions to a pool which would allow the construction of sample exam papers. This latter activity was not a success, since most items produced were found to be unusable – typically being judged too difficult and/or inappropriately constructed. Questions were thought to be too factually and descriptively oriented and typical of the O level questions which NCGE was designed to replace (Lewin, 1981).

The new exam was not markedly different from the old, probably because there was public pressure to retain a degree of comparability with the former GCE O level exam. Questions about whether the new NCGE qualification would have any competitive value in the labour market exacerbated these pressures. The desire to retain the overt objectivity of closed-book, controlled-condition exams also limited the possibilities for significant departures from traditional examining formats, and effectively ruled out school/teacher-based assessment. Previous experience with a teacher-assessed component of public exams had proved controversial. The traditional written exam had only recently been described as the only way of 'screening the candidates in such a way that favouritism, thuggery and low cunning are set at nought in selecting persons for jobs or further education' (Government of Ceylon, 1972).

Another limitation on radical change in examining was the continued unwillingness of the universities to change their admissions criteria. These were firmly grounded in notional comparability with England, and, though it was unlikely that similar educational outcomes could be produced through the proposed – shorter – span of education, such concerns proved very influential. Downward pressure from the universities helped to shape HNCE examinations and curricula and, through these, the shape and content of the NCGE courses. Thus, the GCE O level pattern of a two-paper written exam, the first consisting of multiple-choice questions and the second of structured free-response essay questions, was retained in the NCGE for most subjects.

The proportion of NCGE science knowledge items increased while that of comprehension and application items decreased, when compared with the earlier GCE O level single-subject science exams (Lewin, 1981).

The NCGE exam in a new subject – 'pre-vocational studies' – attracted the most sustained criticism. The subject was introduced with two main components. The first included the existing range of practical subjects taught in schools; the second permitted schools to design curricula individually or collectively for ministry approval based on local economic activities. These designs resulted in 81 courses being approved in 1972, but by 1975 this number had dwindled to closer to 20 as the implications of assessing such a diverse range of programmes became clear. Although teacher assessments were intended to be combined with written, centrally set pre-vocational studies exams, it proved impossible to moderate this process effectively. And in an attempt to encourage teachers and students to take pre-vocational studies seriously, it was made a compulsory subject for progression to the HNCE course. This increased the pressure to examine pre-vocational studies using traditionally accepted styles of examining, despite the likelihood that this would ritualise what was taught.

Growing disillusionment

The consequences of changes in the examination and education system became apparent between 1976 and 1977. Opposition grew around four issues. First, as already noted, the standard of NCGE in most subjects could not be seen as strictly comparable to the GCE O level even though it was argued officially to be so. NCGE was taken in Grade 9, not Grade 10, by non-selective groups from the whole ability range. Curricula were broader. Coupled with a worsening labour market situation, this exacerbated rather than improved employment problems for those with NCGE qualifications. NCGE never became established as an alternative qualification, partly because surplus O level graduates were available for employment in large numbers from previous cohorts of school leavers, and employers generally valued O level as a more reliable and higher qualification.

Second, changes in the name of the NCGE and HNCE examinations and the lower level of achievement represented by them made it difficult to argue that they would be recognised internationally. The middle classes, in particular, felt that their children's chances of studying abroad had been undermined. Many children whose parents could afford it sat the NCGE and simultaneously studied for the London and Cambridge overseas O levels, which required them to travel to Madras or Singapore to sit the exams.

Third, the view that NCGE was 'selling students short' began to spread. Rural parents were not enamoured of changes which gave their children one year less schooling, decreased academic content in favour of pre-vocational content and increased the chances of their children remaining in low-wage casual and traditional employment. Though the evidence on the latter point is complex and it was true that overall numbers progressing to upper secondary education almost doubled when NCGE was introduced, there is evidence to suggest that this disproportionately favoured students attending well-established urban schools with the most competent staff, relatively good resources, and good communication with the Curriculum Development Centre and Examinations Department. Those students were therefore able to adapt to new examinations much more rapidly and effectively, and this was reflected in the initial exam results (Lewin, 1981).

Fourth, pre-vocational studies, a mainstay of the new education system, began to fall into disrepute. After the first NCGE in 1975, when significant numbers of candidates, including urban candidates, were initially denied promotion because of their mediocre performance on the compulsory subject of pre-vocational studies, a public outcry weakened the Ministry of Education's resolve. Urban parents argued that much of the pre-vocational study was irrelevant for their children, who they hoped were destined for modern sector employment, while rural parents and pupils also became cynical of programmes based on skills which they felt the community already possessed and were not best taught by schoolteachers.

Meanwhile, the 'brain drain' of highly qualified, Sri Lanka-educated people continued. Between 1971 and 1976, 1,254 doctors, 1,074 engineers, 494 accountants, 141 university teachers and 1,325 other highly skilled personnel left Sri Lanka to work overseas. These people represented approximately 15 per cent of the total stock of professional and technical personnel in 1971 (N. Nesiah, 1978). Between 1976 and 1978, up to 20,000 skilled and semi-skilled workers were recruited by West Asian oil-producing countries, and by 1979 over 800 million rupees per year was being repatriated by workers in West Asia (*Ceylon Daily News*, 1980). For all these jobs, access depended on the possession of internationally acceptable educational and professional or trade qualifications.

By the time of the 1977 general election there was widespread dissatisfaction with NCGE and HNCE examining, and the economic situation and the mismatch between job seekers and available jobs had not improved. The economy was growing very slowly and there continued a chronic mismatch of supply and demand for educated manpower. Expressed simply, the situation in 1976 was that approximately 330,000 school leavers were entering the labour market each year and fewer than 50,000 modern sector jobs were becoming available (Dore, Humphreys & West, 1976). Nearly half of the school students had reached Grade 9 or higher and were likely to have expectations of modern sector jobs (Lewin, 1981).

The 1977 reforms: return of the old order?

In 1977 the United National Party (UNP) swept to power and sealed the fate of the 1972 reforms. The attractions of returning to the 'golden age' of GCE O and A level examining, comfortably legitimised by long-standing practice and international precedent, fed into a conservative policy to turn back the clock. A party of opposing convictions to the SLFP, which traditionally drew its support from the business community and the conservative establishment, the UNP was committed to a return to educational standards that were 'internationally comparable'. Under its auspices the powerful, though small, lobby whose goal was to re-establish access to internationally recognised qualifications was able to make its voice heard. Students who wished to sit the London University A level exam would now be able to do so (*Ceylon Daily News*, 2 December 1977).

As part of a total package, the Sri Lanka GCE O and A level exams were reintroduced (though much of the curriculum material from NCGE/HNCE courses was retained), the school entry age was lowered once again to 5 years, and the GCE O level, sat at the end of Grade 10, was reinstated. 'Pre-vocational studies' was dropped as a compulsory examinable subject and proposals were advanced for university colleges in each of the island's 22 administrative districts to increase access from HNCE-level to degree-level education. In returning the school entry age to 5 years, the UNP appeased a large segment of the rural population that had felt short-changed by the raising of the age to 6 years in 1972. The UNP gained political capital through the suggestion that one year's less schooling, when compared with England, had created a 'second-class' education system.

It is an indication of the paradoxes of Sri Lanka's education policy that the issues of international comparability and access to external examinations should apparently carry so much weight in influencing the structure and content of the curriculum. The numbers involved in sitting and succeeding in foreign exams were extremely small. In 1978 only around 1,000 students sat the London external A level exams, and of these only a small proportion of candidates was successful (*Ceylon Daily News*, 20 January 1978). These numbers were minuscule when compared with the 75,000 students who took the Sri Lankan A level exams in the same year. Entry fees for an external examination such as the London A level were high compared to typical incomes. Entering one candidate, for example, could cost a parent the equivalent of two months of a graduate teacher's salary. Only the rich could afford to pay that amount. The reform responded to their interests.

The changes in the examining and education systems introduced in 1977 were far less ambitious and more limited than those of 1972. The main changes – changing examination titles without radically affecting their content, reducing the school entry age, returning to the structure that existed before 1972 and abandoning compulsory pre-vocational studies – were rushed through in a flurry of conservatism. They were justified largely by eulogies for the re-capturing of academic quality and the reintegration of the education system into internationally accepted patterns consonant with the open-door economic policy of the new government. Despite the call of the middle classes for international comparability, not every aspect of the 1972 reforms was overturned. The open access/no selection span of education did not fall back to the earlier Grade 8 level; it remained at Grade 9. All students had access to a common mathematics and science curriculum, the control of school examinations lay firmly under Sri Lankan state control, and the medium of instruction throughout the system, from primary to university, remained as either Sinhala or Tamil.

Theoretical perspectives reconsidered

So how might HCM and NMD perspectives contribute to and deepen an interpretation of events presented thus far? The 1972 education reforms were in large measure a response to a deteriorating set of economic, political and social relationships within the country and were catalysed by the upheaval of a violent insurrection. A key feature of the reforms was a change in the structure and administration of examinations held to select students for further opportunities and hence occupational and social status. A temptingly straightforward interpretation of the events leading to the introduction of NCGE and HNCE is simply this: the insurrection focussed attention on the dysfunctionality of the existing education system and its inability to educate, socialise and select young people for roles in society which they were prepared to accept. The reaction of those delegated to resolve the crisis – the legitimately elected government and its professional advisors – was to formulate education policy in such a way that a new 'equilibrium' could be established, with a more balanced set of relationships between educational output and occupational opportunities. The most effective way of achieving this balance was to introduce new curricula with a 'pre-vocational' bias and a new system of examining to support the new curricula. Change followed in the wake of functional breakdown and amounted conceptually to 'systemic homeostasis'. A potential instability was met by concerted actions to 'equilibrate'.[1] This would be consistent with an HCM 'functionalist' interpretation of change.

By contrast, the NMD perspective might suggest that the insurgents were an organised *lumpen proletariat*. Far from the insurgency being a social perturbation that was allowed to get out of hand, it was, rather, an expression of an inevitable conflict of interests between social class groups. The 1972 reforms were thus a compromise forced on the governing elite, but which were not directly in their interests.

The dilution of the 1972 reforms over time and their eventual dissolution can equally be viewed from the two perspectives. Firstly, it could be argued from the HCM perspective that the reforms implemented on the ground were insufficient to guarantee functional stability. Allowing quality to suffer, introducing a broader curriculum which failed to socialise children appropriately, and distancing the examining system from established and internationally recognised patterns had consequences which did not prevent growing instabilities. Under these circumstances a return to the old system, at least in appearance, offered the security of a tried and tested set of procedures widely recognised as 'legitimate'.

On the other hand, the NMD perspective might attribute the gradual undermining of the changes to the slow re-establishment of control over the system by elites. As the imperatives of the crisis created by the insurrection receded into the past, those with power and control over the education system gradually reasserted their dominance and steered its form back to that which had successfully reproduced their class interest for so long. Radical groups lost their influence and the

---

[1] For a more recent account of a systems approach to education see Lewin (2023).

system was re-fashioned in a form which served the urban middle classes more than it promoted the interests of the rural poor. In the ebb and flow of class war the national bourgeoisie had once again gained the upper hand and revolutionary conflict had been staved off.

On this general level it is possible to argue plausibly for either point of view. However, additional analytical power is offered by differences between the perspectives, as discussed below.

Normative consensus, class conflict or punctuated equilibria?

In the HCM perspective, consensus is the societal norm and conflict is considered a pathological deviation. In the NMD perspective, conflict between social classes is the norm while consensus is a pathological deviation from it. Since independence in 1948, conflict had been the exception rather than the norm. The 1971 insurgency represented an atypical sequence of events. Ethnically motivated violence had occurred in the colonial past, but conflict based on class interests was rare. The unusually small size of the armed forces and police in the 1970s reflects this.

Educational change and changes in the examining system appear to have been motivated by a fairly general dissatisfaction amongst diverse groups rather than conflict between different social classes. The 1977 UNP government had a substantial mandate to abandon NCGE and HNCE – a mandate that was given to them by poor rural parents as well as the urban wealthy and middle-class parents.

While an NMD perspective might suggest that these rural parents were suffering from 'false consciousness', their discontent did seem to have a ring of truth about it. 'Pre-vocational' courses did not assist rural children to gain modern sector jobs, qualification escalation meant that rural children needed more rather than fewer years of schooling to gain jobs, and many rural schools were performing relatively worse following the first NCGE exams compared with their performance in the GCE O level the previous year.

Theoretically, it might be more useful to view the educational changes described as a series of 'punctuated equilibria' (to borrow from biological evolutionary theory) rather than as generally functionally stable or conflict-ridden. While significant changes have been associated with crisis, for example the breaks with overseas examining hastened by the Second World War, and the 1972 reforms themselves, there have been extended periods of stability where minor change has taken place and development has been very gradual, as though on a developmental plateau.

Group, individual and professional interests

The second key difference identified between HCM and NMD is the relative emphasis on individuals or social groups as agents of conflict, consensus and change.

Although the insurrection was a conflict between organised groups, the educational response to it depended heavily on the actions of individuals within the Ministry of Education. It would be difficult to maintain that these individuals were acting in a particular group's interests. The initial ad hoc nature of the response suggests a classic bureaucratic reaction to unusual events, with what coordination there was coming from a small number of highly placed individuals. The initiation of examination reforms was inspired by a few individuals and undertaken by small groups of professionals with the capacity to carry them out. Subsequent disillusionment with the reforms was fairly widespread among all groups in society. Similarly, the 1977 reversion to previous patterns of examining was individually inspired, though it apparently had fairly widespread support.

The NMD perspective does offer a novel insight, although – paradoxically – this seems most significant at the individual, not group, level. The account of why NCGE and HNCE examinations did not offer radically different forms of assessment to O and A level must include the possibility that the professionals charged with operationalising the policy rhetoric were dependent on externally defined models of appropriate instrumentation. Staff already steeped in the traditions of examining established by English examination boards may well have turned to them as technical models to be adhered to fairly closely. Even in the absence of direct pressure, a kind of 'law of anticipated reactions' may have operated to keep deviations from existing practice within fairly narrow bounds. Such individual-level dependency can also be used to explain partially why much of the curriculum development of NCGE was modelled on courses in English schools, even though there was little direct external pressure to do so (Lewin, 1981). Similarly, the return of O and A levels in 1977 can be interpreted as resulting partly from an inordinately deferent faith in the British examination system.

Increasing equality of access and maintaining international legitimacy

The HCM perspective is consistent with the view that educational selection through 'meritocratic' examinations is inevitable and essential to the functioning of any socially differentiated society. By contrast, the NMD perspective positions selection as a device for legitimating differences in income and social inequalities in wider society.

The 1972 reforms were motivated, at least in part, by attempts to move away from early selection and streaming at Grade 8, on the grounds that this early selection furthered the interests of high socio-economic groups more than others. This was neither a denial of the need for selection in a labour market where access to most jobs was dependent on educational qualifications, nor was it a rejection of the notion that education could provide useful skills which should be certified. However, in replacing a well-established examining system it created a problem of acceptance of new qualifications which was never resolved effectively. NCGE and HNCE were never widely recognised by employers, and even the government itself was ambivalent about their status and value.

On the surface, the 1977 reforms were a reassertion of the HCM perspective that exam success is a measure of achievement in a meritocratic contest and that rewards should be based on it. While the NMD perspective views all selection exams as a means of legitimising wider inequalities and it is true that individuals with household educational advantage maintained an inside track in the race in both reforms, there is no evidence on whether either reform had the effect of weakening or strengthening social class reproduction in the longer term.

Historical practices and maintaining international professional relations

The HCM and NMD perspectives differ in the importance they accord to historical context; the HCM perspective less and the NMD perspective more. The form that the 1972 reforms finally took was determined in part by pre- and post-independence examining practices which set limits on what was likely to be regarded as legitimate and feasible. The re-establishment of GCE O and A levels after 1977 was more the result of a wish to resurrect the past than a response to needs defined exogenously by, for example, a former colonial power. Mismatches of supply and demand for educated manpower provoked changes in 1972, as the HCM position might predict, but these ultimately had a negligible impact on the changes introduced. The institutional and individual dependence described above can also be seen as a product of a continuing set of international relations between professional educators – less coercive and more voluntary than in the past, but nevertheless powerful factors in conditioning change.

This is not to argue that contemporary factors were not significant. The re-emergence of a governing elite more committed to open-door economic policies with greater sympathy for international flows of labour and capital was obviously important for the 1977 reforms.

Beneficent modernisers and elite group interests

Are policy elites to be seen as beneficent modernisers acting in society's interest as well as their own (an HCM perspective), or are they better described as self-serving agents of transnational capital, satisfying their own needs for the accumulation of wealth and power (an NMD perspective)?

There was little or no direct gain for international interests in the changes introduced by the 1972 reforms. No flows of capital (such as exam fees) were involved, and, since the thrust was towards delinking the education system from a colonially inherited pattern, advantages were argued to accrue to the domestic economy. By and large, policy elites had little to gain from the 1972 reform; indeed, the relative position of their own children was threatened by changes which would democratise access to educational qualifications. It would seem that the conscientiously modernising elite of the HCM model fits the 1972 reform better than the conspiratorial hegemonists of the NMD model.

The 1977 changes, on the other hand, are easier to explain in terms of elite group interests. It was clearly in the interests of elite parents to re-establish access to the lucrative international labour market for their children via exams whose names were familiar in an international or British marketplace. The 'flexibility' of the Sri Lankan civil service is legendary, as is its ability to limit radical changes to those which do not dramatically alter the status quo. In these respects, it is similar to highly bureaucratised organisations elsewhere. But it is not necessary to postulate Machiavellian intent or the conspiracy of elites to explain this.

Summing up

Several possible interpretations of this sequence of events are possible, but none seems to lead clearly to unequivocal support for the greater merit of either the HCM or NMD perspective on the two cases of examination reform presented in this chapter. At the same time, our understanding of the events in 1972 and 1977 has benefited from the use of concepts borrowed from both. Paradoxically, this has sometimes thrown up insights missed by analysts within one tradition which cannot necessarily be predicted by abstract consideration of the strengths and weaknesses of the frameworks themselves. Thus, it was an NMD perspective which highlighted the importance of individual-level professional dependency in shaping change, even though the NMD perspective is, on the whole, concerned more with social class groups than with individual motives, competencies and interests.

This chapter did not set out to affirm or dispute the superiority of either the HCM or NMD perspective on 'development' as a whole. Rather it employed concepts from both perspectives to deepen an understanding of successive reforms in the Sri Lankan public examination system during the 1970s. Excepting the naive excesses of over-zealous acolytes within either perspective, there appears to be much of value in both. Too often theoretical perspectives are atrophied by the unrealistic purity of their assumptions and the refusal of their various proponents and devotees to consider the evidence before perpetuating an ideology. Their contribution to the development process is consequently like the sound of one hand clapping …

5
Human capital, education and development

In this chapter I explore the concept of 'human capital' through an empirical examination of three questions about productivity, earnings and motivation. Is education related to productivity? Do earnings reflect job performance? What are the motivations for learning and working? This research was undertaken in the 1970s and 1980s. I draw attention to extensions of human capital theory and to Sri Lankan studies conducted within it in more recent years.

The concept of human capital

The concept of human capital is traceable to *An inquiry into the nature and causes of the wealth of nations*, written by the Scottish economist and moral philosopher Adam Smith and published in 1776 (Woodhall, 2001). Smith suggested that investment in physical capital through expenditure on machines might have parallels in investment in human capital through expenditure on education and training. Theodore Schultz revived the concept in the early 1960s:

> Measured by what labor contributes to output, the productive capacity of human beings is now vastly larger than all other forms of wealth taken together. What economists have not stressed is the simple truth that people invest in themselves and that these investments are large. (Schultz, 1961, p. 313)

The idea that education is a form of investment was, Schultz suggested, the missing piece in the jigsaw puzzle of the sources of economic growth that was not accounted for by increases in the classical factors of land, labour and physical capital. The propositions of human capital theory were that the skills that people acquire are a form of capital – human capital; these skills are acquired through deliberate investments in education; skills are the capacities that contribute to economic productivity and production; and labour market earnings are the means by which a person's productivity is rewarded.

The idea that education represents investment in human capital is much more than a simple analogy with physical capital:

> it implies that it is possible to measure the returns to investment in education, and to apply cost benefit analysis to decisions about education expenditure, in the same way as rates of return are used to analyse the profitability of investment in conventional physical capital. (Woodhall, 2001, p. 6,952)

The first systematic attempts to measure the economic costs and benefits of education and compute rates of return were made in the US by Schultz (1961) and Becker (1964), and in a range of industrialised and developing countries by Psacharopoulos (1973, 1994) and others. These studies revealed four main findings: (i) social returns are consistently lower than private returns; (ii) social and private rates of return to primary education tend to be higher than rates of return to secondary or higher education; (iii) the rate of return to education is higher in developing countries than in developed countries; and (iv) in developing countries, the rate of return to investment in education is higher than the average rate of return to physical capital, though not necessarily in developed countries (Woodhall, 2001).

Human capital and its critics

Despite its intuitive appeal, human capital theory has attracted extensive commentary and critique. The main theoretical critique is offered by screening theory. Where employers have imperfect information about the likely productivity of job applicants, educational qualifications provide information, albeit imperfect, about the applicant. Education is functioning as much as a screening device as it is an arena where productive skills are created. Qualifications provide employers with a signal of 'some innate productive ability of the individual' (Winkler, 1987, p. 287). Education sorts, sifts and screens individuals according to these abilities. Productive skills are created through on-the-job training. Schooling and higher education offer employers a cheap means of selecting their employees for different grades of jobs.

The 'diploma disease' thesis, introduced in Chapter 2, offers another critique, written more from a sociological than an economic perspective.

> The simple economic argument goes like this: Educate one child and he or she becomes a hundred dollars more productive a year. Educate a million children and they become a hundred million dollars more productive ... If only it were so simple. You see, something happens on the way. To educate a million you have to create systems and institutions. You need to grade and certify, arrange exams and diplomas – and that's where the problem arises, because the business of grading, certifying and awarding diplomas can overshadow the business of educating. The examination tail comes to wag the educational dog. (Dore & Little, 1982, p. 3)

The links between education and economic performance are also mediated by political processes. Writing about industrialised countries, Ashton & Green (1996) suggested that the link between education, skill formation and economic performance is far from automatic. National, international and local politics surrounding education and training influence the strength and nature of the relationship between skills and economic performance. Others have raised methodological issues about the empirical links between education, productivity and earnings. Given that the link between educational levels and earnings is often institutionalised in salary scales and recruitment, selection and promotion procedures, then is it surprising that education and earnings are correlated (Little, 1984)? Wages are a very imperfect indicator of people's relative skills and human capital (Wolf, 2002). The reliability of data employed to calculate 'rates of return to investment' and the exaggerated reporting of results have also been questioned (Bennell, 1996).

The concept of human capital assumes that people *choose* to invest in themselves through education (Schultz, 1961). But what motivates people to invest in education and what motivates them to learn once they have enrolled? A first and fairly obvious point to make is that in contexts where education is not legally enforced, it is parents and communities who expect and encourage their children to enrol in, attend and stay at school, not the children themselves. Where education is enforced, parents exercise less choice about the enrolment of their children in school.

The question of school choice is a different matter. Many parents exercise choice over the school their child attends. At a later stage in life, it may indeed be a young adult rather than a parent that is making a choice about investing in further education. Why is he or she taking that decision? What is his or her anticipated goal(s)? Are all goals economic?

The issue of multiple and non-economic goals of education is addressed through the principle of utility and its maximisation. Utility describes the pleasure, satisfaction or benefit derived from the consumption of commodities. With education treated as an investment rather than consumption, then the maximisation of utility refers to the *anticipated* pleasures, satisfactions and benefits derivable from education. While these may include benefits that go far beyond earnings, few studies of education and earnings explore the conditions under which individuals have been motivated to enrol in and complete their education. That human capital theory takes human motivation for granted is an issue to which I return later in this chapter.

Is education related to productivity?

In 1964 Professor J. E. Jayasuriya of the University of Colombo averred: 'when it is considered how much more competently any job could be done with a little more education than a little less, educated youth are a national asset in whatever numbers they exist' (J. E. Jayasuriya, 1964). This was seven years before the youth insurrection of April 1971 in which educated, but unemployed, young people protested about a lack of jobs commensurate with their expectations and qualifications.

Up to the 1970s, economists tended to measure differentials in productivity in terms of differentials in earnings. However, since salaries and wages are often dependent on educational qualifications and age (particularly in the public sector), it seems tautologous to argue that the more educated are more productive. In the early 1970s, Berg (1970) published results from studies in the US suggesting that people with fewer years of formal school education performed no worse and sometimes better than fellow workers with more education. In India, Chaudhri (1974) examined the relationship between farmer education and productivity, measured by gross value of yield of crop per acre at state, district and household levels of analysis. At the household level in Uttar Pradesh, farmers with no education frequently had yields higher than those with more education. In another Indian study, Fuller (1972) compared company efficiency ratings for workers in two modern industries. In one factory there was no relationship between the number of years spent in formal school education and efficiency ratings, while in the other there was a small positive relationship.

In the mid-1970s I participated in a research collaboration between the Institute of Development Studies (Sussex), the National Institute of Management (Colombo), the Center for Educational Studies, the National Institute for Labor Studies and the National University (Mexico), and the Centre for Development Studies and the Department of Sociology at the University of Cape Coast (Ghana). This research explored how modern sector employers were using educational qualifications to recruit, select and promote employees. This included a series of studies on qualifications and job performance in Sri Lanka (9 groups of managers, 9 groups of clerical workers), Ghana (19 groups of clerical workers) and Mexico (10 groups, including security guards, salespeople, computer programmers and public relations officers) (Little, 1980).

Our measure of productivity was the supervisor's estimate of job performance, using a method adapted from the 'repertory grid' technique of Kelly (1955). Supervisors were invited to describe the job conducted by his/her subordinates in detail and to define the qualities s/he considered necessary for their low and high job performance, using their own rather than externally imposed criteria. After rating workers on a range of these self-generated criteria, supervisors were invited to give an overall rating of performance. Personnel files, shared anonymously by the respective personnel offices, were used to collect information on workers' educational qualifications, years with the organisation and previous work experience. The number of subordinates per supervisor, though generally small, was in most cases large enough for simple statistical analysis. The range in years of education between people doing the same job for the same supervisor averaged 3.9 years in Sri Lanka and 6.2 years in Ghana and Mexico.

The evidence suggested that there was no consistent positive relationship between level of education and job performance for a variety of diverse types of work (Little, 1980). There were a few strong positive relationships, for example in the group of Mexican Government Public Relations Officers and one group of private sector clerks in Sri Lanka, but the size of coefficients across all work groups ranged from +0.71 through to –0.89. The average size of correlation for all 47 workgroups combined was +0.023. Of the correlations which did reach statistical significance, four were negative and only two were positive. The contribution of education levels to enhanced levels of job performance was by no means consistently positive.

Simple correlations can disguise the effects of other variables. One might expect, for example, that experience on the job would correlate positively with performance, but that experience would correlate negatively with education, particularly in times of rapid educational expansion. If experience did correlate positively with job performance and negatively with education, then a positive correlation between education and job performance could be disguised. The partial correlations, controlling for experience, also demonstrated the lack of a consistent, positive relationship between education and performance. The partials, based on small sample sizes, ranged from +0.86 to –0.94, the average size of coefficient being 0.05.

Critics of this work may point to (i) the potential unreliability of using supervisor estimates of job performance and (ii) the possibility that a supervisor's own level of education may influence the way in which s/he evaluates the performance of subordinates. To the first criticism we were able to examine more 'objective' measures of performance among three of the Mexican workgroups. A private airline company measured the performance of its reservation agents by the number of airline tickets sold; a government agency measured the performance of its map draughtsmen by the distance travelled each month by their marker pens, with a weighting for the type of terrain; and a private sector engineering company measured the 'programming velocity' of its computer programmers. In all three cases educational level failed to correlate positively with 'objective' job performance.

The second criticism, that a supervisor's level of education might influence his/her evaluation of the performance of subordinates with higher levels of education, was explored among the 18 Sri Lankan workgroups. These were divided into (i) those where the supervisor's level of qualification was greater or the same as the highest education level of a subordinate, and (ii) those where it was lower than the highest subordinate level. There was no difference in the pattern of relationships between education level and performance between the two groups.

This research does not, of course, suggest that education adds nothing to job performance across the entire occupational structure. Necessarily, we examined a restricted range of education levels and in all three countries every group member had completed at least primary education. We sampled only a few occupations from the range of jobs across the entire occupational spectrum in each country. We did not sample brain surgeons, astronauts, crime investigators, care workers, software engineers or miners. We examined the relationship between education and job performance for particular jobs.

So how do we explain our almost chance relationship between education and performance? Let us examine our evidence in a little more detail. After providing a description of the job performed by his/her subordinates, each supervisor was asked to describe the qualities/skills they considered necessary to perform this job well. An example taken at random from the Sri Lankan data for clerks reads: loyalty, punctuality, good relations with peers, technical knowledge.

Supervisor statements about the qualities/skills necessary for good job performance were divided into two categories: (i) cognitive skills or behaviour directly related to the job itself (for example speed, accuracy, adeptness at planning); and (ii) social/affective skills involving the person's interaction with other people or relating to some moral quality (for example relations with peers, punctuality, obedience). Supervisors of the managerial groups mentioned social skills, such as the ability to deal with people, either supervisors, subordinates, colleagues or customers, more frequently than supervisors of the clerical groups, who tended to emphasise cognitive skills such as accuracy and neatness. While these social skills might today be referred to as 'twenty-first-century skills', they were clearly being recognised as important workplace skills in Sri Lanka in the 1970s.

Do earnings reflect job performance?

Earnings are influenced by a range of factors, not least years of experience and seniority, irrespective of productivity. The following example, from a Sri Lankan public sector organisation in the mid-1970s, illustrates the point. In this organisation there were three grades of clerk with corresponding pay scales.

$$\text{Rs } 312.50 - 15 \times 12.50 - 7 \times 15 - \text{Rs } 606$$
$$\text{Rs } 425 - 20 \times 15 - \text{Rs } 725$$
$$\text{Rs } 800 - 10 \times 40 - \text{Rs } 1200$$

On entering employment, the lowest grade of clerk earned Rs 312.50 monthly. Earnings rise by Rs 12.50 a month for 15 years, then by Rs 15.00 for another seven years. Clerks are usually appointed to the first grade and to a point on the scale that reflects their qualifications and experience. These decisions are taken by the organisation *before* a new recruit starts the job and before he or she has an opportunity to demonstrate his or her performance/productivity. There are just two ways in which job performance can affect the transition from one grade to the next. Many organisations operate an 'efficiency bar' which is interpreted in practice as minimum rather than maximum efficiency. One would need to demonstrate positive demerit not to be promoted from grade to grade. The second way in which job performance can influence earnings is via 'merit increments' awarded for additional responsibilities, exceptional job performance or obtaining a new educational qualification. A third way to move from grade to grade is via promotion 'examinations', though in our research we were unable to examine whether performance in these written examinations reflected present and previous job performance. We found that in practice most salary increments were awarded for simply staying in the job over time (Deraniyagala, Dore & Little, 1978).

The main points emerging from the research reported above were that (i) differences in educational level (across a span of an average five years of education) appeared to be unrelated to supervisors' ratings of job performance among groups of people doing the same job; (ii) supervisors' personal opinions about the 'ingredients' of good job performance stressed the importance of social attributes for job performance and the mix of the cognitive and social attributes varied from job to job; and (iii) income generated through salaries and wages was determined by a range of factors other than job performance.

For the most part, the debate about why the educated earn more continues to rest on the premise that those who earn more *are* more productive and that more education leads to higher productivity and earnings. This research offered a modest questioning of this proposition and the implicit faith which many economists around the world have in the power of educational qualifications per se to generate greater job performance/productivity.

Motivations for education and learning

But let us move on to the people who lie at the heart of human capital theory and who choose to invest in education. What assumptions are made about the process and outcomes of learning once a student has enrolled in a course of study? Reading between the lines we find the assumption that when students enrol in courses, they will be motivated to learn by the anticipated value these skills will contribute to earnings. There is no doubt that this constitutes one potential motivation for learners – but, as teachers, parents and students will be quick to point out, there are many others.

Learning is motivated by many goals, the relative importance of which are likely to change through the life cycle. Many learning goals are determined by societies, communities and families and are driven by the necessity of economic survival. The human needs for food and water are basic goals for the learning of the skills of survival. The search for greater wages, status and prestige also drives people on.

Psychologists have long described how young children's learning is driven by an almost insatiable curiosity about the physical and social world and a desire for 'mastery'. Psychologists contrast this type of learning, often termed 'intrinsic learning', with motivation that is driven by extrinsic rewards, such as treats/gold stars contingent on behaviour. An intrinsically motivated learner derives interest and satisfaction from the content and process of learning. Motivation springs from within the learner and is enhanced through the process of learning. He or she seeks out learning challenges and perseveres. By contrast, an extrinsically motivated learner perceives learning as a means to an end. The end goal (whether that be exam success or ultimately a decent job) is more important than the content and process of learning that leads to the examination.

Deci and Ryan (1985) employed the intrinsic-extrinsic dichotomy to describe motivations across the lifespan, but with a particular focus on young children's informal learning, school learning and work learning. They advanced the controversial claim that when extrinsic rewards are attached to learning tasks undertaken initially for intrinsic reasons, then intrinsic motivation is undermined. Rather than extrinsic and intrinsic motivational goals being additive, they might, under some conditions, be subtractive (Deci, Koestner & Ryan, 1999).

In research cited in Chapter 3, Sri Lankan secondary school students displayed a wide range of self-reported motives for learning. Some reflected an interest in learning and a sense of personal development, such as 'examinations teach us to become self-disciplined individuals', 'studying gives me a lot of personal satisfaction'. Others indicated that assessment and exams provide the main motive for learning, for example 'I study extra hard on those topics which I feel are going to appear in the examination', 'examination success is what I have aimed for throughout my school learning'. Still others indicated a motivation toward the expectations of significant others, for example 'my teacher expects me to do well in class', 'my mother expects me to do well in examinations' (W A. de Silva, Gunawardene & Rupasinghe, 1987).

Linking motives for learning with motives for working

Few economists have ventured to explore the causal links between the motivations developed and demonstrated in school and those developed and demonstrated at work. In an early attempt, Bowles and Gintis (1976) described personality and motivational factors rewarded through high-school grades. They identified three clusters of traits: submission to authority (including 'externally motivated' and 'low creativity'), temperament (including 'not frank') and internalised control (including 'defers gratification'). Submission to authority appeared to be a better predictor of school grades than temperament or internalised control. Their review of studies of motivation at work identified three rather similar clusters, which they labelled rule orientation, dependability and internalisation. Rule orientation showed the strongest relations with supervisor ratings of job performance. From these findings they inferred the 'correspondence principle': – there is a correspondence between the motivations engendered in schools and those in the workplace.

The puzzle for human capital theory is to explore which motivations, at school and at work, are most important for the development of 'human capital' required for economic growth. Are they the search for financial benefits, or the opportunities the job creates for the individual to develop his/her abilities and skills, creativity and originality?

Together with Jasbir Sarjit Singh of the University of Malaya, I designed a study to explore three propositions about the connection between motivations at school and motivations at work (Little & Singh, 1992). These were that: (i) students are motivated to learn by a range of orientations, (ii) workers are motivated to work by a range of orientations, and (iii) inter-individual variation in assessment orientation in school within a society will be associated negatively with interpersonal variation in innovation and creativity in the workplace. The research design involved students describing their learning motivations in the present and expressing their work motivations *prospectively*; and workers describing their work motivations in the present and reflecting on their learning motivations *retrospectively*. The research was conducted in England and Malaysia, but not in Sri Lanka.

A range of motivational goals was identified among students and workers in both societies. The contemporary learning motivations of students were described as: (i) assessment orientation (for example 'examination success is what I have aimed for throughout my school learning'); (ii) interest orientation (for example 'I will continue to study the subjects I like even after the examinations are finished'); and

(iii) an interpersonal orientation (for example 'I work hard to please my parents'). Students expressed their aspirations about a range of job characteristics in the future, including whether they wanted a job that would give them opportunities for creativity and originality.

The contemporary motivational goals among workers were described initially as: (i) material rewards (working for pay, promotion, security or the 'perks that go with the job'); (ii) social rewards (status, acknowledgement, prestige and respect from others); and (iii) self-fulfilment (challenge, a sense of purpose, personal growth and skill utilisation). Dimensions (ii) and (iii), stressing interpersonal processes and self-fulfilment, appeared to be closely related and were subsequently combined for further analysis.

At the risk of oversimplifying a complex body of evidence, our conclusion was that there was evidence for an extremely weak relationship among students between assessment orientation at school and aspirations for innovative and creative work. Stronger and more positive was the relationship between assessment orientation and an aspiration for financial benefits. Of greater interest, perhaps, was a positive link between an expressed interest orientation at school and the desire for work where they could demonstrate and develop their abilities and skills, seek opportunities for creativity and originality, and develop their interests. By contrast, the relationship between interest orientation at school and the desire for financial benefits was almost zero for the English students and negative for the Malaysian students.

The worker data was even more revealing. There was a strong positive relationship between a 'fulfilment' orientation at work and an interest orientation at school (recalled retrospectively). There was a slightly negative relationship between an assessment orientation at school and a current 'fulfilment' orientation at work (that is, a motivation to work based on challenge, a sense of purpose, an opportunity for personal growth or skill utilisation).

Positive and negative correlations do not indicate causality. Aware of this, Singh and I offered possible explanations for our findings on interest orientation at school and at work post hoc. The first was that schools and teachers are succeeding in creating environments in which students derive interest, satisfaction and excitement from the learning tasks they encounter. The interest orientation formed by the school experience endures and transfers to the workplace. This interpretation would, we argued, be consistent with the formation of human capital. A second interpretation was that the relationship may be a function of a disposition to perceive most situations as interesting and challenging – a disposition that is developed in early childhood and which transfers from the family/household to the classroom, to the workplace, to leisure, to parenting. This would be a form of the 'screening hypothesis' referred to earlier in this chapter: schools are not actually forming the orientation; rather individuals are demonstrating dispositions formed elsewhere. A third was that individuals are self-selecting themselves for work. Those who display an interest orientation in school choose to enter or are selected for those jobs that offer the opportunity and environment for creativity and innovation. As educators we were more convinced about the potential role of teachers in influencing the motivation of learners and learning. To date, the relative strength of these post hoc explanations has not been explored.

Human capital theory extensions

With its preoccupation with earnings and economic growth, early human capital theory offered a restricted notion of the benefits of education. Other potential benefits, such as family health, fertility and child mortality, deserved more research and policy attention (Lewin, Little & Colclough, 1983a, b; Woodhall, 2001). Early versions of the theory presented a single story of education and development, where development was defined as economic growth and efficiency. While this is not a criticism of the theory per se, it raised the question of the meaning of 'development' in different societies at different points in time. As we saw in Chapter 2, the definition of development as 'human development' and the positioning of economic growth as a means to that end, rather than as an end in itself, was one example of this type of critique.

Partly in response, human capital theory has been revised in several ways, notably by McMahon (1997, 1999). McMahon's extended conceptual framework for measuring the total social and private costs and benefits of education retains the overall objective of explaining economic growth. It involves four elements: (i) the investor (private or social), (ii) the beneficiary (private or social), (iii) the nature of the return (whether monetary or non-monetary), and (iv) time.

This model for measuring returns to education differs from the old model in two main respects. The first is the specification of non-monetary benefits. Private non-monetary benefits include health effects, higher returns on financial assets, more efficient household purchasing, higher female labour force participation rates, reduced employment rates, more part-time employment after retirement, lifelong adaptation and continued learning, selective mating, and non-monetary job satisfactions. Social non-monetary benefits (public goods) include lower fertility rates, lower population rates, public health, democratisation, human rights, political stability, poverty reduction, property crime rates, environmental effects, higher divorce rates, later retirement, more work after retirement, and community service (McMahon, 1998).

The second is a more explicit specification of time, including intergenerational (benefits passed from one person to his/her children) and dynamic (taking account of earnings trends over time). The more explicit treatment of time, through the notion of the life cycle, is important not just for its power in capturing returns over time, but also for assessing the returns to 'all extensions to the existing provisions for education' (McMahon, 1998, p. 311). In principle, this includes both the 'complete lifespan' and 'life-wide' concepts of lifelong education; that is, education throughout life, from cradle to grave, and education in different arenas (home, work, play/leisure) and through varying modes of learning (for example oral, print, audio, digital). McMahon (1997, 1999) suggested, optimistically, that with better and more comprehensive measures, future estimates of monetary and non-monetary returns will be greater than reported previously.

Other economists have called for greater attention to the measures of education and human capital – and the need to estimate its quality as well as its quantity. Measured by learning achievement or learning outcomes, 'quality' explains more of the cross-country differences in productivity growth than do differences in the average number of years of schooling or enrolment rates (Hanushek & Wößmann, 2007). This notion of quality has, more recently, become embedded in the Sustainable Development Goal for education and its indicator of test scores. There is now an ever-increasing international business in testing, an accumulation of evidence of 'learning deficits' around the world (Chapter 15), and the recent introduction of a measure that combines learning quality with quantity – the learning-adjusted years of education (Filmer et al., 2018).

Still others have extended the discussion of human capital to include a range of capitals. Bourdieu and Passeron (1977) introduced the notion of 'cultural capital' to refer to the social and cultural assets that individuals attain through life to explain social reproduction and the persistence of social inequalities. Coleman (1988) introduced the notion of 'social capital' to refer to school values, associated social networks of students, parents and teachers, and the trust these values and networks engender. While the conceptual distinctions between cultural and social capital are often unclear, and their means of measurement even more so, they are now part of the lexicon of the processes and benefits of education (see for examples Preston & Dyer, 2003; Green, Preston & Sabates, 2003).

Sri Lankan research within a human capital framework

Early research in Sri Lanka conducted within the framework of human capital reported positive private rates of return to education of around 7 per cent in the 1980s to early 1990s (Aturupane, 1993). Estimates of the contribution of human and physical capital to economic growth over a much longer period, 1959–2008, suggest that while investment in physical capital was a key variable in understanding the long-run growth path of the economy, the returns to investment in education, while positive, were modest and 'significantly lower than those found in other developing countries' (Ganegodage & Rambaldi, 2011). More recent studies of the impact of education on household welfare (proxied by household consumption levels) have suggested positive returns to an extra year of schooling of the most educated member of the household, of 5 per cent on average, with a higher effect among the lower income groups (Himaz & Aturupane, 2016). Herath (2022) examined the relative impact of three types of capital found in the home and in the school – financial, human and social – on the achievement of learning outcomes among Grade 8 students. Home financial capital (such as household income level) was more important for learning achievement than human capital (such as parental education) and social capital (such as social interactions outside the family). School human capital (such as teacher qualifications and experience) was more important than either financial capital (such as physical facilities at school) or social capital (such as additional support with schoolwork from teachers).

In its dialogue with the Sri Lankan government, the World Bank recently brought the concept of human capital centre stage. *Realising the promise and potential of human capital* lies at the heart of the Bank's current 'Human Capital Project' for Sri Lanka (World Bank, 2021). Its central message resonates with propositions set out in the writings of Schultz and Becker in the 1960s, but goes beyond them to emphasise the role of human capital in the *global* as well as the *national* economy, its importance to health and nutrition, and its inclusion of socio-emotive as well as cognitive skills.

The recent cross-country metric, the Human Capital Index (HCI), focusses on education and health (World Bank, 2021). The index is based on measures of the (i) 0–5 years survival rate, (ii) expected years of quality-adjusted schooling, (iii) stunting, and (iv) adult survival rates. The HCI bears similarities with the Human Development Index (HDI) developed by the United Nations Development Programme in the early 1990s (see Chapter 2). The HDI combined measures of (i) life expectancy at birth, (ii) mean years of schooling for adults aged 25 years and more, (iii) expected years of schooling for children of school entry age, and (iv) Gross National Income per capita. By contrast, the HCI focusses on education and health indices and excludes the Gross National Income component. By separating it out one can then examine the correlation between it and education and health and Gross National Income.

The HCI includes a sophisticated measure of 'years of quality-adjusted schooling' rather than 'expected years of schooling'. 'Learning-adjusted years of schooling' involves comparisons with learning achievement in other countries. This in turn requires a common assessment of achievement generated through an international survey. To date Sri Lanka has not participated in any international surveys of student achievement. However, one module from the Trends in International Mathematics and Science Study was included in Sri Lanka's National Education Research and Evaluation 2017 survey of Grade 8 mathematics, and the results of this single international module were used to generate the comparative 'learning-adjusted years of schooling' measure.

On the composite HCI measure, Sri Lanka continues to outperform the rest of South Asia but compares somewhat unfavourably with most other countries elsewhere in the Asia region, including those it had surpassed in educational participation and life expectancy in the 1970s when held up as a 'development model'. At that time, these countries included Singapore, Korea, Hong Kong, China, Malaysia, Mongolia, Thailand and Vietnam. On the measure of 'expected years of schooling', Sri Lanka remains one of the top performers in Asia (mean = 13 years), and on a par with high-income countries everywhere. On the measure of 'years of schooling adjusted for learning outcomes', Sri Lanka performs only slightly above average for all lower middle-income countries and well below the mean for East Asia and the Pacific (World Bank, 2021). As explained above, the evidence employed to harmonise Sri Lankan learning outcomes with elsewhere is of a limited nature. Nonetheless, it is a sobering thought that Sri Lankan students may not be learning in line with their potential after 13 long years of schooling and many months and days spent in private tuition classes.

Conclusion

In this chapter I have explored empirically some tenets of human capital theory. I have questioned whether education levels are necessarily related to job performance and productivity. I have questioned whether earnings are a good proxy for productivity. I have suggested that the ingredients of job performance are many and go beyond cognitive skills and abilities to include a wide range of social and personal abilities/ orientations. I have opened up the question of motivation and suggested that there are a range of motivations for learning and for working that go beyond the financial. Finally, I have suggested that although the concept of human capital had been circulating in the international development discourse since at least the 1970s and a few high-quality pieces of economic research were conducted by Sri Lankans in the late 1980s/1990s, it is only quite recently that we have seen the concept entering the education policy discourse in Sri Lanka – and that mainly in relation to technical and vocational education and training and higher education.

Having explored the value of HCM and NMD perspectives on development in understanding the process of examination reform in Chapter 4 and questioned some of the tenets of human capital theory in this chapter, I turn now to a consideration of Dore's (1976, 1997) 'diploma disease' thesis which, with its sharp focus on the 'examinations' interface between labour markets and classrooms, adds the institutional dimension of social selection and allocation to the discussion of the concepts of modernisation, human capital and dependency.

6
The diploma disease

The thesis

In *The Diploma Disease: Education, qualification and development*, Ronald Dore applied ideas about the 'late development' of societies (see Chapter 2) to the articulation of job selection practices and the quality of education. He proposed that

> the later development starts (i.e., the later the point in world history that a country starts on a modernisation drive) the more widely education certificates are used for occupational selection, the faster the rate of qualification inflation and the more examination-oriented schooling becomes at the expense of genuine education. (Dore, 1976, p. 72)

Dore illustrated his thesis through the educational and economic histories of four countries: England – 'an early developer'; Japan – 'a late developer'; Sri Lanka – 'a later developer'; and Kenya – 'a much later developer' (Dore, 1976, chs 2–5).

The use of certificates for the allocation of modern sector jobs lies at the heart of the thesis. A major imbalance in the number of educated job seekers and modern sector jobs available leads to educated unemployment and an intense demand for schooling and the certificates that provide access to those jobs. This mismatch leads to intolerable pressures on government education budgets, to the intense demand for schooling and certificates, even more educated unemployment and the escalation of qualification levels demanded by employers. This leads to exam-oriented learning, a ritualisation of the learning process, a 'deformation' of minds/characters of the 'successful, and constraints on the delivery of 'relevant education', especially primary education.

A pathology of societies or individuals?

The term 'disease' misled many and outraged more (Little, 1997, 2006). Is the disease something which all educated individuals, have caught, especially those in developing countries? Are students and their parents irrational in supporting their children in their pursuit of education and as many qualifications as possible, especially when the pursuit of certificates is a socially legitimate way of improving one's life-chances in a society where resources are scarce, and income and status differences are great?

Dore acknowledged the individual rationality of parents' pursuit of educational qualifications to better the lives of their children. What he questioned, in an uncomfortably radical way, was the underlying social rather than individual rationality of this system of social and economic allocation. The 'disease' was a pathology of societies, not individuals. It was this social pathology that framed the second part of the book. In the 1970s, developments in the education systems of Cuba, Tanzania and China appeared to be pointing the way to alternative forms of social allocation. An analysis of these, combined with Dore's own 'modest proposals for reform', led him to suggest that the *scourge* of the educational certificate can be and indeed must be tempered if millions of the world's children are to have a chance of a meaningful education.

Sri Lanka: a 'later developer'?

I turn now to the discussion of the specific case of Sri Lanka within the more general comparative thesis. The Sri Lankan case rests on 'discern[ing] ways in which Sri Lanka differs from Britain in the same direction as Japan only more so' (Dore, 1976, p. 51).

Dore described educational developments in England and Japan at the point in history when each began its drive towards 'industrialisation', a term which he tended to use synonymously with the sociological term 'modernisation'. In England, industrialisation began in the late eighteenth century, long before even half of its population was enrolled in primary education and long before public examinations were dreamed of.

In Japan, the drive towards industrialisation occurred about a century later. After almost two hundred years of isolation from the rest of the world, the country set itself on a course of a state-directed 'catch-up' with the West from 1868. But this was a Westernisation on Japan's own terms, not those imposed by a Western colonial power. The feudal land system was abolished, a new school system was created, emissaries and students were sent abroad to acquire knowledge and learn new skills, and foreign educators and techniques were imported. Simultaneously, and in contrast to England, the class structure was overturned – 'the samurai gentry became the central government bureaucrats, policemen, schoolteachers, soldiers and pioneer businessmen; the peasants were confirmed as the legal owners of the land to which they had previously been bound; freedom of occupation was roundly declared, and equality before the law' (Dore, 1976, p. 38).

Already by the late nineteenth century, 85 per cent of the labour force in England was employed in non-agricultural occupations, compared with just 17 per cent in Japan. But the contrast in their primary school enrolment ratios was marked. While in England around 40 per cent of children were enrolled in primary education in 1870, almost a century *after* industrialisation had begun, Japan already had 28 per cent enrolled at the time when industrialisation was about *to begin*. By 1900, when Japan's industrialisation had begun in earnest, 81 per cent of her children were enrolled in primary education and 29 per cent of the labour force was employed in non-agricultural jobs. In England in 1900, 83 per cent of her children were enrolled in primary education and 91 per cent were employed in non-agricultural work (Lewin, 1991).

Overall, the 'patterns' of educational development in the two countries were quite different. England experienced slow growth in the provision of primary education; Japan experienced rapid growth. In England primary education growth followed industrialisation; in Japan it accompanied industrialisation. In England, the role of the state in the provision of primary education was weak; in Japan it was much stronger. In England, the use of education certificates in the allocation of jobs did not predominate over heredity and apprenticeship until the mid-twentieth century; in Japan educational certificates played a dominant role in the allocation of jobs from an early stage of industrialisation (Dore, 1976, pp. 35–6; Lewin, 1991).

The pattern of educational development in Sri Lanka compared with England and Japan

So how does the pattern of educational development in Sri Lanka contrast with that of England on the one hand, and Japan on the other? Dore acknowledged that the pattern of education development in Sri Lanka was more complex than that in either England or Japan, for two main reasons. First, Sri Lanka had experience of Western colonial models and practices of education, imposed first by the Portuguese, then the Dutch and then the British. These models and practices overlaid longstanding Buddhist, Muslim and Hindu traditions of education. Second, there was, in Sri Lanka, the complicating factor of language in education: two vernacular languages (the Sinhala of the majority population; Tamil of the minority) and the language of the coloniser, the most recent being English. In the England and Japan of the nineteenth and early twentieth centuries, by contrast, language diversity was more limited.

Notwithstanding these 'complications' of colonial history and language diversity, Dore (1976) suggested that Sri Lanka's state-directed drive to industrialised modernity manifested an acute form of 'later development'. Compared with Japan, the use of educational qualifications in Sri Lanka for job selection had started earlier relative to Sri Lanka's industrialisation and was more complete. Compared with Japan, enrolments in the secondary and tertiary levels of education had grown faster, relative to the primary levels, from an earlier stage in Sri Lanka's educational development. The implications for curriculum and pedagogy in Sri Lanka were judged to be worse than those in Japan.

Exploring the validity of the propositions

The general thesis and the Sri Lankan case revolved around five propositions.

1. Sri Lanka began her drive for economic modernisation following independence.
2. At independence there was a broad consensus that education was a channel for social mobility via 'a single peaked pyramid which everybody could climb'.
3. Asynchronous growth in the numbers of modern sector jobs and the numbers of educated young people seeking modern sector jobs led to increasing levels of educated unemployment.

4. The imbalance between the growth of the modern sector economy and the growth in numbers of educated young people led employers to raise (escalate) the qualifications required for jobs.
5. The more qualification levels were raised, the more exam-oriented teaching and learning became – that is, the learning process became ritualised, and the development of 'relevant' terminal primary education constrained.

Proposition 1: Sri Lanka began her drive for modernisation after independence

Proposition 1 asserts that Sri Lanka, then Ceylon, began her state-led drive for modernisation shortly after independence in 1948. The choice of historical period is important because, as we have seen already, the general thesis rests on the notion of 'late development' (Gerschenkron, 1952) and the consequences for education of *the point in world history at which the drive for modernisation/industrialisation begins*.

The Sri Lankan economist Gamini Corea (1975) suggested that the economic modernisation of the Sri Lankan economy started not at the time of independence but in the early to mid-nineteenth century when the colonial government encouraged the establishment of an export-oriented plantation economy. The majority of labour required for its operation did not require the types of skills that could be acquired through formal schooling. Although plantation processes did change during the long colonial period, and new knowledge and skills were required, these were usually imparted on the job by 'visiting agents' (often expatriates), rather than by the regular employment of educated personnel (J. E. Jayasuriya, 1979, p. 433).

This type of agricultural industrialisation differed from the industrialisation of manufactured goods which, under colonial rule, were generally imported from England under preferential terms. After independence in 1948 and a change of government in 1956, a state-directed strategy of import substitution was pursued. While this involved an expansion of urban-based manufacturing, it did not lead to substantial changes in the proportion of the labour force employed in non-agricultural work. A shift in that direction only followed the change of government in 1977 when the implementation of policies to liberalise an export-oriented economy led to an increase in the proportion of those employed in manufacturing and services.

One of the indicators of economic modernisation used by Dore (1976, p. 40) was the proportion of the labour force employed in non-agricultural occupations. Over the century between 1891 and 1990 there appears to have been only a slow and gradual change in the proportion of the population employed in non-agricultural occupations[1] – a growth that appeared to plateau in the post-independence era between 1953 and 1971. Indeed, the 34 per cent of people employed in non-agricultural occupations in 1901 is higher than the 29 per cent estimated for Japan in 1900. The clearest expression of policies designed to shift the economy away from agriculture and towards manufacturing and services arose thirty years later, following the 1977 change of government. Even then, the shift from agriculture to manufacturing and services was slow, in part because of the rural employment and resettlement effects of major public investment in rural schemes such as the Mahaveli River Diversion Project.

The nature of 'industrialisation' appears to have differed between Japan and Sri Lanka. Japan's industrialisation of the late nineteenth century was state-driven, urban, factory-based and export-oriented. Sri Lanka's industrialisation of the late nineteenth century was also export-oriented, but it was rural, agricultural and private sector based. Sri Lanka's urban and factory-based industrialisation, starting some years after independence, was state-driven import substitution in a first wave, and state-supported and export-oriented in a second. Perhaps the key difference between Japan's late nineteenth-century urban-based industrialisation and Sri Lanka's mid-nineteenth-century agriculture-based industrialisation lies in the composition and levels of skills required of labour and the role that education played in their formation. This was not explored in the thesis.

Proposition 2: At independence there was a broad consensus that education was a channel for social mobility via 'a single peaked pyramid which everybody could climb'

Dore identifies Sri Lanka's independence in 1948 as the point at which education enjoyed a consensus over its role as a channel of social mobility. In England, the drive for economic modernisation during the industrial revolution in the eighteenth century *preceded* the creation of a nationwide system of mass primary education. Education was not perceived to be a channel for social mobility. In Japan, the drive

---

[1] Annual Census 1891, 1901, 1946; Corea (1975), p. 77; Table 5 in Gunatilleke (1974); Table 17 in Alailima (1991); Department of Census and Statistics (1990).

for economic modernisation during the Meiji restoration in the late nineteenth century *coincided with*, and indeed was integral to, a wholesale reform of society which spurred on the nationwide expansion of mass primary education and its integration into a 'unitary pyramid of graded layers' (Dore, 1976, p. 39). Education came to be seen by society as a potential channel of social mobility.

In Sri Lanka, by contrast, the notion of education as a channel of social mobility had emerged even *before* independence. As we saw in Chapter 1, universal franchise was introduced in 1931 and had created the momentum for social and political change. Dr Kannangara, the first minister of education, provided the political force for the realisation of a social egalitarian ideal which resulted in the 'free education act' introduced in 1945. The growth in the power and appeal of the egalitarian ideal was matched by increased responsibility taken by the state for education and evidenced by an increase in the number and proportion of government-run schools. Whereas in 1900 only 13 per cent of the country's 3,917 schools were run by the government, by 1945 this had grown to 42 per cent of 5,726 schools; and, by 1975, to 89 per cent of 9,675 schools (NEC, 1992). Literacy rates, which were estimated to be around 26 per cent in 1900, had reached 58 per cent in 1945 and 79 per cent by 1971 (86 per cent male; 71 per cent female).

After independence, the government set in place measures to create a unified government system of education to replace the dual system of education that pertained during the pre-independence era. The medium of instruction in all government and government-aided schools began to switch from English to one of the vernaculars, either Sinhala or Tamil. From 1948 all primary schools were required to introduce either Sinhala or Tamil as the medium of instruction from Grade 1. Sinhala or Tamil was introduced in the first year of the secondary cycle in 1953; and in the first year of university arts courses in 1959. English-medium school examinations began to fade away in the 1960s, reinforcing the notion that all children, and not just an English-educated elite, could reach the pinnacle of educational success and achieve modern sector jobs that had been out of reach to their parents and grandparents. The denominational schools which had attracted the middle classes and offered English-medium education were nationalised in 1961.

Proposition 3: Asynchronous growth between jobs in the modern sector and growth of the education system led to 'educated unemployment'

Dore suggested that the creation and consolidation of a unified system of education post-independence occurred in an economy which was growing too slowly to absorb the numbers of qualified students emerging from the education system. These young people were seeking modern, largely government, sector jobs. There was a 'mismatch' between employment opportunities and employment expectations. Indeed, the ideas for the thesis were seeded and took root in 1971 at the time of youth unrest. In 1971 Dore had been in Sri Lanka as a member of the International Labour Organization's 'employment mission' to inquire into the large-scale youth unemployment. Reflecting on this experience 26 years later, he wrote:

> Experienced for the first time a country with a sharp division between a modern sector offering salaries and security far superior to life in the traditional peasant economy; and the tremendous strains set up because that modern sector grew only slowly, while the school system, whose certificates had hitherto acted as licenses to enter that modern sector, expanded at a much more rapid rate. I saw this as one more 'late development effect', vastly accelerating processes which were common to all modern societies. (Dore, 1997a, p. 24)

By 1971, nearly 20 per cent of the labour force was openly unemployed, 80 per cent of whom were under 25 years of age (Alailima, 1991). Among 20–24-year-olds with at least three GCE O level passes, 55 per cent of males and 74 per cent of females were unemployed. The level of 'educated unemployment' was extremely high. The estimated imbalance in the labour market was of the order of 3:1. Between 150,000 and 200,000 job seekers with 11 years of general education and who had sat GCE O level exams were pursuing an estimated 60,000 jobs in medium-to-large-scale modern sector enterprises. In white-collar wage employment the imbalance was 7:1. Increasing frustration on the part of educated young people unable to find the kinds of jobs which their education had led them to expect resulted in the 1971 youth insurrection, mobilised by the Janatha Vimukthi Peramuna (People's Liberation Front) against the United Front government.

Proposition 4: The imbalance between the growth of the modern sector economy and the growth in numbers of educated young people led employers to raise (escalate) the qualifications required for jobs

The imbalance between the growth of the modern sector economy and the growth in qualifications led, Dore argued, to a growth in 'qualification escalation'. Qualification escalation refers to the raising of qualification levels for the *same* job over time. The research I undertook with Dore, Chrisanthi Deraniyagala and others in the mid-1970s confirmed that a degree of qualification escalation had occurred during the 1960s and early 1970s (Deraniyagala, Dore & Little, 1978). The qualifications of those who succeeded in clearing the hurdles of both recruitment (that is, qualified to apply) *and* selection rose faster than the qualifications set at the recruitment hurdle alone.

Our research demonstrated that de facto vertical and horizontal qualification escalation was apparent in both the public and private sectors of employment, though it was more marked and visible in the public sector. Vertical escalation referred to an increase in the level of education required, while horizontal escalation referred either to an increase in the performance demanded at a given level or to the addition of a supplementary criterion, for example 'years of experience'. Three examples illustrate vertical escalation. In 1956, a large private sector cinema chain required no educational qualifications for 'sweepers, hall boys and lavatory coolies'. By 1976, a minimum educational requirement of Standard 7 had been established. Before 1972, a public sector corporation required its production supervisors to have achieved GCE O level passes in Chemistry, Maths and Physics. After 1972, this was raised to GCE A level passes in the same three subjects. The personnel manager of a public sector corporation explained how an advertisement for seven vacancies for production assistants, the minimum qualification for which was six GCE O level passes with credits in Physics, Chemistry and Maths, attracted 11,000 applicants. He told the board that he faced an impossible situation and 'they agreed that I should consider only those with GCE A Levels'. He went on to explain to me that that still left 300, so he 'interviewed the whole lot. Next time though the qualification for this job will be GCE A level' (Deraniyagala, Dore & Little, 1978, p. 51)!

The main reason for the escalation of qualifications was logistical; employers needed to reduce applicants to a manageable number. Few employers spoke of a need to raise qualifications because the job would be performed better by a more qualified person. The school system was, in effect, acting as an extension of a personnel office, helping employers to reject some and accept others in a socially legitimate way. The school was acting as a 'screen' (see screening theory, Chapter 5) and doing much of the work that a personnel department ought to be doing for itself.

Proposition 5: The more qualification levels were raised, the more exam-oriented teaching and learning became – that is, the learning process became ritualised, and the development of 'relevant' terminal primary education constrained

The fifth proposition is that an intensive pursuit of examinations and qualifications impoverishes the quality and process of learning. Dore asserted:

> It is not surprising that examinations *dominate* the curriculum, that all learning is ritualised, that curiosity is devalued, that no one is allowed to stray from the syllabus, that no one inquires about the usefulness, the relevance, or the interestingness of what is learned. (Dore, 1976, p. 61)

For Dore, the domination of the de facto curriculum by the assessment process was judged to have at least two negative consequences. The first was the displacement of knowledge and skills which could be of potential use to the majority of children by those assessed through examination and which are of little use to the majority of students (for example, quadratic equations and memorisation of the length of the world's largest rivers). The second was the effect on the abilities of the minority who do reach the top, 'the future controllers of Sri Lanka's destiny'. How, Dore wonders, are they to become 'imaginative managers and administrators noted for their independence and integrity' if they have completed 16 years of training in the 'docile acceptance of the authority of teachers and examiners' and the production of answers 'which we expect those in authority to expect'? (Dore, 1976, p. 64.)

Dore's views on the influence of the selection function of schools on educational quality concurred with those of senior educational professionals in Sri Lanka at that time:

> The qualifying function ... tended to become exalted at the expense of the educational functions. Educational qualifications and not real meaningful education have emerged as the major determinant

of success in life ... the function of education is reduced to that of an expensive means of distinguishing the academically able from the less able, hoping that such a distinction will enable the nation to develop its manpower most effectively. (Ranaweera, 1975, p. 16)

Speaking shortly after the youth insurrection of April 1971 (described in Chapter 4), the minister of education commented that the youth of Sri Lanka had been socialised into a feeling of 'rejection' by an education system that focussed on access to university – a benefit enjoyed by only 1 per cent of students (*The Nation*, 30 May 1971). In his analysis of educational change at the time of the youth insurrection in 1971, a former director of educational planning commented that 'stipulations laid down for crossing a hurdle are likely to have a backwash effect on what goes before that hurdle' (Wijemanne, 1978).

The most systematic evidence for the backwash of public examinations on the secondary school curriculum was collected in 1974–5 by Lewin (1984), who, collaborating with colleagues in the Ministry of Education and Curriculum Development Centre, explored the impact on teaching and learning of the innovative 'integrated science' National Certificate of General Education subject. The integrated science exam was sat by all students and was claimed to have relevance for the lives of the majority of students. Despite statements that the new integrated science curriculum should emphasise the development of scientific concepts, patterns and processes rather than facts, the exam comprised a proportion of items testing knowledge higher than the average of the earlier single-subject science papers (Lewin, 1984, Table 4.3). Moreover, low pass marks (estimated raw scores of around 30 per cent) and multiple-choice formats made it possible for students to pass the exam purely on the basis of the recall of memorised facts. This evidence provided some support for the assertions about the quality of learning set out in proposition 5.

But here I must pause and invite the reader to step back in time. Was the exam-dominated teaching and learning observed by Dore in the 1970s a function of the increasing use of education certificates in the modern sector economy of the 1960s and early 1970s, or was exam-dominated teaching and learning an educational 'issue' of long standing?

That competitive exams have backwash effects on the de facto curriculum inside classrooms was not a new observation. As early as 1867, more than a century before *The diploma disease* was published, examination backwash was an issue of concern to educators. The Revd J. B. H. Bailey submitted a memorandum to the Morgan Committee to complain that the affiliation of the country's elite school (the Colombo Academy) to the University of Calcutta meant that 'the whole curriculum of study is sacrificed to the subjects required for the University Entrance Examination' (Bailey, quoted in J. E. Jayasuriya, 1979, p. 163). In 1928, Ormsby-Gore, a member of the British Parliament and Parliamentary Under Secretary of State for the Colonies, visited Ceylon. He commented on the 'denationalising, de-ruralising, and intellectually and socially cramping results of the system of education', the tyranny of 'an externally and distant written examination wholly out of touch with the needs, traditions, mental gifts, and aptitudes of the people' and the 'anglicizing and denationalizing tendencies of academic or clerical education in the Colonial schools' (J. E. Jayasuriya, 1979, pp. 435–6). The issue surfaced again in Ceylon's 1943 parliamentary sessional papers. An 'examination mentality' was leading to the stunting of imagination, the suppression of originality, the lack of development of a capacity for thought, and the inhibition of emotions (War and Colonial Department and Colonial Office, 1943).

So, while examination backwash may well have been a concern to educators in the 1970s, it was also of concern at least a century before – and remains so today. The historical roots of proposition 5 require further investigation.

Forecast intensification of the diploma disease

In looking to the future of education in Sri Lanka, Dore forecast in 1976:

> Continuous pressure for expansion of facilities, increasing intense competition at every entry port and selection post, increasingly anxious dominance of the curriculum by examinations, and an increasing experience of individual failure within the school system, and of the frustrations of unemployment on leaving it. (Dore, 1976, p. 65)

So, did the symptoms of the so-called disease subside or intensify over the 20-year period between 1976 and 1996? The evidence presented here addresses participation in exams, participation in private tuition, attempts at examination reform, and studies of teaching and learning in the 1990s.

The total number of students in general education grew from 3.5 million in 1981 to 4.3 million in 1992. In terms of sheer numbers, a greater proportion of the school-age population participated in public exams in the 1990s compared with the 1970s. In 1977, 300,000 candidates sat the GCE O level exam; in 1991 it was 526,000. In 1975, 48,000 candidates sat the GCE A level exam; by 1991 it had more than tripled, to 160,000. These numbers reflect a massive growth in the numbers of students enrolling over the period 1976–96.

Over a similar period, participation in private tuition classes preparing students for examinations increased greatly. The editorial of the *Economic Review* (1994) reported that 'private tuition in Sri Lanka is spreading its tentacles rapidly into every avenue'. Estimates from 1989 suggested that 75 per cent of Grade 11 students were taking private tuition for the GCE O level exam. This rose to 92 per cent among GCE A level science students. Since the 1989 data was drawn from all parts of the country, excluding the north and the east (excluded because of the impossibility of collecting such evidence during a time of civil war), and included representative percentages of rural students, we may infer that in most areas participation rates increased (W. A. de Silva, Gunawardene, Jayeweera et al., 1991).

As we saw in Chapter 4, the 1972 examination reform, designed to make the curriculum more relevant to the lives of the majority of children and reduce the backwash effects of exams on the curriculum, was short-lived. The exam returned to the familiar-named GCE O and A levels. Subsequent reforms in the late 1980s were also abandoned. The 1987 reform to include teachers' marks from continuous assessment of project work in selected subjects in the marks awarded by the GCE O level exam was resisted by teachers because of their lack of preparation, by parents because of their mistrust of teacher judgements, and by politicians who argued that it discriminated against the rural child. It survived only one year. A second reform, to include a practical skills component of the GCE A level science exam, did not progress beyond the stage of proposal.

Perhaps the strongest evidence of the hold which exams exert over the daily practices of teaching and learning was offered by Elsie Kotalawala and her team in a study entitled *The Year 5 scholarship examination and the implementation of the primary school curriculum* (Kotalawala et al., 1994). The Grade 5 primary education scholarship exam was introduced in 1944 to provide opportunities for poor able children to enter English-medium 'central schools' in rural areas. Kotalawala's study demonstrated how, in the early 1990s, despite there being fee-free access for all to Grade 11, the Grade 5 exam continued to dominate the teaching and learning practices of teachers and students in most primary schools, especially in Grades 4 and 5. The study found the following:

- only Language and Mathematics are given attention until the time of the scholarship exam ...
- other subjects (viz. environmental studies, beginning science, aesthetics and creative activities) are taught only after the scholarship exam in the majority of the schools ...
- teaching is purely teacher centred. Children are simply coached to answer scholarship exam question papers. The developmental ages of children are not taken into consideration in organising learning activities ...
- in most of the schools surveyed (65 per cent) students were grouped in preparation for the scholarship exam as early as Grade 3 ...
- parental 'interference' contributes to the above situation; this interference is caused by the competition to gain entrance to 'popular' schools ...
- children find little time to engage in play activity. Some children are even deprived of watching TV ...
- principals condone the situation to maintain the popularity of the school, to satisfy the departmental officers and to satisfy the strong request of parents. (Abstracted from Kotalawala et al., 1994, pp. 84–5)

This assessment confirms Dore's proposition about the continuing challenges faced when trying to deliver 'relevant' primary education.

The propositions re-assessed

This chapter has explored the application of the 'diploma disease' thesis to Sri Lanka, the country that had inspired it. With respect to the first proposition, I discussed whether Dore's account of Sri Lanka's drive for economic modernisation and industrialisation might have been strengthened had he distinguished the colonial period of agricultural industrialisation from the much later urban industrialisation based on manufacturing and services, and the skill requirements of labour in each period. This would have assisted his judgement as to whether, in terms of industrialisation, Sri Lanka was a 'later developer' in the continuum of world history, or whether, like Japan, she was a 'late developer' when compared with England's early development.

The second proposition suggested that at independence there was a broad consensus that education was a channel for social mobility via 'a single peaked pyramid which everybody could climb'. By the time of independence, there was indeed a broad social consensus that education was a channel for social mobility and that there was an educational pyramid which everybody could, in principle, climb. Egalitarian education policies designed by Sri Lankan politicians from the 1930 in the years leading up to independence were a core element in Sri Lanka's transition from a colonial to a post-colonial country. This proposition was confirmed.

The third proposition focussed on the consequences of the asynchronous growth in the numbers of modern sector jobs and the numbers of educated young people seeking them. Evidence suggested that there was indeed a high degree of asynchrony in the early 1970s and that was associated with extremely high levels of unemployment among GCE O and A level-qualified young people. This proposition was also confirmed.

The fourth proposition explored whether this asynchronous growth led employers to raise the qualification levels for the same job. We found ample evidence of employers raising qualification levels over time for the same job, not because the job required a higher level of skill, but because it was a socially legitimate way of managing the recruitment and selection process when large numbers of people were applying for a job. This proposition too was confirmed.

The fifth, multi-faceted proposition asserted that the more educated unemployment rises, the more qualification levels are raised, the more intensive the pursuit of qualifications becomes, the more intense exam-oriented learning becomes, the more ritualised the teaching-learning process becomes, and the more difficult it is to implement a 'relevant' terminal primary education. Exam-dominated learning was noticeable in 1976 and attempts to reform exams in ways that would support a more 'relevant curriculum' were thwarted. While this proposition attracted support during the period about which Dore was writing, it was not specific to it. That competitive exams had a grip on the curriculum and serve the needs of the successful minority at the expense of the needs of the majority had been apparent for at least a century and could not be derived from the earlier propositions about unemployment or qualification escalation.

Dore forecast that the diploma disease would grow over time. Evidence presented in this chapter suggested that there had indeed been an increase in exam-oriented teaching and learning as Dore had predicted. The proportions of young people sitting the GCE O and A levels had increased dramatically. Attempts to reform exams were thwarted as various interest groups sought to maintain earlier advantages in access to prestigious educational institutions. The proportions of students preparing for exams through private tuition arrangements increased. Notwithstanding the fact that all students were able to enrol in fee-free education to the end of Grade 11, the grip of the Grade 5 'scholarship' exam over the teaching and learning process in primary education appeared to tighten.

So, has this occurred only through the working out of Dore's propositions, or for other reasons as well? When Dore drafted his book (written in 1973 and published in 1976) he did not anticipate the changes in economic policy that would occur following the change of government in 1977. As we shall see in Chapter 11, economic policy change resulted in a growth of the economy, a growth in GDP per capita and a decline in unemployment in the following decade.

Following proposition 3, one might have expected that a decline in unemployment (that is, a better balance between the numbers of jobs available and job seekers) would have *reduced rather than increased* the degree of examination orientation in the education system. This appears *not* to have happened. So, why, despite economic growth, might examination orientation have increased?

Here we must return to proposition 2, which asserted a social consensus around the belief (at independence) that education was a channel for social mobility via 'a single peaked pyramid which everybody could climb'. That belief, I suggest, remains as strong as ever, even if evidence from personal life histories show that not everybody has been able to climb the ladder. This belief has driven the expansion of the general education system, the examination system, the private tuition system, and the grip that exams continue to exert on the processes of teaching and learning. Expansion had not been smooth. While the unemployment rate among GCE O level-qualified youth declined, that among the GCE A level-qualified increased, the process of qualification escalation continued, and although opportunities for university education expanded slowly, the numbers of those qualified to enter university increased at a faster rate, leading to continued bottlenecks and frustrated job aspirations.

The broader international development discourse and current Sri Lankan policy concerns

Dore's overriding concern with improvements in the quality of primary education resonated with Beeby's (1966) stages of improved quality in primary education (Chapter 2). It also foreshadowed similar concerns expressed at the 1990 World Conference on Education for All, held in Jomtien, Thailand, on the need to expand educational opportunities, improve the quality of education and focus on learning outcomes (World Conference on Education for All, 1990; Little, Hoppers & Gardner, 1994, pp. 230–3). Over the past thirty years the international discourse surrounding 'education for all' (EFA) has focussed largely on the inputs, processes and outputs of education and their inequalities. It has largely ignored the articulation of these systems with the wider institutions of labour/work, and the institutional mechanisms that allocate jobs. Even the most recent Sustainable Development Goals (SDGs), with their array of goals across all development sectors, sidestep the institutional mechanisms through which individuals move from the education arena to that of 'decent work'. The articulation of education with the world of work via selection mechanisms is one of the strengths of the diploma disease perspective and one that is overlooked in the contemporary EFA and SDG discourses.

Meanwhile, the 'qualification chase' symptom of the 'disease' continues and is now being played out on a global scale. With the intensification of globalisation and the integration of national economies, employers are moving jobs around the world, and young people are chasing the most lucrative of them with more and more qualifications. The international assessment business is thriving, international university league tables steer the choices of students whose parents can afford to pay international student fees, cross-border university franchises and campuses are growing, and 'international' qualifications are sought after in the search for jobs in an increasingly globalised economy. All are symptoms of a globalised form of Dore's diploma disease (Little, 1997; Lewin, Little & Wolf, 2019), to which Sri Lanka is not immune.

The qualification chase is dependent on high-stakes public exams. Not unlike the Sri Lankan colonial educators of the early twentieth century mentioned above, the National Education Commission, a century later, deplores examination backwash and the stress and anxiety it generates amongst students, teachers and parents (NEC, 2022). It has proposed a set of 'National Learning Competency Domains' designed to prepare young people for learning outcomes relevant to the needs of globalised workplaces. These include the skills that nurture curiosity, problem-solving and imagination, and are among a package of skills now presented around the world as 'twenty-first-century skills' (see for examples Rychen & Salganik, 2000; Sedere, 2019). As it happens these were also skills that, for Dore, constituted what he termed 'genuine' education, but which were so difficult to promote in the exam-oriented system of education of the 1970s. Will the promotion of these twenty-first-century skills face the same challenges today?

Part III
Basic needs and education for all

Preface to Part III

Rather than applying concepts and propositions from the international discourse to the Sri Lankan context, the chapters in this part of the book offer answers to the question: Which ideas and policies in the international discourse have been influenced by Sri Lankan ideas and policies? The three chapters in this section outline the early advances made by Sri Lanka in the fulfilment of 'basic needs', including education, and in promoting 'education for all'. Sri Lanka's early advances in education are often invoked by those who contribute to the international literature and advocate improvements elsewhere.

Chapter 7 examines the principle of social egalitarianism, which influenced Sri Lankan education policy and practice in the transition to independence and continues to do so today. That policy involved fee-free education for all, the satisfaction of education as a basic need, and education as a key element in overall human development. In later years, Sri Lanka's successes would circulate beyond her shores. The chapter outlines the anti-colonial and social egalitarian principles espoused by Sri Lanka's first minister of education, C. W. W. Kannangara, and his Education Executive Committee during the 1930s following the introduction of semi-autonomous government and universal suffrage. It follows the course of this legislation up to 1990, contrasting the early period up to the 1970s as one framed by the imperatives of independence with the subsequent period 1970–90 as one characterised by successive waves of youth unrest and the government's need to contain it.

Chapter 8 moves forward in time and explores the origins and implementation of the 1997 education reforms through the interaction between political, administrative, technical, human resource and financial drivers. These build from the solid base of expanded access to primary education and consider improvements in the quality of education in both primary and post-primary. The origins of these reforms can be traced to the unrest in the south of the country between 1987 and 1989, the grievances of educated youth about the lack of jobs, despite the growth of the economy witnessed in the early 1980s, and a perceived need to improve the relevance of education. The account of the president's involvement in translating reform ideas into implementation on the ground provides an illustration of the role of strong political will from the top in formulating and implementing policies on 'education for all' – a determination that had also been witnessed fifty years earlier during the tenure of Minister Kannangara. In assessing the implementation of the reforms through the 2000s, it becomes clear that local-level political will can counteract efforts from the top. 'Political will' is a 'double-edged sword' (Little, 2011).

Chapter 9 changes key – from the political to the technical aspects of 'education for all'. Much technical planning work lay behind the scenes of the 1997 reforms, especially in relation to primary education. While some of the chapter's text may strike some readers as rather dry, practical and technical, such work is essential in translating policy into policy implementation. Though dry, practical and technical, educational planning is not immune to micro-level politics which 'technicians' need to contend with and resolve.

7
Education for all, welfare and basic needs: 1931–91

Introduction

By the first decade of the twentieth century, compulsory education between the ages of 6 and 12 years for boys in towns and rural areas, and between 6 and 10 years for Muslim and Tamil girls in town areas, had been prescribed (Ordinance No. 5 of 1906 and Ordinance No. 8 of 1906). They provided an early framework, if not a fully resourced or implemented scheme, for the achievement of 'education for all' (EFA) over a limited age range.

This chapter examines the underlying drivers of education reform policies introduced between 1931 and 1991, designed to expand educational opportunities for all. It also describes the influence of Sri Lanka's early EFA achievements on the concept of 'basic needs' and related policy ideas that were circulating in the international development community in the 1970s and 1980s, the increasing role of political patronage in the day-to-day implementation of EFA policies, and the constellation of education stakeholders by the end of the period in question.

The transition from colonial education

The building of Sri Lanka's unified system of education that is recognisable today began in 1920. It was a slow process, and one where the vested interests of the denominational schools would exert a significant brake for a further forty years. The education ordinance of 1920 gave the central Department of Education the power to fund elementary education in government schools.

The constitutional reforms recommended by the Donoughmore Commission (1928) resulted in the granting of universal suffrage to all men and women over 21 years of age. Popular elections in 1931 led to the establishment of a State Council with both legislative and executive powers and limited self-rule. The extension of political franchise fuelled 'welfarist' policies for education, health and labour conditions. The social demand for education led to a series of social policy reforms and rapid growth in opportunities for primary and lower secondary education in the 1940s and 1950s.

The State Council had both legislative and executive powers. An Education Executive Committee was one of the seven Executive Committees formed. It was chaired by the island's first Ceylonese minister of education, the legendary Dr C. W. W. Kannangara, who would go on to hold that office until 1947. Kannangara was a nationalist politician committed to egalitarian principles and was the person who would make education in Sri Lanka 'unique in the South Asian region' (Jayaweera, 1989, p. 1; E. J. de Silva, 2010).

In the 1930s, the mainstream education 'system' was marked by 'dualities', described succinctly by J. E. Jayasuriya (1979). These included the duality of management (government vs denominational bodies and private individuals), the language of instruction (English vs the vernacular, or *Swabasha*), location (urban vs rural), career destinations (high status vs low status), and school fees (fee-charging vs fee-free). From 1931, Kannangara and his team sought ways to remove these dualities and divisions in order to create a unified and more egalitarian system of education.

Political independence – a relatively quiet affair

Ceylon's political transition to independence in 1948 was a relatively quiet affair:

> At no time was there in Ceylon a mass agitation for constitutional reforms comparable to the Civil Disobedience Movement which took place in India. The Indian nationalist movement was, however, a source of strength for the Ceylonese, and Ceylon enjoyed the fruits of success of the Indian movement. (J. E. Jayasuriya, 1979, p. 426)

Where independence in India was driven by a mass movement, independence in Ceylon was driven by three groups of educated elites.

The first group comprised those educated in high-quality English-medium schools and working in the professions and in the plantation sector; the second were those educated in one of the vernacular languages, Sinhala or Tamil; and the third were English-educated left-wing intellectuals, many of whom had studied and lived abroad, especially in Britain (J. E. Jayasuriya, 1979).

Universal franchise in 1931 and subsequent parliamentary democracy from 1948 engendered a political sensitivity to the needs of voters that distinguished the orientation of policy from that of the colonial era. The welfare goals and measures introduced from the 1930s were influenced by members of the comprador elite of colonial Sri Lanka and were imbued with the liberal social and political values of Victorian England.

> The social legislation during the Donoughmore period (1931–47), relating to child and family welfare, poverty alleviation, social security, education and health bears witness to the ways in which these ideological influences of visionary idealism of social justice and equality, influenced social and political development in the pre-independence period. (D. L. Jayasuriya, 2001)

These welfare measures established an enduring political commitment to social justice that would be pursued to greater or lesser degrees by all political parties. Poverty was addressed through redistributive measures, and a massive programme of social welfare was introduced on the eve of independence in 1948 (Jayaweera, 1986). Free education, free health care, improved nutrition, subsidised food, low cost of living and the fair distribution of income became the 'articles of faith' in the political credos of all parties (Gunatilleke, 1974, p. 17).

The political pendulum influenced the machinery of government as well as general and education policy goals. Control of policies and finance was vested in a newly established Executive Committee of the State Council. However, if the new Committee was to function effectively, the predecessor Board of Education needed to relinquish its role as policy formulator. It took seven years, from 1931 to 1938, to resolve the division of responsibilities between the predominantly Christian Board of Education, 'jealous of its rights under the existing Ordinance' and 'reactionary', and the elected Executive Committee for Education, 'responsible for getting money voted for education, answerable also to the people of the country for the state of education' (J. E. Jayasuriya, 1979, pp. 445–6).

Education Ordinance No. 31 was passed in 1939. It clarified the division of responsibilities for education as between the Department of Education and central/local advisory bodies and committees, set out the powers of the new Executive Committee to make regulations, and gave a ruling on religious instruction.

Policy reforms: anti-colonial and egalitarian

There were three main issues on which Kannangara's committee would work. The first was language medium. Should the medium of instruction be English or one of the vernaculars? Should there be different language policies for different types of school? The second was school fees. Should fees be charged, or should access to all types of school be fee-free? The third was the management of schools. Should schools owned and managed by denominational bodies and private individuals be nationalised?

In 1943, Minister Kannangara's Special Committee on Education recommended that the medium of instruction should be the mother tongue at every stage of education, recommended the removal of fees from all government schools, and recommended that all government-assisted schools be nationalised and 'taken over' by the state – that is, they would become government, rather than government-assisted, schools. If the passage of Education Ordinance No. 31 of 1939 had met with resistance from those who had served the colonial government, the 1943 report would attract criticism from both the conservatives who defended the past and the radicals who described the proposals as too conservative. Widely credited with introducing 'free education' from kindergarten to university, Kannangara's own view was that it should be introduced in stages. He was out-voted by the majority of committee members and fee-free education at every stage of education passed into law (E. J. de Silva, 2010).

Relegation of English

The relegation of English-medium education occurred in phases. From 1945, mother-tongue education was introduced in all primary schools, the mother tongue or a mix of mother tongue and English to the lower division of post-primary schools, and the mother tongue or English to the upper division. By 1948 there was a recognition that secondary and higher education would also employ the mother tongue in due course.

This policy was implemented in the first year of secondary education in 1953, in university arts subjects in 1959, and in university science, medicine and engineering subjects in the 1970s. These were radical changes which would shape curricula, textbook provision, teacher education, and teaching and learning to the present day.

Fee-free education

The second major policy reform was the removal of school fees in all government schools. Policies on school fees were intertwined with language policy. Throughout the British colonial period school fees had not been charged by the vernacular-medium primary schools. These schools were government funded. Opportunities for poor children to gain access to high-status, English-medium fee-charging schools were limited. To combat this, fee-free English-medium 'central schools' were established in some rural areas during the 1940s. This was followed by the removal of fees from assisted primary and post-primary schools, teacher training colleges, universities, and state-funded technical, agricultural and trade schools. The free education scheme 'opened the doors of English education to thousands who could not have afforded such an education' (J. E. Jayasuriya, 1979, p. 524).

In his address to the State Council justifying fee-free education, Kannangara invoked a parable from the gospel of St Matthew:

> I say that Free Education is the answer. I say that it is a pearl of great price. Sell all that you have and buy it for the benefit of the whole community ... [Let it be said that] the State Council of Ceylon found education dear and left it free, that they found it a sealed book and left it an open letter, that they found it the patrimony of the rich and left it the lasting inheritance of the poor. (Kannangara, quoted in *Sunday Times* (Sri Lanka), 23 September 2012)

However, access to fee-free English-medium education for the poorer groups in society would be short-lived, as the policy switch from English-medium education to the vernacular medium for all, described above, worked its way through the entire system of education. While the middle classes would now gain fee-free access to vernacular-medium education where before they had paid, the poor would continue to gain fee-free access to vernacular education as they had done for many years.

Nationalisation of assisted schools

The third major policy reform was eventually enacted in 1961. English-medium assisted schools were given the option of either entering the government scheme and not charging fees or becoming registered fee-charging private schools with no government funding.

Post-independence: the nationalist project

After independence in 1948, the process of policy formulation gradually became embroiled in new tensions between the two main Sinhalese political parties. In education these revolved around education access and the nature of privilege, symbolised through language, religious affiliation, the ability to pay fees and academic selection. More general debates among political parties around official languages and nationalism would also have implications for education policy in the years to come.

The first post-independence government was led by D. S. Senanayake and the right-wing United National Party (UNP). This government reviewed earlier policies and set out its proposals for reform in a White Paper, following the practice then current in Britain. One of the White Paper's recommendations was that entry to secondary education at the age of 11 should be based on ability, assessed through a selection exam. This was rejected by parliament, in favour of a selection exam at 14 years of age.

By the early 1950s, political agitation by the masses for greater access to secondary education led to the increasing use of Sinhala and Tamil as media in the upper division. Sinhala and Tamil became the compulsory media of instruction in all secondary grades from 1953 and in university arts courses from 1960.

In 1956 the left-wing Mahajana Eksath Peramuna (People's United Front), a coalition of the Sri Lanka Freedom Party and various Marxist/left-wing parties under the leadership of S. W. R. D. Bandaranayake, came to power. This coalition appealed to the interests of the rural masses, rural teachers, ayurveda doctors, Buddhist priests and agricultural labourers. Ability-based selection to secondary education at the age of 14 was abandoned. The high-status, privileged denominational schools survived the change of government in 1956, but they could not avoid its gaze in the lead-up to the elections of 1960. Their takeover was hotly debated, and, despite considerable resistance from Christians and Catholics, two Acts of Parliament (1960 and 1961) vested assisted schools and their properties in the state. This contributed to the consolidation of a unified system of education and reflected the ideological push at that time towards the nationalisation of all economic and social institutions. The establishment of new private schools was proscribed in 1961, a legal restriction which remains in place today. The political battle over English and the vernacular languages appeared to have been won, and a unified system of education was created:

> By 1960 therefore major colonial policies had been reversed. Language and religion ceased to be a barrier to educational opportunity. The education system was unified with only sixty-three schools out of over nine thousand schools functioning as private schools. The national languages were the medium of instruction in the secondary school with an English stream for Muslim, and Burgher students. (Jayaweera, 1986, p. 10)

These radical, egalitarian, anti-colonial policy changes in education occurred alongside major policy shifts across the economy and society. When the socialist-oriented coalition came to power in 1956 the direction of the economy also changed. The state assumed a stronger role in the economy and promoted a regime of 'import substitution industrialisation' (ISI), whereby national industries would produce goods for the domestic market and reduce dependence on imports and foreign exchange. There was a retreat from export-orientation and a move towards greater economic self-reliance.

In an attempt to offer access to a diversified curriculum that reflected the needs of the national economy, the National Education Commission's 1961 report recommended that four types of secondary school be established. In keeping with the theme of equality of opportunity, these four streams were to be equal in status and access to them would not be based on academic selection tests. The 1964 White Paper proposed instead that these four types be combined into a single school but with four streams. The government was defeated in the 1965 elections by Dudley Senanayake's National Front and the White Paper stalled.

The new government prepared a new White Paper in which the idea of four types of schools was resurrected, but access to them would be based on academic criteria. The White Paper was debated in parliament for two days and was presented as a draft bill a year later. However, the bill was defeated in parliament because it was anticipated that access to high-status secondary education among the lower social classes would be limited.

The 'national' project and ethnicity

When the coalition government came to power in 1956, one of its first pieces of legislation was the controversial Official Languages Act, commonly referred to as the 'Sinhala-only' Act, which made Sinhala the sole official language of public administration in place of English. Proficiency in Sinhala, not Tamil, became a criterion of access to coveted government jobs. This political move enraged the Tamil-speaking minority. It also contradicted one of the justifications that had been advanced in 1944 for the introduction of Sinhala and Tamil as the media of instruction in all schools – that is, that both Sinhala and Tamil would become the official languages of Ceylon.

The Official Languages Act both responded to and reinforced the growth of Sinhala-Buddhist nationalism among non-Christian and non-English-speaking Sinhalese groups, who were seeking to transform their under-privileged status acquired during colonial rule. In the 1960 elections both of the main Sinhalese parties campaigned on an anti-Tamil line, promising to implement the 'Sinhala-only' Act of 1956 and to repatriate large numbers of Tamils working in the tea and rubber estates to India.

I referred earlier to Ceylon's relatively peaceful transition to independence. In contrast to the violence that led to independence and subsequent partition in India and to the civil war in Burma, Sri Lanka was 'in 1948 … an oasis of stability, peace and order' (K. M. de Silva, 1981, p. 489). But that stability was fragile. Political struggles can lead to the formation of a unified national will. The absence of a violent political struggle in Sri Lanka at that time 'did not provide the conditions for … charismatic leadership' (Gunatilleke, 1974, p. 7).

Although the first prime minister, D. S. Senanayake, had promoted a Ceylonese nationalism that emphasised the common interests of various ethnic and religious groups, including a secular state, a multi-racial policy and a single nation, it was flawed since it enjoyed little popular support beyond the establishment of the political elites. Beneath the aspiration of a nationalism based on the idea of a single, plural and secular state were ethno-nationalisms that were 'as insidious as they were truly formidable' (K. M. de Silva, 1981, p. 496). The majority Sinhalese tended to equate Sinhalese nationalism with Ceylonese nationalism. The Tamils rejected this vehemently and developed instead an 'inward-looking ethnic nationalism' (K. M. de Silva, 1981, p. 496). For their part, the Sinhalese and Tamil Christians resented the tendency of the Sinhalese to equate their version of nationalism with Buddhism. In practice it was the Sinhalese-Buddhist version of nationalism that became the dominant political force in 1956. Language moved centre stage in all versions of nationalism in wider society, and carried particular significance in allocating prized white-collar jobs in the government sector. In the 1960 elections the opposition UNP did little to dispel the idea that national identity meant a Sinhalese-Buddhist identity.

With the change in political regime in 1956, the state became 'the dominant source of almost everything that the citizens desired ... while politicians became the main benefactors, state officials became the key gatekeepers' (Hettige, 2000, p. 10). The expansion of the state into the economic and education spheres began to work against minority youth in several ways. State employment expanded but the imposition of proficiency in Sinhala restricted opportunities for the Tamil-speaking minority. Alongside language proficiency and educational background, political patronage also became a criterion for access to state sector jobs. Since political power was always in the hands of two parties supported largely by the Sinhala-speaking population, political patronage worked against the Tamil minority. Education policy also contributed to a breakdown of relations between ethnic groups. The policy of mother-tongue education was consistent with good pedagogic practice at that time, but it also had the effect of separating the middle-class, English-educated youth of different ethnic groups. In earlier times, these middle-class groups would have studied together and formed longstanding friendships and common identities, albeit identities based on social class and the English language. The majority of all Sinhala and Tamil youth, whatever their social class, would now study separately.

Up to this point, Tamil- and Sinhala-speaking children had been able to join fee-free and fee-charging schools in the same way, and could follow their education in their mother tongue, albeit in different schools. Differences in access to secondary education between social groups were marked more by residence (rural vs urban), wealth and medium of instruction than by ethnicity. An exception to this pattern was Indian Tamil children resident in tea and rubber plantations, whose access to primary and secondary education fell far behind that of all other groups (see Chapter 10). It was in the late 1960s that ethnicity would emerge as a political issue as a marker of access to education – particularly university education.

Political patronage and the implementation of education policy

So far, I have been discussing the political drivers and tensions inherent in the content of policy formulation. The role of politicians in policy implementation is a different matter altogether. By the mid-1960s the day-to-day practices of policy implementation were becoming increasingly subject to political influence, or 'interference' – the more usual term used to describe such influence.

From independence in 1948 up until the early 1960s, the civil service was relatively independent and inhibited the untrammelled involvement of ministers and other politicians in the day-to-day implementation of policies. The influence of politicians in the day-to-day implementation and administration of education was therefore largely absent. That began to change in the mid-1960s with the appointment of I. M. R. A. Iriyagolle as the UNP administration's Cabinet Minister of Education and Cultural Affairs. Iriyagolle was highly active in matters of education policy formulation, but he also took an active interest in implementation. While some would describe this as a positive interest, others would describe it as interference. Widely regarded as arrogant and abrasive in style and personality, he brooked little opposition. His reaction to those in the universities who challenged his ideas was often fierce, and included refusing to give teaching appointments to BEd graduates.

Constitutional change in the 1970s

Constitutional change in 1972 transformed Ceylon into the Republic of Sri Lanka. The governor general was replaced by a president, whose role was largely ceremonial and not aligned to a particular political party. Executive power continued to lie with the elected prime minister and parliament. This constitutional change also altered the constellation of political powers over education and the machinery of policy. One notable change was the loss of independence of the Public Service Commission, which was responsible for the appointment of senior civil servants. The Public Service Commission now fell under the control of the cabinet of the government in power. This new arrangement reduced the autonomy of public servants and increased their dependence on politicians for their day-to-day work, their appointments, and their own promotions and transfers.

The first appointment of a non-career civil servant as the chief bureaucrat in the Ministry of Education had already occurred in 1970, when the Sri Lanka Freedom Party won the general election under the leadership of Mrs Bandaranayake. Mr Premadasa Udagama, a former university lecturer in geography education, was appointed as the new secretary to the Ministry of Education. Although both Mr Udagama and his additional secretary, K. H. M. Sumathipala, were appointed to positions filled previously by civil servants, they would come to be described as 'political appointees' rather than civil servants. In the lead-up to the 1970 elections and beyond, their roles were different from those of traditional civil servants. As one former education officer recalled:

> they conducted the political programme for the government, spoke on political platforms in the 1970 elections and they were given the top posts … And there was a lot of political – not interference – they did not interfere in your work as such, but the curriculum revolves around the political – they were pushing it. They wanted a general comprehensive curriculum. They wanted some practical aspect thrown into the curriculum. (Interview with author, 2009)

This former officer refers to political 'push'. Others might term this 'political will', often considered to be a necessary ingredient of education reform. Gradually this political will and push for change in curriculum policy would be extended to the deployment, transfers and promotions of teachers and education officers. Between 1970 and 1977, a number of teachers who had voted against the government were sent on 'punishment transfers', many to schools in disadvantaged districts far away from Colombo and other large towns. The general public began to use the term 'interference' to refer to the increasing power held by politicians over the day-to-day practices of individuals. While educational qualifications remained important prerequisites in job recruitment, political influence became an important additional qualification. Political patronage was becoming a key ingredient in access to jobs.

The constitutional changes of 1978 were more far-reaching than those of 1972 and only served to increase the power of politicians over the implementation of education policy. In contrast with the constitutional changes of 1972, those of 1978 transformed the presidential role from ceremonial to that of a chief executive, with powers similar to, but greater than, those of a French president. However, beneath the president the former Westminster-style parliamentary system prevailed, with a prime minister, ministers and members of parliament elected every five years. Since the presidential and parliamentary elections coincided rarely this could, in principle, give rise to the cohabitation of a president and a prime minister representing different political parties and policies. Under the 1978 constitution the president could act at will, was not bound by the advice of the prime minister or cabinet of ministers, presided over the cabinet of ministers, and decided how many ministers there would be and their functions (Wickramanayake, 2009). Proportional representation was also introduced in 1978. This had the effect of increasing the power of minority political parties, which the major parties needed to attract in order to form a government.

Waves of political unrest and education reforms

The first wave of political unrest

The welfare measures introduced from the early 1930s had become a welfare tradition. Health improvements led to a steady increase in population. Between 1950 and 1960 student enrolments in general education grew by more than 60 per cent. These students were moving through the system and seeking jobs. But economic growth had slowed and there were insufficient jobs available to meet the expectations of these newly qualified youth. Unemployment increased.

Sri Lanka's first 10-year development plan (1958–68) had placed the reduction of unemployment at its heart (National Planning Council, 1959). Its emphasis on the reduction of unemployment and poverty was unusual, and far ahead of the international discourse on strategies for development at that time (Lipton, 1975). However, the growth of employment opportunities over this period was much slower than required. Between 1959 and 1969 the open unemployment rate grew from 10.5 per cent of the labour force to 14 per cent. This arose in a context of worsening terms of trade, and foreign exchange constraints meant that capital goods imports were cut (ILO, 1971b, pp. 5–10). In 1970 a coalition of the Sri Lanka Freedom Party and smaller Trotskyist and Communist factors came to power, with an election promise of solving the unemployment problem facing school leavers and improving equality of access to education. The left-wing coalition also favoured an intensification of self-reliance and a strengthening of national autonomy in economic, political, cultural and educational arrangements. Members of an Education Review Committee judged that the system was over-dependent on examinations and that the school curriculum was irrelevant to the needs of the economy. The school curriculum needed to be vocationalised and the exam system delinked from its 'colonial master'.

Before education reforms could be implemented, an insurrection in April 1971, led by the Janatha Vimukthi Peramuna (People's Liberation Front) (JVP), gripped the country and paralysed its leadership. The JVP's opposition to education policy was less to do with the relevance of curriculum content and more to do with the continuing monopoly of the English-educated elite on educational and occupational opportunity. Following the restoration of civil order, the Education Review Committee resumed its work, and refined and readied its proposals for implementation.

These proposals would become known as the 1972 reforms. They would be followed by further reforms in 1977 and 1981.

The 1972 education reforms

Chapter 4 has already set out the 1972 reforms. In brief, these were the delinking of secondary school exams from their British namesakes, and a reduction in the length of schooling leading up to the junior secondary exams (now named NGCE, instead of GCE O level) and senior secondary exams (now named HNCE, instead of GCE A level). This reduction in the length of schooling required to reach the restructured O level was accompanied by an increase of one year in the 'open access' span of education. 'Education for all' crept up from the eight grades of the earlier period to nine grades following the 1972 reforms. A new subject – 'pre-vocational studies' – introduced in the junior secondary grades was intended to introduce practical and locally relevant subjects that oriented young people to future livelihoods. Science was made available to all students rather than the minority who had followed them hitherto through the more specialised single subjects such as physics, chemistry, history, geography and civics. Mathematics was made available to all students and replaced the arithmetic, commercial arithmetic and elementary mathematics hitherto studied by the majority. Substantial reforms of primary education were implemented from 1972, based on the ideas of child-centred, activity-based learning prevalent at that time in the West (Peiris, 1983).

In an extremely insightful account of the process of education policy making in Sri Lanka in the period since 1931, Eric de Silva (2003, p. 6) explains how, in the case of the 1972 reforms, there was no time for White Papers, or long-drawn-out debates and discussions. The reforms involved a major overhaul of education undertaken in great haste with, of course, the attendant repercussions. As we saw in Chapter 4, the reforms were unpopular and lasted less than five years. The curriculum reforms were severely criticised by both parents and educationalists as having been unilaterally introduced by the government without carefully examining (a) the suitability of the subject matter, (b) the books, (c) the availability of teachers, and (d) the alignment of the NCGE exam with general practice in other countries.

The 1977 education reforms

The UNP won the 1977 election by an overwhelming majority. The new minister of education acceded to the demands of the small but powerful group with interests in internationally comparable standards of examinations.

GCE O level and A level exams were re-introduced. Many of the 1972–7 curriculum reforms were retained, including a common curriculum for all students up to the end of Grade 11. The status of pre-vocational studies, the curriculum subject that had courted such controversy during the earlier period, was changed from a compulsory, examinable subject to a non-compulsory, non-examinable subject. It was subsequently abandoned and replaced by technical subjects and the curriculum subject of 'life skills'.

The 1981 White Paper on Education

The new government presented a new policy for education in the form of the 1981 White Paper. The White Paper recommended, *inter alia*, the introduction of a system of resource sharing between schools through school 'clusters', with one school designated as the core school and the 'core school principal' responsible for sharing teaching and learning resources across the cluster. The ministry established clusters in many areas, but by 1984 it was already clear that the cluster system would not be adopted country-wide. The human and logistical issues inherent in this new form of school resource management were never resolved.

One of the more controversial reforms proposed by the 1981 White Paper was the inclusion of continuous assessment in the GCE O level exams, specifically the assessment of project work by teachers. Resistance to the reform came from five powerful groups. Teachers opposed continuous assessment because of their lack of preparation for this work; parents opposed it because they mistrusted teachers' judgements; the JVP opposed continuous assessment on the grounds that this form of assessment discriminated against the rural child; owners of private tutorial businesses anticipated that their profits would be undermined; and university teachers were concerned about a dilution of academic standards. Introduced in 1987, it survived for only one year. The practical skills component of the GCE A level science exam was also dropped because of the difficulty of moderating practical skills assessments and a general mistrust of teacher-based assessment (Little, 1999a).

The swings in education policy that followed the metronome of political power in the 1960s continued through the 1970s and 1980s. Each successive democratic election was used by the political party in opposition to feed on the population's dissatisfaction with education. The intimate relationship between party politics and education policy reform was reinforced repeatedly. Cross-party support for education reform was absent and intense efforts by educational professionals and bureaucrats to implement various policies and programmes were repeatedly thwarted.

A second wave of political unrest

Following the liberalisation reforms of 1977, Sri Lanka witnessed increased economic growth and social change. It also witnessed waves of violent political unrest among its youth. Education-related grievances of the Tamil minority voiced in the 1970s led to increasing calls for an independent state of Tamil Eelam, armed combat in 1983 and, by 1987, full-scale ethnic conflict. The 13th amendment to the constitution in 1987 was an attempt to appease the Tamil minority through provincial devolution, including devolution of the control of education. Provincial devolution failed to resolve the ethnic crisis, which continued to disrupt education, especially in the north and east of the country. It led to the deaths of thousands: children, young people, parents, grandparents, teachers, government servants, businesspeople, soldiers, politicians, journalists, academics, religious officers, police, military officers and soldiers alike. The assassinations of the prime minister of Sri Lanka, Ranasinghe Premadasa, and the prime minister of India, Rajiv Gandhi, during this period were attributed directly to the conflict.

A third wave of political unrest

Notwithstanding growth in the economy and employment from the late 1970s, a third wave of youth unrest unfolded in the south of the country involving disaffected, educated, rural Sinhalese youth and supporters of the same JVP political party that had led the insurrection of 1971. More prolonged and bloody than the insurrection of 1971, the 1987 insurrection was met with brutal force by the state. Many thousands of young people died. In the wake of the containment of unrest in 1989 the government quickly established a Presidential Commission on Youth to investigate the causes of the insurrection. Education was identified as the main culprit. The Presidential Commission on Youth urged a definition of a national education policy as:

> one that will be liable to necessary alteration as changed circumstances may require, and as determined through national consensus, but not a policy to be affected by the vagaries of transient political majorities. (Sri Lanka Presidential Commission on Youth, 1990)

The Presidential Commission recommended that a new education policy formulation body – a National Education Commission – be established. This was achieved through a parliamentary bill in March 1991. The National Education Commission's purpose was to make recommendations and give advice to the president on the shape and content of national education policy. Up to that time the policy formulation function had been the prerogative of the Ministry of Education. Questions were raised in parliament about the need for a new policy formulation body. However, the bill was moved through by the powerful minister of education and higher education at the time, Lalith Athulathmudali, who described it as 'one of the most important bills in the history of education in this country' (quoted in E. J. de Silva, 2003, p. 8). The opposition supported the bill, and it was passed without a division. It would take a further eight years for the 1997 Education Reforms Policy to emerge. The drivers of these reforms – focussed on the extension of educational opportunity, curriculum and teacher education and management – and the interests surrounding them will be addressed in Chapter 8.

Education policy stakeholders in the early 1990s

By the early 1990s there was a wide range of stakeholders in education policy and implementation. Some 4.26 million children were enrolled in government schools. More than double that number of mothers, fathers and grandparents were keenly interested in the education of their offspring. Teachers, numbering around 177,000, were employed directly by government. Politicians were more than aware of the appeal of education as an election issue. The national school curriculum embodied and transmitted the values of political regimes.

Different interest groups have different stakes in the curriculum. Educators act politically as they discuss and debate curriculum themes: local knowledge vs universal knowledge, practical education vs academic education, common curriculum vs diversified curriculum, English-medium education vs vernacular-medium education, single subjects vs composite subjects. Elites and the masses have particular interests in some of these themes, especially diversified and common curricula and medium of instruction. Employers engage to an extent in discussions about practical and academic education. All of these interests provide the fodder on which unions, politicians and political parties thrive.

Parents' interests in education reforms are crucially linked to their children's life chances. As we saw in Chapter 4, changes in assessment practices in the early 1970s attracted considerable interest and resistance from the urban middle class and rural parents alike. Proposed changes in the criteria for admission to Grade 1 in prestigious 'national' schools and in the Grade 5 scholarship exam, which in turn improve life chances, arouse considerable interest and resistance among middle-class parents and politicians. By contrast, changes in the detail of what and how children learn during the primary stage of education generate relatively little tension in policy discourse among the general public of all social classes, even if it generates some debate among educators. What concerns parents, and especially middle-class parents, most about primary education is securing a Grade 1 place in a national school which ensures 'all-through' progression to Grade 13.

Teachers actively seek favours from politicians in order to transfer to better schools. Typically, the process works by asking an officer of the local government administration to send a letter (a chit) to a politician, preferably a minister, describing the virtues of the teacher and his/her loyalty to the government in power. The politician then sends a letter to the zonal education office in support of the transfer. These exchanges may or not involve the payment of money by the teacher. What they do involve is an obligation on the part of the teacher to provide continued support for the minister and his/her party. Less formalised than the Job Bank Scheme introduced by the UNP in 1978, the current system relies on the same principle: securing a chit from a politician in order to secure an advantage in the job and job transfer market. In 2003 the National Education Commission would write openly and critically about the political patronage that had pervaded the education system through the 1990s (NEC, 2003, p. 230).

Issues around the allocation of public resources in education are of considerable interest to those who supply services: building contractors, textbook printers and distributors, and equipment suppliers, to name but a few. Politicians may also have direct interests through the involvement of their relatives in the running of such businesses. Changes in assessment practices towards greater reliance on continuous class-based assessment proposed in the 1980s met with considerable resistance from private tutors, who saw the volume of their future business threatened.

Sri Lanka's education policies and international development ideas

In this final section I draw attention to how Sri Lanka's EFA practices between the 1950s and 1970s influenced some of the ideas about development and education that were circulating within the international development community.

The debates surrounding the introduction of the Free Education Act in the 1940s had revealed clear differences between supporters and opposers of the Act and the way they viewed the value of education. For Kannangara and his committee, an increase in educational opportunities for all was a developmental end in its own right and one that was demanded by the people. Education of the people was also the 'best investment a country could make' (Kannangara, quoted in Gunatilleke, 1974, p. 4). This foreshadowed Schultz's (1961) concept of education as a form of capital investment, set out earlier in Chapter 2. Not all who participated in the debates about the Free Education Act would agree with Kannangara. The Financial Secretary, who was opposed to the Free Education Act, was perceived to be of the view that 'education was not a long-term investment, that it did not produce anything, that loan funds should be given only for projects which give a return in money' (Kannangara, quoted in Gunatilleke, 1974, p. 4). Education appeared to be viewed by the Financial Secretary as consumption – a view that was common among economists in the 1940s.

Nonetheless, whether expenditure on education was viewed as an investment or consumption, the percentage of public expenditure allocated to education was increasing and educational opportunities were expanding. In 1925 education accounted for a mere 7.1 per cent of all government expenditure. Between 1930 and 1946 it fluctuated between 12.6 and 15.0 per cent, and by 1947 it had jumped to 18.9 per cent (Ministry of Finance, 1955). Between 1950 and 1960 student enrolments in government schools grew by 62 per cent over a period when the population grew by 25 per cent (see Chapter 1, Table 1.1). Over the same period, education expenditure as a proportion of GDP averaged 2.6 per cent. 'Education for all' was on the march and young people were staying longer in education. Despite the rise in unemployment, disparities in household incomes appeared to be declining. Household Gini coefficients, a conventional measure of income distribution, declined from 0.46 in 1953 to 0.45 in 1963 and to 0.35 by 1973 (Central Bank of Sri Lanka, 2005). Economic growth between 1959 and 1968 was 4.5 per cent, lower than the projected 6.0 per cent (ILO, 1971b, p. 5). Between 1970 and 1977 it would worsen considerably to 2.4 per cent (Snodgrass, 1998).

It was during the 1970s that Sri Lanka was starting to be recognised as a country able to achieve reductions in poverty despite low economic growth (Gunatilleke, 1974; Kelegama, 2000; D. L. Jayasuriya, 2001). International ideas about 'redistribution with growth' (Jolly, 1974) and the 'enthronement' of the concept of basic needs (Jolly, 1976) drew on the Sri Lankan experience. Sri Lanka's welfare achievements in education, literacy, health, reduction in infant mortality and food subsidies, and improving income equality alongside a slow growth economy were being highlighted and explored by those who sought to offer 'development models' and advice to other developing countries (see for example Sen, 1981; Isenman, 1980; Anand & Kanbur, 1991; most recently Richards, 2022). Sri Lanka's 'success' did not go uncontested among economists, and there was considerable debate about whether the achievement of basic needs had come at the cost of economic growth (see for example Isenman, 1980; Snodgrass, 1998).

Conclusion

This chapter has analysed shifts in the political context of education policy reform between 1931 and 1991, subdivided into two periods: 1931–70 and 1970–91. In the first period tension at the regime level lay between those who supported colonial policies and practices and those who supported anti-colonial, national policies and practices. This tension continued to infuse political debate well into the post-independence period but came to be overlaid by tensions between politicians on the socialist left and capitalist right. Education policies were driven by the need to both assert national control over an inherited colonial system and create a unified system of education. After 1970, education policy was driven largely by the need to contain youth unrest.

The nature of engagement of politicians in policy formation and policy implementation would change significantly over the six decades in question. In the initial period politicians confined themselves largely, though not wholly, to debate and decisions about policy content. Policy implementation was undertaken by bureaucrats and teachers, with little interference from politicians. This would change in the 1970s as politicians became increasingly involved in the day-to-day practices of education, especially those concerning teacher transfers. With the loss of independence of the Public Service Commission in 1972, political influence over the appointment of senior and junior members of the education bureaucracy deepened.

Towards the end of the 1980s, considerable powers and financial resources in education were devolved to the provinces, changing the nature of the relationship between the central ministry and schools, and the nature of links between officers, teachers and politicians. This shift in responsibility for the management of education also led to an increase in political influence in day-to-day implementation at the provincial level.

By the early 1990s, multiple and wide-ranging stakeholder interests in education surrounded the National Education Commission as it set about its work developing the next round of education reform proposals. The next chapter considers the Commission's work, the policy tensions it faced, and the major education policy reforms that would emerge from its work by 1997.

8
The 1997 education reforms: origins, political will and implementation

Origins of the 1997 reforms

The origins of the 1997 education reforms lay in the widespread political unrest of the 1980s. As described in Chapter 7, that unrest lay on two fronts: the call of Tamils for an independent state in the north (Tamil Eelam); and the call, mobilised by the Janatha Vimukthi Peramuna (People's Liberation Front), of frustrated rural Sinhalese youth for improved job opportunities in the south. Both sets of frustration had an education dimension.

In 1987, the 13th amendment to the constitution ushered in provincial devolution, including in education, and was intended to ease the conflict in the north. In 1989 a Presidential Commission on Youth was established to examine the causes of the youth insurrections, especially that in the south. In 1991 a National Education Commission (NEC) was established as a policy formulation body that would act independently of the swings of political power and set out proposals for reform of the education system.

This chapter examines the work of the NEC, the role of political will, and the processes of translating policies into plans and action on the ground.

National Education Commission

The Commission was appointed for a period of five years and reported directly to the president, who retained ultimate power over which recommendations to implement. The membership of the NEC and its mandate were accepted by both the government in power and the opposition, but not before detailed negotiations over the draft membership list. Intensive back-room activity resulted in a membership where at least two members had professional expertise in education and others had a broad range of interests and backgrounds, from different ethnic groups and from urban and rural areas. Continuity between the views and aspirations of the Presidential Commission on Youth and the newly formed NEC was achieved by the appointment of the chair of the National Youth Commission as the inaugural chair of the NEC. Shortly after its establishment, the NEC consulted the public in the capital, Colombo, and in the 'outstations'. Representations were made in person and in writing.

In May 1992 the NEC produced its first report, in which nine national goals for education were set out, proposals were made, issues and problems were raised and priorities for action were outlined (NEC, 1992). The report's authors reaffirmed a commitment to providing 'educational opportunities from childhood to old age' and the provision of a 'basic education and initiation into a variety of selected skills … to enable the individual to contribute culturally, socially, politically and economically'. Reflecting the conditions of unrest out of which the NEC had been formed, an overriding goal for the country was 'the achievement of national cohesion, national integrity and national unity'. This and other goals for national development were accompanied by lists of general and specific competencies that the education system could be expected to foster in support of them (NEC, 1992, pp. 5, 7, 11).

The policy formulation process involved a mix of administrators and educators. There were university professors with knowledge about particular subjects in higher education, and other educators with enthusiastic interests in secondary and primary education. There were former university professors with specialised knowledge of education. There were experienced education administrators and managers and experts in teacher education, and curriculum development and ex-officio members from relevant ministries such as Education, Finance and Planning, and the University Grants Commission.

Political will

The term 'political will' refers to the sustained commitment of politicians and administrators to invest resources to achieve objectives and a willingness to make and implement policy despite opposition (Little, 2011). Between 1991, when the NEC was established, and 1997, when the policy proposals were finally published, two executive presidents, President Premadasa and President Kumaratunga, each with an interest in education, held office.

President Premadasa held the portfolios for education and higher education between 1992 and 1993. So much had the power of the presidency grown since the change of constitution in 1972 that, notwithstanding the creation in 1991 of the NEC, education policy continued to be subject to political whim, as the following example illustrates.

A former secretary to the Ministry of Education and Higher Education recalls how the president sometimes took policy decisions 'even of great financial magnitude, virtually on the spur of the moment' (M. D. D. Pieris, 2002, pp. 591–2). The case in point was a quick-fire decision of President Premadasa in 1992 to introduce free school uniforms for all schoolchildren with effect from 1993. M. D. D. Pieris's (2002) blow-by-blow account of a schoolbook ceremony held at Bakamuna, and the announcement about free school uniforms, is worth quoting at length:

> **A spur of the moment policy decision**
> … At these functions the secretary had no particular role … except [to] sit there for three hours on the main stage. Therefore, I did not even bother to take my spectacles along … Everything proceeded smoothly until the project minister for education services began speaking. The president's speech was to follow … Suddenly I saw the president looking back … I quickly got up and went to him. He seemed elated at the largeness of the crowd and their response. He said 'I want to give free school uniforms to the children from next year. Each one would require at least two sets, isn't it?'. I was completely stunned, but stammered 'To all?'. He said 'yes.' I had the presence of mind to say 'but there are 4.2 million children'. He said, 'in that case we can make it one uniform,' and continued, 'Can you work out the costs?' 'When?' I inquired. What he said to this would have killed me if I had a weak heart, 'Now' replied the president, 'I want to announce it in my speech!' That was President Premadasa. He went on the basis that nothing was impossible and many a public servant was faced with an impossible deadline. This day it seemed to be my turn. I walked back to my seat in a daze … Fortunately one of my accountants who happened to be standing at the back of the stage had with him a calculator … In the end we got the figure of approximately 700 million rupees … I walked quickly up to the president, gave him the figure, but warned him that there

could be up to a 20% margin of error. He appeared startled at the cost indicated and said 'can't be so much'. The next minute he had to get up to speak, but he was now more cautious. To the vast cheers of the multitude he announced that 'With effect from next year I will also try my best to give one set of school uniforms free to every child once a year.' The people cheered so loud and so long the effect was clearly visible on the president's face, that I knew there was no going back ... The die was cast. (M. D. D. Pieris, 2002, pp. 589–91)

Given the magnitude of finance involved, the distribution of cotton material for school uniforms to the parents of each and every child in school, irrespective of the means of the household, must surely count as a de facto policy, even if it was not written into the text of a policy document. It is a striking example of 'spur of the moment policymaking'. It is perhaps not surprising then that, notwithstanding the efforts of the NEC to listen to the views of the public, the policy formulation process was described as elitist and top-down rather than pluralist and participatory (Wickramanayake, 2009).

Change of government, continuation of policy formulation

In 1994 a new left-of-centre government and a new president, Chandrika Kumaratunge, came to power. The formulation of the National Education Policy was a priority of the new government. The NEC's members survived the change of government and continued their work. As one education officer commented:

> In most developing countries, when the government changes the education policies and reform are also changed. But in our country for the first time the president followed the recommendations done by a commission of an earlier government. This was a very good indication of the strong desire to do a real reform in education. I admired that. (Interview with author, 2009)

President Kumaratunga worked closely with her minister of education, a former schoolteacher, and asked the NEC to move forward on its recommendations. By this time, the policy machinery for education reform in place in the country comprised several institutions. The NEC had been given a clear mandate for policy formulation but the mandates for other education institutions were rather less clear. In matters of both policy formulation and policy implementation the position of the Ministry of Education had been weakened over the years, in part because of the establishment of the NEC and in part because of the 1987 constitutional amendment which had, in principle, devolved considerable responsibilities for education planning, finance and implementation to the provinces. The dividing line between planning and policy is a fine one in all countries in the best of circumstances, and, in the early years of devolution at least, the provincial education department staff continued to look to the national ministry for guidance on both policy and planning in the traditional way.

Over time, provincial education staff would find themselves caught in ever more complex webs of relationships. A provincial director of education was answerable to the national ministry and to the national minister(s) of education, to the provincial secretary for education, to the chief provincial secretary, and to the provincial minister of education (often, but not always, the chief minister in the province). In the case of the planning of primary education in a province, responsibility lay formally somewhere between the provincial primary education coordinator and the provincial education planning officer, each of whom were, in turn, subject to the higher authority of their provincial director, provincial secretary and chief secretary, provincial politicians, national ministry directors of primary education and education planning, national ministry secretaries, additional secretaries and national-level politicians.

The roles of other national-level bodies for curriculum and education research became unclear, functions began to be duplicated and competition over resources increased. Duplication of functions between the national agencies with responsibilities for education, duplication of functions across the central ministry, the provincial ministries and departments, and long chains of command within and between the ministries and the provincial authorities led to the creation of a management structure that was both inefficient and obsolete (de Silva, 2004). Taken together, these duplications and ambiguities created policy voids between the national institutions and planning voids between the national and provincial institutions (Little, 2003b).

Amidst the ambiguities, the voids and the lack of coordination, there was a growing feeling on the part of the president that the existing institutions were doing 'business as usual' and were not generating the results expected by her (Interview with author, 2009). By late 1996 no policy text had been written for debate in parliament, no steps had been taken to enact new legislation for education, and no financial provision had been made for the implementation of any aspect of the policy.

The Presidential Task Force

Considerable political will was invested by President Kumaratunge in the process of both policy formulation and planning through the appointment of her Presidential Task Force (PTF) for General Education in December 1996. Task forces were also established for tertiary education, and for technical education and vocational training. In appointing each of these task forces the president employed her considerable powers to ensure that the best people were deployed to translate policies into programmes of action. The PTF on General Education comprised a general committee and 12 technical sub-committees with a mandate to create an action plan for the education reforms. To give the work of the PTF added clout, the president declared 1997 the Year of Education Reforms. The PTF was chaired by the minister of education and higher education, with the addition of two deputy ministers as members.

The 12 technical sub-committees comprised professionals handpicked for their technical expertise in different areas. In the case of primary education, a veteran of the earlier 1972 reforms, Ms Kamala Peiris, was invited to lead an 80-strong technical sub-committee on primary and pre-primary education. Her team, handpicked largely by herself, comprised educators from the National Institute of Education, subject advisors from the provinces and practising primary teachers. Each technical sub-committee adopted its own consultative process. In the case of primary and pre-primary education this included consultation with parents, teachers and in-service advisors. This was a largely apolitical process in which each technical sub-committee had its own *modus operandi* and reported through the chair to the president.

Less central to the process was the secretary to the Ministry of Education and Higher Education. The nature of his involvement in the PTF and in other meetings that would lead, ultimately, to the 1997 reforms was indicative of just how far the ministry had relinquished its role as policy formulator. On the one hand, the NEC had been handed the policy formulation mandate in 1991; and on the other the provincial ministries and departments had been empowered with the day-to-day running of education since provincial devolution in 1988. The secretary saw his role as that of running the overall system rather than changing it. And although he was a member of the PTF, constraints on his time prevented him from engaging fully. Recalling his involvement in the 1997 reforms, he said:

> It is true I was there from 1992 to 1997 but what happened was that the secretary as you know has to run the system. And unless meetings are fixed in consultation with him or her, whoever is the secretary, you find last minute notices of meeting. It becomes impossible to go because you are required in parliament, you are required to write to the president, you are required by so many actors and stake holders and in addition to the daily number of people coming to see you and the paper, and the deadlines and the projects and the foreign related issues, whether it's the Asian Development Bank or World Bank or United Nations Economic and Social Commission for Asia and the Pacific or whoever … They [the PTF] did keep me informed, but what they do is, they send a fax and say there is a meeting taking place tomorrow at 3 o'clock. Now tomorrow at 3 o'clock I am [already scheduled to be] at a parliamentary committee … my impression is that the secretary did not play that much of a role because of these constraints. (Interview with author, 2009)

Of crucial importance throughout was a presidential advisor on education, who was also the NEC's vice-chair for policy (De Mel, 2022). She mobilised the technical committees, ensured the active involvement of the NEC, and kept the president closely informed of and involved in all steps of the process. It is generally agreed that she played an extremely significant role in maintaining momentum as the reforms moved from formulation to implementation.

The 1997 reforms outlined

Nineteen reforms were finally set out in the 1997 General Education Reforms. The first set of these reforms were intended to extend educational opportunity and embraced compulsory education, the equitable distribution of educational opportunities, school rationalisation, early childhood care and development, special education for children with disabilities, and non-formal education. The second broad set of reforms related to the curricula in primary, junior secondary and senior secondary education. A third broad area dealt with teacher education and management. While the 1972 reforms had been drafted very quickly in the wake of the youth insurrection in 1971 (see Chapter 4), the 1997 reforms would take a full eight years to emerge after the end of the 1987–9 youth insurgency.

Policy texts: tensions and resolutions

No policy text emerges without tensions, both among those mandated to develop and produce it and among those who are consulted or who make their views heard during the process. The final texts of the 1997 reform documents were no exception.

A first tension was between those who emphasised the role of general education as a selection mechanism for higher education for the few and those who emphasised general education as a terminal stage of education for the majority. In the view of some PTF members, the universities were exerting 'undue influence' on the content of general education for all.

A second tension emerged between political parties in their willingness to allow children of different ethnic and language groups to learn together. As we saw in earlier chapters, the education system had been segregated by the medium of instruction since colonial times. Post-independence policies on the medium of instruction changed the role of English as a medium of instruction for a few to a subject of study for all, reducing to an extent its symbolic power as the colonial sword (*kaduwa*) that cut society into shreds. The post-colonial policy, by contrast, led to ethnic segregation of the entire education system by language – Sinhala and Tamil. In regions where one or other language group was in the majority, segregation arose by default. In urban multi-ethnic areas, the segregation was artificial and enforced; and even in multi-ethnic schools, there was a considerable gulf between communities. The PTF attempted to move forward on the language issue. While the president and others were strongly in favour of strengthening the role of English, both as a second language and as a medium of instruction, those opposed to this position appealed to nationalist sentiments and the oppressive place of English in colonial times.

A third tension concerned the private sector. The president and her advisor would have liked to open education up to the private sector. Other members of the PTF were strongly opposed and drew support from the socialist lobbies. The pro-private sector reforms 'never went anywhere' (Interview with author, 2009).

A fourth tension emerged in relation to differences of view over the powers, roles and functions of the institutions at the centre of government administration and those at the provincial level. Still very new, the devolution of considerable powers of implementation to the provinces led to multiple interpretations of who could, and could not, do what.

The resolution of these tensions took different forms. The opposition to private sector involvement was sufficiently strong to ensure that no recommendations about the private sector would appear in the 1997 policy text. In the case of English as a medium of instruction, the tensions and resistances continued into the implementation phase. Clarity over the respective roles of the ministry and the provinces was never achieved.

While the examples above reflect the tensions apparent among those who participated visibly in the policy formulation process, other tensions, 'silent' during formulation and planning, would surface during policy implementation. Sri Lankan teachers' unions are rarely consulted on macro-education policy, yet they represent the majority of the very teachers who implement change on the ground. Consultation with unions often amounts to little more than the presentation of information about a change of policy that has already been decided. The perception, if not the reality, of exclusion from the formulation process was strong:

> In formulating and drafting the general education reforms, teacher unions or individual teachers were never consulted. At any stage of the designing and implementation process we were never given an opportunity to question, interact or participate in the reforms that were to make a sea change in Sri Lankan school education. The whole process was parachuted from the top and from abroad to the ground. (Ceylon Teachers Union, written submission to the author, April 2009)

Union officials emphasised that the 1997 reforms were introduced largely to contain, rather than resolve, the crisis in education that had emerged through the 1980s. The same challenges continued even after the 1997 reforms: acute shortages of qualified teachers for rural schools, inequality and polarisation of resources, lack of professional training, inefficiency, and corruption within the administration of education. For this teachers' union the most pressing matter of concern was the 'undue influence' of national and provincial politicians in the appointment, transfer and promotion of teachers, and on school admissions (Interview with author, 2009).

Despite the tensions and the production of texts, the proposals themselves went no further than the Parliamentary Consultative Committee on Education. In Eric de Silva's (2003) view the General Education Reforms of 1997 did not constitute National Education Policy as such. The reforms were never fully debated in parliament, they were not based on a consensus which transcended party politics, and no declaration was made by the president under section 2(1) of the NEC Act. The proposals lacked legitimacy.

The drivers of policy formulation

Political will

There is no doubt that President Kumaratunge offered strong leadership to the work of the PTF. The NEC described this as 'strong political will and commitment at the highest level' (NEC, 2003, p. 16). The president used her considerable powers to push reform, to form task forces and to bypass institutions that were not delivering what she wanted. Moreover, as described above, the reforms were never fully debated in parliament.

Where did this strong political will come from? Those directly involved in the work of the PTF recall the president's leadership of the process, her invitations to breakfast meetings at her official home – Temple Trees – and her genuine interest in education. It was said by more than one interviewee that the president's children were at the time being educated in an English-medium international school in Colombo, and she is thought to have wanted all the country's children to have access to an education of similar quality. Political will and determination pervaded not only the formulation of the reform proposals but also the process of translating these into action.

The presidential advisor spoke of the president's 'huge passion for education' and her concern that although access to education was good there was a 'void' in terms of quality. The president was concerned that, despite Sri Lanka's good international ratings in the league tables on literacy, there were still children unable to read and write even at the age of 10 or 11:

> There was urgency on her part. I always knew when people have a soft spot for certain things. Well, she always had a soft spot for education. (Interview with author, 2009)

Widely read, the president was familiar with British prime minister Tony Blair's views on education in England and Wales and was very committed to bringing about change in education. Others referred to the president's earlier interest in education during her time as chief minister of the Western Province, while still others referred to her first-hand experience of the political and personal cost of the youth insurgencies. Her late husband, Vijaya Kumaratunge, a charismatic film star-cum-politician, had been assassinated in the late 1980s by the Janatha Vimukthi Peramuna (People's Liberation Front).

The president's direct involvement in the process of reform led to an acceleration of pace. The first policy element to be translated into action was the steering of the Compulsory Education Regulations through parliament in 1997, enforcing attendance of all children aged 5–14 with effect from 1 January 1998. A second practical step was the launching of the primary reforms in a pilot district – that of the president's own constituency, Gampaha. Yet still, the reports of the technical committees had no status in parliament.

While progress towards tangible change on the ground had been slow in the first half of the 1990s, the continued and committed interest of the president in the second half of the decade created huge pressures for change. The PTF and its 12 technical sub-committees had injected new life into the policy formulation process and the creation of a set of action plans. Thereafter, a special Education Reforms Implementation Unit (ERIU) was established in the ministry to spearhead policy implementation.

The challenge now was to find a person of sufficient seniority and experience to direct the ERIU and lead the implementation process. A former secretary to the Ministry of Education had expressed an interest in the reforms to an old friend of his, the vice-chair (planning) of the NEC. In seemingly no time at all he was invited to head the ERIU at the level of director-general. He recalls accepting the invitation

> on the basis that there was a reform document which will be placed before parliament and before the people. I am being very frank here and have said this in many newspaper articles. Because the whole purpose of having a National Education Commission was to ensure that we have continuity in policies, we cannot just pop and go things. I have seen enough of this happening from the time of the 1981 White Paper. There has to be a consensus, basic agreement, not on everything but the fundamentals, so that we do not waste our time, energy or money. No reform is better than reforms that go

up and down and mess up the whole system. Because I was given the impression that that would happen, I accepted. Then I was told 'OK, set up your own establishment'. (Interview with author, 2009)

The new director-general questioned whether a new unit needed to be established in the national institution responsible for education policy implementation. He was particularly wary of creating a separate, parallel administration, not least because he had been secretary earlier and would not have liked to have had a separate unit established to do what he, as secretary, was mandated to do. His years of public administration experience convinced him that island-wide implementation of complex reforms *ab initio* would be a mistake and he took a tough stand. Together, with the chair of the sub-committee on primary education, he advised the president to agree to a pilot of the primary education reforms (Interview with author, 2009).

Finance

Once the president had agreed to the implementation of a pilot programme, the next challenge was financial. While the PTF technical committee had developed plans for a range of activities (Peiris & Nanayakkara, 2000), these plans had not been costed. No money had been set aside for redesigning classrooms to accommodate 'activity benches' and sinks and provision for running water. An ad hoc solution needed to be found. The president identified money that was left over from a programme in her electorate, the district of Gampaha. So Gampaha came to be chosen for the one-year pilot implementation. Considerable activity and media interest followed. The detail of the programme's implementation was left to the director of primary education in the National Institute of Education.

Over a rather short period of time the director-general of the ERIU became disillusioned; not so much with the technical detail of the programme, which he felt was being handled well by the National Institute of Education, but more with the political economy of the reforms, including their acceptability to the general public and the underlying management structures to take the reforms forward. Among his concerns was the absence of progress in the movement of a 'composite' document detailing all 19 reforms envisaged and available for national debate and discussion. While the primary education reform was thought unlikely to generate resistance, aspects of the secondary reforms, especially those concerning medium of instruction and subject boundaries, were more likely to court controversy. A composite document needed to be taken to parliament. Moreover, there had still been little movement in securing money for the reforms in the longer term. No money had been voted for the reforms. The head of the ERIU was told, 'Oh, we'll get a lot of funds, foreign aid, this and that'. However:

> nothing came ... I had to fight tooth and nail to get the money that was promised to me from Gampaha ... the money was tied and the Treasury ... you know, it is very difficult even when monies are voted in the budget. The Treasury can release monies only if there is liquidity ... If income tax and customs and all these government revenues do not flow in, today you can ask for the 50 million rupees that is provided for in the budget, but they will say 'no money, wait for some time'. Cash has to come. Not mere paper provision ... So, I had to throw my weight around with my juniors to get the money because I wanted the job done. You cannot go on like that. (Interview with author, 2009)

With a view to anticipating implementation challenges that lay ahead, the director-general commissioned an early evaluation of the reforms programme, undertaken by a respected foreign consultant. Ambitious reform programmes confront constraints of time, finance and human resource as well as political will. In the case of the primary education programme, the pilot year in Gampaha was judged to be likely to yield substantial learning benefits for those responsible for moving the programme to scale, country-wide. However, most of the reform components were not 'piloted'. Of concern too was the absence of detailed financial planning and raising of funds for all components of the programme. The commitment of the human resource – the change agents – was a crucial element. The central change agent would be a 'master teacher', a role created back the 1960s whereby an experienced teacher would support and supervise the work of other teachers during periods of reform. Somerset (1998) asked whether master teachers would be available in sufficient numbers to conduct the tasks expected of them and whether they were expected to focus at any one time on a limited or broad set of objectives. Were there sufficient professional development programmes to equip the master teachers to contribute effectively to the reform initiatives and for their role as teacher educators? Were there effective feedback mechanisms in place to promote two-way communication between teachers and project designers?

After little more than a year the director-general resigned. The intrinsic complexity of the reforms and difficulties experienced in raising funds for even the pilot programme in primary education were simply too frustrating and challenging even for a man of his considerable ability and experience.

The frustration experienced by the director-general of the ERIU in securing financial resources illustrates well the point that the term 'policy' has little meaning, beyond ritual, if it is not accompanied by detailed plans for implementation and allocated resources (Little, 2008). It also underlines the point that a demonstration of political will requires not only sustained commitment to a set of ideas but also the commitment of resources.

The allocation of financial resources had been complicated by provincial devolution. From 1987, and as a result of the 13th amendment to the constitution, responsibility for the financing and implementation of education plans lay with the provinces. Up to this point, however, all the work on plans had been undertaken by the technical committees of the PTF, and this work had focussed on activities and not on resources. In the case of primary education, this would be remedied through a technical planning exercise run from the ministry in collaboration with the provincial ministries and departments of education. This resulted in detailed activity and financial plans for the development of primary education, based on the PTF proposals and covering a period of five years from 2000, and will be discussed in detail in Chapter 9.

Evaluations of implementation

Following the early evaluation of the pilot project in primary education, more extensive evaluations of all the reforms were undertaken. The most comprehensive evaluation was undertaken by the NEC during 2002, as part of a major sectoral review of general education (NEC, 2003). The NEC evaluation was based on 23 studies commissioned from Sri Lankan experts who were not themselves involved directly in the implementation of the reforms. Evidence on the primary reforms was drawn from studies undertaken by the National Educational Research and Evaluation Centre (NEREC). These studies were supplemented by 300 written submissions from the public and oral submissions from 39 organisations/individuals.

The results of those evaluations are synthesised here and are supplemented by original material gleaned from interviews by the author with policy implementers and evaluators. This chapter focusses on three of the 19 reforms: (i) equitable distribution of educational opportunities; (ii) school rationalisation; and (iii) primary education renewal, quality and relevance.

Equitable distribution of educational opportunities

The 1989 report of the Presidential Commission on Youth recommended an upgrading of facilities for junior and senior secondary education in rural areas to reduce educational disparities. This proposal harked back to the 1940s and the creation of central schools, which had offered rural children the chance to move from small, vernacular-medium primary schools to higher status English-medium secondary schools with good facilities. In the early 1990s the new scheme, entitled Improvement of Schools by Division (ISD), was launched. Well funded, it targeted 297 junior secondary schools and 62 senior secondary schools for development. These, it was hoped, would become centres of excellence, providing high-quality education to children living in rural, less privileged areas.

Implementation was interrupted by the change of government in 1994. The incoming People's Alliance Government (linked historically with the left-leaning Sri Lanka Freedom Party) launched its own project – the Divisional Schools Development (DSD) project – with similar aims. The DSD project was established in 1995 and targeted 347 schools according to criteria that were unclear:

> It was not merely a change of name from ISD to DSD which would hardly have mattered. There was a fresh selection of schools to be developed as centres of excellence … Only a few of the ISD schools were selected for development under the new project and I have no doubt that the previous selection had also been made on the recommendations made by politicians who belonged to the party that held power at the time. In a country where even nameboards have to be green or blue depending on who runs the government, could we expect even 'excellence' to be neutral in colour! (E. J. de Silva, 2003)

Progress was slower than expected, and after the announcement of the 1997 General Education Reforms 134 of the 347 schools were identified for 'fast track' development. The project continued to attract the political will of the president, and in mid-1999 a 'special unit' was set up in the ministry under a senior administrator and was staffed by provincial coordinators. By 2001, the project was considered to have failed. The NEC noted that it was a matter for regret:

> that a project that was backed by political will and administrative support from 1997 to 2001 failed to produce a single 'centre of excellence' … the original Central Schools had catered to the disadvantaged but the quality of education they had offered had facilitated upward mobility. On the contrary many DSD schools appear to be 'residual schools' that lack the capacity to compete with well-equipped schools. (NEC, 2003, p. 24)

If political will at the highest level and strong ministry backing were present for the creation of centres of excellence across the country, what was holding the programme back? School principals attributed the failure to infrastructure, human resource, social and planning and management factors (Kularatna, 2004). The most frequently cited factor (mentioned by 40 per cent of principals) was the absence of a proper system of supervision and progress monitoring of project implementation at ministry, provincial, divisional and school levels. Teacher shortages and the absence of specialist teachers were also cited by a sizeable number (32 per cent and 27 per cent respectively). Among the social factors cited were the preference of parents with adequate means to send their children to urban schools rather than the rural DSD schools, the admission to DSD schools of children of a lower socio-economic status, political interference in the selection of project schools, and political interference in the allocation of resources to schools and school management. The NEC's (2003) synthesis identified the 'intervention of extraneous factors in the selection of schools, principals and staff' as a 'fundamental flaw'. Extraneous factors were code for 'political interference'.

Crucially, the provincial authorities were not on board. The project was directed from the centre. The provinces felt no sense of ownership over the project and made no special provision in the allocation of teachers to these schools. It would seem, then, that political will at the highest level, backed up by a strong bureaucracy at the centre, was insufficient for implementation on the ground. Political will at the highest level contends with political interference at the lowest levels, which in turn influences the quality of those chosen to lead initiatives on the ground. At the same time, political interference has a demotivating effect on those who have not been singled out for political favours and who are then expected to implement new programmes.

School restructuring and rationalisation

The PTF justified the proposal to restructure and rationalise schools in terms of simplifying a complex array of schools (PTF, 1997, p. 28). An early policy text on restructuring had proposed that schools be divided into junior schools (Grades 1–8) and senior schools (Grades 9–13) (NEC, 1995). Its authors reasoned that students would be more likely to stay in school if that school offered education up to Grade 8 than if they were required to make a transition from Grade 5 to Grade 6 in another location. They also reasoned that a division at Grade 8 would facilitate 'the growth of a school culture more suitable to the two different age groups' (NEC, 1995, p. 5).

In 1996 the ministry took steps to instruct the provinces to begin work on restructuring, justifying this instruction in terms of the need to rationalise the school network and reduce wastage of scarce resources (Wehella, 2001). The policy discourse used the terms 'school rationalisation' and 'school restructuring' almost synonymously. In turn, both were closely related to school 'closure'. For years Sri Lanka's system has been characterised by a large number of small schools, the majority of which are located in rural areas of low population density. In 1997, 26.3 per cent of all schools had fewer than 100 students (Little, 2008b). A proposal to close small schools had been circulating within the Ministry of Education since 1996, and although it fell outside the NEC proposals it ran in parallel with them (NEC, 2003, p. 25).

Early in 1997 the PTF changed the restructuring proposal from Grades 1–8 and 9–13 to Grades 1–9 and 10–13, for reasons that are unclear (PTF, 1997). The NEC and the ministry issued guidelines to zonal directors and zonal education planners on school mapping and preparing the ground for the restructuring exercise. A supplementary circular was issued in March 1997 advising the provinces that if any serious inconvenience or hardship for pupils had resulted from the implementation of the previous circular then the provincial authority should take reasonable and proper action (Wehella, 2001).

During 1997 and 1998 the restructuring met with community resistance, from local politicians concerned about school closures in their constituencies and from educators concerned about the impact of closures on student dropout (Jayaweera, 2004). By 1999 a World Bank Review Mission recognised that the policy framework for the school restructuring programme required a revision of criteria that was sensitive to ethnicity, religion, and the cultural and historical background of schools, as well as cost effectiveness. A crucial factor in the call for this revision may have been the gradual realisation that the likely costs of restructuring were prohibitive. The NEC's assessment of restructuring referred to the 'sheer impracticability of the scheme ... the possibility of increased dropouts ... wide opposition and an abortive pilot project in a Colombo suburb' (NEC, 2003, p. 25).

The restructuring and rationalisation circular was withdrawn in March 2003. Fifteen years after the NEC's 1995 proposals for restructuring, the basic structure of the system remained more or less intact. As more parents moved to urban and semi-urban areas in order to increase their children's chances of accessing popular schools and good exam results, enrolments in rural schools declined. The proportion of schools with enrolments of less than 100 increased from 23.3 per cent in 1993 to 30.2 per cent in 2007 (Ministry of Education, 2008).

Curriculum renewal, quality and relevance in primary education

Key elements of the primary education reforms were: child-centred education; an integrated curriculum based around first language, religion, mathematics and environment; division of the primary education stage into three 'key stages' – Key Stage 1 (Grades 1–2), Key Stage 2 (Grades 3–4) and Key Stage 3 (Grade 5) with combinations of guided play, activity and desk work appropriate to each key stage; and the introduction of oral English from Grade 1 and formal teaching of English from Grade 3. These would be supported by syllabus revision and the production of textbooks, workbooks and supplementary materials, teacher education, class-based assessment, infrastructure, school-based management, monitoring and supervision (see Little, 2010 for further detail).

The primary education reforms were launched rapidly in 533 schools in the pilot district of Gampaha, the president's constituency. The authors of the General Education Reforms indicated that 'this district was chosen because, already, there was an ongoing primary school project sponsored by UNESCO' (NEC, 1997, p. 13).

Considerable effort had been expended in designing curriculum materials, developing classroom infrastructure, and supervising teaching and learning. However, teachers felt that more effort was needed to integrate the teachers' guides, textbooks and workbooks. They would have welcomed more practical demonstrations by in-service advisors and teacher educators as to how they should implement the new pedagogy (L. Perera & Dharmawardana, 2000). The NEC confirmed that the primary education reforms were 'well-designed and implemented systematically and ... all stakeholders – students, teachers, officers and parents – had responded positively' (NEC, 2003, p. 36).

Many classes continued to be desk, blackboard, book and teacher-centred, and teachers complained of resource gaps, large classes and time-consuming record-keeping (NEREC, 2004). Wide disparities in infrastructure, learning, and teaching processes and performance continued between the primary classes in different schools (NEC, 2003, p. 37). The primary reforms benefited from a clear vision of what primary education could, and should, offer to all children. The PTF technical committee was led by Kamala Peiris, who, though well into retirement from public service, continued to advocate a philosophy of child-centred, activity-based learning. The notion of 'tiny saplings' developing into 'sturdy trees' (Peiris, 1983) pervaded much of the discourse around primary education as the foundational stage of education. While parents expressed misgivings about the role of 'play' in learning, others viewed play as 'nice and exciting' (Interview with author, 2009). Parents generally saw education as something for the 'experts' to decide and while they did not demand or push for the reforms, they did not oppose them either. Teachers were judged to be generally supportive of the reforms in primary education. They engaged enthusiastically in in-service training programmes, and in the development of curriculum material. They organised the school meals programme and participated in surveys of out-of-school children. There may have been resistance from older teachers. The authors of two evaluation studies suggested that many teachers were not translating the intended pedagogy into practices envisaged by the reform designers (L. Perera & Dharmawardana, 2000; National Education Commission, 2003).

Implementation was not all plain sailing. Interviewees spoke of the continuing distortion of the teaching and learning process by the spectre of the Grade 5 scholarship exam, the first public exam sat by students, the results of which could lead to admission at Grade 6 into a popular school and a financial bursary for the poorest. Coaching of children for this exam, both inside school and through private tuition after school hours and at the weekends, was undermining the pedagogy promoted by the reforms, limiting teachers' and children's attention to the types of items and knowledge areas that were likely to appear in the exam.

Teacher morale varied and was affected by myriad factors. While newly graduated and trained teachers approached their work with enthusiasm, some longer-serving teachers fell prey to the frustrations of the system. Delays in salary increments, lack of school facilities and few possibilities to transfer to better schools, especially from rural to urban areas, were disincentives that undermined teachers' commitment to the work of teaching and learning inside the classroom.

Trade union members identified additional implementation issues, such as the neglect of the needs of teachers in small schools who had responsibilities for teaching across grades. They were also concerned about the logistical challenges of translation and delivery of textbooks and teacher manuals, especially in difficult-to-reach areas in the north and east during the ongoing civil war.

Drivers and inhibitors of policy formulation and implementation

It is clear from the above that that the underlying political driver of – or imperative for – the 1997 reforms lay in widespread youth unrest in the 1980s, to which the political and administrative response was the creation of a Presidential Youth Commission and the National Education Commission. Other political, technical, administrative and financial considerations then came into play. All the reforms above benefited from the establishment of the Presidential Task Force on Education, led by the president and the minister of education, and the subsequent establishment of an administrative/management unit inside the Ministry of Education. The education bureaucracy at the national and provincial levels mediated the intentions of those in the task force technical committees who constructed the plans and the practices of the teachers in schools who implemented them. The bureaucracy inhibited some aspects of the reforms and facilitated others. During the first four years of policy implementation, the Ministry of Education was headed by four secretaries, disturbing the continuity of policy implementation. Patronage politics between politicians, teachers, officials, parents and communities underpinned the day-to-day practices of education.

The reforms, designed to redistribute opportunities for high-quality education beyond primary for children in rural areas, were judged to have failed. Although two schemes had attracted high-level political will and ministry administrative support, as well as financial support from donors, both schemes were inhibited by a lack of ownership at the provincial level, community perceptions, and political interference in the selection of schools.

The rationalisation reforms also failed. Driven by high-level 'will' from the National Education Commission, the minister of education and the ministry, and financial support from the World Bank, they were inhibited by communities and local politicians whose schools were likely to be 'closed' as part of the rationalisation process and by initial ministry guidelines that were insufficiently sensitive to the particular conditions of schools, especially small schools in rural areas. The ministry and World Bank's gradual realisation that the financial costs of rationalisation would be huge led to a slow-down on implementation. In short, these access reforms enjoyed high-level political and administrative support as well as financial support from the international community. However, those ingredients alone did not guarantee smooth implementation.

The primary education reforms were judged to have been the most successful. They enjoyed high-level political involvement, from their formulation as action plans to the choice of the district for the pilot scheme and on into country-wide implementation. They enjoyed high-level technical involvement from the National Institute of Education. The provinces became involved in detailed activity planning and budgeting, and external financial and technical support was available from the international community. The reforms were backed by media campaigns and activities designed to increase awareness and involvement of all teachers in the reforms, but these drivers were tempered by inhibitors throughout. Structurally, the Grade 5 scholarship exam inhibited curriculum objectives, especially in the upper primary grades. Teachers' needs varied, some wanting more guidance and support, some less. Disparities in material resources impeded the implementation of curriculum and pedagogic reforms in some schools. The reforms relied very heavily on the provision of support for teachers by supervisory or 'master' teachers, but many of these had been appointed on political criteria rather than on merit and this compromised their effectiveness. Underlying all of these issues was the relentless process of teacher transfers between schools – a process supported by local and national politicians and officials.

Overall, then, it is clear that high-level 'political will' was a strong driver of the formulation of the 1997 reforms, alongside a range of administrative, technical and financial factors. Indeed, it was so strong that the proposals were able to be come to fruition without the due political process that usually confers wider legitimacy on a 'policy'. The proposals came into being through a drive from the top, but in the longer term they lacked political authority, laws, regulations – and, crucially, resources. As a range of actors moved the reforms to the ground level, myriad political influences at the local level came to the fore. Political will is a 'double-edged sword' (Little, 2011), where the positive impact of high-level political will can be cancelled out by myriad political wills acting at ground level to hinder implementation.

9
Behind the scenes: the technical work of planning for 'education for all'

Introduction

The Master Plan for Primary Education project (MPPE) began life in 1996 in response to the publication of the 1995 National Policy on Education. That policy was designed to improve access to primary education and to improve its quality; its objectives were repeated in the more detailed 1997 education reforms published a year later, as described in Chapter 8. MPPE was designed to plan for the implementation of the reforms in primary education. It culminated in the production and dissemination of eight provincial plans and one national plan for primary education in 2000. For reasons that will be described later, the MPPE project would be renamed the Primary Education Planning Project (PEPP) shortly after its inception.

This chapter focusses on the technical aspects of education planning. But it also recognises that:

> Educational planning is actually a series of untidy and overlapping episodes in which a variety of people and organisations with diversified perspectives are actively involved – technically and politically. (Haddad, 1995, p. 17)

In contrast with Chapters 7 and 8, it is largely a technical and detailed account. However, while planning is largely a technical activity, it is not immune to political considerations.

Who are the planners?

While education planners may sit within a primary education or education planning department in the national Ministry of Education, myriad actors in myriad organisations perform a wide range of education planning tasks that impact education access and quality.

At the school level, teachers plan lessons in line with a national curriculum, teacher guides, textbooks and available resources. School principals plan the lesson timetable, the management of school-level financial resources and, together with their teachers, the annual school plan for a range of activities. At the zonal level, officers collate resource requests from schools and communicate these to the provincial level. They administer resource allocation to schools once provincial-level budgets are known, and they disburse teacher salaries. Their key role is to implement development plans agreed at the provincial level, especially in the provision of in-service training. Officers of the provincial education department play a key role in planning and resourcing primary education. They prepare yearly estimates of financial and human resource needs, including teacher deployment and in-service training. At the provincial ministry level, the education minister and relevant officers play more of a political and less of a technical role in planning. Their chief role is to negotiate within the provincial council for the annual education budget, without which education plans cannot be developed. At the national Ministry of Education, the key players in planning for primary education are the director-general of the policy planning and review division, the director of primary education and the secretary for education. All play roles in negotiating the annual education budget with the national parliament.

Other national organisations are involved in education planning. The National Institute of Education plans the national curriculum for students and the curriculum for teacher education institutions, and plans and runs in-service training at both the national and provincial levels. The Ministry of Finance and Planning is responsible for the construction of national development plans across all sectors, including education. These generally have a five-year rather than annual time horizon. The Finance Commission allocates block grants for education directly to the provinces rather than through the national Ministry of Education. The National Education Commission (NEC) has a remit to develop policy, but it does not have a responsibility to translate policy into plans and action.

Short-term education planning – daily, termly, yearly – occurs closer to the point of education delivery: at school level. Planning of human and capital resources for schools is also annual and occurs at the provincial level. Longer term planning occurs at the national level.

Development of national and provincial plans for primary education

The technical language employed to structure the MPPE reflected that of the 'log frame' used by the Department for International Development in 1997: Goals, Purposes and Outputs. The log frame was a planning tool in wide use at that time, promoted by the international aid community, and although I personally had a number of misgivings about its use as a tool for planning, as distinct from a monitoring tool (which was of greater concern to foreign funders), it was a tool with which we were obliged, for contractual reasons, to work.

The goal of the project was to strengthen the capacity of the Ministries of Education and Higher Education and provincial authorities of education to plan, manage, monitor and evaluate primary education programmes, within an agreed policy framework. The more specific purpose was to develop and agree five-year plans at the provincial and national levels and move them to implementation. The plan had five main activities: (i) training of national and provincial primary education and planning staff; (ii) working alongside planning teams at the national and provincial levels; (iii) producing and disseminating long-range national and provincial plans for primary education; (iv) raising public awareness about issues in primary education; and (v) developing a set of guidelines for the preparation of education development plans (see Figure 9.1).

The interface between policy formulation and planning

The various outputs listed above were conceived as a set of activities that would serve and support the long-term implementation of the National Education Policy and the 1997 General Education Reforms. While 'supportive', the relationships between policy formulation and planning are neither static nor one way. On the one hand, new policies emphasise change and education planning needs to be responsive to those changes. On the other, the exercise of planning generates insights to which policy formulators need to be responsive. In principle, relationships between policy and planning are reciprocal, organic and emergent.

Figure 9.1 The Primary Education Planning Project (PEPP): goal, purpose and activities.

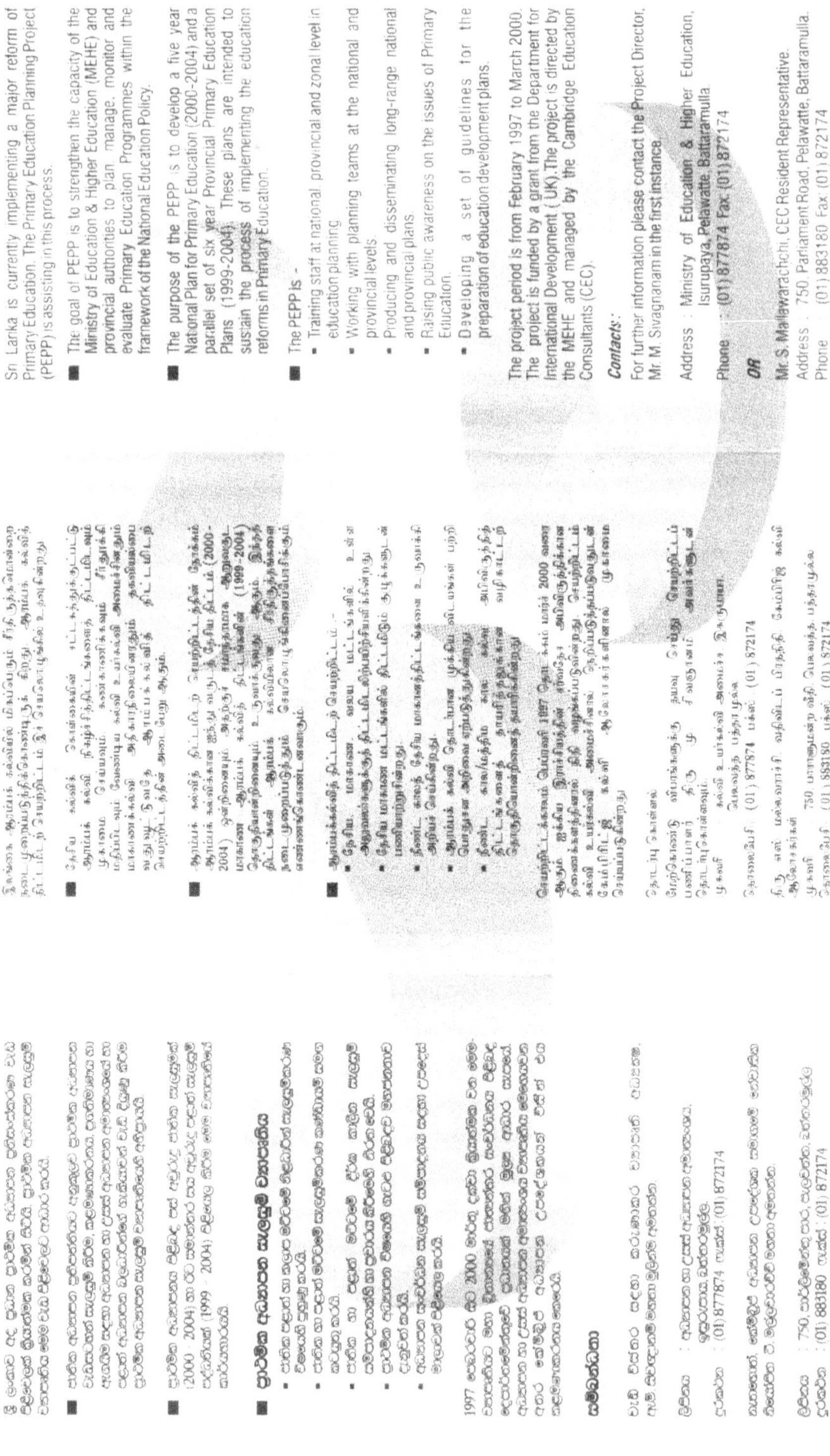

Sri Lanka is currently implementing a major reform of Primary Education. The Primary Education Planning Project (PEPP) is assisting in this process.

- The goal of PEPP is to strengthen the capacity of the Ministry of Education & Higher Education (MEHE) and provincial authorities to plan, manage, monitor and evaluate Primary Education Programmes within the framework of the National Education Policy.

- The purpose of the PEPP is to develop a five year National Plan for Primary Education (2000-2004) and a parallel set of six year Provincial Primary Education Plans (1999-2004). These plans are intended to sustain the process of implementing the education reforms in Primary Education.

- The PEPP is :-
    - Training staff at national, provincial and zonal level in education planning.
    - Working with planning teams at the national and provincial levels.
    - Producing and disseminating long-range national and provincial plans.
    - Raising public awareness on the issues of Primary Education.
    - Developing a set of guidelines for the preparation of education development plans.

The project period is from February 1997 to March 2000. The project is funded by a grant from the Department for International Development (UK). The project is directed by the MEHE and managed by the Cambridge Education Consultants (CEC).

Contacts:

For further information please contact the Project Director, Mr M Sivagnanam in the first instance.

Address : Ministry of Education & Higher Education, Isurupaya, Pelawatte, Battaramulla
Phone : (01) 877874 Fax: (01) 872174

OR

Mr. S. Mallawarachchi, CEC Resident Representative.
Address : 750, Parliament Road, Pelawatte, Battaramulla.
Phone : (01) 883180 Fax: (01) 872174
E-mail : cec@eureka.lk

Though organic and emergent in principle, there is also a powerful sense in which project design, and especially foreign-funded project design, has a static quality. A project is designed in response to a perceived need. The perceived need in 1995 was a planning mechanism that would give momentum to translating the 1995 policy into planning and on into implementation. The secretary to the ministry, who was also a member of the NEC, had enthusiasm for a three-year project to develop a 'Master Plan for Primary Education' (MPPE). It would be funded by the UK government's Department for International Development. The design work was undertaken in December 1995. The designers included a financial analysis that led to a project budget (to develop a plan, as distinct from a budget to implement the plan in schools), a financial contract and a budget discipline. A UK management company was awarded a contract to work alongside the Ministry of Education in November 1996. Work started officially in February 1997.

An extremely important set of planning activities was emerging in parallel. This was the work of a technical sub-committee of the Presidential Task Force (PTF) on Education. Given its presidential mandate, the work of this sub-committee would, naturally, attract political support.

In Chapter 8 I explained how the president felt that the 1995 policy was losing momentum. She had also become aware of the disappointing results of the survey on learning achievements among primary schoolchildren. Towards the end of 1996, the president established her Task Force on Education and declared 1997 the Year of Education Reforms. The PTF comprised 12 technical sub-committees, each of which was charged with translating the 1995 policy into detailed and implementable work plans. MPPE members worked alongside the sub-committee on primary education and early childhood development.

The technical sub-committees of the PTF were essentially planning committees. They were located outside the ministry structure, though selected ministry staff were members of them. They met intensively in the early months of 1997 at the same time as the project formally commenced. The work plan of the PTF technical subcommittees was presented to the president on 3 March 1997. The MPPE had begun its planning work just the previous month. Would the existence of two groups of planners, one led from the ministry, the other from the president-appointed Task Force, lead to duplication, competition and a slow-down in the process of developing plans and translating them into practice?

Duplication and competition?

From the beginning, those working on MPPE from inside the ministry worked hard to establish their 'space' and remit. They needed to explain how what they were doing was complementary to, rather than in competition with, ongoing policy and planning work. At least one member of the NEC thought that the purpose of the ministry project was to create a new and competing policy (that is, a 'master policy') for primary education. Others felt that intensive planning activity by a group that included foreigners would lead to proposals for foreign funding and foreign intervention in primary education. As early as 1995 the then chair of the NEC said that it would be a 'sad day for Sri Lanka if foreign aid was required to support Sri Lanka's primary education' (Interview, December 1995).

Those inside the ministry argued that their activities complemented rather than undermined or competed with those of the technical sub-committee on primary and early childhood education. Their objectives included strengthening the capacity of both the ministry *and* provincial education authorities to plan, manage, monitor and evaluate primary education programmes, within an agreed policy framework. Hitherto, the NEC had focussed on national policy and the technical sub-committees of the PTF had focussed on national work plans. In view of the provincial decentralisation of the management of education and its funding, the establishment of a planning system for primary education within provincial departments of education was viewed as essential if national policy reforms were to be implemented within the provinces.

Those inside the ministry argued that the timeframe of the PTF sub-committee was short term whereas the planning timeframe of MPPE was long term. The president wanted to forge ahead rapidly and implement changes from Grade 1, with effect from January 1998 in a pilot district (her own constituency), and needed an action plan. Her technical sub-committee was focussed on the immediate and short-term political imperative of implementing the reforms as quickly as possible. It focussed on school-level activities but made no reference to costs. The ministry staff did not consider this short-term aim to be in competition with their own. On the contrary, they would rely on and work from the activity plans of the PTF technical sub-committee. And they would assess the feasibility of the immediate implementation of the reforms during 1998 to hone the content of the long-term (five-year) Master Plan. They would also place emphasis on linking activities, programmes and goals with costs, and would seek to identify domestic and other sources of finance to sustain the implementation of policy over a prolonged period of time.

The naming of the project: MPPE or PEPP?

The name of the ministry's Master Plan for Primary Education became problematic: there appeared to be sensitivities surrounding the use of the English term 'Master' and the parallel Sinhala term *Pramuka*. Although the term had been chosen by the project designers in line with terms common in the public administration system of Sri Lanka (for example the Tea Master Plan, the Highways Master Plan), its association with a set of planning activities which in turn were associated with foreign consultants and foreign funds may have conveyed an unintended – and unfortunate – political message to senior policymakers in the NEC. It was difficult to pinpoint the root of the issue. Possibilities included the association of the Master Plan with foreign funds stemming from the current government of the former 'colonial master' (the United Kingdom), the lack of a conceptual distinction between a *policy* and a *plan*, and, by implication, the possible conflation of the term 'Master Plan' with 'Master Policy'. A separate nomenclature issue concerned the relationship between national plans and provincial plans at a time when some provincial authorities were questioning the relationship between national and provincial government in the determination of provincial policies and plans, albeit in a sector other than education.

There were three responses to these concerns. First, the name of the overall activity was changed from Master Plan for Primary Education (MPPE) to Primary Education Planning Project (PEPP). This had the dual advantage of removing the term 'Master' and focussing on the processes of planning. From then on the acronym of the project became PEPP, and will be used in this chapter henceforth.

The main output of the project was changed first, from a Master Plan for Primary Education to a 'National Plan for Primary Education', and second, from the National Plan to the 'Five-Year Plan for Primary Education' which incorporated both the provincial and the national plans. After these changes were made a comfortable working equilibrium was achieved.

The planning-cum-training strategy

Following an assessment of planning activity in 1997, it was decided that the provincial and zonal levels were the levels at which improvements in long-term planning should be made. Shorter-term school management planning was already the focus of extensive training programmes for school principals organised under the World Bank's General Education Programme 1. Its General Education Programme 2 was expected to continue this programme. The focus of PEPP on provinces and of the World Bank on schools were perceived by PEPP staff to be complementary.

While the production of plans would be central to the work of the planners at the national, provincial and sub-provincial levels (that is, zones), training was also key. This was especially important at the provincial and zonal levels, where few staff had received training in planning. At the national level, some staff had already received formal training in planning and others had some experience of donor-funded project planning. The pressing issue here was less the training and experience of actors and more the absence of a planning culture or environment in which planners could act and work: there was an absence of expected processes, structures and timetables of planning. The planning environment appeared to be oriented to the short-term needs of politicians or foreign funders.

If long-term planning was rarely a concern of the national ministry, it was certainly low on the list of priority activities among the provincial education authorities, to which powers to develop education plans had been devolved under the 13th amendment to the constitution nine years earlier. PEPP set about establishing provincial planning teams (PPTs) in each of the provinces. The PPTs comprised the director of the provincial education department, the deputy director of educational development, the deputy director of planning, the primary education coordinator, an officer from the finance section, and a representative from the provincial ministry of education. Zonal officers, divisional and school-level officers were co-opted as appropriate. The work of the PPTs was supported through workshops and on-the-job training.

Training of these teams was very practical and went hand in hand with the development plans. Those who designed training exercises used issues and information from the zones and the provinces in which training took place. The training was perceived to support the development of plans directly and immediately. Training exercises became part of the set of 'planning guidelines' that would be drafted and that would eventually emerge as a self-study manual for education planners. On-the-job plan development and feedback via training workshops would influence the planning guidelines. Training, the development of planning guidelines and the practice of developing plans would all feed from and reinforce each other.

The training of PPTs was guided by a national-level 'core training team'. The development of provincial plans was undertaken by PPTs, guided and supported by members of the training team and other members of the ministry co-opted to support particular needs (such as student and teacher projections). For further details of the content of the training programmes and planning guidelines see Little (2003b).

Unanticipated challenges

Two unanticipated challenges were faced in the implementation of the training strategy. The first was the frequent turnover of planning staff, especially the key provincial primary education coordinators (Sarvi, 1999), and thus the need for continuous retraining. The second was the time required for the design, negotiation, agreement and application of basic planning criteria, norms and tools.

Throughout the planning period there was an absence of agreement at the highest levels about both the norms for school rationalisation and the number of teachers per school. Under its loan agreement with the World Bank, the ministry was reviewing the management and financing of the education system, from Grades 1–13. The Bank was backing the NEC's proposal to restructure the school system into just two types of school, spanning Grades 1–9 and 10–13. Simultaneously it was concerned that the ministry and provincial authorities should improve the efficiency of resource allocation and the equity of teacher deployment between schools. The work of PEPP depended on these planning norms. The norms of school restructuring were designed to ensure that schools would achieve minimum student enrolments and to determine which schools would offer education across which grades. The application of these norms would have implications for the number and types of schools in each province, and in the projected number of students per school. In turn the projected student numbers would have implications for the number of teachers per school at a time when the teacher norm national target was an average of 1:28.

The development of the norms on school restructuring were influenced strongly by political and community resistance to the initial proposals. In 1995 the NEC had proposed two tiers of schooling: Grades 1–8 and Grades 9–13 (NEC, 1995). In 1996 the ministry took steps to instruct the provinces to begin work on restructuring, justifying this instruction in terms of the need to rationalise the school network and reduce wastage of scarce resources (Wehella, 2001). Early in 1997 the PTF changed these to Grades 1–9 and Grades 10–13 (Presidential Task Force on General Education, 1997).

Early in 1997, the NEC and the ministry issued guidelines to zonal directors and zonal education planners on school mapping and preparing the ground for the restructure. A supplementary circular was issued in March 1997 advising the provinces that if any serious inconvenience or hardship for pupils had resulted from the implementation of the previous circular then the provincial authority should take reasonable and proper action. As we saw in Chapter 8, community and political resistance to school restructuring was strong and the criteria needed to be changed, illustrating the fluidity of the informational environment in which the PEPP team worked.

Building on complementarities

Despite early misgivings about the respective objectives of the PTF sub-committee and PEPP, an easy relationship developed between them. The sub-committee focussed on work plans for the launch of the reforms in one pilot district. A range of preparations was needed – in curriculum design, the assessment of learning outcomes, the physical development of classrooms, training of teachers, and creating public awareness. To assist them in this urgent work, another primary education sub-committee was established, this time within an Education Reforms Implementation Unit (ERIU) within the ministry itself. Its main objective was to support the pilot district in reform implementation.

The work of PEPP focussed on the development of longer-term plans and planning capacity. PEPP supported plans at the provincial level as well as at the level of the national ministry. It focussed on the costs of implementing plans, and the greater coordination of activity and budgetary plans and planning cycles. It also sought to institutionalise planning mechanisms that would serve the long-term implementation of the reforms into the next century. Its overall goal was to strengthen the capacity of the national and provincial authorities to plan, manage, monitor and evaluate primary education programmes, within an agreed policy framework. This goal came to be recognised as substantially different to that of the PTF sub-committee and its successor in the ERIU – whose goal was to develop implementable work plans in the short term.

Where functions were different but complementary, they could feed into and enhance the other. For example, the ERIU prepared orientation booklets for the parents of new entrants to Grade 1 in the pilot district of Gampaha in 1998. When the reforms began to be implemented nation-wide from January 1999, PEPP organised the funding and distribution of 400,000 booklets for parents, an exercise that was repeated in 2000. Similarly, the ERIU and National Institute of Education prepared a useful booklet for school principals setting out the purpose of and outlining the reforms for primary education. Ten thousand copies were produced, one for each school. As part of its awareness programme, PEPP revised the booklet and produced 100,000 copies, enabling every teacher and education officer to have his/her own copy. When PEPP mobilised provincial planning teams from across the country to present their draft long-term plans to the NEC and to one another in January 1999, members of the ERIU mobilised a panel of teachers to discuss their early experiences of the reforms at the same event.

Establishing connections between policy, ongoing implementation and long-term planning was an overarching goal of PEPP.

Deepening education networks

National conferences on primary education served to deepen networks within the education sector. The purpose of the first, held in 1997, was twofold: to raise awareness of the Primary Education Reforms Policy, and to promote discussion of more specific strategies/sub-policies that would function as a bridge between general policy statements and detailed plans of action. The first conference was national in its orientation and brought together policy, planning and implementing stakeholders. The number of participants exceeded planned numbers by over 100 per cent, indicating the depth of interest in the reforms and the conference.

Strategy papers were commissioned from a range of stakeholders on the themes of the Education Reforms Policy. The themes included decentralisation and planning; initial and continuing teacher education for teachers at the primary stage; career development for primary-stage teachers; curriculum and the assessment of learning at the primary stage of education; planning, monitoring and educational management information systems; the supply, demand and cost characteristics of the primary stage of education; career development; and professional and administrative support for primary-stage teachers. Emerging from the papers prepared for the first conference was a book on the primary education reforms (Little, 2000). Because of the lapse of time between the conference and finalising the book, it was possible to include an evaluation of teachers' reactions to the reforms and an early evaluation of the reforms piloted in one district (L. Perera & Dharmawardana, 2000). In short, the process of producing the book served to strengthen professional networks and further the dialogue about the policy reforms and their implementation via planning. The book itself, published first in

English and later translated to Sinhala and Tamil, would be used subsequently for dissemination and training purposes among the academic and professional education community.

While this first conference brought together national-level stakeholders, it also brought provincial and national officials together. It underlined the need to strengthen networks between the two levels and improve the flow of information about the goals of the policy (Sarvi, 1999).

PEPP learned from this experience. Provincial-level staff wanted and needed more orientation to and knowledge about the detail of the policy. They also wanted clarification of their powers under the new regime of provincial devolution. National-level policymakers and planners needed new ways of working with the provinces if decentralisation of planning and budgetary control were to take root. In a bureaucratic and hierarchical culture of public administration, this supportive rather than directive way of working would present a challenge. At a more basic level, the conference experience exposed the need for training in communication techniques – how to make clear, focussed and brief presentations; how to respond to the presentations of others; and how to stimulate and manage debate.

Listening to the provinces and the teachers

A second national conference, a year later, adopted a different focus and attendance was restricted to 100 delegates. It afforded the PPTs an opportunity to present their draft plans to the other teams, and, importantly, to members of the NEC, the body that had formulated the 1995 policy and its 1997 elaboration. A second purpose was to listen to teachers' accounts of how they were implementing the reforms in pilot district schools. The underlying message of the conference was that there was much to be gained in terms of planning and implementation practice from listening to the provincial planners and teachers.

The conference timetable gave precedence to provincial officers and teachers. The intended role of the national-level policymakers and planners was to listen, comment and synthesise. Presentation rehearsals were run the day before the conference to give the presenters an opportunity to improve their content and delivery. The presentations included a wide range of policy and practice matters alongside planning matters. In contrast with the conference held the previous year, points made and issues raised were more grounded and specific. But it was clear that some staff in the provinces remained unaware of all the policy intentions. The PPTs were still calling for more guidance from the centre on strategies, policies, planning criteria and norms. In a final discussion chaired by the chairperson of the NEC, a list of specific recommendations for action, mostly to be taken by the national ministry, was drawn up. While there was enormous excitement at the end of the conference, the list of recommendations was never finally delivered – in the main because no member of the NEC, PTF or ministry felt they had the authority to issue it. This was perhaps yet another illustration of the planning voids referred to in Chapter 8 that had been created in the wake of the establishment of the NEC.

Extending the network beyond education

PEPP was also able to extend the network beyond education. It invited officers from the Ministry of Finance and Planning, the National Planning Division and the Finance Commission to its conferences and held regular meetings. The work of PEPP with the Finance Commission on the development of a separate budget line for primary education laid down a structure for financial allocations that would serve primary education for years to come. It brought together professionals in the Ministry of Education, the provincial ministries and the Ministry of Finance and Planning. It resulted in a change of financial policy and administrative procedure at the highest level.

Communicating with multiple stakeholders

All parties – the NEC, the PTF, PEPP and the ERIU – recognised that an awareness campaign would be an essential element in communicating policies and putting plans into action. Communication with education officers, teachers, parents and students was key to the process. PEPP embarked on an awareness programme that employed three channels or media of communication in all three languages: (i) print; (ii) music and drama; and (iii) exhibitions of teaching and learning materials.

Alongside a wide array of print materials distributed to every school, music and drama and exhibition activities involved every school in the country. Music and drama festivals were built around the themes of the primary education reforms. This was a nation-wide activity – every school was invited to write, produce and stage a small drama or musical performance based on one of the themes. Exhibitions displayed teacher-designed and -made teaching and learning aids, including storybooks, in line with the reformed primary education curriculum. The school activities were followed by competitive performances at the zonal and provincial levels.

Twenty-seven schools (three per province plus three extras from the north-east) and an estimated 1,000 students and 500 teachers then participated in a National Primary Education Programme in July 2000. Such was the standard achieved that at least two of the 20 drama/ musical performances were subsequently filmed and broadcast on TV to raise awareness of the reforms among the wider public.

Multiple roles

Coordination was also effected through the involvement of key actors in PEPP's work and in other related work within the ministry. Initially a core team of staff seconded on a full-time basis to the Primary Education Branch was to have been established. In practice, permanent secondment was difficult to arrange and by the end of the first year of project implementation only two staff were engaged in the planning work on a full-time basis. Although part-time regular attachments had been negotiated and agreed in principle, the priorities of their other work (involving work on the World Bank General Education Programme 2 and Teacher Education and Teacher Deployment projects) meant that they were usually unavailable for the PEPP work. An alternative strategy emerged: to co-opt ministry staff as and when work on specific tasks was required; and to supplement this with local consultancy inputs, as necessary. This arrangement became the norm as the planning work progressed. It had the advantage of involving staff in the work of PEPP who were simultaneously involved in planning work elsewhere in the ministry, with which PEPP wished to co-ordinate its efforts.

Overlapping membership of committees provides another example of the same principle. The ERIU sub-committee for primary education and the steering committee of PEPP had distinct but overlapping membership. Key members of the ERIU sub-committee were co-opted to the PEPP steering committee. These members had also chaired/deputy chaired the PTF sub-committee at an earlier stage and so were in an advantageous position to inform, influence and support. This increased the potential of information sharing, mutual influence and complementarity of function.

Multiple roles across time

It became apparent that the mobility of staff – especially senior staff – across roles and across time was another crucial element in building consensus about the reforms and support for the emergent five-year plan. Actors changed their positions across and within various key organisations over time, bringing the experience gained through their involvement in a prior stage of the policy-planning-implementation process to each new role (for examples see Little, 2003b, p. 49). Policy formulators moved into senior planning and implementing positions. Monitors and evaluators moved into more senior planning positions. Provincial officers moved to become national officers. There is nothing unique about such a process. Professionals everywhere move to new positions, taking with them their experience of previous roles. The quality of the skills and experience that actors bring to each new role and position within the policy-planning-implementation process *over time* is often overlooked in academic discussions of the political economy of education. Yet it is an important dynamic that can both promote – and hinder – change.

The language of planning

The multilingual character of Sri Lanka was described in Chapter 1, and reference was made above to the need to publish awareness materials in multiple languages. The official languages of government administration at the national and provincial levels are Sinhala and Tamil. Circulars sent by the Ministry of Education to the provinces and schools are in either Sinhala or Tamil, depending on the language of the majority population in a particular area. English is used in documents that need to be used in negotiations with external partners. The involvement of external partners in PEPP meant that English needed to be used orally and in writing for selected planning and training activities, alongside Sinhala and Tamil. All three languages were used during training, facilitated by the impressive trilingual skills of key actors. Figure 9.1 above is one small example of the many trilingual documents produced by PEPP.

A major and concerted effort was made to publish key planning documents – especially the five-year plan, the abridged versions of the provincial six-year plans, the planning guidelines, books and booklets – in all three national languages. Key documents were published in all three languages within the same covers, with key planning information presented in a single table using trilingual headings.

Though not envisaged in the original project design, the translation and production of planning and other written documents became a publishing project in itself. The ministry mainstream did not have the capacity to produce and translate planning documents in multiple languages to an acceptable standard for a mass audience. The project status of PEPP, with its grant from an external partner, provided the financial flexibility to enter a partnership with a small private sector company that was able to organise and coordinate the chain of writing/editing/printing activities. The ministry – with its strict financial regulations and its tradition of servicing itself or 'buying' services from other government departments – would never, in the four-year life of PEPP, have been able to produce documents to the standard and with the speed of a small and efficient private sector company.

In most cases the initial planning work was undertaken in English. In retrospect this was a mistake, especially at the provincial level, where the English writing facility of most officers was severely limited. It was less of a problem at the national level, though even here draft text needed to be heavily edited. An alternative (albeit more costly) strategy would have been for planners to write in their language of choice and to have organised extensive translation from the earliest stages of plan development. This experience will resonate in countries where English, French or Spanish is not the language of national or provincial education planning. An international language needs to be used at the interface of the international and national; but official and national languages need to be used at the interface of the national and intranational.

Environmental flux

Throughout the project, project managers faced frequent challenges posed by the fluidity of the political and internal security environments. Aspects of the environments beyond the ministry and from which the planning process drew support and legitimacy were themselves changing. Although this flux originated outside the ministry, it impinged on its work.

Civil strife and internal security

The internal security environment was also in a constant state of flux throughout the period of the project. The civil war continued unabated, and the president survived an attempt on her life. Staff in the North Eastern Province maintained their involvement in the development of long-term plans for education throughout.

During the period in which the five-year plan was developed, no democratically elected provincial council operated in the combined North Eastern Province. The provincial ministry was responsible to the president-appointed provincial governor. Parts of the province were controlled by the government and others by the Liberation Tigers of Tamil Eelam. The areas under the control of the Tigers were referred to in government circles as the 'uncleared areas'. PEPP's planning team members in both the North Eastern Province and in the central ministry in Colombo worked in an atmosphere of great uncertainty. Travelling and communication within the North Eastern Province and between that and other provinces was difficult. Despite this, the education secretary for the North Eastern Province showed great interest in the preparation of a long-term development plan for primary education in his province and motivated the planning team to work with 'missionary zeal' (Interview, PEPP project director, May 2002).

Political flux

Provincial council elections were held in April 1999, presidential elections in June 2000, and parliamentary elections in October 2000. Prior to each election, education officers could be called for election duty, education offices were closed, and meetings and conferences were postponed. After each election, holders of political and education posts would change, and technical staff inside the ministry needed to create and maintain dialogue with politicians at the national and provincial levels each time. Informing and securing support from a group of provincial chief ministers and their secretaries, the provincial education ministers and their secretaries, and the provincial directors of education was no mean task for an education officer. Few politicians could be expected to know and be interested in the finer detail of education plans. Few of the politicians could expect to be in post long enough to follow a plan to which they had been a signatory through to its implementation. Their concerns were more immediate and focussed on the next set of elections. Yet the education planners needed their support for their painstaking work. Thus, relationships between planners and politicians needed constant renewal.

As we saw in Chapter 8, national and local politicians are heavily involved in education, from the stage of policy formulation, through planning, to day-to-day implementation at the school level. The symbiotic relationship between teachers, politicians and education officers, especially at the local level, is well understood. In matters concerning teacher deployment and transfer, this relationship is regarded by some as 'unhealthy interference', and by others simply as part of the accepted culture of educational practice.

Given this political environment, PEPP planners considered ways of involving politicians in the development of and commitment to educational plans. The need to 'get the politicians on board' was tempered by the knowledge that politicians come and go. The vagaries of democratic and not-so-democratic elections, combined with the regular swings of political mood in Sri Lanka, mean that some politicians stay in post for a time, others move around, and yet others disappear from the political scene altogether. Having 'got the politicians on board', education planners and implementers cannot depend on sustained political support for the policy-planning-implementation phases of reform. This is especially so in the case of long-term planning and long-term implementation phases (Lewin, 2007).

Planners must keep their eye on their target and not bend with the political winds. They have technical skills that politicians do not possess. The average planner is usually in his/her job much longer than the average politician. Planners can provide stability and continuity within the policy-planning process. They need to be aware of the value of their technical skills and build on them. They also need to understand the power – the political power – that well-constructed plans convey. As one ministry insider said:

> The availability of long-term plans discourages politicians from resorting to *ad hoc* measures that divert scarce resources to a vote-catching patchwork and to satisfying politically popular but developmentally unsound demands ... Unhealthy political interference could be prevented if the long-term plan is well formulated, incorporating valid and officially accepted norms and criteria to guide the disbursement of funds. (Interview, ministry officer, May 2002)

Previous experience of the planning-implementation interface bears out this view. Faced with the plans and the criteria that described how and why particular schools had been included in sub-district development plans oriented to the most disadvantaged communities, politicians who wished to secure financial resources for particular schools found themselves unable to penetrate the education bureaucracy. The plans provided the planners, other education professionals and schools with a technical-rational defence against both political favouritism and punishment.

The creation of a separate budget line for primary education was considered by PEPP staff to be an issue on which political support at the highest levels was required. It was ministry practice for the minister and his deputy to discuss key issues with ministry staff on a monthly basis. The separate budget line was placed on one of the agendas by PEPP staff. The good interpersonal relations established by PEPP staff with members of the Finance Commission and the General Treasury was also important in generating discussion with politicians at the provincial level. The separate recurrent budget line for primary education was established by the Finance Commission with the political consent of the provincial chief ministers and provincial ministers of education.

Conclusion

This chapter has described in detail the process involved in developing a long-term plan for primary education in Sri Lanka. It has shown how the development of a plan has been accompanied by a deliberate and systematic attempt to develop planning capacity. It has also demonstrated how planning capacity and responsibilities for planning lie at myriad levels of both the education and the financing system. Educational planning is not the preserve of a small group of people located at the centre. The process of provincial devolution that began in 1987 has extended the network of activity and financial planning responsibilities considerably. While this extension suggests wider participation in planning amongst education officials at least, it has also underlined major challenges for staff development, training and the creation of an environment that supports high-quality technical work. The case study above underlines the importance of establishing, maintaining and extending networks of professional contacts beyond and within education in building consensus around the goals of the plans for primary education.

The relative power of various planning cultures can conflict with innovative approaches to planning. The development of the long-term plan within a trilingual context also raised critical issues for planning at the interfaces between the intranational, national and international arenas. If planning is to lead to implementation, it needs to be undertaken in familiar languages.

Planning occurs in political contexts that are sometimes marked by civil war, extremely difficult working conditions and political flux. Despite the challenges of a long-running civil war, long-term plans for primary education were created by Sri Lankan planners for all areas of the country. The special arrangements that emerged in the war-torn 'uncleared' areas were described above and were shown to have created the foundations for current plans for rehabilitation in the post-conflict period.

The vagaries of political support and interference for the development of plans were described. We saw in Chapters 7 and 8 how political will is fundamental for education reform. But the political dimension extends to many levels of interaction – and 'interference'. Provincial devolution deepens the imperative for political support and mobilisation. Yet, as the above case study has shown, educational planners often need to work long and hard at getting politicians 'on board' and keeping their eyes on the 'education for all' ball.

Part IV
Globalisation, education and social disparities

Preface to Part IV

Throughout the 1970s, my research attention in Sri Lanka focussed largely on children in school, rather than those out of school, and on job seekers for modern sector employment in urban areas, rather than employment in rural areas (Chapters 4, 5 and 6). At that time, my interests in policy and practice were informed theoretically by the 'development' ideas of modernisation, human capital and dependency. Sri Lanka's political issues of the day, including nationalisation of the plantations, the takeover of plantation schools by the government, the incipient ethnic crisis, major changes in the economic direction of the country following the 1977 elections and the onset of late twentieth-century globalisation were attracting little of my attention. That was about to change.

Sri Lanka's engagement with globalisation in the 1980s was not a new phenomenon. Positioned for millennia at a crossroads of trading networks, religions, and Asian and European empires, Sri Lanka has been – and remains – a place defined 'by its openness to movement across the Indian Ocean' (Biedermann & Strathern, 2017).

Historians describe several phases of the globalisation of ideas, cultural contacts and exchange of goods around the world. Sri Lanka's engagement in the maritime jade and spice road and the maritime silk routes stretched over many centuries BCE (Bandaranayake, 1990). Greco-Roman trade relations with Sri Lanka stemmed from 600 BCE (D. S. A. Munasinghe et al., 2021). The Greeks and Romans referred to Sri Lanka as Taprobane, while the Arabs, who also traded with Sri Lanka from ancient times, referred to the country as Serendib (Dasanayaka, 2017). These early waves of globalisation are referred to as 'archaic globalisation'.

A later wave – 'early modern' or 'proto-modern' globalisation – refers to the rise of the European maritime empires, with, in the Sri Lankan case, the 450-year period of colonial rule by the Portuguese, followed by the Dutch and the British (described briefly in Chapter 1).

Historians trace the 'modern' wave of globalisation, starting from the early nineteenth century, to the international transport revolution in steam, the first industrial revolution in Britain and a general increase in international trade. The 'modern' phase began in Sri Lanka from the early nineteenth century with the annexation of the Kandyan Kingdom by the British in 1815 and the gradual establishment of a colonial plantation economy based on the export of agricultural goods. By the end of the nineteenth century the plantation economy had contributed to a rise in Sri Lanka's economic prosperity, and, by the early years of the twentieth century, was generating surpluses that facilitated the development of the welfare state, as described in Chapter 7.

By the middle of the twentieth century, following independence and a change of government in 1956, there was a brief period of 'de-globalisation' when economic strategy became inward rather than outward oriented. Import substitution industrialisation strategies were implemented to reduce import bills, to build up nationalised industries and to reduce economic dependency. Export-led globalisation slowed and there was a retreat from international trade.

The most recent wave of globalisation worldwide started in the 1970s. In a bid to halt declining rates of economic growth and rising inflation, industrialised countries deregulated the finance sector, reduced taxes, privatised state-owned companies and reduced government spending. International finance institutions encouraged low-income countries to adopt export-oriented economic strategies and to reintegrate with the global economy (Chapter 2). The growth of information technology contributed to a reduction in communication costs around the world and accelerating international trade of goods and services. Following the 1977 elections, Sri Lanka liberalised the economy and resumed an export-led economic strategy.

The three chapters in this part of the book examine the growth of educational opportunity alongside issues of social disparity during the waves of globalisation in the nineteenth and late twentieth centuries. Chapter 10 covers the period from 1840 to the present day and addresses the growth of education within the plantation economy and the enduring social disparities between plantation communities and the rest of the country. My interest in the people who lived, worked and were educated inside the plantations was piqued in the early 1980s when I was invited to undertake an evaluation of a proposal for educational support within an integrated rural development programme aimed at poverty reduction in the rural district of Badulla, where 25 per cent of a culturally diverse population were Indian Tamils living and working inside tea plantations. Within this social group adult literacy and school enrolment rates were the lowest in the country and the differences between males and females were marked. School dropout rates among both boys and girls were high.

This evaluation led to a part-time involvement in a series of international collaborations focussed on improving educational opportunities in disadvantaged rural and plantation areas over a period of 16 years – a period in which Sri Lanka's twentieth-century wave of globalisation would come to overlay the nineteenth-century wave. It was also a period in which several international development organisations became involved in the economic and social infrastructure of plantations. Positive change in educational opportunity in the plantations was beginning to be observed. Members of international development organisations were quick to attribute much of the change to various 'projects' they were promoting. I was less certain: surely the explanation for a rise in educational opportunity was more complex than this. Once my participation inside the project had ceased, I stepped back to learn more about the drivers of educational opportunity in the plantations.

I would also begin to reflect on how the international discourse on basic needs, especially that part of it which lauded Sri Lanka's achievements in education (Chapter 2), appeared to overlook questions about the means – especially the economic means – through which those achievements came about. Social and economic disparities between those who lived inside the plantations and those who lived outside them were marked. As we shall see, it was the communities residing beyond the borders of the plantations that were to benefit most from the revenues generated by the labours of those who lived and worked within them.

Chapter 11 moves the discussion of globalisation to the period following the United National Party's return to power in 1977 and the introduction of liberal economic policies. These were driven by a worldwide decline in economic growth and the introduction of monetarist policies in industrialised countries (dubbed 'Thatcherism' and 'Reaganomics'), followed by the international finance community's recommendation to low-income and low-growth countries to follow suit and increase exports. In education terms, globalisation was manifesting itself in the increased mobility of students across national boundaries, increased levels of educational provision, training and qualifications across national boundaries, and increasing numbers of highly educated people seeking foreign job opportunities (Little, 2000). Would these changes also be apparent in Sri Lanka? Would some social groups benefit educationally more than others during this new phase of globalisation? And what impact, if any, might there be on the aspirations and expectations of young people from different social classes for education and employment? These are the research questions addressed in Chapter 11.

Chapter 12 focusses on twentieth-century globalisation in the Asia region. While much of the 'developing' world, including Sri Lanka, had adopted policies of import substitution industrialisation advocated by international agencies in the 1960s and early 1970s, several Asian countries eschewed this advice, embarking instead on a strategy of export orientation. This chapter addresses two main questions. First, what were the economic, political and educational features of the so-called Asian 'Tigers' and other 'High Performing Asian Economies' that contributed to their integration into the global economy? And second, how did the Sri Lankan experience compare? It concludes by raising questions about what it means to globalise 'successfully', in the context of Sri Lanka's civil war on the one hand, and the burgeoning international agenda of 'sustainable development' on the other.

10
The export-led plantation economy and educational opportunity: 1840–2020

Introduction

Plantation systems of agricultural production originated in the Portuguese Canary Islands in the fifteenth century and the American New World in the sixteenth and seventeenth centuries. Despite the formal abolition of slavery around the world during the nineteenth century, plantations based on indentured and migrant labour continued to spread. In their book *Class, patriarchy and ethnicity on Sri Lankan plantations* (2015), Kumari Jayawardena and Rachel Kurian trace the development of the plantation economy in Sri Lanka and the lives and struggles of plantation workers across two centuries of power and protest. Vijayapalan (2015) has written of the 'endless inequalities' of the plantation community of Sri Lanka and the denial of their rights in housing, wages, health and civic rights as well as in education.

Nineteenth-century plantation production in Sri Lanka emerged following Britain's abolition of slavery, ending a period during which the port of Colombo had been used as a transhipment base in the Indian Ocean region. The export-oriented plantation economy, based first on coffee, then tea and rubber, was central to the British colonial regime's economic strategy from the 1840s and was a nineteenth-century example of modern economic globalisation.

There was little role for education in Sri Lanka's early plantations. During the coffee period migrant male labourers moved periodically between India and Sri Lanka. They were not a settled community. That would change from the 1880s when tea, an all-year-round crop, replaced seasonal coffee, and male labourers brought their families with them.

Women were employed as tea pluckers, and children were also employed in a range of plantation work (Kurian, 1982).

Historically, plantation production systems have been defined by three characteristics: (i) an external market controlled by metropolitan interests; (ii) authoritarian and hierarchical management–labour relationships; and (iii) an institutionalisation of the productive and social spheres of life and work (Kemp & Little, 1987). Writing about the Caribbean, Beckford (1983) emphasised the all-embracing nature of plantations. A plantation is not simply an economic system of production; it is also a cultural system of social reproduction – or, as might be said in Sri Lanka, a plantation is a system in which one is born, lives, works and dies – from 'womb to tomb'.

The development of educational provision within the plantations was slow, for:

> education was not part of plantation culture; it was neither technically necessary nor did it have any survival value. For labourers' children, education is a means of emancipation, but to the planter it is a potential threat to the labour supply. (S. B. D. de Silva, 1982, p. 346)

During the 1970s and 1980s, analyses of education in plantation communities in other parts of the world tended to focus on educational stasis, continuity and social reproduction rather than educational progress and social mobility. Since plantations did not require skilled labour, only minimal educational provision was necessary for social reproduction. In the 1960s Marimuthu (1971) described the education of the children of plantation workers in Malaysia as serving a custodial function that failed to facilitate social mobility and served as a means of social control. Most early analyses of education in plantations advanced the reasons why educational progress does *not* occur, rather than *when, why and how it does*. As such they are invaluable in understanding the enduring aspects of education, resistance to change and the maintenance of the status quo. But they are less powerful in explaining why and how change occurs. However, a long view of history indicates that change has occurred in plantation settings, albeit often rather slowly, and that this progress cannot be explained simply by changes in the nature of the plantation production system.

One of the best accounts of educational change in plantation communities is offered by Bacchus (1990, 1994). His long view of history in West Indian colonies traces changes in education to changes in occupation and stratification systems and to shifts in the relative power of social groups over education. Conflicts between planters and missionaries, between metropolitan and local elites, between missionary organisations, and between teachers and managers all played their part in generating the conditions for change in education.

This chapter focusses more on change than on continuity. It explains how and why opportunities for education have increased in Sri Lanka's plantations over decades. My analysis of those changes was not tied to a particular theory of social change or continuity. I wished to remain open to the possibility that change is influenced variously by interests and drivers in the economic, political, social and cultural domains at different points/periods in time. Educational change is a straightforward outcome of neither international declarations nor national legislation, nor is it a straightforward consequence of industrialisation and modernity.

Phases of educational progress

As we saw in Chapter 1, there are at least two main groups of Tamils. The first, the Sri Lankan Tamils, are concentrated in the north and the east of the island. Their ancestors migrated to Sri Lanka over 2,000 years ago. They currently (2023) comprise about 12 per cent of the population. The second, the Indian Tamils, are concentrated in the south-central 'up-country' highlands. Their ancestors came to Sri Lanka when the British established an export-oriented colonial economy based on coffee, and subsequently tea and rubber. Indian Tamil labour was recruited by plantation owners from among Tamils living in the areas of the Madras presidency in India. Indian Tamils currently comprise about 5 per cent of the population (2023). At independence in 1948 they comprised 12 per cent of the population. The majority – those that reside inside tea and rubber plantations – are often referred to as 'plantation', 'up-country' or 'hill-country' Tamils. By contrast with Sri Lankan Tamils, the Indian Tamils are drawn disproportionately from low-caste groups. It is the educational story of the Indian (up-country, hill-country) Tamils that I present in this chapter.

In 1911 the Sri Lankan literacy rate was 31.0 per cent; in the plantations it was 12.3 per cent. By the 1980s, the country-wide rate had grown to 88.6 per cent, with rates of 92.2 per cent for males and 85.2 per cent for females. The comparable rates in the plantation sector were 68.5 per cent, 80.0 per cent and 58.1 per cent respectively. By 2003–4 the country-wide rate was 92.5 per cent, with rates of 94.5 per cent and 90.6 per cent for males and females. The comparable rates for the plantation sector were 81.3 per cent, 88.3 per cent and 74.7 per cent (Consumer Finances and Socio-Economic Survey, cited in World Bank, 2007). There had been progress – but how had this come about?

Educational progress in plantation communities between 1840 and 2020 may be divided roughly into six phases.

Phase 1 – 1840–69: diffuse inception of line and mission schools

From the 1830s the British colonial government encouraged large-scale clearances of land for the cultivation of coffee. Coffee planters employed local up-country Sinhalese labour to clear the land. Thereafter labour requirements were seasonal. Planters' early attempts to employ up-country Sinhalese labour for this type of work failed and Tamil workers were imported from South India. They were recruited by Tamil *kanganies* (labour supervisors), who also hailed from South India and often recruited from their home villages. The labourers were economically poor and of low-caste ascription. The 'push' was the avoidance of starvation during periods of famine. Male labourers, mostly illiterate, migrated seasonally between the coffee plantations in Sri Lanka and their home villages. The lives of these men were harsh, their culture impoverished. Yet it was under these conditions that the rudiments of education in the plantations began to be promoted by three agents of change.

The *kanganies* were the labour recruiters and supervisors, but they were also money lenders and debt collectors. They established night schools for the labourers, probably for two purposes – to reinforce their control over their labourers, and to conserve the values of the labour community. These 'schools' were held on the verandas of the line rooms where labourers were housed and became known as 'line schools' (Gnanamuttu, 1976, p. 15). Limited historical evidence suggests that a second group of change agents comprised a handful of individual planters. The names of prominent planters – Ferguson, Bird, Tytler and Wall – appear to have been associated with the ad hoc establishment of schools inside the plantations they managed. And one or two not so prominent planters – for example Finnimore and Simmons – resigned their posts as plantation owners/superintendents to become religious missionaries working among the labourers (Gnanamuttu, 1976, pp. 17–18). A third group of change agents were individual Christian missionaries, whose work in the plantations was an extension of their religious work elsewhere on the island and of the corporate work of their churches globally (K. M. de Silva, 1965).

Alongside these agents for positive change was a set of interests that inhibited the establishment of schools. These were primarily economic. The colonial export economy was expanding and needed a growing supply of unskilled, docile and low-paid labour. The purpose of labour was labouring, not learning. Planters perceived education to represent a threat to the supply of labour. By 1854 the planters had formed the Planters' Association, which would become a powerful lobby group. Overall, the plantation owners, superintendents and *kanganies* were the agents of economic and social reproduction rather than change.

Phase 2 – 1869–1900: slow growth of line and mission schools

The leaf virus *hemileia vastatrix* appeared in 1869 and decimated the coffee plantations. During the period 1869–1900 tea was introduced and became a successful plantation crop. In contrast to coffee, tea required year-round labour, and it was during this period that the colonial authorities encouraged wives and children to migrate from India along with their husbands and augment the labour force. Labour became more settled. *Kanganies* became more active in the provision of 'line schools'. Simultaneously, religious missionaries became more active in the establishment of schools inside the plantations and in the small towns that grew at their edges.

The economic interests that had inhibited education in the earlier period had not changed. The plantation production system continued to require an uneducated, docile, low-paid guaranteed supply of labour. Ever more men, women and children migrated from India to live, work and die inside the plantations. Women were employed as tea pickers. Children were frequently employed, but since their labour was not required full time, rudimentary schools were provided for, mainly, custodial care. The dependent position of women and girls within the plantation system would manifest itself in myriad ways throughout the nineteenth and twentieth centuries. Women were paid less than men for a day's work and girls' enrolment in school lagged behind that of boys.

Beyond the plantation sector, the colonial state government responded to a growing social demand for education among Ceylon's population more generally. There was a growing awareness amongst Sri Lanka's middle classes of educational developments in England, and there were religious revivalist movements within Ceylon that called for the expansion of educational opportunities. The colonial state supported education through a financial grant-in-aid scheme available to missionary and private organisations. Although this would have only a very modest impact in practice within the plantations, the expansion of schools beyond the plantations was supported by legislation, norms and benchmarks and, eventually, plantation community aspirations and demands. The schools established by missionary organisations in the areas surrounding the plantations created an avenue of opportunity for plantation children, especially the children of mid-level supervisory staff. Thus, a degree of co-action between the colonial state and missionary bodies resulted in an expansion of education in the country at large, from which there was some small benefit for the plantation community.

Phase 3 – 1900–48: widespread establishment of plantation schools

Over the next forty years, schools in plantations became more widespread. The Ceylon census report of 1901 indicated that across the country less than a quarter of elementary school-age children were attending school. There were enormous gaps in the literacy rates of Europeans and Burghers on the one hand, and Sinhalese and Tamils on the other; between males and females; and between those living in urban, rural and plantation areas.

In 1903 the lack of educational facilities in the plantations became the subject of political debate in the UK parliament. Questions in Westminster were put to the Secretary of State for the Colonies (Hansard, 6 April 1903 and 4 May 1903). Under pressure from Westminster, the colonial governor of Ceylon (Sri Lanka) sought to influence the group perceived to hold the greatest sway with respect to the education of children in the plantations – the planters. At this time almost all the tea crop was exported to Britain and British interests controlled almost all stages of production, processing and marketing. The tea crop was yielding a healthy economic surplus for both the private sector tea companies and colonial government revenue.

In such an economic climate the colonial governor felt able to address questions to the plantation owners and managers about the conditions in which labour lived and worked. By now the planters were acting in a coordinated manner and expressing their views and concerns via the Planters' Association. While a handful of individual planters continued to lend active support to a handful of schools, most were content to offer passive support to the *kanganies* who ran the inferior line schools. The planters continued to resist educational change. Despite the profits from tea and the availability of grants-in-aid for education from the colonial government, they fell back on two excuses: the start-up costs of a school, and the potential threat to the supply of child labour in the plantations.

External influence on the colonial government was also exerted periodically by the colonial Indian government, keen to see that the welfare needs of Tamil labour were being met. A series of ordinances on labour conditions and health and medical provision starting in the mid-nineteenth century continued to be revised into the twentieth (Wickremaratne, 1973; D. L. Jayasuriya, 2001). In 1906 and 1907, government ordinances established guidelines for the country-wide provision of elementary schools in town and rural areas, with some financial support from the colonial government. Attendance was made compulsory in aided and government schools. However, because of the rather separate nature of labour in the plantation community and, perhaps more importantly, the political and economic strength of planters' interests, the 1907 rural schools ordinance contained less restrictive clauses on schools in the plantations. Planters had a 'duty' to provide arrangements for the vernacular education of all children of labourers employed in the estates 'between the ages of six and ten, and to set apart and keep in repair a suitable classroom' (Ordinance No. 8 of 1907, section 6, quoted in J. E. Jayasuriya, 1979). Unlike children in the other rural areas and town areas, school attendance was not compulsory for children in the plantations.

Although education at this stage was not compulsory for the children of labourers, the duty to provide it had finally been incorporated into a system of norms and expectations which would gradually become more binding over time. Where educational provision in the plantations had been a matter for an individual *kangany*, planter or religious agency in the nineteenth century, by the early twentieth century it had become a matter of colonial state government and legal ordinance.

The 1920 ordinance made education in plantation schools compulsory for the first time and obliged plantation superintendents to appoint competent teachers. It was illegal to employ children between the ages of 6 and 10 years before 10 am, though it was not illegal to employ them after 10 am. The government made financial grants available to schools that registered. Between 1923 and 1939 the number of registered schools had grown from 272 to 820. The number of girls enrolled in plantation schools also began to grow, from just 9.5 per cent of those enrolled in 1903 to 30 per cent by 1930.

During this period, the trade union movement was established, and political franchise was extended. Both would have direct implications for education. The first plantation labour trade union was established in 1931. Unsurprisingly, the planters resisted the formation of trade unions. Union demands for improvements in wages coincided with the onset of the global economic depression and retrenchment of plantation labour. The union collapsed after only two years. The second, the Ceylon Indian Congress Labour Union, later to become the Ceylon Workers' Congress (CWC), enjoyed more success. It attracted a large membership during the 1940s and contributed to the success of politicians representing plantation labourers in the 1947 elections (Jayewardene, 1972, pp. 337–54; Nadesan, 1993, pp. 136, 149–50).

Political franchise was extended to most sections of the Sri Lankan population in 1931, including the plantation community. Sections of government and the electorate questioned the political rights of plantation labourers. They were regarded by many as a migratory population having no abiding, long-term interest in the nation of Ceylon (Sri Lanka). Despite restrictions on their numbers able to vote, plantation Tamils proved a significant minority force in the first post-independence election. By the end of this period there were 955 'registered' plantation schools.

In Chapters 1 and 7 we saw how British colonial polices in education had created a 'dual system of education' (J. E. Jayasuriya, 1979) – urban English-medium schools for the middle and upper social classes, and vernacular-medium schools for the lower classes. However, as we can see above, there was at least one other school 'system' running in parallel with these two: plantation schools, owned and managed by plantation companies.

The plantation economy was prosperous and contributed indirectly to the financing of welfare programmes introduced across the rest of the country from the 1930s. By 1938/9 there were substantial foreign exchange earnings, substantial tax revenues from imports, and government revenue surpluses from government-owned utilities, including the railways, ports and electricity on which the plantations depended (Moore, 2017). In the lead-up to independence, parts of these revenues were providing the financial means to expand educational opportunities among the majority population. Those who laboured inside the plantations would have to wait many years to catch up.

Phase 4 – 1948–77: stagnation of low-quality schooling in plantations

At independence, the economy was strong. The plantation economy generated substantial government revenues, including 90 per cent of all foreign exchange earnings. Export taxes on plantation crops were introduced in the 1950s. The welfare state, which had developed from the 1930s based around food subsidies, health and education, was an integral characteristic of the newly independent government and was 'kept going basically through taxation of plantation exports' (Kelegama, 2000, p. 1,478).

Political independence was a turning point for the plantation community. At the first post-independence election the Indian Tamil community won seven seats and joined the opposition. The new government responded with the introduction of the Indian and Pakistani Residents (Citizenship) Acts of 1948 and 1949. Large numbers of those previously enfranchised were now effectively disenfranchised. The governments of Ceylon and India agreed, in 1954 and again in 1964, to grant Indian citizenship to and repatriate certain numbers of Indian Tamils, while others would be granted Ceylonese citizenship. For the plantation Tamil community this created a situation of extreme uncertainty about their futures. Those who applied for repatriation to India would wait many years for their papers to be processed and their passage secured.

The repatriation scheme led to a decline in the percentage of Indian Tamils in the total population, from 11.7 per cent in 1946 to 9.4 per cent in 1971 and 5.6 per cent by 1981. During this period of uncertainty and repatriation, enrolment ratios (the number enrolled compared with the number of children in the relevant age group) remained stable. So, although large numbers of Indian Tamil families left the country, among those who were left behind the period may be regarded as one of educational stagnation.

In Chapter 7 the 'Free Education Act' of 1945 was described as having been of enormous significance for the enfranchised masses of the Sinhalese and also the Sri Lankan Tamil communities. It had much less significance for the plantation Tamils. Although a 1947 ordinance prescribed that the state would be responsible for establishing *new* schools in plantations, there is no evidence of the state establishing any new schools under the provisions of this ordinance. In 1948 there were 955 plantation schools. Between 1951 and 1955 just 24 schools were 'taken over' by the government. There followed some closures and amalgamations among the remaining schools owned and managed by the plantation companies.

Questions were raised in parliament about the 'takeover' of plantation schools and reports were written, but up to 1970 little action was taken. 'Takeover' became an election issue in the manifesto of the United Front in 1970, and between 1972 and 1976 a further 14 schools were taken over. Following communal attacks on plantation workers in early 1977, police shootings of workers and trade union strikes, the United Front government realised that it could not rely on the vote of the plantation community at the forthcoming election and embarked on a hasty, last-minute series take-overs of 255 schools. The anticipated votes from the plantation community did not materialise, the government changed and the plantation community's trade union-cum political party leader, Mr Thondaman, joined with the government. Mr Thondaman would become a key player in the implementation of school takeovers, especially in the securing of plantation land to build new schools.

A major obstacle to the integration of estate schools into the emerging national system of education had been the question of language. The Sinhalese who supported integration recommended that Sinhala be taught as a compulsory language, or that rural Sinhala and plantation Tamil children be taught together in the same school, with Sinhala as the medium of instruction. Plantation Tamils were keen on the integration of their schools into the national mainstream but wished that the schools be maintained as separate institutions or streams, in which children learned through the medium of Tamil – a position that has prevailed.

So, if the period 1900–48 had been a phase in which political influences were exerted by colonial interests from outside the country, and which led to an expansion of plantation schools, the period from independence in 1948 to 1977 saw political influence take its toll in the opposite direction. Plantation revenues were important for the newly independent government and were crucial for funding education and health programmes among the Ceylonese population residing outside the plantations. The revenues generated by labour inside plantations had become the means to the welfare ends of those outside. Plantation labourers' economic subsidy to the rest of the society was matched by little political compromise on the part of the national government. Plantation labour unions, the only corporate channel for the collective expression of labourers' demands, lacked substantial political power to achieve effective compromises. Declining terms of trade for plantation crops and the dawn of the nationalisation of plantation assets by socialist governments led to disinterest on the part of both planters and the newly independent government to invest in the welfare of a substantially disenfranchised minority population.

Phase 5 – 1977–2000: state takeover and widespread increases in enrolment

During the period 1977–2000 considerable progress appears to have been made in the expansion of enrolments, in the nationalisation of schools and in teacher numbers. As we saw above, country-wide literacy rates grew from 88.6 per cent to 92.5 per cent between 1986 and 2003. Rates among the plantation community grew from 68.5 per cent to 81.3 per cent. The increase in the female plantation community rate, from 58.1 per cent to 74.7 per cent, was particularly striking.

But were these increases also being perceived on the ground in changes at the school level for members of the younger generation? Did parents, teachers and plantation managers perceive educational change and progress, and if so, to what did they attribute them?

Views and voices on the ground

Interviews were undertaken with parents in the Gordon Estate (Nuwara-Eliya district), with parents and teachers in the Nayapane Estate (Kandy district), and with 19 estate superintendents and corporation officials in three plantation districts (Nuwara-Eliya, Badulla and Kalutara – see Little, 1999b, ch. 5 for more detail). Parents, teachers and plantation superintendents were unanimous in their view that there had been considerable educational progress in the period between 1977 and 1994. The following extracts from interviews conducted in 1994 provide a flavour. Describing the nature of educational progress, a father in the Nayapane Estate said:

> Now there are more teachers, new buildings, free books and uniforms, children stay at school longer, especially beyond primary school. There is an opportunity to study for longer, and we parents are more interested in our children's education.

The principal of the Nayapane school confirmed and extended this view:

> Now there are free books, free uniform and food stamps. Parents are much more interested in educating their children and they seem to have an awareness of higher education. The estate schools have been brought in under the national system of education, new

teaching methods are being used and there are comparatively better buildings, furniture and equipment.

And an estate corporation official described the change in graphic terms:

> Before nationalisation there was the *pilla kambara* (the baby's room) run by a toothless old lady. Today that is the crèche with an educated and trained crèche attendant. Then for the 6–14-year-olds there was something called the school, managed by one person – all grades managed by one person. God only knows what kind of education they received. Today there is the school with several teachers. The purpose of both the crèche and the school was to look after the child while the parents were at work. Let me illustrate the change by telling you about a ceremony I attended recently. The Deputy Minister of Education was giving out spectacles. Afterwards I turned to him and said that not one of the children looked malnourished and also that one of the GCE O-level boys who came forward for spectacles was in fact taller than the Deputy Minister himself – around five feet and six inches!

The views of parents, teachers and superintendents confirmed an overwhelming sense of progress in educational provision in estate schools between their takeover and the mid-1990s. Tangible evidence was produced by all three groups to support the description of change and the perception that estate schools were at last being integrated into the mainstream education system. Whatever the indicator – school enrolment, the average level of education reached, number of teachers, number of buildings, facilities, parental interest, the interest of education bureaucrats – the perception of progress was the same.

The perceived value of education expressed by parents for their children was also positive, and similar to opinions expressed by parents in the country at large. Education opens up the possibility of gaining employment, especially government employment. In the case of plantation parents this meant the opening up of employment opportunities for their children beyond the boundaries of the estates. Teachers, too, most of them of plantation origin, spoke of benefits in terms of new employment opportunities, especially government teaching jobs which had expanded in the plantation schools in recent years.

Plantation superintendents were quick to acknowledge the expanding employment opportunities for educated youth afforded by education. They were also quick to note that educated plantation youth would eventually face the same employment constraints as youth elsewhere in the country. In contrast with their longstanding resistance to education in an earlier period, their new-found support for educational developments can best be understood in terms of (i) the plantation companies divesting monetary responsibility for schools to the government, and (ii) a general labour surplus and growing unemployment problem. It was now in the superintendents' interests to see a proportion of young people seek their futures outside the plantation. Children's aspirations for their own futures reflected those of their parents for them. Occupational aspirations were high and mirrored the generally high level of aspiration among schoolchildren elsewhere in the country.

It would be misleading to suggest that the dynamic and positive change environment attested to by all parties was constraint-free. Teachers in particular were quick to identify a range of constraints on the functioning of their schools. Superintendents continued to exert control over land needed for school development. Teachers' housing conditions were less than satisfactory. And conditions in the classrooms were often cramped and noisy. This last point is a good example of how the solution to one constraint (low enrolment ratios) can lead to the creation of another (overcrowded classrooms).

The explanations of change, by parents, teachers and superintendents, as distinct from their descriptions, were wide-ranging and perceptive. No group was quick to claim credit for itself. Hence superintendents and teachers attributed much of the change to increased parental interest in education. Parents and teachers attributed much of the change to the takeover of the schools by the government, to government subsidies for textbooks and uniforms, and to the implementation of special development schemes for estate schools. Parents and teachers were aware that much of the economic resource for the special development schemes originated from development agencies operating outside the country. Superintendents were keen to highlight the particular effects on parents of an enlargement of contacts outside the plantation boundaries through television, travel within and beyond Sri Lanka and, indirectly, through the experiences of those who leave the plantation and then return to live with their families for short or extended periods. They also attributed part of the increase in parental interest to increased income levels. All three groups identified a decline in employment opportunities inside the estates and an opening up of opportunities outside as a reason for a greater interest in education. All three groups pointed to the key role played by the major plantation union, the CWC, especially at the national level. And all acknowledged the more recent influence of the grant of citizenship to all members of the plantation community, opening up employment opportunities in the government sector and affirming the futures of the plantation labourers within Sri Lanka. The role of leadership, and of specific leaders, was highlighted. All groups referred to the positive political role played by Mr Thondaman as leader of the CWC. Teachers mentioned the names of influential education officials at the regional and national levels.

The general impression of educational progress projected by parents, teachers and superintendents in the 1990s was one of cooperation and unity of purpose within and between these groups, supported by political leadership at the national level and educational leadership from officers within the educational bureaucracy. No longer were most teachers isolated from each other in their single-teacher schools, no longer were large numbers of parents withdrawing their children from school after just one or two years, and no longer were superintendents resisting the idea of educating plantation children.

Broader underlying drivers

Underlying these on-the-ground impacts was a range of broader economic, educational and political changes. The economic decline of tea and the growth of a labour surplus was an indirect driver of educational change. During the 1980s employers had a guaranteed labour supply, there was little need to employ children, and unemployment was beginning to surface. The plantation superintendents preferred to see children enrolled in schools rather than roaming around the estates. Moreover, the fact that the schools had been or were about to be taken over meant that plantation managers were no longer required to include the costs of running a school in their costs of running the plantations. The plantation companies and their managers could afford to adopt a more relaxed attitude to the question of educating labourers' children.

An influx of teachers of plantation community origin also created more opportunities in education. In the mid-1980s the Ministry of Education established a scheme called the Plantation Sector Teachers Programme, which encouraged young people with GCE O level qualifications to become government teachers in the plantation schools. Similar schemes followed and contributed to an increase in the number of teachers in the estate schools from 1,146 in 1984 to 4,843 in 1994.

These young people of plantation origin provided role models for planation parents and their children and raised aspirations.

Through the 1980s 'stateless' families were granted Sri Lankan citizenship and families could now begin to look forward to a future as citizens of Sri Lanka. This in turn strengthened the demand for education from plantation workers for their children and a growing number of children were gaining jobs through education.

The availability of foreign funds for development assistance (from multilateral and bilateral development agencies) was also important in the translation of plans into action on the ground. These supported, *inter alia*, the building and rehabilitation of schools and crèches, and comprehensive measures for improving the quality of teaching and learning. Independent evaluators pointed to programme characteristics that had contributed positively to the implementation process (Jayaweera, 1990; Metzger, Stenback & Athukorala, 1997; Gunasekara, 2008). These included clear programme aims, a long-term commitment on the part of the external agency to achieve those aims, regular monitoring and evaluation, and a pragmatism that enabled contentious issues to be successfully negotiated without damage to the bilateral relationship. Planned and implemented by mainstream government personnel, the programme was not a 'special project' that took teachers or officers away from their schools and normal day-to-day work. Over time, programme actors moved on to more senior roles in government programmes related to the plantation community that ensured a measure of continuity of commitment and approach (McGillivray, Carpenter & Norup, 2012). A recent account of a range of programmes in the plantation sector supported by the Swedish International Development Authority is provided by Vijayanandan (2023).

During the 1980s and through the 1990s the political and ethnic crisis intensified. The specific position of plantation Tamils within this had, I would suggest, a paradoxically positive impact on educational change inside the plantations. This part of my analysis will come as no surprise to those who understand the political tapestry of Sri Lanka. But external audiences are often puzzled by a story of progress among an ethnic minority. How and why, they ask, was increasing state and external donor intervention in plantation schools possible in a period when (i) the Sri Lankan state had been accused internationally of human rights violations against minority Tamils; (ii) there was open warfare between Tamil extremists and state security forces; and (iii) thousands of young, educated Tamils and Sinhalese died. Moreover, they ask, why would a government encourage investment in plantation people's welfare when the economic contribution of the plantations was waning?

As we saw in Chapter 1, the Tamils of Sri Lanka comprise two main groups – the Sri Lankan Tamils and the plantation Tamils. The ethnic crisis involved sections of the Sri Lankan Tamils, not the plantation Tamils. Politically, the vote of the plantation community was important in delivering the United National Party to power in 1977 and remaining in power up to the mid-1990s. It was also important to the People's Alliance in the mid-1990s. Both of the major political parties had grasped the power of the plantation minority, its political party-cum trade union the CWC, and its unrivalled leader, the late and charismatic Mr Thondaman. Rather than joining the call for a separate Tamil state, Mr Thondaman chose instead to work within the framework of government to promote the interests of the plantation Tamil community. Seizing every opportunity to wring concessions from the state, he promoted education, housing, income generation, the resolution of the citizenship issue, and the general development of the community. Political agency and political forces more generally provide a major part of the explanation for increased access to education among the plantation community between 1977 and 2000.

Phase 6 – 2000–20: continued expansion of opportunity and disparities

Increased access to education in schools inside plantations and in the surrounding areas continued to 2020. A belief that education had the potential to forge socio-economic integration with mainstream society was becoming widespread among the plantation community (Centre for Policy Analysis, 2005).

However, obstacles and bottlenecks remain. A detailed study of students between 2000 and 2006 showed that the percentage of plantation sector children qualifying to enter GCE A level classes from GCE O level is much lower than in the country as a whole, and the number of GCE A level students who achieve high enough scores to be admitted to university are also much lower proportionately (Vijayanandan, 2008).

In 2009/10 the percentage of the population aged 5+ with no schooling across the country was 4.2 per cent; in the urban sector it was 2.5 per cent; in the rural sector 4.0 per cent; and in the plantation sector 13.1 per cent. By 2019, the latest year for which figures are available, the respective figures were 3.1 per cent, 2.1 per cent, 3.0 per cent and 8.3 per cent (Department of Census and Statistics, 2021). These indicators demonstrate educational progress in all sectors over time – but the plantation sector continues to lag behind.

In 2019 the percentage of the population with GCE A levels in the urban sector was 23.1 per cent, in the rural sector 13.8 per cent and in the plantation sector 3.6 per cent (Department of Census and Statistics, 2021). Major disparities between the plantation sector and the rest of the country in pre-school provision, in the quality of general education in Grades 1–11, and in access to senior secondary and post-secondary education continue. Disparities in access to undergraduate and post-graduate education are particularly glaring.

Increased participation in education does not translate, automatically, into poverty reduction. In 2012 the Swedish International Development Authority commissioned an independent evaluation of its 50-year programme of work with Sri Lanka across the sectors of family planning, agriculture, water supply and irrigation, and education. The evaluators considered that the most successful area of the Authority's work across all sectors over fifty years of engagement lay in its long-term support for a pro-poor education programme in the plantations. However, they also pointed out that 'the effects of these gains on levels of poverty – an ultimate objective of Swedish assistance – remain uncertain, due to the complex and shifting dynamics of estate communities and prevailing conditions in the labour market' (McGillivray, Carpenter & Norup, 2012).

This observation was apposite. Between 1995 and 2016 the poverty headcount index had decreased from 28.8 per cent to 4.1 per cent across the country as whole, with decreases in all three sectors – urban, rural and plantation. But large gaps between these three sectors remained. Between 2009 and 2016, the percentage of poor households decreased from 7.0 per cent to 3.1 per cent across the country, from 3.8 per cent to 1.3 per cent in the urban sector, from 7.5 per cent to 3.3 per cent in the rural sector, and from 8.9 per cent to 6.8 per cent in the plantation sector (Central Bank of Sri Lanka, 2019). In 2019, the headcount index of monetary poverty (based on a revised 2012/13 poverty line) was 14.3 per cent country-wide, 6.0 per cent in urban areas, 15.0 per cent in rural areas and 33.8 per cent in estates (World Bank, 2021).

There has been no shortage of national development plans to reduce poverty in the plantations. In 2005, the Ministry of Estate Infrastructure and Livestock Development (previously known as the Ministry of Estate Housing Infrastructure and Community Development) prepared a three-year national development plan for poverty reduction and the social advancement of the plantation community, including projects in housing, health, gender equity and education. The time horizon of this plan was extended to 2006–2015 in line with the global initiative to achieve the Millennium Development Goals, and then to 2015–25 by the Ministry of Hill Country New Villages, Infrastructure and Community Development. The time horizon was reduced subsequently to 2016–20. As for implementation, each of these plans faced a series of financing obstacles and a lack of political will to drive them forward.

The expansion of educational opportunities has not always been smooth, as is amply illustrated by tensions in both teacher recruitment and teacher education. In 2006 a large number of teachers were recruited for plantation Tamil-medium schools in accordance with the subject-based vacancies existing in each plantation school across the plantation provinces – Central, Uva, Sabaragamuwa, Western (Kalutara district only) and North Central. The recruitment criteria included the requirement that applicants hold at least a minimum pass in GCE O level Hinduism or Christianity. Potential Muslim candidates claimed that the omission of Islam in the recruitment criteria was discriminatory. Eventually, the criteria were changed and Muslim candidates were given the opportunity to apply for teacher vacancies in Muslim Tamil-medium schools.

The Sri Pada teacher education college at Kotagala has continued to admit students for training to serve the plantation sector. In 2007, out of an enrolment of 509 students, 380 were Tamil and 129 were Sinhalese. Admission to the Tamil- and Sinhala-medium primary education courses has been restricted to the children of Tamil and Sinhala estate workers' children. Admission to the science and maths course is restricted to Tamils of Indian origin from 11 plantation districts (that is, parents do not necessarily have to be estate workers). These changes in admission criteria have increased opportunities for plantation youth to enter the teaching profession.

In 1999 Mr Savumiamoorthy Thondaman, the powerful leader of the plantation Tamil community, died. His place as leader of the CWC was taken by his grandson, Arumugan Thondaman, who had first entered parliament in 1994. Arumugan held a number of positions and aligned himself with both the United National Party and, later, the Sri Lanka Freedom Party. Before his death at the relatively early age of 55 in 2020, he was the cabinet minister for Community Empowerment and Estate Infrastructure Development, and, like his grandfather before him, was an advocate for the plantation Tamils, alongside others including the late Muthu Sivalingam (deputy minister), V. Radhakrishnan (state minister) and Palani Thigambaram (minister).

Continuing challenges into the 2020s

Just as increased educational enrolment does not necessarily translate into a reduction in relative poverty, so it does not translate into a reduction in disparities in learning outcomes between social groups. While the number enrolling in the upper grades of education is certainly increasing and will continue to do so, it is important to track the relative performance of plantation students in national assessments of learning and public exams. Across the country we know that learning achievements at the same level of schooling vary considerably between schools, locations, media of instruction and gender. At Grade 4 and Grade 8 urban schools perform better than rural schools, students in Type 1AB 'popular' schools perform better than students in all other types of school, and students in Tamil-medium schools perform worse than students in Sinhala-medium schools (NEREC, various years). The coarse-grained category of 'rural' does not, to date, distinguish rural and plantation schools. The inclusion of plantation schools as a sampling criterion would facilitate the evaluation of progress in this subsector and inform strategies for improvement.

Current challenges in education in the plantation areas remain, especially in senior secondary school education and higher education. As noted above, there are bottlenecks in progression from GCE O level to A level – and in the transition from A level to university admission. There is a need to improve the quality of education in both the primary and secondary stages of education to increase the number of students progressing to A level. There are acute shortages of maths and science teachers for the plantation schools that currently offer a science stream at A level. Added to this is the fact that few schools offer the A level science stream (either or both biological science and physical science). As at 2023, there are just four schools (including one Muslim school) in the Uva Province providing science stream courses, and all have limited facilities. In the Sabaragamuwa Province, only one plantation school provides an A level science stream. The districts of Nuwara Eliya, Badulla, Moneragala and Ratnapura are identified as disadvantaged districts and are given a 5 per cent disadvantage quota in university admission for students who qualify to enter university. However, schools in disadvantaged districts are not allowed to admit A level students from other districts as they might enjoy this 5 per cent disadvantage quota in university admission. Hence, the Nuwara-Eliya district has closed admissions for students from other districts, including disadvantaged plantation districts. Opening up more streams in science will require even more staffing and equipping

(Vijayanandan, 2023). In terms of educational administration there remains a shortage of Tamil-medium officers in the central Ministry of Education, provincial ministries, provincial departments and zonal education offices.

Summing up

The long view of progress in education among the Indian Tamil estate community of Sri Lanka suggests that the dominance of economic, political and social influence on it has varied from phase to phase. In the mid-nineteenth century, the cultural needs of plantation labourers to maintain contact with their kin in India, the religious goals of missionary organisations and philanthropic pressures on a colonial government influenced the establishment of a small number of schools offering a rudimentary education. In the early to mid-twentieth century (1900–48), politicians in Westminster and India pushed for improvements in the working conditions of labour. This, combined with political developments in Sri Lanka generally (such as the growth of political franchise and the growth of trade unionism), contributed to an expansion of education in the plantations.

The period from independence in 1948 to 1977 saw political influence take its toll in the opposite direction. The newly independent government continued to rely on plantation revenues for foreign exchange to fund education and health programmes among the population residing outside the plantations. But this subsidy to the rest of the economy and society was matched by little political compromise on the part of the national government. Declining terms of trade for plantation crops and the dawn of the nationalisation of plantation assets by socialist governments led to disinterest on the part of both planters and the newly independent government to invest in the welfare of a substantially disenfranchised minority population. The much-vaunted praise for Sri Lanka's performance in education and satisfaction of basic needs came at the expense of the educational performance of the very children whose parents provided the economic means for expansion of education in the rest of the country.

Between 1977 and 2000, several drivers coalesced to exert a major influence on educational expansion. Political drivers included the gradual resolution of the citizenship question for 'stateless' labourers. An economic driver exerted its impact indirectly: the decline of the tea industry and the growth of a labour surplus reduced the resistance of plantation managers to the education of workers' children. Government policy commitments to take over plantation schools and incorporate them into the mainstream gathered momentum in the mid- to late 1970s. A government scheme to encourage young people with GCE O level qualifications to become teachers in the plantation schools in 1984, followed by similar schemes later on, resulted in a marked increase in the number of teachers in the estate schools. The availability of foreign funds for development assistance which supported the building and rehabilitation of schools and crèches, and comprehensive measures for improving the quality of teaching and learning, along with programmes to improve housing, health, water supply and sanitation, also played their part. Undoubtedly, 'political will' was a powerful driver throughout this period, not least the individual political will of the powerful trade union and political party leader Mr Thondaman, who was able to skilfully wring concessions for the plantation Tamils from a government gripped by a civil war and other political crises.

Since the 2000s several of these drivers have continued to play their part. A succession of politicians of plantation origin have championed the cause of plantation education and the development of the community. A succession of carefully crafted national plans of action have had some impact, but changes in government and financial limitations have reduced their impact. There have been improvements in teacher supply and teacher education but still there remain structural challenges – continuing questions of quality of education at every stage of the system, acute shortages of teachers in the secondary grades, the absence of science streams in most plantation schools, shortages in science and maths teachers in the schools that do offer the science stream, and shortages of Tamil-medium officers at every level of educational administration. The expansion of education has created new challenges as students move ever further upwards through the system.

11
Late twentieth-century globalisation, education and social disparities

The interface between late twentieth-century globalisation and education

The relationship between late twentieth-century globalisation and education is reciprocal. On the one hand, education creates the knowledge and skills that are important in the increasingly globalised competition for knowledge-based goods and services, and for the capacity to benefit from the best and mitigate the worst effects of globalisation. On the other hand, globalisation influences, *inter alia*, education policy, the shape of the labour market and employment opportunities, the demand for skills, the purpose, shape and provision of educational opportunity, the role and employment of teachers, the aspirations and identities of students, and the control and affordability of education. Education is both influenced by globalisation and contributes to engagement with it (Little & Hettige, 2013).

This chapter explores the interface between late twentieth-century globalisation and education through a comparison of labour markets, skills and education, and social disparities between Sri Lanka's retreat from the global economy (from the mid-1950s to 1977), followed by reintegration with it (from 1978). I address three questions: Has the shift toward globalisation been accompanied by shifts in labour markets and skill requirements, shifts in education policy and provision, and a widening/narrowing of social disparities? Have there been shifts in the expectations of youth across the two periods? If so, are these marked by an increase or reduction in social class differences across the two periods?

The benefits of twentieth-century globalisation are uneven. Economic globalisation can have differential social group effects on poverty and income, unemployment and underemployment, security of employment, violence and conflict, and educational opportunities. A World Commission on the Social Dimension of Globalisation was established 'to respect the needs of the people as they cope with the unprecedented changes that globalisation has brought to their lives, their families and the societies in which they live' (Gunter & van der Hoevan, 2004).

There are several mechanisms through which globalisation and education interact. Some are direct. For example, education policies may be changed to reflect the new priorities, knowledge and skills necessary to navigate the challenges of globalisation. These policy changes may be influenced by national and local concerns and/or by supranational (regional and international) bodies (see for example Dale, 1999; Sebatane, 2000; Samoff, 2003).

There are also a number of indirect mechanisms through which globalisation and education interact. A first is via changes in the composition of the economy and the labour market. A second is via employer demands for new skills, new forms of education, training and certification. A third is via economic policy reforms which encourage inward foreign investment, access to foreign exchange, private sector incentives and new forms of privately financed foreign education and training arrangements. A fourth is via the aspirations of youth, who become aware of new job and skill opportunities, both at home and abroad, and demand the new types of qualifications that provide passports to them.

Retreat from nineteenth-century globalisation

The previous chapter described the development of education in Sri Lanka's plantation sector – an economic sector that had been integrated in world markets for coffee, tea and rubber from the nineteenth century. Within a history of globalisation stretching back millennia, the plantation economy represented the beginning of what historians describe as the modern period of globalisation. In Sri Lanka, this period ran from 1840, through the early years of independence, to 1956. After independence and up until 1956 the plantations were a mainstay of the economy.

In 1956 a socialist-oriented coalition led by the Sri Lanka Freedom Party came to power. This regime retreated from engagement with the global economy and introduced a 20-year regime of import substitution industrialisation (ISI). ISI was characterised by 'high tariff levels, import and exchange controls, price controls, industrial licensing, an over-arching presence of state enterprises and central planning' (Lakshman, 1997, p. 7). The terms of trade declined (that is, the price of exports fell relative to the price of imports), imports were heavily restricted, foreign-owned oil companies were nationalised in 1961, and plans to nationalise foreign-owned plantation companies were announced. The United National Party returned to power in 1965. For a brief period, the government re-liberalised imports, devalued the currency, modernised agriculture, cut food subsidies and encouraged foreign aid. The ISI policies were re-strengthened when, in 1970, the socialist United Front returned to power. By this time, however:

> A vicious circle had … been developing. The public were cushioned against the effects of Ceylon's deteriorating foreign exchange position. But this also made it harder to solve the basic economic problems – and thus to provide any real basis for meeting the public's expectations. Ceylon was increasingly often described as a welfare state, but in fact its social problems, including unemployment, were now growing, not diminishing. (ILO, 1971a, p. 15)

Between 1959 and 1969 the open unemployment rate grew from 10.5 per cent to 14 per cent. Education expenditure as a proportion of GDP during this period averaged 2.6 per cent and more young people were staying on for the middle and upper grades of schooling. Since the labour force had been growing at about 2.5 per cent per year and employment at only 2.0 per cent, unemployment was emerging on an explosive scale. Amongst those aged 20–24 with GCE O level qualifications the unemployment rate was a massive 63 per cent (ILO, 1971a). The youth insurrection of April 1971 underlined the scale of the challenge.

Sri Lanka's 20-year economic experiment with ISI was characterised by increasing state control over the economy, growing unemployment, especially among the educated, and declining economic growth. As we shall see in the following chapter, the East Asian Tiger economies (Korea, Singapore, Hong Kong and Taiwan), which had eschewed ISI in favour of export-led development, were surging ahead in terms of economic growth, income equality, education and health. Income equality was moderate over the period 1948–77, with a low-income Gini coefficient of 0.35 (that is, relatively high equality) (Central Bank of Sri Lanka, 2005). However, while a low Gini coefficient may indicate greater equality, it can also indicate a greater degree of 'shared poverty', especially when economic growth is slow and unemployment high, which was the case in 1973.

Reintegration and export-led growth post-1977

In 1977 the United National Party was returned to power on a ticket of export-led development – the strategy that had been followed by the East Asian Tigers from the 1950s. But the contrast with the Tiger economies could not have been greater. These societies had emerged from political conflicts of varying kinds in the 1950s to become 'strong states' based on national unity legitimated through shared economic growth via exports and international trade (see Chapter 12). Sri Lanka, by contrast, made the transition from a colonial to an independent state with relative calm. Subsequently, when Sri Lanka embarked on her export-led development strategy the state was becoming increasingly divided by ethno-nationalisms.

Sri Lanka's economic 'reintegration' strategies came in two waves. The first, in 1978, liberalised and deregulated the economy, promoted exports, and eliminated restrictions on imports including terminating the public monopoly on certain imports. Tariffs were reduced, export duties revised, exchange controls liberalised, most price controls were removed, and the Sri Lanka Rupee was devalued. Private sector investment, including foreign investment, was encouraged and 'export processing zones' were established. There was a substantial increase in foreign aid. The role of government as 'entrepreneur as well as a provider' was reduced and the goal of economic growth took precedence over income distribution. Food subsidies were drastically reduced (Lakshman, 1997; Abeyratne, 2000, p. 41; Jayatissa, 1993, p. 6). Education expenditure, as a proportion of total government expenditure, dropped from an average of 12 per cent between 1955 and 1975 to 6 per cent over the period 1976–86. As a proportion of GDP expenditure remained at 2.6 per cent.

A second wave of reintegration was launched in 1989 under the umbrella of 'structural adjustment'. This promoted the privatisation of semi-governmental corporations, a further rationalisation of tariffs, the partial liberalisation of the capital account and the relaxation of export processing zone restrictions. The strategy attracted major support from the International Monetary Fund and the World Bank (Salih, 2002). The targeted food stamp scheme was supplemented by targeted cash subsidy schemes – Janasavaya (from 1989) and Samurdhi (from 1994).

Socio-economic transformation

Alongside changes in the economy, changes in social stratification have also occurred. Hettige (2000) provides an overview of socio-economic transformation from the British colonial period to 2000. During the colonial period, the economy is described as a 'dual' economy (plantation and rural), with a colonial state bureaucracy and urban service industries. The main social groups were landowners, peasants, plantation workers, urban workers and public servants. Following the elections of 1956, many private businesses were nationalised, import substitution policies were introduced and social expenditure increased. Now the main social groups were state sector industrial workers, small-holders, peasants, plantation workers, white-collar workers and urban indigenous capitalists.

The elections of 1977 ushered in further transformations. The economy became more open, with direct foreign investment and free trade zones encouraged. Labour migration increased, privatisation increased, the state sector contracted to a degree and the private sector was promoted as the engine of growth. The peasant economy remained a substantial component. A 'new urban middle class' began to emerge (Hettige, 2000).

Changes in education policy

In Chapter 7, we saw how education policies on fee-free education, the medium of instruction which separated students into Sinhala and Tamil streams, and the state takeover of assisted schools were key to the independence and post-independence political projects for education. The implementation of these policies shaped the status of education and the expectations and skills of youth both before and following liberalisation. By 1981 the adult literacy rate had reached 87 per cent and there was an abundance of young people educated to GCE O level and A level seeking new employment opportunities. While this was a potential incentive for foreign investors and a growth in private sector employment, the aspirations and expectations of youth remained focussed on scarce government jobs. Through the segregation of the education system into separate language streams, the majority of Sinhala and Tamil youth, especially middle-class youth, lived their lives apart, not together. Moreover, levels of English proficiency among the population as a whole had declined and would potentially limit engagement with the English-speaking world.

Following the change in economic direction in 1977, the first change in education policy was the swift overturning of the reforms introduced five years earlier in 1972 (Chapter 4). The 1972 reforms had sought, *inter alia*, to change the curriculum to make it more 'relevant' to the world of work. They also sought to alter education qualifications in ways that disrupted their symbolic link with foreign exams, especially those conducted by British examination boards. By 1977, sections of public opinion were voicing concern about the (lack of) international currency of the new qualifications; others expressed concern over the economic and employment value of the new curriculum. Widespread dissatisfaction had contributed to the downfall of the government (see Chapters 4 and 7). Committed to a return to educational standards which were 'internationally comparable', the United National Party government re-introduced the GCE O level and A level exams.

Subsequently, few education policies were linked explicitly with global reintegration and the world of work. Indeed, few education policies, either before or after economic liberalisation, had been linked overtly with economic growth. Stirling Perera's review of education reforms between 1943 and 2005 concluded that of the few education reforms linked, in principle, with future economic performance, most were generally abandoned during implementation. By contrast, the education reforms oriented towards increasing equality of opportunity generally survived into the implementation phase, even if they often fell short of their aims (S. Perera, 2005).

Between 1977 and 1994 the general education reforms concentrated mainly on improving quality through curriculum development, teacher training and management reforms. The 1995 reforms included two reforms more related to economic performance and to the changing technological environment of the twenty-first century. The first was an intensification of the teaching of English, which was intended to enable young people to find employment, proceed easily into tertiary education and benefit from information available through multi-media systems (NEC, 1997). The second was the development of technical and practical skills throughout the system. A revised primary curriculum was to be based on activity learning, activity rooms were to be introduced for Grades 6–9, science and technology O level was to be revised, and a technology stream was to be introduced at GCE A level. As we will see in Chapter 13, the role of English in education had been relegated from the 1950s, but attitudes to its place in education began to change, slowly, following liberalisation.

The education policies which anticipated global reintegration were those emerging from the technical education and vocational training (TEVT) sector. TEVT policies were designed explicitly to meet the additional demand for skilled, semi-skilled and unskilled labour in the expanded secondary and tertiary sectors of the economy, through both public- and private sector training institutions. The call for more and improved TEVT continued through the 1990s and on into the new century. Concluding its 2005 review of myriad policies, the World Bank noted that progress of the TEVT sector in implementing the proposals introduced since the mid-1990s was modest (World Bank, 2005).

Although education policies have made relatively little overt reference to the knowledge and skills needs of economic reintegration, this does not mean that globalisation had no impact on educational provision. As we will see below, there has been change, but these changes have generally been mediated by changes in economic rather than education policy. The chain of influence of globalisation on education has been indirect.

Changes in the labour market

Following 1977, structural changes in the economy, in particular the emergence of a vibrant private sector, led to changes in the labour market. Unemployment and educated unemployment were both major political issues at the 1977 general election, as the general rate stood at about 20 per cent of the labour force at the time. Post-liberalisation labour force employment rates increased for both males and females. However, unemployment rates continued to be high among those with higher education qualifications (GCE A level) and higher for females than for males.

Following liberalisation there was a significant expansion of livelihood opportunities outside the state sector. Paradoxically, and contrary to the expected outcomes of liberalisation, state sector employment remained significant, though in absolute numbers it began to account for a smaller share of total employment than the private sector.

In 1973, prior to liberalisation, agricultural employment accounted for 54.5 per cent of the employed population. By 1996/7 it had declined to 37.7 per cent. Manufacturing, which had represented an insignificant share of employment in the 1960s, became an increasingly significant area of employment. Service sector employment increased even more rapidly than the manufacturing sector. Casual employment also increased, from 21 per cent in 1973 to 30 per cent in 1996/7. Self-employment also increased. Foreign employment in the Middle East, which had already started to increase from 1975, prior to liberalisation, became even more important. Where, in 1975, just 1,039 people migrated abroad for employment, in 2007 this figure was 217,306, of whom 53 per cent were men and 47 per cent women (Central Bank of Sri Lanka, 2008). Foreign employment was important not only for those who found employment but also for the wages and salaries they remitted to their families. Such remittances were also important for the foreign exchange they generated for the government.

There were significant reductions in unemployment especially among the unskilled and semi-skilled categories. Free trade zone factories created new employment opportunities for women, while young men found semi-skilled employment in the hospitality trade, security services, retail trade and personal services. Employment rates among those with GCE A level qualifications remained low, although the rate increased among university graduates. Much of this increase was accounted for by successive government employment schemes that created jobs for graduates and contained protests and revolt. The liberal economy appeared to have generated opportunities for the low-skilled but not the high-skilled (Little & Hettige, 2013).

Overall, this implied that following liberalisation young job seekers were more likely to be employed than their peers in the immediate pre-liberalisation years, more likely to be employed in manufacturing and services than in agriculture, more likely to be employed as 'casual employees' than regular employees, and more likely to find employment in the private than in the public sector. Those with GCE O level or higher qualifications were more likely to be unemployed than those with less than GCE O level. (This was also the case in the pre-liberalisation period.) And, like the youth before them, it was the youngest job seekers, those aged 15–19 years, who were most likely to be unemployed.

Changes in skill requirements

In 2002, 17 employers from the government and private sector were interviewed about the qualifications they required for various skill areas and on skill needs and shortages (Little & Hettige, 2013). Skill requirements for middle- and higher-level positions in both the government and private sector were English language skills and writing, and information technology. Since high-level positions in joint-venture companies were often filled by foreigners, English language skills were also being sought for clerical positions.

In contrast with the private sector, recruitment practices among government employers are bound by rules and regulations and qualification and experience criteria. Vacancies are advertised in the daily and weekend press and in the government gazette, in all three national languages. GCE O and A level qualifications are normally required for clerical-level vacancies and a degree is required for executive-level positions. The number of applicants for government positions is always extremely high.

Private sector employers said they would always look inside the company first and resort to external recruitment and advertising only if there was no one suitable. Most private sector employers recruited those with GCE O and A level for clerical-level positions (including clerk, secretary, storekeeper, personnel assistant), while a degree in a relevant field was required for some higher positions. In fields such as accountancy, audit, administration and management, some employers recruited those with foreign professional qualifications such as CIMA and CIM in preference to those with degrees. These employers were of the view that most graduates of Sri Lankan universities did not have the required skills, knowledge and attitudes suitable for the private sector. In addition to the qualifications, private sector employers placed great stress on work experience, leadership qualities, communication skills, English language proficiency and personality traits. These requirements are similar to those we found among private sector employers even before liberalisation (Deraniyagala, Dore & Little, 1978; see Chapters 5 and 6).

Both government and private sector employers spoke of skill shortages, especially for middle- and upper-level positions. A government employer said in 2002:

> At the moment there are some vacancies in the accounting, auditing and administration sections. We advertised all these positions in the paper yet cannot find qualified persons. Most of the professionally qualified people have more opportunities in the private sector with lucrative salaries and other benefits which the government sector does not offer. And we cannot fill up these vacancies with lower qualified persons because of government rules and regulations.

Government sector employers spoke of senior officers leaving their high-level positions for more lucrative opportunities in the private sector.

Periodically there were reverse trends. In 2005, for example, there was the extensively reported finding of large numbers of graduates who had been recruited to the private sector seeking government sector employment through a new government graduate placement scheme. The status, prestige and security of government employment relative to private sector employment appeared to be preferable to these young people. The work environment in the public sector was also preferable, being perceived as more relaxed compared to that of the private sector where productivity considerations exerted considerable pressure on employees. Non-governmental organisations also suffered from this exodus when they faced difficulties retaining the graduates they had recruited for casual jobs.

Changes in education and training provision

I noted above that, following liberalisation, the economic structure shifted away from agriculture and towards manufacturing and services. Employment rates and women's participation in the labour force increased. Private sector employment, self-employment and casual employment increased. Foreign employment opportunities, especially in the Middle East, increased, though the majority of these opportunities were for unskilled labour.

Among the new opportunities within Sri Lanka, many were low skill, mainly in the garment manufacturing sector (Kelegama & Wijayasiri, 2004). Employers, both foreign and local, recruited young people, especially women from rural areas with a basic secondary education, and trained them on the job. New courses and qualifications in garment manufacturing also appeared. The service sector expanded greatly, with demand for skills in information and communications technology (ICT), English, and management and finance (Little & Hettige, 2013).

Growth in demand for these skills is evidenced by a plethora of new types of skill training provision, public and private, Sri Lankan and foreign. Public provision in basic crafts and trades and higher technical skills expanded alongside opportunities in ICT and English in the general education system (Little & Hettige, 2013).

A marketplace survey of advertisements conducted at eight points in time over the period 1965–2000 indicated the growing importance of skills training opportunities in management, communications, computing, tourism, sales and exports (Little & Evans, 2005). In 1965 the majority of advertised courses were those leading to GCE O level qualifications

(36.6 per cent). Between 1975 and 1985 the majority of courses on offer led to GCE A level qualifications. By 1990 the overwhelming preference was for higher education courses and degrees. Over time there was a gradual shift in supply of and demand for ever higher levels of general education qualification courses, a trend that has long been apparent in the Sri Lankan education system and employment market. This is referred to as 'qualification escalation' (Deraniyagala, Dore & Little, 1978).

Courses in languages peaked in 1970 but declined over the next three decades. However, these courses remained significant even in 2000, indicating the value placed on language skills. General higher education's pre-eminent position in 1995 was eclipsed in 2000 by courses and qualifications in the ICT sector on the one hand (24.6 per cent), and courses in 'clothing technology' on the other (23.1 per cent). Management and accountancy courses accounted for a further 10.1 per cent of courses.

Changes in the types of courses offered at university and secondary levels were apparent. In the period prior to liberalisation only 6 per cent of university students had graduated from the commerce and management stream; by 2001 this had grown to 27 per cent. This growth in commerce and management was also apparent in the number and percentage of graduates who followed Sri Lankan university external degree courses. The universities created more opportunities for students to undertake courses in the medium of English, rather than Sinhala or Tamil, especially in medicine, engineering, law and science. In 1984 there were just 250 students following Colombo University's courses in English, taught by just 10 members of staff. By 2001 this number had increased to 3,799 students and 82 staff. New in-house and external degree university courses in ICT were established. At the secondary school level, there was also a shift in Grades 12 and 13 towards the commerce stream. Between 1975 and 2006 the number of students enrolled in all GCE A level courses grew by 368 per cent. The percentage of students enrolled in the commerce stream grew from 12.2 per cent to 27.4 per cent. The percentage following arts subjects dropped slightly, but the largest percentage drop (from 36.3 per cent to 22.8 per cent) was in science (Little & Hettige, 2013).

In the post-secondary, non-university government sector there was evidence of growth in craft apprenticeships in the auto trade, building, hotel and catering, electrical, electronics, and textiles and garment industries. At the undergraduate level there was growth in engineering apprenticeships. The English language began to play a growing role, in both schools and universities, both as a subject and as a medium of instruction. There was growth in courses offering skills in English, ICT and management and accountancy at post-secondary, non-university private sector institutions.

Changes in public and private educational provision

While the involvement of private providers increased following liberalisation, this does not appear to have been at the expense of the public sector. Public provision in the general education system expanded at many levels – from basic crafts and trades to higher technical skills – and in the provision of opportunities in ICT and English.

Private educational provision expanded very slowly at the primary and general secondary education levels and more rapidly at the tertiary level. Following nationalisation of the denominational schools in 1961, a small number of 'aided and non-aided' private schools remained and were registered with the Ministry of Education. Their numbers have remained fairly constant over time, estimated most recently to be 90. Before liberalisation there was just one 'international school': the Overseas Children's School was established in 1958 and catered for the children of expatriate workers and foreign diplomats. The number of 'international schools' has mushroomed since the early 1980s. These schools generally use English as the medium of instruction, follow non-Sri Lankan curricula and enter students for foreign exams (such as the Cambridge Overseas Syndicate and EdExcel). Unlike the private schools referred to above, they are not registered with the Ministry of Education; they are registered instead with bodies established under post-liberalisation legislation (such as the Board of Investment Act, the Companies Act or the Business Names Ordinance). In 2019, 143,123 students were estimated to be enrolled in 397 private international schools. Together with the 136,230 students enrolled in government-registered private schools, the total number of students in private education was 278,291. Of the total 4.42 million students in all types of school (government, special, pirivena (monastic college), private registered, international), only 6.3 per cent were enrolled in private education (NEC, 2022; Ministry of Education, 2020). This is a very small percentage when compared with other countries in the region.

In Chapter 6 I presented evidence on the growth in 'private tuition' up to 1990 following liberalisation. Private tuition provision, ranging from one-to-one tuition to small groups to large groups held in lecture halls, has continued to grow since then. A 2002 study of youth in one urban and eight rural areas showed that 67 per cent of all youth were attending or had attended private tuition. This compared with just 10 per cent of their mothers and 10 per cent of their fathers, most of whom would have been enrolled in school before the period of economic liberalisation. Private tuition participation rates in rural areas varied, with the lowest in the Muslim village of Nachchaduwa (39 per cent), the tea estate of Park (56 per cent) and the rubber estate of Vogan (41 per cent) (Little & Hettige, 2013). A recent ethnographic study of Sinhala-Buddhist girls attending a national school in Kandy underlines the personal and social, as well as the educational, reasons for opting for private tuition. Tuition offers a space to socialise outside of school, to meet boy 'pals', to develop their ideas about their 'self', and to play out some of their personal aspirations (Batatota, 2020).

Many students following courses in the new skill areas consistent with the liberalised economy enrolled in small and large institutions in the post-secondary, non-degree public and private sectors. The public sector offered craft and technical courses and certificates at vocational training centres, technical colleges and advanced colleges. The number enrolled for trade apprenticeships between 1977 and 1997 increased elevenfold, notably in the areas of the auto trade, building, hotels and catering, electrical, electronics and telecommunications, fitting and fabrication, textile and garments, woodworking, and clerical industries. Between 1997 and 2011 the number enrolled for apprenticeships in ICT grew from 592 to 4,037. Private sector provision grew in both the technical and vocational education skill areas as well as in professional level courses in English, ICT and management/accountancy. Student numbers for English language courses have expanded greatly. In one popular private sector college, Aquinas College, enrollees on the Diploma in English course had grown from 2,160 in 1984 to 8,267 in 2011 (Little & Hettige, 2013).

At the higher education level there was growth in fee-levying private higher education institutions. Sri Lanka's university system is almost entirely funded by the state, and it has not expanded in line with social or skill demands. While some have argued, unsuccessfully, for a greater involvement of the private sector in university provision, others have resisted this on the grounds that private universities will charge high fees, cater to the rich, and lead to a polarisation between poorly endowed state universities and well-equipped private universities and between students whose parents can and cannot pay fees. Responses to the demand included an increase in the intake of the National Colleges of Education which offer pre-service teacher training to those with high GCE A level grades, and the establishment of private sector institutions offering post-secondary education at diploma and certificate level, but not degree level. A third response was an increase in the number of students seeking study opportunities abroad, often via local recruitment consultants and agencies. A fourth was the establishment of franchise and access arrangements with overseas universities which enabled students to follow all or part of their degree in Sri Lanka (Little & Hettige, 2013).

Internationalisation of education and training

The economic liberalisation policies of 1977 and 1989 facilitated foreign private provision through two main measures. Currency restrictions were lifted, and Sri Lankans could convert Sri Lankan Rupees into foreign exchange. Those with the financial means could enrol in fee-charging courses offered by foreign universities, colleges and schools. Secondly, and as part of the general move towards foreign direct investment and the establishment of foreign partnerships, foreign education companies and universities could find a local partner and register as a company so that they could operate in Sri Lanka. Some registered through the Board of Investment and the majority through the Sri Lankan registrar of companies.

Much of the expanded private provision is oriented towards foreign qualifications outside the quality assurance purview of the government. Foreign education and qualification suppliers established new arrangements for provision in myriad ways. Some provided only the exam syllabus, the exam itself and the qualification, with course delivery by Sri Lankan education institutions and businesses. Others provided both the course and the qualification through franchises, access pathways, correspondence materials, online tutoring and assessment (Little & Evans, 2005). Following liberalisation, students had more opportunities to enrol in education institutions in Australia, Canada, India, Ireland, Japan, Malaysia, Russia, Singapore, the UK and the US.

The proliferation of so-called international schools in Colombo and other urban centres has added a new dimension to school education in Sri Lanka. These schools are diverse in terms of size, physical infrastructure and the socio-economic background of pupils, and cater to more affluent segments of society, including the country's elite. In contrast to the government schools which prepare students for the Sri Lankan GCE O and A levels, the international schools prepare students for 'international' or foreign exams, in particular those linked with English examination boards. This trend needs to be seen in perspective. The vast majority of school students attend government schools and sit the exams of the Sri Lankan Department of Examinations.

The number of foreign-controlled courses and qualifications has increased since liberalisation. Foreign qualifications created opportunities for migration to other countries and were attractive for youth living and working in the unsettled situation that prevailed in the country from the early 1980s onwards. Private sector firms and international agencies based in Sri Lanka readily recruited youth who possessed international qualifications. But this is not to say that foreign qualifications predominate or have displaced domestic qualifications. The number of domestic-controlled courses and qualifications has also increased markedly since liberalisation.

The internationalisation of education in Sri Lanka over the last three decades ran alongside structural changes in the economy, and the significant changes in the labour market are highly relevant. Sri Lanka's pre-liberalisation, state-dominated economy gave way to a more diversified economic structure driven largely by private capital, both local and foreign. The private sector grew in importance, particularly in the export-oriented industrial sector and the large-service sector. But, contrary to the expectations of those who advocated liberalisation, the absolute number of employment opportunities in the medium- and large-scale government and semi-government sector continued to grow, even as their percentage share of the total declined. In all sectors and types of employment the percentage share of government employment declined from 22 per cent to 13.8 per cent between 1991 and 2007. The relative significance of the state sector declined after economic liberalisation, due largely to the privatisation of public enterprises including state-owned commercial plantations. Increasing integration of the local economy with the global economy facilitated the expansion of economic activities such as financial services, travel, exports and imports, and shipping. The relaxation of rules governing foreign exchange transactions and international travel enabled Sri Lankans to travel abroad for business, education, work and leisure.

Socio-economic disparities

Not all social groups have benefited equally from the growth in new employment opportunities. Liberalisation was accompanied by employment shifts towards female, low-skilled and urban labour (Lakshman, 1997). It reduced rural female opportunities for off-farm employment. While it increased opportunities for young females in low-skill jobs in 'export processing zones', their work was confined largely to repetitive assembly-line jobs with few opportunities for upward occupational mobility and job security, and questionable working and living conditions. It was accompanied by a marked increase in foreign employment, mostly in the Middle East, and also an increase in sexual abuse, violence and family disruption (Jayaweera, 1994, 2001, 2003).

Despite the continued expansion of the education system, socio-economic disparities persist in educational opportunities and attainment in schools. Between 1971 and 2008 the number of government schools increased by 12.5 per cent, and the number of students enrolled in them increased by almost 40 per cent. The number of teachers increased by 236 per cent. Student-teacher ratios decreased from 30:1 to 18:1, while the adult literacy rate increased from 79 per cent to 93 per cent. From the 1980s birth rates began to decline, resulting in a decline in total enrolments in government schools from 4.3 million in 1991 to 4.0 million in 2001 and 3.9 million in 2008. Over the same period, the student-teacher ratio improved from 24:1 in 1991 to 18:1 in 2008 (Aturupane, 2009). The proportion of the population with no schooling declined from 22.9 per cent in 1973 to 8.6 per cent in 1996/1997 and to 3.1 per cent by 2019. However, an upward trend in the general education level of the population has been apparent since the 1880s and it would be misleading to attempt to trace this directly to the effects of twentieth-century economic globalisation. Traditionally, the Sri Lankan population accords high value to formal education, and, throughout the twentieth century, formal education was perceived as the main channel for social mobility by rural and urban students alike. In the ten years prior to liberalisation and after, the majority of educational opportunities remained in the public sector.

While the children of poor and non-poor households participate equally in Grade 1–5 education and almost equally in lower secondary, social class discrepancies arise in Grades 10–13 and at the tertiary level (World Bank, 2005). In the early 1990s, mothers' education and parents' income had a strong influence on length of schooling achieved (Ranasinghe & Hartog, 2002). Household and child characteristics also influence performance at specific grade levels. At the child and household level, educated parents, better nutrition, high daily attendance, enrolment in private tutoring classes, exercise books, electric lighting, and children's books at home have an impact on learning achievement at Grade 4 (Aturupane, Glewwe & Wisniewski, 2011).

Learning outcomes are also influenced by the school type attended (Type 1AB students perform best), location (urban students perform best), language medium of instruction (Sinhala-medium students perform better than Tamil-medium students) and gender (female students outperform male students). Access to higher education remains skewed towards richer groups. And while females outnumber males in GCE A level courses and in university education, they experience higher levels of unemployment. Education opportunities have increased and diversified in terms of available courses and public/private provision for all social groups, but social disparities in access to them persist.

Economic liberalisation has had differential impacts on opportunities and aspirations for education and qualifications. Higher-income groups, especially those based in the Western Province and around Colombo, are able to access opportunities that lead to foreign qualifications and high paid jobs, both at home and abroad (Little, 2007). The shift towards English-medium education is occurring more rapidly in schools and universities in Colombo and other parts of the Western Province than elsewhere in the country.

Better-off families spend more on education, both absolutely and as a proportion of monthly income, than worse-off families. Fees charged by private and international schools and by private sector post-secondary providers vary considerably, but it is reasonable to assume that where access is rationed by price, the better off can afford to pay the highest fees. Access to foreign qualifications is heavily skewed by income group. The most expensive route is 'study abroad'. Only the richest can afford to send their children abroad for an entire course of study. More young people follow part of the study in Sri Lanka and move to a foreign country for a final year. This is a cheaper option. Still others follow the entire course in Sri Lanka and gain a foreign qualification. This is cheaper still. Others, in the technical and vocational field, can gain dual certification from a government ministry and foreign qualification provider at relatively low cost. Students in urban areas, especially the Colombo district, have the greatest level of access to training for the skills demanded by the new economy and through the medium of ICT.

Schools in the Colombo district achieve the highest levels of English language proficiency and rural districts such as Moneragala and Nuwara-Eliya the lowest. The shift towards instruction through the medium of English is occurring more rapidly in schools in the Western Province (which includes the city of Colombo). Opportunities for learning about and through ICT are greatest for students in the Western Province. There are also higher percentages of students following courses in the science and commerce streams in the Western Province. The increasing demand for these courses is fuelled by a growing concentration of wealth in urban areas. While poverty has declined across the country, the distribution of household income has worsened. The pre-eminent position of the Colombo metropolitan region in this respect has been greatly reinforced following economic liberalisation in 1977.

Developments since 1977, particularly in post-secondary education, point to a steady diversification of education institutions towards private provision. Misgivings about the rise of private education among political groups representing rural disadvantaged communities have not halted the growth of private institutions, particularly in urban centres which largely cater to the more affluent segments of society. The private sector has benefited from the expansion of post-secondary private education as this provides the skills and attributes that private firms demand. At the general education level there has been growth, from a tiny base of enrolments in both registered private schools and international schools. The registered private schools are regulated by the Ministry of Education and are owned by Sri Lankan interests; the international schools are regulated by private companies and are owned by a mix of foreign and Sri Lankan interests. However, legal and regulatory frameworks have contained the growth of private and international schools and, at just 6.3 per cent (2019 figures), the percentage of students enrolled in them remains modest. Participation in private tuition, in which students enrol alongside participation in full-day schooling, has grown extensively. New synergies and complementarities between the public and private sectors of education have emerged.

As regards employment, particularly at higher levels, there is a close correspondence between the education sector and the employment sector. Foreign employment and security sector employment have provided new opportunities for those with lower qualifications from lower-income backgrounds. But correspondence is different from employability. High unemployment rates persist at the upper end of the education system. Attempts to establish public–private partnerships to train public university graduates through internship arrangements with private firms showed considerable promise initially but eventually failed, forcing the government to revert to the politically expedient method of mass recruitment of unemployed university graduates into government service.

New job opportunities emerged in industrial production, service industries and personal services. Many of the private sector employers demanded new skills. In response to this demand, training institutions providing such skills, particularly in urban centres, have grown. At the same time, the public education system did not respond rapidly to new market pressures. As a result, graduates from the publicly funded education system in general could not easily find their way into the newly emergent segments of the employment market. Even though new employers created new employment opportunities, many school leavers and university graduates remained unemployed for extended periods. Young people with educational qualifications continued to wait for white-collar employment in government institutions.

Youth expectations and social class

So far in this chapter I have outlined educational changes that resulted from economic liberalisation and globalisation, including the growth of the 'education business', the growth of qualifications, foreign and domestic, the growth of private tuition, the growth of cross-border student mobility and the growth of foreign educational provision, especially at the post-secondary level. In the jobs sphere, unemployment declined, foreign employment opportunities expanded, the expansion of private enterprise increased earnings differentials and government sector jobs declined. This meant that the avenue for employment which the educated, but poor, rural youth had come to expect narrowed (Hettige, 1992). Young people were now exposed to the competition of the global economy where before they had sheltered within a nation-state that had protected them from competition. The liberalised economy was pushing 'nationally oriented youth from the centre stage to the margins of society' (Hettige, 1998, p. 100) and drawing them into political resistance movements. What impact, if any, did the effects of these changes have on the aspirations of youth for education and jobs?

Studies of youth aspirations and expectations conducted before 1977 had demonstrated a preference among youth for government jobs and a gradual rise in aspirations and expectations over time (for example ILO, 1971a; Deraniyagala, Dore & Little, 1978) and a rise in the aspirations of girls for a university education (Jayaweera & Rupasinghe, 2007). In the period following economic liberalisation, youth aspirations and expectations remained high. A 1998 study of 951 students in GCE O level classes found that the majority of girls (60.3 per cent) and boys (54.6 per cent) aspired to a university degree (Jayaweera & Rupasinghe, 2007). Chandra Gunawardene (2002) reported that 70 per cent of youth (aged 15–29) wished to continue their education beyond their current levels. There was a continuing 'mismatch' between job expectations and the jobs available in the economy (C. Gunawardene, 2002; Jayaweera & Sanmugam, 2002). A majority of schoolchildren in 2004 preferred governments jobs (Hettige, Mayer & Salih, 2004). Higher-level private sector jobs were sought after but these often placed a premium on English and favoured the urban English-speaking middle classes (Hettige, 1998; C. Gunawardene, 2002).

So, has there been a shift in the expectations of youth across the pre-liberalisation and post-liberalisation periods? If so, are these marked by an increase or reduction in social class differences? These questions were explored through evidence collected by Siri Hettige and his team and analysed by Ricardo Sabates and myself.

With a general expansion of educational opportunity and shifts in occupational structure and opportunities from agriculture towards manufacturing and services, we predicted that today's youth would display higher levels of educational and occupational expectations than their fathers and mothers when they were educated in the pre-liberalisation period. We also predicted that social class background would have an effect on the level of expectations in both periods (Little & Sabates, 2008; Little & Hettige, 2013). With the growth of domestic and foreign private sector opportunities in education following liberalisation, especially at the post-secondary level, and the growth of the private corporate employment sector since liberalisation, we predicted that the gap between the social classes would widen. Youth from higher social classes – with greater access to the upper grades of senior secondary schools and national schools, the ability to pay for supplementary education, a greater proficiency in English, greater social capital and more connections in the private sector of employment – would, we predicted, be able to take advantage of these new opportunities more readily than youth from lower social classes. This would be reflected in the levels of occupational expectation. The gaps between the expectations of youth from the higher and lower social classes today would, we predicted, be greater than that between youth of higher and lower social classes in the previous generation.

In sum we predicted that there would be (i) cross-generational shifts in expectation levels; (ii) social class effects on expectations; and (iii) cross-generational shifts in social class effects.

Cross-generational shifts in expectations
1. The educational and occupational expectations of youth will be higher than those of their mothers and fathers (when young).

Social class effects on expectations
2. The level of educational and occupational expectations of youth of a higher social class will be higher than those of youth of a lower social class.
3. The educational and occupational expectations of mothers and fathers (when young) of a higher social class will be higher than those of mothers and fathers (when young) of a lower social class.

Cross-generational shifts in social class effects
4. The social class effects on expectations of today's youth will be stronger than the social class effects on expectations among mothers and fathers when young. In other words, the social class gap in expectations (predicted in Hypotheses 2 and 3 above) will widen over time.

These propositions were explored through evidence from a household survey conducted between 2001 and 2003 among youth aged 15–29 and their parents. The sample consisted of 455 youth, 385 mothers and 299 fathers (further differentiated by age, gender, ethnicity (Sinhala, Tamil, Moor) and location (urban, rural, plantation)). For a full description of the sampling criteria and characteristics, the selection and characteristics of communities, measures of social class and of educational and livelihood expectations of youth and their parents, and statistical tests employed see Little and Sabates (2008).

The cross-generational shift in educational and occupational expectations was confirmed. While youth expected to achieve a mean level between the GCE O level (11 years) and GCE A level (13 years), both fathers and mothers reported mean levels between primary and GCE O level. This is consistent with the structure of education in the 1960s and 1970s when a selection exam at Grade 8 (representing nine years of education, including a first 'kindergarten' year) marked the end of the open-access span of education, after which there was selection to subsequent stages of education. It was only between 1972 and 1977 that the open-access span was extended to 10 years of free, non-selective basic education, and from 1977, to 11 years. Youth reported mean occupational expectations at around five on a nine-point scale compared with their parents of around two. This reflects the general upward movement in the structure of the economy, from the elementary occupations of agriculture to the semi-skilled and skilled occupations of manufacturing and services.

The effects of social class on expectations showed different patterns for youth, fathers and mothers. Middle-class youth reported higher levels of educational and occupational expectations than low-class youth, irrespective of whether the sample of youth was paired with fathers or mothers. This confirmed our prediction. Middle-class fathers and mothers reported educational expectations (when young) that were higher than those reported by low-class mothers and fathers. This also confirmed our prediction. However, there were no social class differences in the occupational expectations reported by middle- and low-class fathers and mothers. Comparisons between the lower-middle and low class showed no differences in either educational or occupational expectations for youth, fathers or mothers.

This last set of findings influenced the testing of the final proposition that predicted an increasing social class gap in educational and occupational expectations *over time*. When the middle class were compared with the low class, our prediction was confirmed for occupational expectations, irrespective of whether youth were compared with fathers or mothers. In all other cases, the gaps were positive, indicating a widening rather than a narrowing of the gap, but none attained statistical significance. The finding of a widening of the gap in occupational expectations confirmed our prediction, but a detailed understanding of how and why this arose deserves further attention in the future. It is possible that the gap was due to the pull of the expanding private corporate sector and that middle-class youth were able to find jobs in this sector more easily than the lower-middle and lower classes. The reasons for this are likely to be because of qualifications sought by employers, proficiency in English and social networks. It is also possible that the gap would have been even wider if the expanding private sector had not simultaneously afforded new opportunities for low-skill jobs in manufacturing, especially for females from rural areas.

The empirical investigation focussed on levels of expectation. We did not examine the sectors of employment expected (whether public, private, corporate private or small-scale private). Nor did we explore the type of education institution (whether public or private) expected. These deserve investigation in the future. Further investigation is also required of young people's gender and ethnicity, perceptions of the criteria required for the occupations they expect, their proficiency in English, their ability to pay for specific types of educational qualification, and their social networks for recruitment to jobs in the different sectors of employment.

Conclusion

Changes in the structure of the economy and the labour market following liberalisation have led to shifts in skill demands, especially in ICT, English language and commerce. Changes in economic policy have opened up opportunities for private sector education and training providers in Sri Lanka and for youth to seek education and training opportunities abroad. With the exception of the technical education and vocational training area, education policy was not influenced substantially by the new skill demands, nor did it promote a liberalisation of private education and training provision. Education policy reform continued to reflect longstanding principles of equality of educational opportunity, resulting in a gradual expansion of the education system at all levels. Nonetheless, the greater access of richer groups to the best government schools, the best private tuition, the best training opportunities in the post-secondary private sector, and access to education and training abroad indicates the differential impact of liberal economic policies on richer and poorer classes. While youth expectations for education and livelihoods have increased in line with an underlying growth in educational opportunity, the effects of social class on those expectations appear to have increased. It may be concluded that in this current phase of Sri Lanka's globalisation – that of reintegration – there has been a de facto impact on educational provision, and a differential impact on social groups. Increased opportunity has been accompanied by continued socio-economic divisions. These impacts have largely occurred in spite of, not because of, education policy reforms.

12
Globalisation, education and skills: comparing Sri Lanka with elsewhere

Introduction

Almost a century ago Sri Lanka's export-led economy was strong enough to give her 'a standard of living well ahead of that in the rest of South Asia and most of South-East Asia, with the possible exception of Singapore and parts of the Federated Malay states' (K. M. de Silva, 1981, pp. 376–7). As noted in Chapter 1, Sri Lankans often recall that when Lee Kwan Yew visited Sri Lanka shortly after independence in 1948, he averred that the country provided a development model for emulation by Singapore. By the late 1970s and early 1980s the international development community was celebrating Sri Lanka's human development record in the face of rather modest levels of economic growth (Isenman, 1980; Sen, 1981; Kelegama, 2000). Indeed, Sri Lanka's strong human development record has been regarded by mainstream economists as something of a puzzle, since it is often believed that improvements in human development follow, rather than precede, economic growth and rising incomes (Lakshman, 1997).

Compared with some of her Asian neighbours, Sri Lanka's record on human development has been strong, but her record on economic growth has not (Kelegama, 2000). By 1990 the economic performance of South-East Asian economies, notably Hong Kong, Singapore, South Korea and Taiwan, achieved high economic growth rates of around 7 per cent per annum between the early 1950s and the 1990s, far outstripping Sri Lanka's average growth. Internationally, these economies came to be known as the Four Asian Tigers, or the Four Little Dragons. They were to be joined through the 1990s by Thailand, Malaysia and Indonesia, who, along with the Tigers, were considered to be High Performing Asian

Economies and part of the 'East Asian miracle' (World Bank, 1993). Unprecedented levels of economic growth were accompanied by low levels of inequality, declining poverty and a rise in living standards. All were considered to be countries that had globalised 'successfully'.

This chapter analyses the common economic, political and educational characteristics of these successful globalisers and compares the Sri Lankan experience along the same characteristics. The final part of the chapter considers the concept of 'successful globalisation'. Based on the Sri Lankan story, I suggest that the concept of successful globalisation needs to incorporate the dimension of peace and – based on the contemporary agenda for sustainable development – ideas of sustainable growth, sustainable equality and sustainable peace.

Common political and economic characteristics of successful Asian countries

A number of writers have outlined the common political and economic characteristics of Asian countries which have experienced high rates of economic growth (for example World Bank, 1993; Castells, 2000; Green, 2007). While key differences between them are acknowledged, the focus here is on common characteristics.

The World Bank's analysis of the East Asian miracle (1993) focussed on the High Performing Asian Economies (HPAEs) during the period 1960–85 and the positive relationship between high economic growth rates, redistribution of income and human welfare, measured in terms of life expectancy, poverty reduction and improvements in education. In this analysis the HPAEs included the four Asian Tigers and Japan and the newly industrialising countries of Indonesia, Malaysia and Thailand. While the World Bank authors cautioned against the identification of a single model of development, they identified common threads in the development strategies adopted.

Common characteristics included sustained economic growth over extended periods between 1960 and 1990, and investment rates exceeding 20 per cent of GDP over the same period, increasing equalisation of income distribution and high and rising endowments of human capital due to universal primary and secondary education. Economic policy interventions took many forms – targeting and subsidising credit to selected industries, protecting domestic import substitutes for a time, developing export marketing institutions, imposing mandatory savings schemes, and ensuring flexible labour markets. Although agriculture's contribution to the overall economy declined, the sector nonetheless experienced rapid growth and productivity. Education policies contributed to more equitable income distribution, helped by an initial condition of low inequality which set up a virtuous circle in which education expansion reinforced low inequality and a rapid demographic transition. Between 1960–70 and 1980–90 population growth rates declined sharply in Hong Kong and Korea, though less so in Singapore (the World Bank report does not cite figures from Taiwan).

Politically, the leaders of each country sought legitimacy by promising 'shared growth' – as the economy expanded, all social groups were promised benefits. Effective systems of public administration were established, albeit within authoritarian and paternalistic systems. While authoritarian, the leaders of the HPAEs were 'willing to grant a voiced and genuine authority to a technocratic elite and key leaders in the private sector' (World Bank, 1993, p. 13).

Focussing on a more limited group of HPAE countries – the 'Asian Tiger' countries of Hong Kong, Singapore, South Korea and Taiwan – Castells (2000) identified five common characteristics. The first was the outward orientation of the economy, specifically the export of manufactured goods to the US market. Although import substitution industrialisation (ISI) policies protected the initial industrial base in both South Korea and Taiwan, significant economic growth came only after exports increased. The second common characteristic was the absence of a rural landowning class. There were no landowning classes in Hong Kong and Singapore. In South Korea and Taiwan, US-inspired land reforms were implemented during the 1950s and many former landowners became major industrialists. The third was the availability of educated, productive, cheap, disciplined and re-skillable labour. Initially this was enforced by repression but in later stages improved living standards quelled potential rebellion and promoted social integration. The fourth was the ability of economies to adapt to the informational paradigm and the changing pattern of the global economy, via technological upgrading, market expansion and economic diversification. Research and development for the high technology sectors of the new global economy were matched by growth in science and technology education.

The fifth – and, for Castells, the most fundamental common characteristic – was the *politics of survival*, the development of a nationalist project with a strong cultural/political identity and the emergence of the 'developmental state'. The term 'developmental state' was introduced by Johnson (1982) in his analysis of industrialisation in Japan and South Korea (see also Johnson, 1999). A 'developmental state' exerts autonomous, political power, and state intervention that 'governs the market' (Wade, 1990). Each of the Asian Tigers discussed by Castells faced external threats and crises and a need for political survival. Singapore experienced race riots in 1964, prior to her expulsion from the Federation of Malaysia. In Taiwan, the Kuomintang, defeated by the Communists in mainland China, imposed martial law on the majority, impoverished Taiwanese. The Korean war led, in 1953, to a divided North and South Korea. The Chinese revolution in 1949 led to Hong Kong's loss of role as an entrepôt for Chinese trade. Meanwhile, successive waves of political and economic migrants sought refuge from mainland China. Lee Kwan Yew's People's Action Party in Singapore, Park Chung Hee's regime in South Korea, the Kuomintang in Taiwan and the colonial state in Hong Kong shaped their states 'around the developmental principle of legitimacy' (Castells, 2000, p. 285).

The role played by political crises in the initial phase of the Asian Tigers' economic and political trajectory featured very strongly in Castell's analysis but much less so in that of the World Bank. The role of state-led macro-economic planning, otherwise known as the 'developmental state', featured in both accounts.

A review of literature by Green (2007) identifies a number of additional reasons that might explain this period of economic history in the Asian region. Geopolitical factors include strategic position, peninsular states with long seaboards, centres of entrepôt trade, and an absence of natural resources which meant that countries were less likely to pursue economic development through agriculture or extractive industries. Historical timing may also have been a key factor – for example, the industrial take-off of the Asian Tigers in the 1960s coincided with a buoyant world economy. The cultural impact of Confucianism may have been a key factor in the economic trajectory of Confucian societies, but does not explain the economic rise of Malaysia, Indonesia and Thailand.

Common and uncommon education and training characteristics of successful Asian countries

A number of authors have identified similarities and differences in the education and training strategies followed by the successful Asian countries (Morris & Sweeting, 1995; Tilak, 2002; Green et al., 2007).

Similarities include the role of education in serving (i) the maintenance of strong states, (ii) rapid economic and technological advancement, and (iii) the creation of a distinctive sense of national solidarity and identity. In all countries high levels of basic education and literacy for males and females were available to the population before initial economic take-off and the subsequent expansion of secondary and then tertiary education. In Taiwan, South Korea and Singapore, school curricula have been used to promote a powerful sense of social cohesion, patriotism and national identity. All the school systems have been equitable, open, competitive and largely meritocratic, offering all sections of society the prospect of upward social mobility. Additional characteristics include the development of communication skills that facilitate international economic transactions.

Alongside these common characteristics are others that have been uncommon. These include variations in sources of funding for education; the responsiveness of the state in educational provision, in particular tertiary education; the extent of state control in education; the relative emphases on general and technical education; and the nature and role of school curricula.

Sri Lanka compared

So how does Sri Lanka's history following independence match any or all of the above characteristics?

Economic strategies
Manufactured exports

Unlike each of the countries discussed above, Sri Lanka's economy has long been export oriented. As we saw in Chapter 10, the British colonial government promoted an export-oriented economy based on agricultural commodities, which, at independence in 1948, left Sri Lanka as one of the wealthiest countries in Asia. After 1956 the development strategy changed substantially and became inwardly rather than outwardly oriented. This orientation would last until 1965, when a cautious liberalisation strategy was introduced, which was replaced again with an inward orientation between 1970 and 1977. In 1977 economic liberalisation policies designed to attract inward foreign investment and promote exports were introduced (Snodgrass, 1998). Coincidentally, 1960–80 was the period when the Asian Tigers began their drive towards manufactured exports. The shift to manufacturing and away from agriculture was evident in Sri Lanka only in the 1990s.

Transition to higher value-added activity

Sri Lanka was slow to move to the higher added value sector of manufactured exports. The traditional reliance on substantial revenues from agricultural exports had led to complacency on the part of post-independence governments (Kelegama, 2000).

With a degree of prescience, the International Labour Organization report of 1971 noted that 'on average the medium-sized countries of Asia (with between 5 and 30 million inhabitants) doubled the value of their exports in this period, and most of them more than trebled their exports of manufactures'. Sri Lanka sat back while others in the region embarked on manufacture-led export drives.

Availability of foreign exchange

From the 1950s, Sri Lanka experienced serious foreign exchange problems (Kelegama, 2000). In 1971 the ILO Employment Mission noted that, with the exception of Burma, Sri Lanka was the only Asian country earning less foreign exchange in 1968 than in 1958 (ILO, 1971a, p. 14 n. 1). The foreign exchange crisis of the 1960s and 1970s arose, Kelegama suggested, because 'the exigencies of electoral politics bound the country to welfare-oriented inward-looking policies' (Kelegama, 2000, p. 1,477). In the 1960s and early 1970s Sri Lanka eschewed support from the West and oriented herself instead to the non-aligned movement. But since liberalisation in 1977, inward foreign investment and aid from the West has been considerable. And substantial financial support from the World Bank and others enabled her to fund income support programmes for those living in poverty as well as improvements in both access to and the quality of education.

Investment and savings rates

The World Bank (1993) identifies high and rising rates of savings and investment as a key element in the growth strategy. For all HPAEs, the average (unweighted) mean of investment as a percentage of GDP was 19.5 per cent in 1965 and 35 per cent by 1990. The comparable rates of savings were 17 per cent to 30 per cent.

Historically, Sri Lanka's investment and savings rates were much lower. The investment rate increased from 12.5 per cent of GDP to 22.2 per cent between 1965 and 1990 (Central Bank of Sri Lanka, 2005) while the savings rate increased from a low of 4.5 per cent of GDP in 1959 to 14.7 per cent in 1978 and 14.3 per cent by 1990 (Atapattu, 1997).

By 2005 the Central Bank noted that levels of investment and domestic saving (25 per cent and 15.9 per cent in 2004) remained inadequate to raise growth and the standard of living substantially and that 'a concerted effort must be made to raise savings and investment at least up to 30 per cent of GDP in the near future' (Central Bank of Sri Lanka, 2005, p. 1).

Rural landowners and rural productivity

During the colonial period in Sri Lanka, landlessness was a major issue. After independence, the Paddy Lands Act of 1958 strengthened the hands of tenants and reduced the power of landowners. Radical and controversial land reforms in 1972 and 1975 were implemented in the run-up to liberalisation in 1977. Lands owned by foreign plantation companies were nationalised, large areas of land owned by Sri Lankan nationals were broken up, and parcels of land were redistributed to the rural landless. After nationalisation, productivity in the plantation sector declined and in 1992 a process of privatisation of the management companies commenced with the objective of improving productivity. Productivity in the main non-plantation crop, paddy, increased in the first six years after economic liberalisation but dropped back thereafter (Nakamura, Ratnayake & Senanayake, 1997).

Income inequality

As described in Chapters 1 and 4, Sri Lanka's development strategy had, since the 1930s, combined the objectives of social justice/equity and economic growth. A series of welfare measures established an enduring political commitment to social justice, pursued to greater or lesser degrees by all political parties. The greatest equality of income was apparent in 1973 (Dunham & Jayasuriya, 1998) but this was also a time when economic growth rates were at their lowest. This is sometimes referred to by Sri Lankans as a period of 'shared poverty', rather than 'shared wealth'. Figures quoted in the 2004 Human Development Report (United Nations, 2004) indicated a Gini coefficient of 0.34 – that is, low inequality; Korea at 0.31 was similar. Singapore and Hong Kong displayed higher levels of inequality (0.43 and 0.44 respectively).

Technology

By 2005 Sri Lanka's uptake of information technology had been slow. In 1999, the estimated number of internet users was 65,000 (out of a population of c. 18 million), rising to 200,000 by 2002. Personal computer use grew from 5.8/1,000 in 1999 to 13.2/1,000 in 2002. Telephone use expanded from an estimated 51 fixed lines and mobile telephones per 1,000 in 1999 to 95.8/1,000 by 2002 (World Bank, 2004).

Demographic transition

As countries develop economically and invest in education, especially female education, birth rates fall and lead to decreases in the rate of population growth. Hong Kong, the Republic of Korea and Singapore experienced sharp falls in birth rates between 1965 and 1980.

With a birth rate of 33.1/1,000 in the early 1960s, Sri Lanka was already well on the way to low population growth. The percentage change between 1965 and 1980 was -12.7, and between 1980 and 1990 -30.7 per cent (Central Bank of Sri Lanka, 2003). These resulted in an annual average growth of population of 2.4 per cent over 1960–70 and 1.48 per cent over 1980–90, a demographic transition almost identical with that of Hong Kong over the same period, and lower and faster between 1980 and 1990 than both Korea and Singapore.

Politics and the state
Initial political conditions

Castells (2000) had suggested that the political conditions facing the Asian Tigers in the initial stage of transition to high economic growth were unstable. For the purpose of the Sri Lankan comparison, it is difficult to know where to identify the 'initial stage' of transition to high growth – whether at independence in 1948 when growth was high (GDP growth rate in 1951 was 6.2 per cent), or in 1977 when economic policies changed and growth rates began to increase again. Either way, the idea that unstable political conditions accompanied the initial stages of growth, either in 1948 or 1977, does not hold.

Unlike India, Sri Lanka did not experience a bloody nationalist campaign against the British colonial regime. The nationalist movement was mild in comparison and the dawn of independence in Sri Lanka was a by-product of Indian independence. While governments swung regularly from right to left, the period from independence to 1977 was not characterised by major conflict or tension. Ethnic conflict leading to civil war characterised the period since 1977, coinciding with the period of economic liberalisation. The origins of the conflict may be traced to the pre-independence period, but it was from 1956, when the Sri Lanka

Freedom Party imposed Sinhala as the official language of government administration in place of English, that the politics of the independent state began to deteriorate, and the minority Tamils perceived gradual and systematic discrimination. Notwithstanding the 'invitation' by the Sri Lankan government to the Indian army to 'intervene' in the civil war in 1988, the conflict in Sri Lanka was internal. Unlike the cases of the Asian Tigers there was no significant external threat to Sri Lanka's sovereignty.

Coincidence of the period of the civil war with economic liberalisation is not causation. The simmering mutual grievances of the majority Sinhalese and minority Tamils did not cause the introduction of liberalisation policies, nor did the liberalisation policies cause the conflict, though they may subsequently have fuelled it.

The developmental state

Education and skills policies have been created and delivered by the 'developmental states' discussed above. Education has generally supported rapid economic growth through encouraging foreign investment, enabling technology transfer, promoting productivity and progressively upgrading the skills base as required for each successive economic shift to higher value-added areas of manufacturing and service industry. Education has also played a generally positive role in promoting relatively cohesive national identities and in enhancing state capacity by producing a cadre of well-educated and, on the whole, extremely competent civil servants who are the ones that have planned and implemented the industrial policies and all the complex mechanisms that have been used to implement successful strategic trading policies (Green, 2007).

Political and technical elites

Most analyses of the rise of the Asian countries have played down the authoritarian character of some of these states. Emphasis has been placed more on the willingness of the political elite to grant authority for action and policy implementation to technocratic elites and the private sector. Sri Lanka compares unfavourably on this point, particularly in relation to the preparedness of political elites to delegate authority to technical elites and policy implementation to the civil service. In 1963, the long-established Ceylon Civil Service, created during the colonial period, was replaced by the Ceylon Administrative Service – an event described by some as 'the beginning of the present plight of public administration in Sri Lanka' (Somasundram, 1998 quoted in Ranugge, 2000). In 1972, the constitution of the newly designated republic transferred all powers in connection to public administration appointments, promotions and transfers to the Cabinet of Ministers, thus wresting control away from the Public Service Commission.

The long-held tradition of respecting the seniority and merits of senior public servants when making appointments to higher positions was displaced by the appointment of outsiders, some of whom had neither the skills nor the experience to hold such positions. The only qualifications they had were their connections with the political party in power or their relationships to the ministers (Ranugge, 2000, p. 53).

Education strategies and characteristics

The educational record of Sri Lanka resonates in most ways with those of the successful Asian countries. High levels of basic education and literacy have been a feature of Sri Lanka's population for several decades. Access to education for both males and females has also been actively encouraged. The expansion of secondary education followed the expansion of primary education, but this arose more in response to social demand than in response to the manpower needs of the economy. The expansion of tertiary education followed the expansion of secondary education, but expansion was slow, largely because the economy expanded slowly (and much slower than rates observed in the four Asian Tigers), employment opportunities for graduates were limited and the costs of tertiary education in a system that discouraged private initiative was a heavy burden on the public purse. Education expenditure has been equitable, especially at the basic and junior secondary levels of education, with inequities appearing from Grade 10 onwards. Comparable data from the Asian Tigers is not available to gauge the comparative levels of inequity. Given the level of public expenditure devoted to education historically and currently, Sri Lanka has achieved remarkable levels of expansion. Estimates of qualitative improvement are more difficult to gauge. The numbers of young people achieving qualifications at Grade 11 (GCE O level) and Grade 13 (GCE A level) increased dramatically over the years. Pass rates at GCE O level increased from 22 per cent in 1993 to 37 per cent by 2002 (World Bank, 2005). Pass rates at A level have changed little, though the number of students admitted to the exam has increased steadily. The relative equity of the system has gone hand in hand with a continued dominant perception that the education system is open, competitive and largely meritocratic. Indeed, it has been argued that in the face of civil war over the past twenty years the education system has been relied upon to offer hope for economic opportunity and social mobility (Little, 1997).

In contrast to Korea and Taiwan, Sri Lanka has not invested heavily in technical and vocational education, nor, in contrast to all four Asian Tigers, has she permitted the establishment of new private schools since the early 1960s. University enrolments have been severely capped and the few attempts made by Sri Lankans to establish degree-awarding tertiary institutions have been resisted fiercely by those concerned with social equity and the widening of the gap between rich and poor. In general, expansion of education has not followed manpower planning principles, though it could be argued that the restriction on tertiary-level enrolment was one way of doing this, given the low level of average skill demand in the economy. The unplanned growth of secondary education and the slow growth of the economy have led to high levels of youth unemployment, frustration and breakdowns in social cohesion. The extremely slow growth of the Sri Lankan economy in general and of the private sector in particular during the 1960–77 period led to unemployment, frustration and, to a degree, civil war. The slow growth of non-government employment reinforced the expectations of youth that their educational achievements qualified them for government jobs which, under liberalisation, were set to decline as a proportion of all employment.

Perhaps most significant has been the failure of the Sri Lankan education system over the past half-century to build a sense of national identity, solidarity and cohesion. Since the relegation of English as a medium of instruction, the separation of students by ethnicity and language and the failure of link language programmes, education has not forged national values that transcend ethnicity. In a sense, this comparison is invalid since the population composition of three of the Asian Tiger countries is homogeneous. In terms of the ethnic composition of the population, Singapore provides the better comparator for Sri Lanka's population. In Singapore the dominant population group – the Chinese – comprise the same proportion of the population (77 per cent) as the Sinhalese in Sri Lanka, with Malays and Tamils comprising 14 per cent and 8 per cent respectively. In contrast to Sri Lanka and its two official languages, Singapore has four official languages – mandarin Chinese, Malay, Tamil and English. English is treated as a common, neutral language and is the main language of government, education and commerce. When Singapore became an independent republic in 1965, education was seen as a means of forging a common national identity and of establishing harmony between races in a multinational society.

By contrast, following the 1956 elections in Sri Lanka, education was seen as a means of promoting social mobility and the economic opportunity of, especially, the majority social group. English was replaced by Sinhala as the language of public administration.

Summing up

At independence in 1948, Sri Lanka's economic performance and her educational achievements were ahead of most other countries in Asia. The countries that came to be known as the Asian Tigers were early integrators into the global economy, from the 1960s. Through policies of export-led growth they sustained high rates of economic growth between 1960 and 1990, enjoyed high rates of investment, and equalised incomes and access to welfare services. By contrast, and as we saw in Chapter 11, Sri Lanka adopted the economic policies of ISI between 1956 and 1977 (with a period of cautious liberalisation 1965–70) and while income distribution measures remained fairly stable, economic growth declined. During the 1960s investment was low and shortages of foreign exchange became acute.

Sri Lanka's pursuit of ISI economic policies from 1956–65 and 1970–7 reduced her ability to provide economic growth and increase her strong lead in human and social development. The volume and type of employment generated during this period was incommensurate with the volume and aspirations of qualified youth seeking employment. The economy was dominated by an inefficient public sector and by a privately run plantation sector that did not require skilled labour. Concurrently, the Asian Tigers eschewed ISI strategies despite the recommendations of the international finance community and introduced export-oriented policies based on manufacturing. Historically low levels of savings and investment and shortages of foreign exchange meant that Sri Lanka's early lead in economic performance stalled. Despite this, Sri Lanka has stood out in relation to the Asian Tigers – and to developing and industrialising countries as a whole – in terms of her enduring commitment to education and income equity.

The common features of the developmental strategies followed by the successful Asian countries are complex and multi-dimensional. They embrace the economic, technological and political as well as the educational. Policy 'cherries' should be picked with caution, and only in the spirit of identifying options worthy of further discussion rather than tried and tested recipes for implementation. Sri Lanka followed similar education policies to those followed by the Asian Tigers and experienced similar demographic transitions. It was in the spheres of economic policy and the state, in the context of an ethnically diverse population, that Sri Lanka diverged.

While it is easy to point to the failure of the education system to promote social cohesion through curriculum and language, it is also salutary to ask how much difference education could have made, per se, within a political system which sowed the seeds of ethnic conflict from the mid-1950s and within a society that had not seen a meaningful end to more than twenty years of civil war.

Politically, each of the Asian Tigers had experienced internal and external conflicts of varying kinds in the 1950s prior to embarking on export-led growth. These conflicts gave rise to 'developmental' states which sought to gain and maintain their legitimacy through growth and its redistribution. In Sri Lanka, by contrast, a prolonged period of political conflict coincided with the period of reintegration and the adoption of export-led growth. But this was not the only reason. Sri Lanka's economic performance had been stymied by poor governance, a lack of understanding of the policies, institutions and reforms required for globalisation, and pervasive politicisation.

In the education sphere Sri Lanka has performed well in comparison with both our early and later integrating countries, especially in primary and secondary enrolment rates and in gender equity at these levels. But school leavers, unable to find jobs commensurate with their expectations and their qualifications, experienced unemployment that created stress and conflict. Youth insurrections among the Sinhalese in the early 1970s and again in the late 1980s, combined with a 30-year ethnic civil war between Tamils and Sinhalese, inhibited economic growth and social development.

Sri Lanka has performed less well in post-secondary, technical and vocational and higher education. She has also done much less well than our comparators in creating common national identities among her youth. Medium of instruction policies, challenges faced in the implementation of programmes for the teaching of English and of the second national language (Tamil or Sinhala), and classes and schools segregated by ethnicity have undermined the ability of the education system to socialise youth identities that transcend the particularistic identities of ethnicity, religion and region. Just when the Asian Tigers were embarking on their drive towards greater integration into the global economy, Sri Lanka was nationalising her education system, relegating English as a medium of instruction and segregating all the country's youth, particularly middle-class youth, into separate media of instruction. Competition for scarce jobs and even scarcer university places was played out between groups that had strong ethnic but weak national identities.

Notwithstanding the contribution of education polices to the story of Asia's rise, economic policies have probably played a more important role. Sri Lanka's poor economic record of growth can be attributed to, *inter alia*, a wholesale import substitution policy resulting in low economic growth and extremely high unemployment among the educated, leading to political unrest. Foreign exchange and domestic savings and investment were low. The public sector was inefficient, and policy implementation in all sectors, including education, became increasingly politicised.

The relative absence of political conflict in the transition to independence in Sri Lanka may also have been significant. In Japan, post-war reconstruction following crushing defeat in the Second World War was important in the rise of the 'developmental state'. In Korea, Taiwan, Singapore and Hong Kong, the economic project of growth arose out of political conflicts of various kinds and the need for political survival. In Sri Lanka, the transition to independence was relatively peaceful and the post-independence government continued pre-independence economic policies through the 1950s and 1960s. Internal conflicts would arise later. The end of the civil war in 2009 presented Sri Lanka with an opportunity to use education as one means of building peace and reconciliation – one that is still not being exploited to the full.

Conclusion

I conclude with the suggestion that any discussion of globalisation needs to proceed hand in hand with a discussion of 'successful globalisation', of peace and of sustainable development. This arises from this chapter's discussion of Sri Lanka's attempts to implement economic globalisation strategies during a period of civil war. It also arises from a review of other studies in the Asia region, case studies on China, India, Kenya and Sri Lanka and a discussion of 'successful globalisation' (Green et al., 2007; Little & Green, 2009). In that review we suggested, initially, that a country might be judged to have been a 'successful globaliser' if it demonstrated income equality, equitable access to social services including education, and rising living standards for all alongside moderate to high economic growth. However, and drawing from our analysis of the Sri Lanka case, we concluded, *inter alia*, that any notion of successful development must include the dimension of 'peace'. Here was a country that in the early 1980s was hailed by many in the international community as having offered a model for development. Sri Lanka showed how, through choices made by policy elites, welfare provision could be achieved even when economic growth was low. And here was a country that, following the introduction of export-oriented liberalisation strategies in 1977, had grown moderately and had more or less maintained levels of income equality that, historically, had been considered 'good' in relation to countries with similar levels of wealth. On these criteria Sri Lanka might have been considered to be a moderately successful globaliser. Yet, as we have seen above and in several earlier chapters, Sri Lanka had been in the grip of civil war starting in the late 1970s – a war that did not end until 2009. How could we possibly assert that a country is a 'moderately successful' globaliser when thousands of young people have died and many more have been injured and maimed for life in the competition for economic, political and social resources (Little, 2007)?

The second reason for including 'peace' as a constituent of the definition of 'successful globalisation' was that social cohesion and national unity appeared to us to be critical elements in the 1970–80s story of East Asia's economic growth on the one hand and growing equality on the other. Although, as we saw above, conflict had characterised the early transitions to growth in some of the East Asian countries, for most of the past forty years these countries have enjoyed relative peace. We judged, as would most, that peace was a more desirable developmental outcome than conflict, war and societal breakdown and needed to be emphasised, not only as a characteristic of a successful model of development in the past, but also as a goal for development in the future.

A third reason to focus on peace stemmed from our analyses of the role of education in promoting social cohesion as envisaged by the literature emerging from the Decade of Education for Sustainable Development (Chapter 2). While much of that literature regards education curricula as a source of peace, human security and social justice, our case studies highlighted how the systemic structure of education can act as a source of both cohesion and conflict. In the Kenya case we judged that post-independence programmes to use a common medium of instruction for ethnically mixed student bodies contributed positively to ethnic tolerance in the early post-independence years (Oketch, 2007). In the Sri Lanka case, by contrast, the post-independence policy of two media of instruction (Sinhala and Tamil) promoted a stratification of education which ensured that Sinhalese and Tamil middle-class youth were socialised separately. Peace education, population education, environment education, life skills education and education for conflict resolution have all had their place in the Sri Lanka curriculum – but these may have been less powerful influencers and drivers of knowledge, values and ways of thinking than the hidden or implicit curriculum of daily, informal experiences of learning together in the same schools and building trust across ethnic groups. The Ministry of Education recently set out proposals to establish 20 well-resourced trilingual schools. Assuming that these are implemented, a systematic evaluation of them will provide invaluable insights into the potential of the hidden curriculum and the structure of education to influence young people's values.

However, none of the research cited above explored the related ideas of *sustainable* globalisation, *sustainable* development, *sustainable* growth, *sustainable* equality or *sustainable* peace. In Chapter 2 I described the entry of the concept of 'sustainable development' into the international development policy discourse when the Brundtland Commission used it to connote a development strategy that 'meets the needs of the present without compromising the ability of future generations to meet their own needs' (World Commission on Education and Development, 1987, p. 43). The more complete definition of sustainable development contained the key concepts of (i) 'need', in particular the essential needs of the world's poor, to which overriding priority should be given, and (ii) limitations imposed by technology and social organisation on the environment's ability to meet present and future needs (World Commission on Education and Development, 1987, p. 43). The Rio agenda in 1992 introduced the idea of 'sustainable consumption' and called for people in rich countries to change their consumption patterns so that sustainable development might be achieved (United Nations, 1992). At this same conference the Sri Lankan physicist, engineer and economist Mohan Munasinghe introduced the *Sustainomics* framework with its three spheres of activity – environment (including water and waste), society (including employment, human rights, gender equity, peace and human security) and economy (including poverty reduction, corporate responsibility and accountability) (Chapter 2). Sri Lanka's recent strategy for sustainable development makes a number of recommendations to this end (M. Munasinghe, 2019a).

Future research on globalisation and education needs to be framed within the ideas of sustainable growth, sustainable equality and sustainable peace. The concluding part of this book, to which I now turn, discusses sustainable development, education and learning.

Part V
Sustainable development and learning

Preface to Part V

In 2015 the United Nations advanced 17 global goals for Sustainable Development (United Nations, 2015a, b). These replaced the previous eight Millennium Development Goals (United Nations, 2000). Mohan Munasinghe's early conceptualisation of the need to harmonise the three spheres of development – the environmental, the social and the economic – influenced the sustainable development discourse around the world (M. Munasinghe, 1992, 2019b), a vision that is also fundamental to *Sustainable Sri Lanka: 2030 vision and strategic plan* (M. Munasinghe, 2019a).

The Sustainable Development Goal on Education, often referred to as SDG4, aims to 'Ensure inclusive and equitable quality education and promote lifelong learning opportunities for all'. SDG4 has 10 targets, seven of which are presented as primary targets and three as 'enabling' targets. Alongside these 10 targets are no fewer than 43 indicators and hundreds of sub-indicators. In contrast to the earlier MDGs, the SDGs are characterised by a proliferation of targets and indicators on education, information and social media surrounding their determination and monitoring of progress towards them, and on agencies with interests in them, especially national and international non-governmental organisations and international private sector interests (Lewin, 2015b).

Education has synergistic potential and can be expected to contribute to sustainable development both directly and indirectly – directly through improvements in learning outcomes, and indirectly by contributing to other SDGs, such as reducing poverty and hunger, and contributing to health and well-being, gender equality and climate action (Little, 2008b; Waage et al., 2008).

SDG4 Target 4.1 reads: 'by 2030, ensure that all girls and boys complete free, equitable and quality primary and secondary education leading to relevant and effective learning outcomes'. This target has attracted enormous interest among international agencies and research groups with expertise in measuring learning outcomes. Since 2004 the University of Colombo's National Education Research and Evaluation Centre has conducted surveys of learning outcomes in maths, first language and English in Grades 4 and 8. Over 20 years the findings have been very consistent – students in Type 1AB schools perform better than students in other types of school; Sinhala-medium students perform better than Tamil-medium students; girls perform better than boys; students enrolled in urban schools perform better than those in rural schools; and students in the Western, Southern and North Western Provinces perform better than those in the Northern and Eastern Provinces and those containing relatively large proportions of plantation schools.

Internationally, there has been an overwhelming emphasis on measuring learning outcomes and international comparisons of such measures. There has been less emphasis on the relevance and effectiveness of these learning outcomes in specific countries. Measurement in itself, whether employed in a national or international survey, does not lead to better teaching, better learning and improved learning outcomes. As we have already seen in several chapters, learning outcome assessment practices have not exactly been lacking in the Sri Lankan context, since at least the nineteenth century.

Sri Lanka's *Sustainable Sri Lanka: 2030 vision and strategic plan* sets out myriad recommendations on education spanning early childhood, general, technical, vocational and higher education. In general education the main recommendation is for a 'better articulated outcome-based curriculum integrating and embedding skills (cognitive as well as socio-emotional) focussed on the underlying objective that all children should be successful learners, confident individuals, responsible citizens and effective contributors' (M. Munasinghe, 2019a, p. 11). Here is an example of a conceptual framing of an international idea – sustainable development – generated by a Sri Lankan, educated in Sri Lanka and abroad – and then applied to the Sri Lankan context in order to formulate a sustainable development policy for Sri Lanka.

The achievement of SDG4 is not simply about target-setting and indicators. It is fundamentally about the content (skills and values) of learning, the methods through which learners learn, both individually and in groups, and the ways learning is assessed. Crucially it is about nurturing the motivation of learners to *sustain* their learning, their personal development and their contribution to wider society *throughout* life. Sustainable development is as much about sustainable learning and personal development as it is about environment, society and economy.

In Chapter 4 different types of personal motivations for learning were explored. The chapters in this final part of the book focus on learners and the means by which the motivation for learning is nurtured. Chapters 13, 14 and 15 address teaching methods, student grouping practices and the assessment of learning respectively.

Chapter 13 addresses the methods employed by teachers of English. As we noted in earlier chapters, the role of English in the general education curriculum has seen swings of democratic politics since the time of independence. In the current era, English has come to be regarded less as the language of colonial oppression and more as an international language of importance within an internationalised economy and society. This chapter presents the results of a large-scale survey in the Central Province of Sri Lanka. It evaluates equality of opportunity for the learning of English, and variations in the teaching methods employed on the ground.

Chapter 14 also examines 'on-the-ground' classroom practices. Its focus is on the ways in which teachers organise groups of students for teaching. Worldwide, ability grouping and streaming between and within schools is widespread, with mixed results in the literature in terms of learning outcomes of low and high achievers. Ability grouping is a practice little used in Sri Lanka. In recent years the multi-level approach, which recognises the diversity of student learning achievement levels found in every classroom, has been adopted in some areas. In this approach students are grouped within their classes according to their learning progress. Chapter 14 evaluates the relevance and effectiveness of this multi-level approach in four provinces (Northern, Eastern, Central and Uva) and draws comparisons with similar programmes found elsewhere in the world.

Chapter 15 focusses on the methods through which learning is assessed. It contrasts the summative assessments of national and international surveys with the difficult-to-capture, but arguably more important, formative assessments that teachers and students can employ in their everyday teaching and learning practices. Through reflections on a series of on-the-ground examples of classroom-based formative assessment drawn from across Sri Lanka's provinces, I suggest that 'learning for all' might be enhanced by a greater investment of time and expertise in a wider understanding and practice of formative assessment. I suggest that the concept of sustainable development be broadened to include the ideas of sustainable personal development and sustainable learning.

Finally, in Chapter 16 I review what I have learned from development and education in Sri Lanka. I revisit the status of some of Sri Lanka's exceptionalisms, I revisit development and education concepts in the light of the Sri Lankan experience, and I comment on recent proposals for education reform in Sri Lanka. The book's overriding messages are: (i) that education's undoubted potential to contribute to development is realised when accompanied by reforms across myriad development sectors including employment, health, law and finance, and in the institutions of political, economic and social life; (ii) the course of education and development needs to be understood first and foremost in a country's own terms; and (iii) learning needs to be placed at the heart of education policy and situated within broader conceptions of the purpose, values and means of development.

13
The teaching of English in the early twenty-first century

Introduction

Within the South Asia region, proficiency in the English language is valued for its role in educational opportunity, employability and social mobility, both within and across borders, global business and international dialogue. English does not always sit easily within those education systems where the country's official languages do not include English and where it has been associated historically with the British colonial period and educating an elite. Its place within the systems of the Asia region has fluctuated over time and 'a number of challenges remain around ensuring equitable, high-quality provision of English language teaching and learning for all who want or need it' (Indrarathne & McCulloch, 2022). The place of English within Sri Lanka and the issues that have surrounded its role as a medium of instruction and as a subject of study since the 1950s are no exception (K. Nesiah, 1945; M. E. S. Perera, 2000; Punchi, 2001; L. Perera, Wijetunge & Balasooriya, 2004; Attygalle, 2009; Hayes, 2010; C. P. Davis, 2020; National Education Commission, 2022).

This chapter examines opportunities for learning English, and teaching and learning methods employed in the teaching of English, in 60 schools. These are framed by English language teaching policy in the past and the present, and current curriculum and pedagogy guidelines. The empirical study reported does not explore the impact of these opportunities and teaching and learning methods on learning outcomes. It addresses three main questions: How much time is allocated for the teaching of English in schools and classrooms and how much time is delivered and lost? In what types of student-centred and teacher-centred lesson activities do English teachers engage and how frequently? What factors are associated with the amount of time spent on student-centred learning?

English language teaching policy past and present

Chapter 4 described the radical policy education reforms introduced in the immediate run-up to and in the years following independence. These included the gradual introduction of mother-tongue education in primary and secondary education in all government schools from 1945 and the nationalisation of denominational schools in 1961. English-medium classes in Grade 1 of government schools ceased in 1971 and by 1983 all students in government schools were taught in either the Sinhala or the Tamil medium from Grades 1 to 13. English was a core subject of study but was not a medium of instruction for other subjects. In the early years of the post-independence period the relegation of English as a medium of instruction reflected its status as a symbol of colonial oppression and the nationalist ideals of self-reliant development.

In later years, especially in the years following economic liberalisation, proficiency in English has been emphasised for its utility as an international language, in information and communications technology, and in international business and communications (National Committee on Education, 2009; Little & Hettige, 2013; Wettewa, 2015; National Education Commission, 2022). Following the 1997 education reforms, oral English was introduced from Grade 1, with formal teaching from Grade 3. English became a core subject at GCE O level, and a general English paper was introduced at GCE A level. By 2004 the Ministry of Education recognised that the standard of English teaching had declined, but the 'increased pace of globalisation and the advances made in IT' meant that English was now an 'international language' and the standard of teaching English had to be improved (Ministry of Human Resource Development, Education and Cultural Affairs, 2004). During the 2000s English as a medium of instruction was re-introduced cautiously in science, arts and commerce streams through the Bilingual Education Programme. Information technology and computing courses, as well as computing hardware, were introduced.

Variations in learning outcomes

In the 2012 national assessment of English language performance amongst Grade 4 students, variations in performance were identified by province, school type, school location, medium of instruction and student gender. Western, Southern, Sabaragamuwa and North Western Provinces achieved mean scores above the national mean, while Central, North Central, Northern, Eastern and Uva Provinces achieved below the national mean. Students in Type 1AB, urban and Sinhala-medium schools performed better than those in Type 1C, 2 and 3, rural and Tamil-medium schools. Girls performed better than boys. This pattern of performance was repeated in the subsequent national assessment conducted in 2015 (NEREC, 2016).

Current policy on teaching methods

Current policy in Sri Lanka indicates that students should be introduced to activity-based oral English from Grade 1 and to more formal instruction from Grade 3 (Premarathna et al., 2016). A bilingual medium policy, in which some subjects are followed from Grade 6 in one medium and others in another, is also being implemented in a small number of government schools – Sinhala/English (5.16 per cent), Tamil/English (1.55 per cent) and Sinhala/Tamil (0.41 per cent). In a tiny percentage of schools – just 0.3 per cent – instruction is offered across all three media (NEC, 2022).

The recommended approach to the teaching of English is in line with the learner-centred and activity-based approach endorsed most recently by the National Education Commission (NEC, 2022). Curriculum developers in Sri Lanka are influenced by ideas about the teaching of English that flow around the world. Sri Lankan English language specialists have conducted studies in the teaching of English as a foreign language in universities abroad, as well as in Sri Lanka (see for example M. E. S. Perera, 2000). The British Council in Sri Lanka has supported the teaching of English for many years through its own teaching programmes and links with the Ministry of Education and the National Institute of Education (Indrarathne & McCulloch, 2022). From the late 1990s, the UK Department for International Development supported the National Institute of Education's Primary English Language Programme, which comprised a major reform of curriculum content and materials and a systematic cascade training programme (Hayes, 2000). The British Council works worldwide and conducts international research on and surveys of policies and practices in the teaching of English as a foreign language. The results of such surveys are shared with Sri Lanka English experts (see for example Rixon, 2013).

With its stress on communication rather than grammar, the teaching and learning approach in Sri Lanka is consistent with the prevailing discourses on the teaching of English as a second or foreign language around the world (Zhou & Ng, 2016). With its stress of student-centred activity methods, the recommended approach is consistent with learner-centred models of teaching around the world. Moeller & Catalano (2015) describe changes over time in the dominant approaches to teaching and learning of foreign languages internationally – from the imitation and practice approaches consistent with behaviourist stimulus-response psychology, to the discovery of the rules of grammar in line with biological programming, to the interactionist position in which learners are 'active co-constructive participants' who interact with teachers who need to be able to modify their input to the ability of the learner. Although not explicitly stated in Sri Lanka's curriculum policy guidelines, it is likely that those who promote the current student-centred approach have been influenced by this last set of ideas.

Guidelines on learning time and activities

English language curricula, syllabi, teacher guides, pupil texts and workbooks were revised following the policies outlined in the 1997 General Education Reforms. The official school timetable allocates 180 minutes (3 hours) a week to English teaching in Grades 3 and 4, and 210 minutes (3.5 hours) in Grade 5. School principals and teachers have discretion as to how they distribute this time across the week.

The curriculum is divided into three key stages. Teacher guides indicate that at Key Stage 1 (Grades 1 and 2) a greater part of the time should be devoted to play and activities, with less time given to desk work. At Key Stage 2 (Grades 3 and 4), play, activities and desk work are given equal prominence. At Key Stage 3 (Grade 5) desk work predominates.

Guidelines vs practice

Previous chapters have underlined myriad disjunctions between formal policies and school and classroom practices – disjunctions that are apparent in education systems worldwide. The rest of this chapter reports on the results of an empirical study undertaken in 2014 to address the questions set out at the beginning of this chapter: How much time is allocated to the teaching of English and how much of that allocated time is used? In what types of English language activities do teachers engage? And are there any school, teacher and class characteristics associated with the amount of time spent on student-centred learning?

The study is reported in full in Little et al. (2019). It was undertaken in the Central Province, where the mean achievement in Grade 4 English language lay midway among all nine provinces in both the 2013 and 2015 national assessments (NEREC, 2014, 2016). Teaching in either the Sinhala or Tamil medium was observed in 307 classes, divided almost equally between Grades 3, 4 and 5 and on two occasions for each teacher teaching the same grade. Analysis of school timetables and logbooks indicated the amount of academic time allocated in the school calendar to the teaching of all subjects and other school activities as well as the time allocated to English teaching in Grades 3, 4 and 5. Analysis of interviews with 60 school principals and 112 teachers generated evidence on school and class characteristics, the time available for formal teaching and learning, and teacher qualifications. Classroom observation schedules and class information sheets generated evidence on how teachers use the available time for teaching and learning.

Time for learning English: opportunity and loss of opportunity

The time available for the teaching and learning of English was estimated through five measures:

(i) **School opening/closure days plus 'special event' non-teaching days, compared with guideline**
According to the school activity calendar, the Ministry of Education allocated 210 days for all school activities. The number of days on which schools were closed during the 2014 school year ranged from

0 to 5 days (average 0.9 days). Not all school days were used for teaching: some were used for special events (such as sports days and exams). These averaged 18.9 days per school. School closures and special events reduced the amount of time available for teaching to 190.2 days: a loss of time of *9.4 per cent*.

(ii) Timetabled time, compared with guideline

As noted above, the official school timetable allocates 180 minutes (3 hours) a week for the teaching of English in Grades 3 and 4 and 210 minutes (3.5 hours) in Grade 5, and principals and teachers can determine their school timetable. In the 60 schools in our sample, English was allocated, on average, 6.4 fewer minutes per week than the official amounts. This translates to a further time loss of *3.4 per cent*.

(iii) Teacher absences

The original sample was 360 English classes, 120 from each of Grades 3, 4 and 5. However, only 307 classes (85 per cent) could be observed. Reasons for the shortfall included: (i) a substitute teacher was teaching a subject other than English; (ii) the teacher was on leave from the school (on training, attending an education office on official work, illness, maternity leave or casual leave); or (iii) the teacher was in school but attending to other duties. This leads to an additional time loss of (360 – 307) / 360, or *14.7 per cent*.

(iv) Early/late lesson start and finish, compared with guideline

In classes everywhere, teaching can sometimes start late and/or finish early. In our 307 observed classes the average time loss due to a late start and/or early finish was just 1.4 minutes per class period, which meant that students lost on average *4.4 per cent* of time in one lesson.

(v) On or off task during lesson

Once a lesson has started, a wide range of activities can be observed. Here, we focussed only on whether teachers were engaging students in an activity (on-task) or no activity (off-task). Our observations suggested that 97.9 per cent of time was spent 'on-task' and *2.1 per cent* 'off-task'. If 'on-task' activity that is devoted to classroom management and discipline rather than teaching is treated 'on-task but non-academic', the proportion of 'off-task' time increases to *4.2 per cent*.

Combining the sources of time loss

A simple addition of the above sources of time loss amounts to 9.4 + 3.4 + 14.7 + 4.4 + 2.1 = 34 per cent (or 36.1 per cent including 'on task' classroom management and discipline). In other words, only two-thirds of the prescribed time is used for teaching and learning, and one-third is lost. However, this is an overestimate of time loss since percentages of time loss should be treated as compound not simple.[1] The compounded time loss reduces to 30.0 per cent or 31.4 per cent respectively. In other words, just over two-thirds of prescribed school time is employed, while just under one third is lost.[2]

Lesson activities

Classroom observations involved the use of a classroom snapshot tool developed from Stallings (1980). The tool was time-based, with the main teaching activity noted every three minutes. Eighteen types of observed activity were classified into 'on-task' and 'off-task' activities. These are summarised in Table 13.1.

Table 13.1 indicates that similar amounts of time are devoted to on-task student-centred (40.7 per cent) and teacher-centred (43.9 per cent) activities, with smaller amounts allocated to rote learning activities, classroom management and teacher off task. This compares rather favourably with Marie Perera's (2001) estimates of 'on-task' activities in case studies of English teaching in Sri Lankan secondary schools, in which only 50 per cent of available time was used for teaching in her best case.

Variations in time spent on student-centred learning

The evidence presented above disguises variations across schools, classes and teachers in terms of time spent in classrooms on student-centred activities. These variations are explored further through correlations of school, class and teacher characteristics and outcome variables. The *School* variables explored were location (urban/rural/estate), facilities (toilets, classrooms, desks, chairs), and the

---

[1] Compounded loss applies the percentage to the previous percentage of time loss.
[2] Note that due to a correction of a calculation error the percentages of time loss reported in this chapter are higher than those reported in Little et al. (2019).

Table 13.1 Hierarchy of on-task and off-task teaching and learning activities, time percentages. Source: Author.

On-task	Academic tasks	Student-centred tasks	Kinaesthetic	6.6	
			Discussion/questioning	18.7	
			Focused listening	1.3	
			Remedial work/ corrective feedback	14.2	40.7
		Teacher-centred tasks	Reading aloud	12	
			Demonstration	4.8	
			Assignment/desk work	17.7	
			Verbal instructions	9.5	43.9
		Rote learning tasks	Practice/drill	8.5	
			Copying	2.5	11.1
	Non-academic tasks	Tasks not purely academic	Classroom management	1.9	
			Discipline	0.2	2.1
Off-task	Non-academic tasks	Student off task	Student interactions	0	
			Student uninvolved	0	0
		Teacher off task	Teacher interactions	0	
			Teacher management	0	
			Teacher uninvolved	0	
			Teacher outside class	2.1	2.1
				100	100

availability of English learning and materials, including play material. The *Class* variables were class size (large/small), grade, and a teacher estimate of student numbers attending private English tuition outside of school. *Teacher* variables were (i) whether the teacher allocated to teach English had been appointed as an 'English teacher'; (ii) the teacher's educational qualification, professional qualification in English, and years of experience; (iii) whether the teacher had undertaken the Primary English Learning Programme training some years ago; (iv) the number of teacher absences during 2013; (v) whether the teacher discussed their child's performance and behaviours in learning English with parents; (vi) whether the teacher provided remedial teaching for English; (vii) time spent by the teacher on lesson planning and preparing teaching and learning materials; (viii) the amount of time spent in in-service training; (ix) whether the teacher received training away from school; (x) whether the in-service advisor for English visited the school; (xi) the use of teacher guides, pupil book and workbook; and (xii) whether the teacher used extra material for teaching (such as manipulatives, pictures, stories, newspapers, computers, radio).

A hierarchical linear model (where teachers are 'nested' in classrooms, which are in turn nested within schools) was employed for the analysis (Raudenbush & Bryk, 2002). The analysis indicated that 65.5 per cent of the total variance in the frequency of student-centred tasks could be accounted for by differences in class and teacher characteristics rather than differences in school characteristics (Little et al., 2019).

School and within-school effects

There were wide variations between schools, classes and teachers in the amount of time devoted to student-centred activities. Greater time spent on student-centred activities was observed among teachers who reported using remedial teaching methods frequently, were observed teaching Grade 3 rather than Grade 5, and who had been appointed to schools as specialist English teachers (as distinct from appointment as primary school teachers who taught all subjects as well as English). These observations were consistent with expectations.

Less expected was the finding that student-centred activities were less likely to be observed among trained teachers than among those with no professional qualification, those that reported using the teacher guide frequently and those that had attended between 11 and 30 days of in-service training during the previous year. Were these trained teachers more aware than the untrained of the amount of syllabus content they needed to cover in a school year, more skilled in teacher-centred methods, and more aware of parental expectations about test results? Did they believe that these constraints could most effectively be overcome through teacher-centred methods? Future research might explore these hypotheses further.[3]

Comparisons with elsewhere

The length of the Sri Lankan school year – 210 days in 2013 – compares favourably with countries elsewhere. In OECD countries the average number of instruction days is 185, with a range from 162 days in France to 223 in Israel (OECD, 2016). In 2013 the average number of school days across the States of India ranged from 220 to 225 (Sankar & Linden, 2014). Our estimates of lesson time 'on task' – at around 97 per cent – are

---

[3] At the 1 per cent, 5 per cent or 10 per cent level; for full account of results see Little et al. (2019).

high compared with an international benchmark recommendation that 85 per cent of class time be used for instruction (Bruns & Luque, 2015). However, it should be noted that these numbers and percentages are not strictly comparable with our study since evidence generation methods and variable specifications are likely to have been different.

Conclusion

This research has compared policy guidelines with school, class and teacher practices in the teaching of English in Grades 3 to 5, with a particular focus on time opportunities for the teaching and learning of English and variations in the time spent on student-centred learning across schools, classes and teachers. Our estimates suggested that almost one-third of official teaching time was lost in school and class practices, and that broadly similar amounts of time were devoted to student-centred and teacher-centred activity. Although the official guidance indicates that more emphasis should be placed on student-centred activities, no guidance is given as to which types of student activity, and over what periods of time, are likely to be the most effective. Our findings also pointed to a number of expected and unexpected findings, the latter concerning teacher education and training.

Future research surveys of English language achievement in Sri Lanka could build on the current national assessments to include measures of home language environment and parental background. Such surveys could also employ a longitudinal research design to analyse observations of teaching and learning practices across a school year and identify those which contribute most to gains in learning achievement between the start and the end of the school year. Such research designs have been employed elsewhere and could usefully be adapted to the Sri Lankan context (see, for example, Azubuike, Moore & Vaidya, 2023). Such surveys should also include and extend the school, teacher and class variables included in the study reported above in order to confirm/disconfirm our findings and to explore post-hoc explanations for the unexpected findings described above.

Reviews of current education policy in the teaching of English recommend introducing the teaching of English from Grade 1 primary, raising the level of proficiency in English, and developing modes of assessment to monitor learning progress (Presidential Task Force on Sri Lanka's Education Affairs, 2020). Our research suggests additional policy areas for review. These include, *inter alia*, (i) the time expected to be devoted to English teaching in relation to the number of official school days and the length of the school day; (ii) curriculum aims in relation to syllabi and teacher guides, textbooks and workbooks; (iii) alignment between the guidance on play, activities and desk work with that on student-centred and teacher-centred activities; and (iv) alignment between curriculum intentions, the content and process of professional and in-service training courses, the knowledge, experience and qualifications of trainers and teacher educators, and the content of teacher guides across all subjects of the primary curriculum.

The positive findings on teachers' use of remedial approaches resonates with research on formative assessment reported in Chapter 15 and its potential role in improving learning outcomes for all children. The positive finding on the link between student-centred teaching and the teacher having been appointed to the school as a specialist trained English teacher underlines the attention that the national and provincial ministries of education and respective education officers must continue to pay to teacher supply and deployment to ensure that appropriately qualified English teachers are deployed to each and every school. More generally, the research underlines the need for equitable and implementable policies on the deployment of teachers in all subjects to provinces and schools.

14
Multi-level teaching in Sri Lanka and elsewhere

Introduction

In this chapter I introduce and present an evaluation of an innovative method of grouping students for learning and teaching in rural Sri Lanka – the multi-level teaching method (ML) – and contrast it with a range of similar ongoing programmes in Latin America and Asia.

Until quite recently, Sri Lanka's education system included many small, largely rural, schools. In these schools teachers were required to combine classes and teach more than one grade at the same time. In other words, they engaged in multi-grade teaching. In 1986, 5.6 per cent of schools had just one teacher. This meant that a single teacher was responsible for all grades of primary education. Almost a quarter of all schools had some classes in which two or more grades were combined (Abhayadewa, 1989). By 1998, 18 per cent of all primary and post-primary schools had four or fewer teachers. Since primary schools comprised five grades, teachers had to 'double up' their classes and become multi-grade teachers and/or reduce the time available for learning for some part of the school day (Vithanapathirana, 2006). Over time, and as a result of rural–urban migration and a parental preference for student enrolment in urban schools, some of these multi-grade schools closed, while others benefited from successive rounds of politically driven teacher recruitment programmes, increasing their staff complement and reducing student-staff ratios.

By 2019, about 14 per cent of schools were still small, with enrolments of between 1–51. The average student-teacher ratio across all schools in the country was just 4.7:1 (Ministry of Education, 2019). While this ratio will surprise readers unfamiliar with Sri Lanka, and education planners may raise an eyebrow at its implications for 'cost efficiency', it suggests that by the second decade of the twenty-first century most teachers, even in small schools, were responsible for a single grade at any one time. Classes in these small schools were moving away from being multi-grade to being mono-grade.

In the late 1980s, Abhayadewa (1989) anticipated the idea that 'multi-level teaching' is relevant to both mono-grade and multi-grade classes in Sri Lanka. She supported her case with evidence from a large-scale survey of variations in student learning outcomes at both grade entry and exit, and pointed to the cumulative effect of lack of mastery in basic learning competencies on grade repetition and early school dropout. Although teachers have long known that the learning levels of students in all types of class, whether multi- or mono-grade classes, are diverse, few education policymakers have been able to translate this reality into curriculum and teacher education practices that support this diversity. It is the recognition of this reality that foreshadowed the introduction of the ML teaching programme that is the main focus of this chapter.

Multi-level teaching

The Ministry of Education offers the following definition of ML. It is a pedagogical approach

> that enables one to teach lessons to an entire group while meeting the individual needs of learners, to 'teach individually all at once'. [It is a method that accommodates] … a range of learning, teaching and assessment methods in which students can engage according to their own developmental needs along the continuum of learning. (MOE presentation at a ML Stakeholder Roundtable, 21 January 2020)

ML addresses issues faced by teachers and learners worldwide as they strive to meet the learning targets set out in the Sustainable Development Goals (United Nations, 2015a). ML recognises the diversity of learning achievement levels found in every classroom in Sri Lanka (NEREC 2009, 2014, 2016). It recognises that children learn at different speeds, and focusses especially on the learning needs of slow learners. It also focusses on the causal link between prior and subsequent learning and the difference that changed teacher and learner practices make to reducing achievement gaps between learners. As described by a senior Ministry of Education officer, ML is based on the following principles:

> When cognitive skills are strong, learning is fast and easy; when weak, learning becomes a struggle. Irrespective of age, cognition can be improved with the right training. Multi-level teaching provides success for every student within rigorous standards and acknowledges diverse learner characteristics. Students who are absent do not lose out. They are able to start the learning ladder where they left off. (ML Evaluation Stakeholder Roundtable, 21 January 2020)

There are two versions of ML in Sri Lanka. In the first, the ML lesson is divided into phases. Teachers introduce the same learning material to the same age-group students who undertake the same learning activities. This is followed by a task that assesses the achievement of learning activity up to that point in time. Based on the result of this assessment, students are divided into subgroups for 'remediation' or extension activities.

In the second version, students select individual work cards. These cards lead students through a stepped sequence of tasks which culminate in self-evaluation, followed by teacher evaluation, the result of which determines whether the student moves on to the next step of a learning 'ladder' of learning steps, or through a stepped series of remediation activities.

In both versions, the assessment activity is embedded within a series of learning activities across the lesson. It is an example of 'formative assessment' in which teacher and student gain information about learning achievement in a timely way (see Chapter 15 for a discussion of formative assessment). Rather than waiting for the results of a monthly or termly test, adjustments to the order of learning activities can be made by the teacher immediately and on the spot. The ML scheme acknowledges that within the same age-grade group there are multiple levels of achievement among students and that formative assessment is key to ensuring that students maintain progress at their own pace. To date the ML approach in Sri Lanka has been employed exclusively in mono-grade classes.

The idea of learning diversity is central to the discourse surrounding both the ML approach and the broader literature on learning exclusions and inclusions. Figure 14.1 sets out a model of access, transitions and equity in education systems with seven 'zones of exclusion' (Lewin, 2015a; Lewin & Little, 2011; http://www.create-rpc.org). The model charts the progress of a cohort of students through education from pre-school to the end of secondary education. The model pinpoints where actions are required in order to transform educational exclusions into educational inclusions.

In Sri Lanka, the primary school enrolment ratio is high and dropout from primary school is low compared with other lower-middle-income countries. The zone of exclusion of greatest relevance to ML is a subset of Zone 3, which describes, *inter alia*, those who are at risk of dropping out of learning through 'silent exclusion'. The 'silently excluded' are

> those who are at risk of remaining in school but dropping out of learning because of a failure to achieve sufficient learning at one level in order to learn effectively at the next. (Little, Indika & Rolleston, 2009)

ML focusses squarely on the teaching and learning challenges faced by children in Zone 3 – that is, children who are at risk of dropping out of learning, rather than school, because they fail to achieve sufficient learning at one level in order to learn effectively for the next. ML is essentially a teaching method designed to deliver the national curriculum in ways that enhance learning outcomes. ML objectives and ideal practices align closely with those of the national mainstream curriculum approach, but there are also key differences. The ML approach:

- simplifies the competency levels expected to be achieved by all children;
- emphasises the importance of learning activities at all stages of the lesson;
- re-stages lessons in terms of Introduction, Practice, Assessment, Remediation and Enrichment (this contrasts with the mainstream stages of Introduction, Lesson Development, Assessment and Closure);
- advocates the use of one or more assessment activities at an earlier stage in the lesson than in the mainstream approach, with a greater emphasis on the 'formative', remediation activities for those children likely to fall behind, and a parallel set of enrichment activities for those who are succeeding in attaining the required learning levels;

Figure 14.1 Zones of inclusion in and exclusion from learning. ECD refers to early childhood development. Developed from Lewin & Little, 2011.

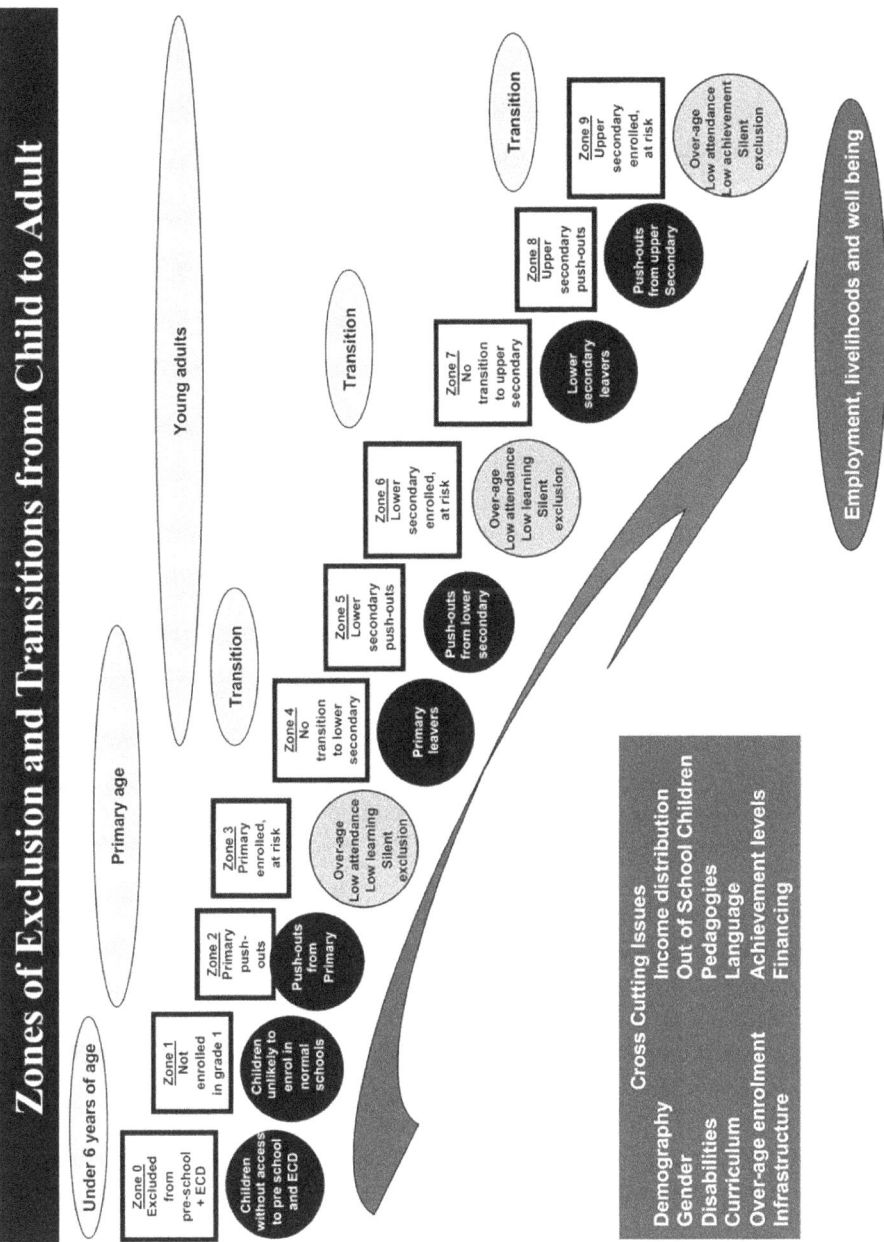

- employs 'learning ladders' to guide the lesson planning of the teacher and to chart personal and inter-personal progress;
- uses a wider range of within-class student grouping practices than the mainstream.

Relevance of ML in practice

In early 2020 an evaluation of ML was undertaken in four provinces on behalf of the Ministry of Education (MOE) and UNICEF (Little et al., 2020). The MOE had been promoting the approach in the country's nine provinces, in four of which UNICEF had funded aspects of the work. Since no achievement data had been collected from the beginning of the ML implementation, the evaluation was unable to assess the impact of ML on gains in learning achievement. Its focus was on the 'relevance and effectiveness' of the programme.

The evaluation methods employed included observations of teaching and learning, interviews with teachers, parents and education officers working at the provincial and central levels, and documentary analysis. Sixteen schools were included for detailed study, four in each of the four provinces (Central, Uva, Northern and Eastern) where UNICEF had been supporting the ML approach. In each province two multi-level schools (hereinafter ML) and two non-multi-level schools (hereinafter non-ML) were included. The schools were further differentiated by a 'difficulty' index (an official measure of school remoteness, community disadvantage and difficult terrain). The selected schools lay at the extremes of this index.

Twenty-nine teachers were observed teaching 46 maths, Sinhala-language and Tamil-language classes using an observation schedule and a follow-up teacher interview (Grade 2 and 3 classes in Central and Uva, and Grade 2 classes in Northern and Eastern). Classroom observation schedules were developed in pilot form and trialled and revised before final use. The study captured teaching and learning practices of both ML and non-ML settings. An additional 54 ML teachers invited to a one-day Teacher Workshop completed questionnaires and engaged in discussions about ML. Discussions were held with education officers from the four provinces who attended an initial workshop (31), Ministry of Education officers (7), National Institute of Education officers (12), and UNICEF-Sri Lanka and South Asia region officers (6). In the field additional interviews were held with provincial officers (9), zonal officers (11), divisional officers (5), in-service advisory teachers (8), community service organisation officers (3) and parents (152).

The relevance of ML was explored in four ways: (i) the relevance of ML to the needs, policies and priorities as expressed by the Sri Lankan policy research community; (ii) the relevance of the ML teaching approach for delivering the primary curricula; (iii) the relevance of the training of teachers in preparing them to adopt the ML approach in the classroom; and (iv) the relevance of ML teaching and learning materials to the ML approach.

Need, policies and priorities

The recent ML approach arose in response to two main influences. The first, stemming from the late 2000s, was the evidence flowing from research studies that showed lower than expected performance in Grade 4 learning assessments and wide differences across provinces, school type, medium of instruction, school location and student gender. Through its monitoring role, the Ministry of Education was concerned about performance shortfalls in relation to the National Institute of Education's (NIE's) 'Essential and Desirable Learning Competencies' at the end of Key Stage 1 (Grade 1), Key Stage 2 (Grades 2 and 3) and Key Stage 3 (Grades 4 and 5).

The second influence was exposure to the Indian model of multi-grade and multi-level learning (MGML). In 2010, the then director of primary education took a team of Sri Lankan educators from the MOE, NIE and provincial education departments to the Rishi Valley Institute for Educational Resources (RIVER) in the district of Chittoor, in the state of Andhra Pradesh, to observe and learn about the ideas and practices of the MGML approach. The RIVER-MGML approach starts from the proposition that within any class of learners there is diversity of learning levels among children, a proposition echoing Abhayadewa's observations on Sri Lanka in 1989. Most of the Sri Lankan educators who observed the RIVER-MGML approach saw it as a way forward to combat the learning achievement challenges identified in earlier studies of learning outcomes among Sri Lankan students.

MGML and ML: fidelity and adaptation

In curriculum theory the terms 'fidelity' and 'adaptation' are used to describe curricula and pedagogy that remain faithful to the model that inspired them and those that diverge and are adapted to new circumstances. In the RIVER-MGML model, the pace and sequencing of learning is managed by the children, a concept encapsulated by the expression 'the child is in the driving seat'. The MGML method is 'individualised learning' guided by 'ladders of learning' that sequence learning tasks and respective evaluations. Children proceed through the learning sequences at their own pace and learn in diverse types of groupings: teacher-based, partly-teacher-based, peer group-based and individual (Müller, Lichtiger & Girg, 2015).

Sri Lanka subsequently adapted the RIVER-MGML model. ML represents a curriculum adaptation of the RIVER-MGML model, rather than being a faithful copy of it.

- The Sri Lanka ML model focusses on maths and language, while RIVER-MGML includes environmental studies. The ML model includes environmental studies in the Northern and Eastern Provinces and excludes it in the Central and Uva provinces.
- The RIVER-MGML model is used in multi-grade as well as mono-grade classrooms; ML is used only in mono-grade classrooms.
- The ML model is based around the lesson format of the school timetable – one-hour periods for Grades 1 and 2; 40 minutes for Grade 3. In RIVER-MGML time-use is more flexible.
- In RIVER-MGML children engage in activities without teacher direction or supervision for the majority of the time. In ML, students work with teacher direction or supervision for the majority of the time.
- In the RIVER-MGML model, students self-mark their assessment activities prior to the teacher marking their work. In ML the teacher marks most of the student work.

In 2012 the MOE Primary Education Branch embarked on a small-scale ML innovation in 14 schools. By the end of 2019, the MOE had been directly involved in the training of more than 1,000 ML 'resource persons' across the country – that is, those who could train and advise teachers. The ministry estimated that between 1,000 and 2,000 schools had adopted the approach for at least part of the day across the country. From 2012 onwards ML-related activities were include within the MOE's Education Sector Development Plan (2012–16). UNICEF became involved with the project in 2016 and focussed its support on 450 schools in the Central, Eastern, Northern and Uva Provinces. The following observations derive from these four provinces.

ML and primary curriculum delivery

The overwhelming perception among a range of stakeholders was that ML was a relevant approach for delivery of the primary education curriculum. Its relevance lay, in part, in its alignment with the learning objectives, content and competencies guidance as set out by the NIE. ML neither threatens the overall goals of primary education nor does it suggest radical revisions of what content should be taught. It is not an alternative curriculum. It is, rather, a different method of delivery. ML aligns with national learning objectives, and learning outcomes are clearly specified. ML was considered to have the potential to help *all* students achieve the essential learning competencies set out by the NIE and reduce learning gaps between students. ML is relevant because it caters for diverse levels of learning, while promoting support for the weakest students. It helps teachers identify the learning levels of students, build lessons from simple activities to more complex ones, and manage lessons.

School principals and education officers were asked whether they considered ML to be relevant for the early grades of primary education. The overwhelming answer was 'yes', from seven of the eight ML school principals and 17 out of the 19 support system officers at provincial, zonal and divisional level. Two went further and suggested that it was a method that should be applied across all five grades of primary school, and on into the lower secondary stage, Grades 6, 7 and 8. Teachers explained how ML helps students reach the required competency levels, caters to all students in the classroom, promotes student engagement and motivation, and lays the foundations for the rest of their education.

ML teacher training

In the ML schools visited, 12 of the 15 teachers interviewed had received some form of ML training; three had received none. Among the 54 teachers who attended a teacher consultation workshop, all of whom had been invited because they were currently teachers in ML schools, 13 had received no ML training. Conversely, a surprising number of teachers in the non-ML schools visited had received ML training (7/14). Four main reasons for this apparent anomaly were identified. The first is that teachers are transferred from school to school frequently. A teacher who was posted previously to what was deemed by province officials to be an 'ML school' may have been transferred subsequently to a non-ML school. Second, zonal and provincial officers may have decided to invite all teachers, irrespective of school history, for ML training because of its perceived relevance for *all* teachers. This was found to be the case in the Central Province. Third, new, untrained teacher recruits may have received no training in any of the techniques of primary education, including ML, and may have been allocated to an ML school to teach Grade 1, 2 or 3. Fourth, a teacher in an ML school, now teaching Grades 1–3, may previously have taught Grade 4 and 5 and not been called for the ML training for Grade 1, 2, or 3 teachers. Conversely, a teacher in an ML school who has received ML training may have been allocated to teach Grade 4 or 5, where ML is not currently practised. These are the realities of teacher deployment between and within schools.

ML training modalities

Sri Lanka has a complex system of pre- and in-service training (Sethunga et al., 2014). In-service training for ML is undertaken by teams of province-level or zonal-level teams of officers. Teachers who follow ML courses are neither assessed nor certificated. The length of ML training received by the teachers we interviewed varied. The majority had attended a three- or five-day course in a central location, organised by the zone or the province. Others had received only one or two days of training, while still others had received between nine days and two weeks of training. At the time of the evaluation, ML training had not been included within the primary education teacher education curricula of the nationally managed colleges of education, teacher training colleges, the NIE or universities. However, a unit on ML teaching had been included in the crash-course 300-hour primary education training programme for graduate recruits who had received no training in primary education prior to their school appointment.

Of the nine teachers we met in the eight ML schools who had received ML training, eight reported finding it relevant/useful. Among the much larger group of teachers we met at the teacher consultation (N=54), a substantial number commented that the training had helped them to use activity cards, implement the distinct stages of an ML lesson, teach for diverse levels in the same classroom and prepare aids for teaching. Just two reported being dissatisfied with their training on the grounds that 'it was insufficient'. This was hardly surprising since these two teachers had been given the opportunity to attend training for only one or two days. This can have done little more than create a general awareness of the approach.

ML teaching and learning materials

The teachers we met identified a wide range of materials used in their ML classrooms. The majority reported using activity cards (98 per cent), worksheets (91 per cent), learning ladders (89 per cent) and additional materials (80 per cent). The proportion of hand-made and disposable materials made by the teachers and those designed by teachers but produced in large numbers for use by all teachers varied from class to class and school to school. The majority of the teachers interviewed in schools who had received activity cards, ladders or worksheets (over 75 per cent) found them relevant for ML. These teachers reported that activity cards helped children reach the competency levels, catered for diverse levels of student achievement, were easy to use, reduced the workload of the teacher and were a good practical activity. They said that the learning ladders helped them to identify the level of their students, encouraged and motivated the students, helped them to achieve competency levels, and increased students' ownership and understanding of their learning progress.

Overall, then, both the concept and practice of ML are relevant to and consistent with the dominant policy discourse of child-centred education that has pervaded the Sri Lankan education discourse since the 1970s (Peiris, 1983). The ML approach is aligned with NIE curriculum content, learning competencies and expected learning outcomes, and is of potential value in contributing to the delivery of current and revised national curricula. The majority of stakeholders at national and provincial levels with experience of ML perceived the ML concept and method as both relevant and useful for the delivery of the primary education curriculum, especially in the early grades where it is currently being practised.

Effectiveness of ML in practice

Effectiveness was addressed through the question 'to what extent has the ML approach achieved its objectives?'.

The challenge in applying this criterion to ML lies in defining the expected results of this intervention. At the time of the evaluation no theory of change or results chain/causal pathway, setting out clear and measurable objectives, had been developed. However, some ML objectives could be inferred from documentary sources. Some sources referred to cognitive learning outcomes, such as achieving the NIE's

Essential and Desirable Learning Competencies, whilst others referred to non-cognitive outcomes such as student 'personality and social skills', 'holistic all-round development', communication, collaboration and leadership. Some referred to system indicators such as minimising dropouts and improving school attendance. Still others referred to the teaching and learning process, for example promoting enjoyable learning opportunities or inputs and development of teacher skills.

Prior to the fieldwork, national, provincial and zonal-level officers made positive claims made about the effectiveness of ML in relation to the Essential and Desirable Learning Outcomes, attendance, reduction in dropouts, student personality and social skills. During the Stakeholder Roundtable and during fieldwork respondents were invited to provide us with evidence for their claims. Despite the fact that no evidence was presented to us in the course of the evaluation, it was clear that the implementation of ML had clearly been effective in *creating a positive narrative* around which teachers and education officers can enthuse. This positive narrative suggests that ML objectives were, to some extent at least, being met.

Integration of ML into daily teaching and learning practices

The integration of ML into daily practices was assessed through an observation schedule, as described earlier. Practices that could be expected to be observed in both ML and non-ML classes were included. Given the key role played by learning resources in the ML approach, the availability of resources was examined in both ML and non-ML classes. Forty-six lessons (24 ML and 22 non-ML) were observed, Grade 2 and 3 classes in the Central and Uva provinces, and Grade 2 classes in the Northern and Eastern provinces.

As noted earlier, some teachers in some schools identified by provincial officers as ML schools had received no training in ML methods. Conversely, some teachers in schools designated as non-ML schools had followed some ML training. Hence, the observation data were analysed using two types of comparison group: (i) teachers in classes in ML vs non-ML schools, and (ii) teachers with some training in ML vs teachers with no training in ML, irrespective of whether their school was labelled as an ML or non-ML school. During the course of the fieldwork, it also became clear that the length of classes varied. So, in order to control for the length of lessons observed, the analysis was restricted to the number of times any one of the practices was observed in three-minute intervals over a 45-minute period.

Table 14.1 presents the practices which differed in these two analyses between (i) ML schools and non-ML schools, and (ii) ML trained teachers and non-ML trained teachers. There were no significant differences between the classes observed in the ML and non-ML classes on 33 of the 43 practices/behaviours observed. These behaviours were observable to similar degrees, on average, in all classes, and all represented good pedagogic practice. These included, for example, 'teacher marks assessment', 'informal student interaction', 'students engage in same individual task, sat in groups', 'whole class in which teacher demonstrates while children watch', and 'teacher disciplines student(s) in positive manner'.

Table 14.1 indicates that the differences between ML and non-ML schools lay in 10 behaviours. In all cases the mean frequency was higher in the ML schools – that is, the behaviour was observed more frequently on average.

The analysis was repeated between the lessons conducted by teachers who had received training in ML, compared with those who

Table 14.1 Comparing findings from teaching and learning behaviours, by schools and training of teachers.

	Schools: ML vs non-ML	Teachers: ML vs non-ML trained
Observed behaviours reaching statistical significance in both comparisons	Whole class: student asks question of teacher, teacher responds Most students appear engaged Teacher provides feedback on incorrect answer to whole class or to individual	Whole class: student asks question of teacher, teacher responds Most students appear engaged Teacher provides feedback on incorrect answer to whole class or to individual
Observed behaviours reaching statistical significance in one comparison only	Whole class: teacher asks question of student, student answers Whole class: teacher evaluates or probes student answers to question Group: students engage in activities that vary across groups Following evaluation teacher assigns students to remedial/enrichment groups Teacher monitors/supports all groups equally Students place mark on class ladder Overall class management	Teacher organises groups and materials Group seating: students undertake individual work

had not. There were no significant differences between the teachers who had received ML and those who had not on 38 of the 43 practices/behaviours observed. But there were statistically significant differences on five – student asks questions of teacher, students are engaged, teacher provides feedback on incorrect answers, teacher organises groups, and students work individually in groups. In all cases the behaviour was observed more frequently on average among teachers with ML training.

These findings are broadly consistent with the ML objectives. Both analyses show higher levels of student engagement in ML schools and amongst ML trained teachers. While neither analysis showed differences in the propensity of teachers to provide feedback on incorrect answers, both show that teachers in ML schools *and* those who had received ML training were more likely to provide feedback on incorrect answers. This practice is not mentioned in the MOE's draft ML Guidelines, but it is a characteristic of good formative assessment practice. Encouragingly, both analyses show that ML students were more likely to ask a question of a teacher in a whole-class setting than were students in non-ML classes or students taught by teachers without ML training. This is suggestive of student engagement and participation in learning, and the development of confidence to engage with the teacher.

Other significant differences found in only one of the two analyses are also consistent with ML objectives. Differentiation of activities across groups is seen more often in ML classes than non-ML classes, whereas differentiation of activities within groups is seen more often when teachers are trained in ML as compared with those who are not. It is more common to find students in ML classes being assigned to differentiated activities, designed to remediate or enrich, following assessment.

Parent perceptions of ML effectiveness

The group outside the school setting who may benefit the most from ML is parents. During school visits, the evaluation team met groups of parents – mainly mothers. They were asked whether their children were following the ML method in any subjects. Five out of the eight groups met in the ML schools were aware of the ML method. With the exception of one comment made in relation to a declining interest in the Tamil language, the comments were overwhelmingly positive:

> There is a clear difference. Children are more interested to learn Maths.

Even when at home doing gardening work, children use rocks, leaves, seeds to do mathematics.

We are very happy with the teacher … we notice a difference between the ML subjects and non-ML subjects taught … the children are more enthusiastic and have more activities with ML subjects.

I have 100 per cent confidence in the school and the teaching approach.

Yes, they enjoy … the children compete to learn as they want to get further with the [activity] cards.

Implementation challenges

As described in Chapters 4, 7 and 8, the implementation of curriculum or pedagogy reforms is rarely smooth. The most frequently cited challenge to the implementation of ML by provincial support system staff was 'resistance from teachers', though this varied widely across the provinces, from 75 per cent in the Northern Province to 38 per cent in the Central Province. Provincial support system staff also reported that teacher resistance had reduced over time, usually because of heightened awareness of ML and/or more training or because teachers had started to see the approach 'working'.

The challenges faced by teachers and school principals revolved around the time spent on preparing materials and the cost of their development. Materials, time, budget and space/facilities were mentioned by around 40 per cent of teachers. Other barriers mentioned were insufficient numbers of in-service advisors, in-service advisor workload and shortage of transport facilities for them. Only five people (14 per cent) cited lack of support from the school principal.

Teachers and support system actors were invited to suggest 'ways in which ML could become more effective'. ML teachers cited a range of ways in which it could be improved. The most cited were training, teaching materials, resources and monitoring. Others referred to the classroom environment, space, facilities and equipment.

There were broad similarities across the four provinces, but also differences. ML teachers in the Northern Province were less likely to mention monitoring/supervision as requiring improvement. Teachers in the Uva Province were more likely to mention funding, while teachers in the Eastern and Central Provinces were more likely to mention classroom space and facilities than those in the Northern and Uva

Provinces. A similar pattern of responses emerged from the staff in the provincial support system. Training, materials and monitoring were top of the list, though, again, respondents in the Northern Province were less likely to mention monitoring than those in the other three provinces. Almost 30 per cent across the four provinces suggested scaling up the programme and integrating it within the national curriculum, though there was variation in the frequency of this suggestion across the provinces (Northern 50 per cent; Eastern 20 per cent; Uva 33 per cent; Central 12.5 per cent).

System barriers

The absence of sound arrangements for governance and quality control can pose a major challenge for implementation, especially sustained implementation over time. By the beginning of 2020, governance structures pertaining to ML had not been outlined. There was no government circular, no recognition of ML within curriculum guidelines from NIE, and no guidance manual issued by either the MOE or the provinces.

The flow of financial resources to schools also has implications for the ability of teachers to implement ML. As described in Chapter 7, financial resources to provincial schools now flow from the Treasury to the provincial ministries and provincial departments of education via the Ministry of Local Government and Provincial Councils. If the latter does not direct provincial ministries to ringfence funds for ML training, materials and monitoring, then the ML work lacks a degree of legitimacy and officers must make a special case for expenditure. Lack of legitimacy also has implications for teachers who worry that they are implementing a programme that is not the mainstream programme and does not cover all the primary grades up to the all-important Grade 5 scholarship exam. As one UNICEF field education officer said, 'still we do not have a national level/MOE approved guideline or book'. Key elements of good governance involve legitimacy and funding. The ML programme has reached a stage where, if it is to be sustained, it needs to be legitimated.

Overall, then, the lack of a clear and consistent definition of objectives limited the evaluation team's ability to address related questions of effectiveness. Stakeholders working at various levels of the education system made positive claims about the effectiveness of ML. The implementation of ML appeared to have been effective in creating a positive narrative around which educators enthuse. A wide range of 'good' teaching and learning practices was found in all classes, whether

ML or not. However, in ML-related settings, student engagement in learning was observed to be higher, teachers were more likely to provide feedback on incorrect answers, and students were more likely to ask their teachers questions in whole-class settings. These were all consistent with the broad objectives of ML and indicate that ML has been integrated into daily classroom practices. Whilst the target beneficiaries of ML are children, parents also appeared to be benefiting in terms of their engagement with and enthusiasm for their children's learning. This in turn was likely to generate more support for their children's education. However, the implementation of ML has faced challenges. For teachers, these are lack of materials, time spent developing materials, the cost of materials, and classroom space and facilities.

ML compared with similar programmes elsewhere

The past forty years have seen the introduction of programmes around the world bearing similarities to the ML programme in Sri Lanka. At their heart is the recognition that student achievement levels are diverse and that 'differentiated' approaches to teaching and learning can be effective. The RIVER-MGML programme in India has already been described briefly (Müller, Lichtiger & Girg, 2015; Rishi Valley, 2021). From 2003 it was adapted and extended in stages across the entire state of Andhra Pradesh in a programme known as activity-based learning (ABL) (Akila, 2009; National Council of Educational Research and Training, 2011; Harihan, 2011; Singal et al., 2018). Subsequent adaptations were implemented in the states of Gujarat, Jharkhand, Karnataka, Madhya Pradesh and Rajasthan (UNICEF, 2015). Various Indian states have also experimented with a separate programme known as Teaching at the Right Level (Banerjee et al., 2017). This initiative is currently being promoted in countries beyond India (TaRL, 2023; Global Education Evidence Advisory Panel, 2020).

On the opposite side of the world, the Escuela Nueva (EN) (New School) programme was developed with school principals and teachers in rural Colombia in the 1980s and was later adapted for use in other Latin American countries (Colbert, Chiappe & Arboleda, 1993; Psacharopoulos, Rojas & Velez, 1993; Little, 1995b; McEwan, 1998; Mogollon & Solano, 2011; Hincapie, 2014). The EN programme went on to inspire the government of Vietnam to establish the Vietnam Escuela Nueva Programme (VNEN) (Parandekar et al., 2017).

Understandably, the originators and implementors of all the programmes described in this chapter have been keen to demonstrate the positive impacts of their respective innovative programmes. Some have attracted international attention, have been adapted for use elsewhere in the world, and have won awards from the international education community.

Where evaluations have addressed the impact of the above programmes on learning outcomes, some have reported a positive impact on mean learning achievement, some have reported a positive impact on both high and low achievers, and others have reported no discernible positive impact on either group. In no case has a negative effect on achievement been reported.

Programme designers and implementors in all of these programmes have much to learn from each other, and it is unfortunate that there is, to date, little indication that this learning and sharing is occurring. The ML programme as practised in Sri Lanka is less holistic in its approach than EN programmes in Colombia and Vietnam and MGML and ABL programmes in India. Unlike ML, the EN, VNEN, RIVER-MGML and ABL programmes attempt to promote a wider range of socio-emotional outcomes including self-esteem, friendship and leadership, behavioural development, democratic behaviours and peaceful social interaction. Teacher-student interactions in Sri Lanka's ML programme are more teacher directed than in other programmes. The EN programmes in Latin America place a strong emphasis on school-community behaviours and within-school democratic practices. This has not been a feature to date of Sri Lanka's ML programme.

In EN, RIVER-MGML, ABL and VNEN, student assessments are individualised. Students undertake self-evaluation as one element in a series of learning tasks, followed by teacher evaluation at the end of a learning unit. Assessment is both summative and formative. If the student achieves the required standard, s/he moves to the next step on a ladder of learning; if not, s/he reviews and repeats the learning unit, or parts of it. Students ascend the levels of learning at their own speed. This practice is followed by ML in the Eastern and Northern Provinces. A different practice is followed in the Central and Uva Provinces. Here, the teacher sets an assessment task which is marked first by the student and then by the teacher. Each student marks her/his 'level' on a board which all students can see. The teacher then allocates students to different learning groups for extension activities or remediation. These groups reconvene as a whole class when they meet again for the next class.

The EN, RIVER-MGML and ABL programmes were designed to be as relevant and effective in multi-grade schools as in mono-grade schools. In Sri Lanka multi-grade schools are disappearing fast – and while Sri Lankan educators recognise the potential for the ML approach to work in multi-grade schools, the few remaining multi-grade schools have not been included in the ML programme to date. It should be noted, however, that in a study of Grade 3, 4 and 5 students in rural multi-grade schools, Vithanapathirana (2006) introduced teachers to a method that foreshadowed the Sri Lankan ML approach currently employed in the Central and Uva Provinces. Teachers identified themes and topics in the maths syllabus that were common to Grades 3, 4 and 5, albeit at different levels of difficulty, and identified the learning outcome expectations prescribed in respective syllabi and teacher guides. Lessons commenced with whole-class teaching, followed by differentiated tasks for different grade groups, followed by whole-class revision and consolidation. In a pre- and post-assessment of achievement, with experimental and control groups, the intervention resulted in a positive effect on gains in learning achievement among Grade 4 and Grade 5 students. The 'non-significant' effects of the intervention on Grade 3 gains in learning were attributed to a possible 'ceiling' effect of the test instrument.

Sustainable development

I conclude with observations on the sustainable development of these programmes. The sustainable development of a programme may be thought of as the extent to which the net benefits of an intervention continue or are likely to continue. Innovative programmes attract attention and often additional finance for their launch and extended implementation, especially when early 'results' are positive. Attracting rather less attention is the question of their sustainability over time – whether in terms of financial resources or in terms of the motivation of teachers and other education stakeholders to maintain, extend, evaluate and improve programme implementation.

It is clear that programmes similar to ML have been sustained over time, but the mix of factors driving each case probably differs. Individual personalities have played a key role in all programmes. The examples from Colombia and India, and the more recent expansions elsewhere, have been heavily dependent on financial support from the international education community. Strong political will and state funding were major forces in the institutionalisation of the RIVER-MGML programme across the entire system of government schools in the state of Andhra Pradesh. By contrast, the Teaching at the Right Level programme in India was driven by a non-governmental organisation and has enjoyed less success in its institutionalisation within the mainstream system.

It is clear from the observations of and discussions with teachers that considerable technical capacity in ML has been created in the provinces, zones, divisions and schools, providing proof of concept that could be used for scaling up. However, systemic issues around the functionality and resourcing of provinces, zones and divisions to strengthen school improvement still prevail. Most stakeholders near the ground believe that ML can be owned and run by government. There is immense potential and political will at the ground level to scale up the ML approach, its content and its implementation modalities. Whether that potential is realised depends in part on the ability and willingness of the NIE to become more involved in the content of teacher education curricula, national curriculum revisions and teacher instruction manuals. There are opportunities too for the Department of Publications to encourage textbook writers to develop materials suitable for self-directed as well as teacher-directed learning, the need for which has been underlined in a most forceful way by the recent COVID pandemic. Sri Lanka's General Education Sector Development Plan for 2020–5 includes the promotion of multi-level teaching methods and inclusive education (Ministry of Education, 2020). The transition of this plan into classroom implementation and its sustainability over time will be observed with interest.

15
Assessment for sustainable learning and development

Introduction

Within the UN's Sustainable Development Goals, the first and main target of Sustainable Development Goal 4 (SDG4) is ensuring that 'all girls and boys complete free, equitable and quality primary and secondary education leading to relevant and effective learning'. One indicator within this target is the summative assessment of learning outcomes:

> the proportion of children and young people: (a) in grades 2/3; (b) at the end of primary; and (c) at the end of lower secondary achieving at least a minimum proficiency level in (i) reading and (ii) mathematics, by sex. (Indicator 4.1.1)

In recent years, the summative assessment of learning outcomes in line with SDG4 has attracted considerable interest from international agencies and businesses, as well as from those who organise international and national surveys of learning outcomes.

This chapter sets this recent spate of testing into a more comprehensive framework of learning that examines: (i) the myriad purposes and types of assessment; (ii) the technical challenges of summative assessment; (iii) the political economy of assessment; (iv) the value of formative assessment for learning; and (v) recent advances in formative assessment for learning in primary education in Sri Lanka.

Purposes of learning assessment

The purposes of learning assessment vary (Little & Wolf, 1996). Throughout history, the dominant purpose of assessment has been educational and occupational selection. As we have seen in earlier chapters, the Sri Lankan tradition of using assessment for education and occupational selection purposes is deeply ingrained. In Chapter 6 we saw how the 'diploma disease' drove the curriculum. The Sri Lankan interest in exams for selection were described in the mid-1990s as 'obsessive' (Kariyewasam, 1996). The same remains true today (see for example Education Forum of Sri Lanka, 2020; National Education Commission, 2022).

A second purpose of learning assessment is certification. This indicates that a course of study has been completed to a particular standard. In some – but not all – systems of education, certification feeds directly into selection systems. In the case of Sri Lanka, the GCE A level exam certifies levels of achievement at the end of Grade 13, while simultaneously acting as a criterion for entry to university. A third is the monitoring of system performance – a role that was apparent in the US by the 1980s (Madaus & Raczek, 1996), in England and Wales in the 1990s (Broadfoot & Gipps, 1996), in the education programmes supported by loans to developing countries by the World Bank in the early 1990s (Lockheed, 1996), and in the proliferation of international surveys of student achievement (Goldstein, 1996). Increasingly the monitoring function has morphed into a fourth purpose: 'accountability' (Wyatt-Smith & Cumming, 2009), whereby school test results hold schools accountable for expenditure of public finances. A fifth purpose is the improvement of learning through diagnosing learning errors and providing feedback to teachers and students (for examples see Gipps, 1996; Somerset, 1996; Umar, 1996).

Large-scale international and national surveys of learning outcomes

Since the establishment of the International Association for the Evaluation of Educational Achievement in the early 1960s, successive rounds of international and regional student assessments have been conducted and new surveys launched. These are intended to benchmark the learning levels of one country against others, and to generate an understanding of system and other influences on mean levels of learning and its distribution among diverse groups in society. They are not used for student selection or certification.

Participation in the Programme for International Student Assessment (PISA) grew from one-fifth of all countries in 2000 to one-third of countries by 2015 (Lockheed, 2015). Participation in PISA was higher for members of the Organisation for Economic Co-operation and Development (OECD), countries in Europe and the Central Asia region, high- and upper-middle-income countries, and countries with previous national and international assessment experience.

During the post-Jomtien decade (1990–2000), 70 countries conducted at least one national assessment and during the post-Dakar period (2000–13) the figure stood at 142 (UNESCO, 2014). Many of the national assessments in the developing world were funded by loans and grants from the World Bank. Growth in national assessments has been observed in both developed and developing countries: in developed countries from 5 in 1990 to 36 in 2013; and in developing countries from 8 in 1990 to 64 in 2013 (UNESCO, 2014).

The international education community has supported much of this expansion, including the establishment of the Learning Metrics Task Force, a working group with representatives and members from international organisations (including UNESCO, UNICEF, the World Bank and the United States Agency for International Development (USAID)) and work undertaken by the International Commission on Financing Global Education Opportunity (2016). The EFA-Fast Track Initiative, later to become the Global Education Partnership, included the monitoring of learning outcomes as a criterion for the endorsement of country-funding. The US State Department and USAID require countries to demonstrate an increase in the proportion of children attaining minimum grade-level proficiency in reading at the end of Grade 2 primary and on completion of the full primary stage as a condition for funding. As Bruns (2018) has commented, 'with an $800 million international basic education budget on the line, there are high stakes around how "minimum grade-level proficiency" is defined and measured'.

In Sri Lanka, national assessments of learning outcomes (NALOs) in maths, English and students' first language in Grades 4 and 8 have been repeated every three years since the first round in 2003 and are undertaken by the National Education Research and Evaluation Centre (NEREC) (NEREC, various years). In principle the results are to be used to inform curriculum planning, improve learning and teacher education, and monitor achievement by province, location, school type and language medium of instruction. Year-on-year results have shown the highest achievement in the Western and Southern Provinces and the lowest in the Northern and the Eastern, the superior performance of Type 1AB schools, better performance of schools located in urban areas, and Sinhala-medium students performing better than Tamil-medium students. The dissemination of results among relevant stakeholders has improved year on year and more are aware of the NALO-NEREC surveys. However, despite twenty years of research on the learning achievements of Grade 4 students there is little evidence to date of a marked impact of the survey results and analyses on the practices of curriculum development, the curricula of teacher education or pedagogy in the classroom.

With the exception of the inclusion of a few items of the Trends in International Mathematics and Science Study in one of the NALO-NEREC surveys, Sri Lankan engagement in international assessments has been minimal to date.

Technical challenges of learning assessment

The international call for more evidence on student achievement and learning outcomes has gathered momentum. This is reflected in the 2021 World Bank report on education in Sri Lanka – *Realizing the promise and potential of human capital* – which calls for a well-developed system for assessing learning outcomes, including increased capacity in the technical aspects of assessment and in making use of results. It also recommends that Sri Lanka should accelerate efforts to participate in international assessments in order to benchmark learning outcomes against international standards and to inform the quality of the system.

Many international and regional assessment surveys have been conducted in recent years and these provide experience from which the international community – including Sri Lanka – can draw. Trevino and Ordenes (2017) compare 15 international and regional assessments in current use (Table 15.1).

Trevino and Ordenes (2017) identify three criteria for comparing and evaluating these surveys. All pose technical challenges for global ambitions to create cross-nationally comparative assessments. The first criterion is assessment design – the overarching purpose of the assessment, the intrinsic rationale of the instrument and the conceptual framework to be assessed. Design dimensions include: purpose of the assessment (for example system monitoring, programme evaluation,

Table 15.1 Student assessment surveys – international, regional and foundational skills (Trevino & Ordines, 2017).

International assessments (non-regional)	Regional assessments	Assessments of Foundational Skills
ePIRLS: Progress in International Literacy Study (online reading) **LANA:** Literacy and Numeracy Assessment **PIRLS:** Progress in International Reading Literacy Study **PISA:** Programme for International Student Assessment **PISA D:** Programme for International Student Assessment for Development **TIMSS:** Trends in International Mathematics and Science Study	**LLECE:** Latin American Laboratory for Assessment of the Quality of Education **PASEC:** Programme for the Analysis of Education Systems **PILNA:** Pacific Islands Literacy and Numeracy Assessments **SEA-PLM:** Southeast Asia Primary Learning Metrics **SACMEQ:** Southern and Eastern Africa Consortium for Monitoring Educational Quality	**ASER:** Annual Status of Education Report **EGMA:** Early Grade Mathematics Assessment **EGRA:** Early Grade Reading Assessment **UWEZO:** Uwezo Annual Learning Assessment

baseline definition, student population diagnosis); target population (age groups, grade groups); what is being assessed (knowledge vs competencies); domains (specific knowledge and skills); inferences (the validity of inferences made from the assessments); sample (the subgroup within the targeted population); modes of assessment (for example paper vs computer-based); test administration site (school, household, test centre); and individual vs group administration (Trevino & Ordenes, 2017, p. 6).

The second criterion is standard setting. This is important for SDG Indicator 4.1.1 because one needs to identify the proportion of students who perform at or above a minimal standard. This involves identifying the cut-scores on a scale that define the threshold between various levels and the writing of substantive descriptions of what students classified into these levels can do.

The third criterion considers statistical characteristics, of which three are especially important. The first is the scaling technique chosen to create the measure of achievement (for example classic test theory, Rasch modelling and multi-parameter models). The second is the way individual achievement results are estimated. The third is 'equating' – the procedure used to make assessments comparable.

Within the first criterion above is 'purpose'. The 15 assessments listed in Table 15.1 vary in their purposes. While the majority aim to monitor the performance of a school system over time and/or in relation to other systems, some (for example EGMA, EGRA, ASER and UWEZO) conduct system diagnosis or programme evaluations at the national or sub-national level. These assessments are not designed to produce cross-national comparisons.

The 'target' populations of these surveys also vary. Some of the assessments are age-based; others are grade-based. PISA surveys are based on a single-age group and are designed to generate evidence across systems and/or over time. By contrast, ASER and UWEZO are based on an age range (5–16 years) and are not designed for cross-system comparisons.

A content-based assessment measures 'the extent to which students know the contents or standards of a particular subject matter' and a competency-based assessment measures 'the extent to which children can apply competently the knowledge and skills they have learned in the education trajectories' (Trevino & Ordenes, 2017, p. 9). This distinction remains somewhat obscure, especially if 'subject matter' involves the application of knowledge, skills and principles to unfamiliar situations. Nonetheless, the authors claim that the distinction is important for reasons of external validity and feasibility of comparison. Five of the surveys are classified as content-based (including EGMA, EGRA, PISA) and 10 as competency-based (including SACMEQ and TIMSS). To define commonality among different assessments, it is important to know whether they are assessing the same thing. For example, in Grade 2/3 literacy tests (EGRA, LLECE and PASEC), the domains and sub-domains range from phonological awareness and reading fluency to text comprehension. In Grade 2/3 numeracy tests, they vary from number identification, quantity discrimination, number patterns, addition and subtraction and word problems (EGMA) to proficiency in numbers, geometry, measurement, statistics and variation (LLECE).

Significant variations are also found on all other design, standard-setting and statistical criteria. These variations indicate not only the magnitude of the challenge of combining the results of these various surveys to attain global coverage, but also the challenge in deciding which type of international survey one might choose to participate in.

The political economy of assessment

Involvement in international assessments involves several considerations, some of which are political. A main issue is the relationship between the content of a national curriculum and the content of test items included in an international survey. If the extent of overlap is limited – if, say, students in a particular country have had no opportunity to learn or practise the skills assessed in the international survey – then what is one assessing? What does a country's education system gain from a survey result that shows that its students are performing much worse than elsewhere? What might be the benefits of participation in an international assessment? While a number of OECD countries have taken action to adjust aspects of their education systems in response to lower-than-expected results (Greaney & Kellaghan, 2008; Kellaghan, Greaney & Scott Murray, 2009) we know little to date about the benefits to non-OECD countries that have performed very much lower.

This raises the question of who designed the survey items, when, and in relation to whose conception of relevant knowledge. It is likely that there is a *primacy* effect: the countries who joined the survey initially selected content/skill domains and wrote items that most reflected the content and skills already included in their respective national curricula. How might this dilemma be resolved? Have late-joining countries resolved this dilemma, and if so, how?

Alongside a consideration of anticipated benefits is the question of cost of participation. PISA is a major advocate of and player in assessment surveys and has an interest in conducting more surveys in more countries in the future. It encourages countries to participate using their domestic financial resources, some of which are then sought from multilateral donors. Stakeholder interests also potentially skew the benefits of international assessment systems for individual countries. UNESCO's Institute of Statistics had a major stake in creating Indicator 4.1.1 and holds a major stake in the creation of measures. All the organisations and associations involved in the testing programmes listed above in Table 15.1 have stakes in the survival of their programmes and in the funding and continuation of their activities. These stakes, which are both financial and political, may lead to competition rather than cooperation between these powerful international players.

A broader view of stakeholding in assessment systems indicates a very wide range of possible stakeholders, both within and outside national boundaries. The World Bank's 2018 global report outlined the multiple interests that govern the actions of education stakeholders within countries (World Bank, 2018, Table O.2) and distinguished learning-aligned interests from other, competing interests. So, for example, teachers have an interest in student learning and practice in line with professional ethics, but they also have an interest in their own continued employment, job security, salary and private tuition, some or all of which may be in competition with their interest in student learning. Other stakeholders include school principals, bureaucrats, politicians, parents and students, the judiciary, employers, non-government schools (such as religious schools, private for-profit schools) and suppliers of educational inputs, all of whom have some learning-aligned interests and some of whom may have additional interests in competition (see Chapter 7 for an outline of education interest groups in Sri Lanka).

The business of assessment attracts several interest groups. The private sector includes many who sell assessment tests, analyses and reporting mechanisms. They are joined by, *inter alia*, those who represent teachers through international trade unions, international civil society organisations, international research consortia, international curriculum providers and textbook publishers, international computer software firms, and international and national firms that seek to attract highly skilled labour from specific countries, creating skill deficits within those same countries. These groups perceive opportunities for budgets, contracts, expansion of jobs and increased power. Some may perceive threats – a national government if its system is exposed internationally as a low performer; teachers if their class or their school is exposed as a low performer; national examination boards if there is a move over time to merge selection and monitoring assessment systems; trade unions if teachers are expected to increase their workload and/or change their practices to increase national levels of achievement. Political responses are likely to range from embracing proposed assessment reforms to active resistance, sabotage and avoidance of implementation. In Sri Lanka private tuition was banned officially in the 1970s but that ban was lifted subsequently – and today private tuition is now a thriving business that attracts hundreds of thousands of students and employs large numbers of retired and serving teachers.

Summative vs formative assessment

I turn now to assessment as a means of diagnosing and improving learning. Central to this discussion is the distinction between summative and formative learning assessment – a distinction that underlines the diverse roles that assessments play in society and which form part of the underlying political economy of educational assessment discussed above.

Sri Lankan students, teachers and parents are all too familiar with summative learning assessments. The purpose of national exams, end-of-year tests and end-of-term tests is to provide evidence of the level of student learning at the end of a course of study. Evidence is judged in relation to a set of criteria (criterion-based assessment) or the performance of others (norm-based assessment). When this evidence is used to select students for future education and occupations or life chances in general and when these life chances are limited and highly sought-after, the stakes are high. These may be referred to as 'high-stakes summative assessments'.

By contrast, when the purpose of an assessment is to improve student learning then we need to understand a different type of assessment, known as formative assessment. Formative assessment is intended to provide timely feedback for teachers and students. The critical words here are *timely* and *feedback*. Formative assessments help teachers and students to identify strengths and weaknesses and content/skill areas that require extra and/or remedial work. They help both teachers and students to address and remediate problems immediately and help teachers identify students in need of extra support.

The key difference between formative and summative assessment lies in the use made of the information generated by the assessment. Formative assessment is the process of seeking and interpreting evidence for use by learners and their teachers to decide where the learners are in their learning, where they need to go and how best to get there. Formative assessment provides both teacher and learner with information about performance on learning tasks that is available immediately and can be used to modify the next steps of teaching and learning. *Inter alia*, formative assessment is part of effective planning for teaching and learning, is central to classroom practice, focusses on the task, and identifies the steps needed to perform the task well. Formative assessment refers to activities that teachers and students undertake to gain evidence that can be used diagnostically to alter teaching and learning. These may include teacher observation, classroom discussion, quizzes, and analysis of student work, homework and tests and self-evaluations. Formative assessment can also be built into the lesson itself as an integral learning task (for example, students demonstrate their understanding of a subtraction task in mathematics and other students are invited to comment; or the teacher deliberately offers a wrong answer to a problem and asks the students to point out where s/he has erred). Assessment becomes formative when the information generated is used to adapt teaching and learning to meet student needs (Boston, 2002; Black & Wiliam, 1998; Assessment Reform Group, 1999).

Expressed succinctly, one may say that summative assessments are intended to *prove* learning while formative assessments are intended to *improve* learning; or to put it another way, summative assessments are assessments *of* learning while formative assessments are assessments *for* learning.

Formative assessment of students relies on the notion that the identification of errors in learning and their diagnosis provide valuable information for both student and teacher. There is a long tradition of mathematics education research that analyses the errors that children make in solving mathematical questions. Let us consider two examples.

> *Example 1* The teacher shows Siri a picture in his workbook of 10 children and 20 sweets. She asks him to use his pencil to draw lines and give each of the children the same number of sweets. Siri gives each child one sweet. The teacher asks, 'What about the others?' Siri replies, 'They are for me!'

From the teacher's point of view Siri has made an error in tackling this task. In an assessment 'test', Siri's answer would be marked 'wrong'. From Siri's viewpoint he had done what he was asked to do – he gave each child the same number of sweets (one sweet each). The teacher expected him to give out all the sweets to all the children, excluding himself. Siri had not yet learned a basic 'rule' of this type of workbook task (that the answer is contained within the information provided on the workbook page). He is expected to distance himself from the task in hand. The teacher does not expect him to seek any reward for himself. Example 2 presents a different type of 'error'.

> *Example 2* The teacher gives Kumari the following information and question: Pradeep had only 50 cents left with him. So, his mother gave him another 10 rupees. How much money does he now have altogether? Kumari's answer was 60 cents.

After further teacher questions Kumari was able to read out the question correctly and she knew the meaning of cents and rupees when considered outside the boundaries of the test. She knew that she had to add the two amounts together, so she added 50 + 10, disregarding the different units of money, rupees and cents.

The errors that children make in mathematics tell us as much about the processes of learning as do the correct answers. Research on children's errors in arithmetic stretches back to at least the 1920s in the US, Germany and Russia. That research largely remained confined within national boundaries and was only rarely exchanged, due in part to differences in learning theory traditions, education politics, the structure of education and curricula, and language (Radatz, 1979, p. 163). Since that time, research findings have been more widely shared across national boundaries (within the limitations posed by language and the availability of language translations) and include errors in place value, ordering, problem solving, decimals and percentages, ratio and proportion, shape and area. Emphasis has been placed on diagnosing the underlying causes of error and the specific actions that teachers can take to help children overcome error.[1]

Researchers classify the sources of error in overlapping ways. Radatz (1979) distinguished errors due to language difficulties, obtaining spatial information, deficient mastery of prerequisite skills, facts and concepts, incorrect associations or rigidity of thinking and the application of irrelevant rules or strategies. Carpmail et al. (n.d.) outline a variety of reasons as to why and how children make mathematical errors. These include the child's experience and background knowledge, understanding the 'rules' of the task, inappropriate choice of application strategies, imagination, mood and attitude, and confidence. The task itself can produce errors – a task may simply be too difficult for the ability of the child, the presentation of a task may be over-complex or unfamiliar, the task may be presented in language that is unfamiliar or too complex. The teacher too may contribute to children's error for a number of reasons, including a lack of confidence in or dislike of mathematics, pressure and mood, too much mathematical knowledge leading to a lack of appreciation of the difficulties children encounter, lack of experience in teaching mathematics and encountering the errors that children make, and, finally, too little knowledge and mastery of mathematics.

A large-scale study of primary teacher first-year undergraduates in Australia and a smaller study of primary teacher second-year

---

[1] For just a few examples, see the work of Hansen et al. (2014), Ryan & Williams (2007) and Carpmail et al. (n.d.) in England; Newman (1977, 1983) in New Zealand; White (2005, 2009) in Australia; Nanayakkara (1992) in Sri Lanka; White & Clements (2005) in Brunei; Radatz (1979) in Germany; and Resnick et al. (1989) in the US.

undergraduates in England identified errors made by trainee teachers (cited in Ryan & Williams, 2007). Teacher trainees were given a test based on a primary teacher curriculum. Items assessed number, measurement, space and shape, chance and data, algebra, and reasoning and proof. Teacher trainees made errors in place value and the conversion of a fraction to its decimal notation. For example, 24 per cent of the sample could not write 912 + 4/100 in decimal form. Out of three options, 12 per cent of the teachers selected 912.004 and 6 per cent 912.25. Errors were also apparent in the division of decimal numbers by 100, as for example, 300.62 ÷ 100. Two options given were 3.62 and 3.0062. 22 per cent selected 3.62. Fractions, computation, chance and measurement also generated errors. It would surprise nobody if these errors were passed on to children. More recent examples of teacher knowledge from developing countries include Bold et al. (2017) and Cueto et al. (2017).

Training in formative assessment for learning in Sri Lanka

In this section, I describe an extensive in-service training programme in Sri Lanka designed to help teachers and in-service advisors identify, diagnose and remediate errors in mathematics. Between 2014 and 2016, a series of residential workshops for provincial education officers, in-service advisors and teachers on the use of formative assessment to improve the quality of primary education were held in each of Sri Lanka's nine provinces. The initial idea for the teacher workshops on ways to improve primary education quality came from one of the provincial directors, who was frustrated at the type of information that was being generated and fed back to him by the national assessments of learning outcomes. He was (naturally) dissatisfied with the low performance of his province in a national assessment. He was frustrated by the design of a national study, with its attendance sampling characteristics, which did not permit him or his officers and teachers to compare performance across the schools, divisions and zones within his province – and take remedial action to support them. Aligned with this was a concern that a school principal and its teachers needed to know not only where it stood compared with other schools and teachers, but also how teachers could improve the performance of students.

The initial workshops were conducted over two to three days for different staff cadres. The training team moved from one province to the next and, through experience and regular evaluation, improved the workshop programme. In its final form the programme consisted of two components: five days for assistant directors of education (primary education), in-service advisors (primary education) and primary education teachers; and one day for senior provincial education officers and theme convenors of the provincial plan. The one-day programme for the senior staff, conducted towards the end of the parallel five-day programme, included inputs from those who had participated based on their work in the week-long programme. A significant feature of the five-day workshops was the two half-days spent working with individual students in schools. In some provinces, separate Sinhala and Tamil workshops were organised; in others, Sinhala and Tamil participants attended the same workshop, with separate language streams for specific sessions. Between 2014 and 2017, around 700 in-service advisors, education officers and teachers participated in the workshops.

The content of the workshops included a series of linked activities: (i) brief reviews of international research on 'effective teachers', and an exploration of the purposes of formative and summative assessment; (ii) the identification of common errors through an item analysis of the Grade 5 test performance of the workshop participants and of Grade 5 students in two to four schools in each province; (iii) a review of common error types; (iv) the development of an interview protocol to diagnose errors; (v) interviews with children to identify and diagnose a range of errors; (vi) review of relevant curriculum units/learning tasks and the development of remedial activities; (vii) trialling remedial activities; (viii) writing up and sharing of error, diagnosis, remediation notes; and (ix) the development of future work plans. All teaching materials were prepared in Sinhala, Tamil and English, and copies of all training materials were shared digitally with provincial staff to be used and adapted in the future by staff in the provinces. The Sri Lankan teacher educators and teachers found the work of Newman (1977, 1983) to be especially helpful and it was her outline of nine types of errors that informed much of the professional development work.

At the beginning of each workshop, participants worked anonymously through a Grade 5 primary curriculum test, drawn from the doctoral research of Nanayakkara (1992). This was then used as a basis for item-analysis, a subsequent item-analysis of Grade 5 student performance, and the creation and application of remediation strategies. The error rate of the adult workshop participants averaged 14.4 per cent across four provinces which, while being a cause for surprise, and echoing the Australian study reported above, generated a strong motivation to understand how and why item errors had occurred.

The workshops included time spent in schools with students who had produced errors on the same Grade 5 test as that taken by the adult workshop participants, and the preparation of interview protocols. On their first day in the schools, two participants each worked with an individual student and invited him or her to retry the items on which they had produced errors in the earlier paper-and-pencil test. This was followed by a question-and-answer discussion employing the interview protocol (for one example see Box 15.1).

Having diagnosed error types, workshop participants reconvened and developed remediation plans to try out with the same student the following day. So, in the case of Malith, two of the participants developed a plan to help him overcome/remediate his transformation error.

Box 15.2 presents this example plan. It is presented here step by step to indicate how teacher educators might collaborate with teacher trainees to sensitise them to the depth of skill involved in helping students overcome errors.

Since the programme was designed to enhance the professional development of teachers, in-service advisors and education officers, and since each programme involved an evaluation of how it might be improved in its subsequent provision, its effects have not been evaluated in a systematic fashion. We have no 'before' and 'after' results, in terms of either changes in everyday teacher educator or teacher practices, and no 'before' and 'after' results on the impact on student learning. Nonetheless, the programme generated teacher enthusiasm and a desire to learn more about the practices of formative assessment. This is a sound starting point for future developments. As well as providing a wealth of material for the continuous professional development of teachers in the future, this type of material has enormous potential for use in curriculum manuals for teachers and as a training module for teachers and teacher educators at the national as well as provincial level.

Prospects for formative assessment in Sri Lanka

On the question of formative assessment – intended to measure learning progress in order to diagnose learning problems and provide feedback to students – we learn from the NEC that formative assessment has 'descended to a level where the teacher administered tests and compiled the marks to add to a total for the summative assessment of learning' (NEC, 2022, p. 129). In other words, 'formative assessment' appears

Box 15.1: Example of an error diagnosis

A Grade 5 student had answered the following paper-and-pencil assessment task incorrectly (in the Sinhala language):

> 435 children were being prepared to go on an excursion. Each bus can carry only 20 children. To carry all the children how many buses are needed? (Correct Answer = 22)

At his first attempt Malith had written '8,700'. When the teacher educators met him the following day and presented him with the same question, his answer was the same: 8,700.

He was then asked Q1 and Q2 below (in Sinhala).

Q1 Can you read the question to me, aloud? If you do not know a word, leave it out. (To check for a possible reading error.)

Q2 Can you tell me what the question is asking you to do? (To check for a possible comprehension error.)

His answers suggested that he could read the question and understand what the question was asking him to do. He was then asked Q3 below.

Q3 Can you tell me how you are going to find the answer? (To check for a possible transformation error.)

He responded:

> '435 has to be multiplied by 20 to get the number of buses needed'.

He then calculated this multiplication correctly and arrived at his answer, 8,700. The interviewer diagnosed his error as one of 'transformation' – that is, he had chosen to *multiply* 435 by 20 rather than *divide* 435 by 20.

The interview stopped there. Had Malith answered Q3 satisfactorily the interviewer would have proceeded to Questions 4 and 5, below:

Q4 Can you show me what you do to get the answer? Talk aloud as you do it, so that I can understand how you are thinking. (To check for a possible process error.)

Q5 Can you now write down the answer to the question? (To check for a possible encoding error.)

Box 15.2: Example of remediation plan

Step 1: Give a similar but simpler problem with number of children less than 10 and a single digit number of children per taxi. Select two numbers that are exactly divisible. Example 1:

> There are 9 friends in a group. They are planning to go to the temple in a three-wheeler taxi. If one taxi can carry only 3 persons, how many taxis are needed to carry all the friends?

Ask the student to solve the problem using Dienes blocks. Provide help, if necessary. Repeat the process with one or two similar problems, with increasing difficulty – but with no 'carry over'. Discuss with the student and try to find out the underlying mathematical operation. Provide help, if necessary. Try to establish that the underlying operation is 'division'.

Step 2: Ask the student to answer the first problem that he/she answered in Step 1, using paper and pencil. Provide help, if necessary. Ask the student to repeat the process using paper and pencil for the other problems that he/she solved using Dienes blocks. Ensure that the student has understood the 'transformation' step correctly.

Step 3: Give a problem similar to the original question but simpler, with the number of children and number of children per taxi each smaller than the numbers in the original question. Select two numbers that are exactly divisible. Example 2:

> 36 children were being prepared to go on a trip in vans. A van can carry only 9 children. To carry all the children how many vans are needed?

Ask the student to find the number of vans needed, using Dienes blocks. Provide help, if necessary. Repeat the process with one or two similar problems, with increasing difficulty. Ensure that the student is able to find the number of vans needed, when the two given numbers are exactly divisible.

Step 4: Repeat Step 3 with a problem involving two numbers that are not exactly divisible. (Use Dienes blocks.) Example 3:

> 50 children were being prepared to go on a trip in vans. A van can carry only 9 children. To carry all the children how many vans are needed?
>
> Ensure that the student is able to find the number of vans needed, using Dienes blocks, when the two given numbers are not exactly divisible.
>
> *Step 5:* Ask the student to answer Example 3 using paper and pencil. Provide help, if necessary. Ensure that the student is able to find the number of vans needed, using paper and pencil, when the two given numbers are not exactly divisible.
>
> *Step 6:* Ask the student to answer the original question again (using paper and pencil). Observe the working and provide additional help if necessary. Ensure that the student is able to answer problems related to the given context.
>
> *Step 7:* Give a similar problem under a different context. Observe the working and provide help, if necessary. Example 4:
>
>> A waiter is preparing the tables for guests at a wedding. One bottle of aerated water is placed on the table for each group of 4 guests. How many bottles are needed to serve 54 guests?
>
> Repeat with additional examples drawn from different contexts.
>
> Source: Based on teachers' plan, edited by G. L. S. Nanayakkara.

to be interpreted by many as continuous summative assessment. As suggested above, formative assessment at the classroom level is of enormous potential value to students and teachers alike. Unlike the myriad structural organisational, technical and financial issues that beset the timely use of both national and international survey data for student learning at ground level (UNESCO, 2023), formative assessment provides teachers and students with information that can be used immediately to guide subsequent learning tasks and teacher inputs. Employed alongside graded learning materials and wider 'remedial' teaching strategies, including those described in Chapter 14, formative assessment has the potential to improve learning and provide a sound basis for sustainable learning into the future.

Conclusion

The development of internationally comparable tests of student performance in primary and secondary education involves formidable technical and considerable political challenges. But if national curricula are to continue to be valued and not be determined by the backwash effects of international assessment, we might ask why the evidence garnered for SDG4 Indicator 4.1.1 or other learning outcome indicators needs to be internationally comparable. At the heart of SDG4 are learners. But the SDG framework of Goals, Targets and Indicators seems to leave them, their teachers, their teaching and learning processes, teaching and learning materials and daily learning assessment practices out of the chain of activities and processes required for the improvement of learning and for the type of 'mastery' that provides the student with confidence and a desire to go on learning in the future – in other words, learning that sustains learning.

Formative assessment occurs in diverse classrooms with diverse teachers and diverse learners facing myriad local learning and teaching challenges. The 'results' of formative assessment cannot be homogenised across students, schools and systems and used by education managers to 'test' the efficiency and effectiveness of an education system. The process of formative assessment by teachers and students can make an important and timely contribution to learning outcomes, especially when employed alongside a range of 'remedial' learning materials. In the future all Sri Lankan test developers, teacher educators and teachers might be expected to learn about – and use – formative assessment tools and all curriculum developers and textbook writers might be expected to include formative assessment tasks within student texts, student workbooks and teacher guides.

16
Lessons and reflections

This book has charted flows of ideas and policies that have influenced today's education system in Sri Lanka. It has highlighted those ideas and policies generated in Sri Lanka and by Sri Lankans which have influenced the broader international discourse on development and education, especially that on human development, the satisfaction of basic needs, education for all, poverty reduction, and sustainable development. Conversely, it has identified ideas and policies generated by the international finance and education community which have influenced the course of development and education in Sri Lanka.

In Chapter 3 I shared my inaugural professorial lecture, 'Learning from developing countries', delivered in 1988 at the UCL Institute of Education. At the time of its delivery the terms 'developing countries' and 'the South' were in widespread use to describe economically poor countries, where the social conditions of the mass of the population needed improvement. While noting that the majority of countries in Latin America, the Caribbean, Africa, Asia and Oceania fell into this broad category I acknowledged that the economic, political and social conditions of these countries varied enormously. I also recognised that despite the political independence of many countries since the end of the Second World War, many continued to follow or emulate education models from elsewhere, supported often through development 'aid' and other arrangements, with relatively little adaptation to local conditions, values and needs. I called for greater voice to be given to education researchers and educators well-grounded in the societal, cultural and economic contexts of the countries with which 'aid' relationships were conducted. I called for cross-cultural theoretical models to be grounded in diverse empirical realities and for a more equal knowledge exchange on the North-South knowledge superhighway.

So, what have I learned from my research journey about development, education and learning in Sri Lanka across time and space, in the company of fellow travellers?

Continuity and change

The first lesson is one of continuity and change. Sri Lanka is a culturally diverse society with settler roots and ancient civilisations originating mainly from India, stretching back over two thousand years, and with diverse social, economic, political and education traditions. Over time these were overlaid by the colonial policies and practices of the Portuguese, the Dutch and the British.

Present-day post-colonial studies of education focus critically on enduring colonial legacies in contemporary education systems around the world (Chapter 2). Some contemporary policy issues in Sri Lanka are traceable to the British colonial period and earlier and have endured. These include the language of instruction, the ethnic, religious and language identities of schools, and the enduring educational disadvantages of some minority communities (Chapters 7, 10, 13). Contemporary GCE O and A level exams are designed and implemented by the Sri Lankan Department of Education. Their formal links with the examination boards of the universities of Cambridge and London ceased before independence and they were abolished in 1972. They were reinstated in 1978 and renamed GCE O and A level, a symbolic renaming that appealed to those who valued the long tradition of links with the Cambridge and London examination boards and who sought to retain names that resonated internationally (Chapter 4). The history of Sri Lanka's contemporary universities is rooted in the Ceylon University College, affiliated with the University of London in 1921.

Other current policy debates, decisions and practices may more properly be traced to the 1930s and 1940s, when the bold recommendations of the Kannangara Committee led the semi-autonomous State Council to pass legislation on fee-free education from kindergarten to university, the relegation of the role of the English language in the curriculum, and the introduction of mother-tongue education for all (Chapters 7, 12, 13). These radical anti-colonial reforms occurred in the years immediately preceding formal independence.

Post-colonial studies tend to underplay *changes* in policies and practices that have occurred during both the colonial and post-independence periods, colonial legacies that may have been absorbed deliberately into contemporary systems, and the role of post-colonial national elites in policy reform. Portuguese, Dutch and British colonial policies and practices differed from each other, and changes were introduced during each of these periods. Suppressed by the colonial powers, pre-colonial traditions in education were not extinguished completely and re-emerged in new forms, especially in the late nineteenth century. Policies on school exams changed several times during the British colonial period; so too in the post-colonial period. To write of either the colonial or post-colonial period as if there was a single continuous policy is to overlook the many changes, twists and turns during both periods. Following constitutional change in 1987, provincial decentralisation of education led to major shifts in the financing and management of schools. Policies on curriculum, textbooks and teacher education changed several times before and following independence and continue to do so. The political orientation of national elites has changed several times since independence, with consequent changes in education policy (Chapters 4, 11).

That all contemporary systems of education are shaped by legacies from the past is neither a new nor a startling insight. What is startling is that, perhaps with the exception of education historians, most social science researchers understand little about the history of the education system in which they undertake their research, irrespective of whether this is the 'familiar' system in which they themselves were schooled, or an 'unfamiliar' one in which they embark on research.

In sum, analyses of current-day policies and practices benefit from an understanding of policy continuities *and* changes during both the colonial *and* post-colonial periods.

Myriad conditions for and drivers of education reform

A second lesson is for those who seek to influence the literature on development and education (Chapter 2). Much of that literature has focussed on a definition of development defined largely as economic growth. Some, especially that stemming from the World Conferences on Education for All, the Millennium Development Goals and the Sustainable Development Goals, conveys the idea that the setting of international and national goals and targets, in and of themselves, provides a sufficient spur for educational change to take place. History suggests otherwise.

Let us for a moment step back in time and across space. Worldwide, education has served many purposes and arisen out of myriad conditions. The purposes have been, *inter alia*, to civilise through religious education, to socialise and reproduce societal norms and ideals, to prepare young people for diverse types of work, and to create a modern and cohesive nation state. While these definitions of purpose may have been driven by the vision, mission and zeal of individual reformers and organisations, their efforts have always been situated within broader economic and political conditions out of which those efforts arose.

Military defeat, economic rivalry, revolution, religious reformation, restoration, political independence and post-war reconstruction – all have shaped education reform in various places at different points in time. Religious reformation in Scotland led to widespread reform of basic education from the 1660s. Defeat in the Napoleonic Wars in the early 1800s convinced the Prussian leadership that a modern army required, *inter alia*, a massive expansion of compulsory education. Following the French Revolution, Napoleon created a centralised educational administration which opened new schools, appointed teachers, and defined and controlled school curricula. Germany's political federation in 1871 and consequent economic performance contributed to England's drive to 'catch up' and to introduce compulsory education in 1880. The fledgling independent nation of the United States of America needed to foster unity among culturally diverse peoples and achieved this in part through education. The Meiji restoration in Japan was followed by the introduction of compulsory education in 1872. The Russian Revolution and the Chinese Cultural Revolution led to major reforms in education in 1918 and 1978, respectively. The prospect of political independence provided an impetus for radical education reforms in many former colonies in Asia and Africa from the late 1940s.

Some of these drivers resonate in some of Sri Lanka's history. Religious socialisation and conversion played a major part in defining the purpose of education from the time of the first Sinhalese and Tamil settlers, through the three waves of European colonisation, and on to the present day (Chapter 1). The colonial government's need for educated and loyal functionaries was achieved in part through the medium of English instruction for a small elite. During the twentieth century the extension of universal franchise, the prospect of political independence and strong ideals of egalitarianism underpinned radical changes in education policy (Chapter 7). Demographic transitions, rural-urban migration and population increase are conditions that continue to shape the challenge of equitable provision of education (Chapters 12, 14). Insurgencies, political crises and the need for political stability were powerful imperatives that led to policy changes in the 1970s (Chapters 4 and 7) and late 1980s (Chapter 8). This is not to say that these were sufficient conditions for change. The cessation of the civil war in 2009 led to few substantial changes in policy or practice.

Reforms – and resistance to them – are driven by the interests of particular socio-economic-political groups. Chapters 7, 8 and 9 underlined the role of 'political will', of national and local politicians and bureaucrats, of school leaders, of elites and masses, of teachers and private tuition masters in both promoting and resisting reform. Actors external to the country also play a role in promoting and supporting certain types of reform at various times, from membership of colonial government committees, church councils and employer groups through the nineteenth and twentieth centuries, to officers and consultants to multilateral banks, aid agencies and international non-governmental organisations through the late twentieth and early twenty-first centuries.

The account of the growth of educational opportunity among the minority plantation community extended this list of underlying conditions and drivers of education change – and of interested actors – over time (Chapter 10). From the 1970s national-level drivers of change included legislation on the nationalisation of the plantation schools and changes in citizenship legislation. Economic drivers included the growth of a plantation labour surplus and new employment opportunities in national and international labour markets. Political drivers included the electoral strength of the plantation community and trade union pressures. A growing number of government-employed teachers of plantation origin provided role models for the next generation of plantation children and fuelled parental demands for education. Over the years exogenous actors and organisations played a role in moving education forward. These included the activities of religious missions with a global reach (late 1800s), pressures from the home (British) parliament (early 1900s), foreign-funded grants to education in the plantations (from the 1970s) and global pressures on human rights (1990s). The drive, ambition and leadership of a wide range of individual actors have played a vital part in this story of reform over time.

Drivers of change in the twenty-first century

The main drivers of educational change in the early 1970s and late 1980s were the insurgencies and the need for government to regain political stability. The insurgencies provided unexpected shocks to the education system, led to the loss of life of large numbers of Sri Lanka's youth, and disrupted opportunities for education for many more. Since the turn of the twenty-first century there have been three more unexpected shocks – the tsunami of 2004, the COVID-19 pandemic of 2020–2, and the economic and political crisis of 2022. To what extent have these driven education reform?

Tsunami 2004

On the morning of 26 December 2004, a subduction earthquake occurred near northern Sumatra. The resulting tsunami struck the eastern coast of Sri Lanka at 8.35 am. There was no early warning system, leaving most people on the coast unprepared. The tsunami claimed 35,000 victims, a third of whom were children, and injured a further 23,000. It destroyed upwards of 100,000 homes and displaced one million people. Around 80,350 students and 3,300 teachers were displaced from their schools across 10 districts. It orphaned 932 children, and 3,477 children suffered the loss of one parent (UNICEF, 2009). December 26th was a school holiday, and it is not clear whether the impact of the tsunami would have been greater or smaller had it occurred on a regular school day. Seventy-four schools were destroyed and 108 were severely damaged. Nearly 300 schools were converted into camps for internally displaced persons (Education Rehabilitation Monitor 2009, in Cels et al., 2022).

Schools were rebuilt and some were re-sited away from the coast. Families were rehabilitated and schools reopened. Despite this epic human tragedy which claimed almost a quarter of a million lives in 14 countries surrounding the Indian Ocean, schools, principals and teachers remain unprepared for a future tsunami (Cels et al., 2022). Only half of the 430 Sri Lankan schools in coastal areas exposed to the threat of a potential future tsunami are within audible range of a tsunami early warning tower. Schools rarely conduct fire drills or construct tsunami evacuation plans.

This is an example of an unexpected shock to education of unimaginable proportions. In the immediate and short term, it prompted major rehabilitation efforts. Yet, to date, no clear and coordinated policies, guidelines or practices at the national or local level have been created to prepare principals, teachers and students for a similar event in the future. The potential of this shock to drive forward a reform of policies and/or guidance has not yet been realised. There are several reasons why this may be the case. First, tsunamis have been a rare occurrence in Sri Lanka's history and may be judged unlikely to recur in the future. Second, the tsunami affected coastal areas, mainly on the east and south-east coast. It did not affect the entire country and the families of most national policymakers were unaffected.

COVID-19 pandemic 2020–2

In March 2020, as I completed the field research reported in Chapter 14, I became aware of a minuscule rise in the number of reported cases of COVID-19 in Sri Lanka. The first death was reported on 11 March. Schools closed two days later and reopened at the beginning of July to allow students in Grades 5, 11 and 13 to sit exams. They reopened for all, bar Grade 1, in late August, closed again in October and reopened for Grade 6 and above in late November.

Unlike the devastation of tsunami, COVID spread across the country, affecting people of all ages, ethnicities, social groups and places of residence. The Ministry of Education, TV channels, internet providers, provincial education officers and schoolteachers assembled a range of internet, print, hybrid and blended learning and teaching materials (Ministry of Education, 2020). Although teachers adapted to this unprecedented situation very quickly, students from socio-economically disadvantaged groups were affected disproportionately, due in part to their lack of access to the internet via PCs or smartphones and home support (Dayasiri et al., 2022; Fukami, 2022). Even by September 2021 it was estimated that fewer than half of all students were able to follow teaching and learning remotely (De Mel, 2021). Just one day of school closure was leading to an estimated loss of student learning opportunity of around 25 million hours and teaching of around 1.4 million hours (UNESCO-UNICEF, 2021).

Unlike the tsunami, the COVID-19 pandemic appears to be driving policies and plans of action for change in education today, less in terms of how to mitigate the health effects of a similar pandemic in the future and more in terms of the delivery of education. The National Education Commission asserts that Sri Lanka is moving through 'an initial phase of development in the process of transforming a conventional education system to a technology-enhanced one' (NEC, 2022, pp. 189 ff.). Calling for all education institutions, irrespective of location and student numbers, to be provided with ICT facilities, connectivity and software, the need for training of 'competent personnel' (in technology-enabled curriculum development and pedagogy) is recognised. It remains to be seen how and whether these calls will be met.

Economic and political crisis 2022

Early in 2022 the world heard about Sri Lanka's worst economic and political crisis in more than seventy years. The national and international news headlined Sri Lanka's violent anti- and pro-government protests; acute shortages of fuel, cooking gas, medicines and essential items; debt repayment defaults; the torching of politicians' houses; and the ransacking of the president's palace. The incumbent prime minister, Mahinda Rajapakse, was forced to resign, to be replaced by Ranil Wickramasinghe. Two months later, the president, Gotabaya Rajapakse (the former prime minister's brother), was also forced to resign. He fled the country. The recently appointed Prime Minister Wickramasinghe (a former minister of education in the 1980s) became the country's new president.

The economic crisis of 2022 was attributed variously to a range of proximate causes, including the Easter Sunday church bombings in 2019 and the consequent decline of tourism; the COVID-19 pandemic from 2020, the slow-down of economic activity and the curtailment of foreign tourism; the banning of imported fertilisers and decline in food production; tax cuts; corruption and mismanagement; and international – especially Chinese – 'debt traps'. By January 2022 foreign exchange reserves had reduced to just $1 billion, a massive decline from the $14.5 billion just two years earlier (International Monetary Fund, 2015).

Economic analysts point to vulnerabilities, economic mismanagement and a lack of fiscal discipline over an extended period of time (Moramudali, 2022). In the early 1990s, when still classified as a low-income country, Sri Lanka had been able to access concessionary loans from, *inter alia*, the World Bank, the Asian Development Bank and Japan for a range of sectors, including education. In 1997 Sri Lanka was classified as a middle-income country and in 2018 as an upper middle-income country. This affected the country's ability to access concessionary loans. Already by 2007 the country was borrowing heavily from international capital markets, issuing international sovereign bonds and accumulating debt. The debt included Chinese loans taken out to fund large infrastructure projects. Where in 2005 non-concessionary debt accounted for less than 3 per cent of GDP, by 2020 it had reached 50 per cent. Over the period 1990–2014, and despite rises in per capita income, the country's tax revenue declined from 19.1 per cent to

10.1 per cent of GDP, due to weak revenue administration and a lack of government effort. From 2000 there had been a failure to diversify exports away from low value-added plantation crops and apparel and to attract substantial amounts of foreign direct investment. Throughout, the government subsidised fuel and electricity, supplied mostly by loss-making state-owned enterprises. By the time the COVID-19 pandemic swept across the island, the economy was already vulnerable.

At the beginning of 2022, schools were returning to a normal pattern of opening following the COVID pandemic. But the economic and political crisis of April 2022 forced many to close again. Parents could not buy fuel to transport their children to school, and bus services were restricted. As the crisis worsened, the poorest parents found themselves having to choose which child would be sent to school on a particular day, for although schools are fee-free and uniform material is free, parents still pay for exercise books, pens, shoes, socks and satchels. When the overriding priority for households is finding food to stay alive, paying for children's education become prohibitive.

So, what, if anything, does the current economic crisis have to do with education? The failure to raise revenue through taxation has had an impact on all social sectors, including the inability of the government to meet demands for an increase in education budgets which, as we saw above, have been hovering around 2 per cent of GDP over many years. Teachers are already poorly paid, the COVID-19 pandemic closed schools for prolonged periods of time, and the government effort to introduce remote learning was slow and ineffective for those without access to the internet. Without a huge injection of effort and resource, the system will struggle to create educational opportunities to recover the learning losses experienced during the pandemic equitably.

Exceptionalisms revisited

A third lesson is the need to examine critically some of the exceptional features of Sri Lankan education – exceptional, that is, when compared with elsewhere. At the beginning of this book I set out seven distinctive features of the Sri Lankan education system: historically high levels of literacy driven by principles of equality of opportunity; gender parity in education; mother-tongue education offered in the language of the minority as well as the majority population; fee-free education; a small private education sector; guaranteed non-selective access for all students to Grade 11 (and soon to be Grade 13); and a low percentage of both

GDP and government budget allocated to education. Here I revisit three of these features – equality of opportunity in education, gender parity and the financing of education.

Equality of opportunity in education revisited

Chapters 1, 2, 6, 7 and 14 underlined the influence of the political rhetoric of social egalitarianism on policies of equality of opportunity in education in the years leading up to and following independence. These included, *inter alia*, fee-free education from primary education to university, the nationalisation of denominational schools and private teacher training institutes in 1960, the prohibition on establishing new private schools in the early 1960s, a steady increase in 'open and non-selective access' to the senior grades of secondary education, a common curriculum through 11 years of schooling, the absence of 'streaming by ability', and the provision of free textbooks, free school uniforms, subsidised public transport and free or subsidised school meals. These provisions remain in place today alongside the phased implementation of 'guaranteed education' for all up the end of Grade 13.

Formally legislating for equality of opportunity in education and equality practices are not the same. Legal provisions on free education and equality of educational opportunity for all have proved challenging to implement in practice for reasons, *inter alia*, of governance, service delivery, fee payments by parents for admissions to popular schools, and teacher deployment practices that disfavour the schools in the most disadvantaged areas and communities (Wehella & Balasooriya, 2014). Equality of enrolment has not always translated into equality of learning outcomes (Chapter 13). A range of social class factors inhibited efforts to provide all children with a 'relevant' curriculum, not least because different social groups viewed 'relevance' in diverse ways (Chapter 4). A range of other factors, including political 'interference', undermined efforts to upgrade schools in disadvantaged areas during the 2000s (Chapter 8). Political will in education can be double-edged. A strong national-level political will driving policies and plans forward can be undermined by local political wills which undermine the daily operation of schools. Social disparities in education and youth aspirations have been present for decades but these appear to have grown since 1977 (Chapter 11). Inequalities in the deployment of trained English teachers to primary schools are associated with differences in teaching and learning methods (Chapter 13).

The principle of equality of opportunity of access to education is long-held in Sri Lanka – but if it is to translate into equality of learning outcomes, more attention needs to be paid to the resources and processes that surround learning and teaching. 'Equitable' education involves the notion of 'fairness' and the need to ensure that all schools and students receive the inputs promised by policy and, in some cases, the need to compensate already disadvantaged learners, teachers and schools with additional support.

Gender parity revisited

The second exceptionalism is gender parity. By the 1980s Sri Lanka was approaching gender parity in enrolments in primary and secondary education. Today that parity has been replaced by female advantage in education. Several chapters pointed to the consistent superiority of girls' performance in tests of achievement in recent years. In 2015 females comprised 63 per cent of all state-level university enrolments across all subjects. Only in engineering were female enrolments lower than male enrolments. One might suggest, then, that it is boys not girls who are subject to gender disparities in education and that remedial action is required to reduce them (Aturupane, Shojo & Ebenezer, 2018).

This reality seems to have been overlooked by the Global Partnership for Education, a multi-stakeholder partnership and funding platform that aims to strengthen education systems in developing countries, created in 2002 as a successor to the Education for All Fast Track Initiative. A media announcement in March 2023 stated that, following the COVID-19 pandemic and the sudden downturn of the economy, Sri Lanka would be included for the first time in Partnership funding. The statement read: 'the Global Partnership for Education looks forward to working with the government of Sri Lanka and a wide range of development partners to get more children, particularly girls, into school and to improve the quality of learning for all children …' (Global Partnership for Education, 2023). While there is no doubt that recent events have impacted all children, especially the poorest, and that strenuous efforts must be made to support their education into the future, one must wonder how much homework members of this organisation have done on the relationship between gender and education in Sri Lanka and how much effort is required to support the education of poor boys as well as poor girls. Economists and many members of international advocacy organisations tend to assume that the knowledge they generate or the advocacy they mobilise is based on universal knowledge, with universal application. This is rarely the case.

Girls' advantage in educational outcomes does not extend to equality of opportunity in the workplace. It is here that the Sri Lankan experience is non-exceptional and converges with that of many countries. Female unemployment rates are higher than male unemployment rates and have been so historically (Chapter 8). In equivalent jobs, the mean level of education and cognitive skill is, on average, higher for females than for males, the mean level of non-cognitive skills valued by employers is the same for females and males, while the mean level of earnings is, on average, lower for females than for males (Himaz, 2010; D. Gunawardene, 2015). Recent research also suggests that households spend more on girls' education than boys' (Himaz & Aturupane, 2018). Taken together, these studies suggest that despite girls' superior enrolment rates and academic performance in schools, their 'returns to education' are lower than for boys. They also point to positive discrimination in favour of males in the labour market.

Education finance revisited

The third exceptionalism of Sri Lanka's education system to be revisited is the low percentage of GDP allocated to educational expenditure – around 2 per cent. This compares with around 6 per cent in Malaysia, South Korea, Thailand and Vietnam in 2011. The most recent evidence, from Sri Lanka's Central Bank and the Ministries of Education and Higher Education, suggests further deterioration – just 1.93 per cent in 2019, 1.85 in 2021 and 1.52 in 2022 (provisional). This compares with an average of 4.5 per cent in low- and middle-income countries (Dundar et al., 2017; National Education Commission, 2022).

That Sri Lanka has succeeded in enrolling so many children in a largely state-supported system of primary and secondary education over so many years remains remarkable and exceptional. It raises the question of how Sri Lanka has outperformed and continues to outperform many other countries in the region at every stage of general education, achieves this without charging fees for enrolment in government schools and universities, and, additionally, offers free textbooks, uniforms and subsidised travel and meals for schoolchildren.

There are at least three reasons. The first is the relatively low level of salary paid to teachers. The second is a thriving private tuition business that runs parallel to the state system. Most students in general education attend two systems of education simultaneously – the state system on weekday mornings/early afternoons and an array of private tuition arrangements in the late afternoons, early evenings and weekends

(Chapter 11). The third is the historically low percentage of students attending university and higher education and the reduced impact this has had on the overall education budget.

However, questions have been raised many times over about the quality of education (Chapters 6 and 13; National Education Commission, 2022; World Bank, 2018, 2021) and the level and types of learning outcomes achieved across the country. It is hardly surprising, then, that in 2022 the National Education Commission called for an increase in public expenditure on education over the next ten years to 4.5 per cent of GDP, alongside a fairer distribution and efficiency of fund utilisation (NEC, 2022). Education finance is an essential ingredient of reform policies, for which there are currently a number of proposals. Policies may be resource-rich or resource-poor. Statements of goals, objectives and means cannot be credited with the label 'policy' if resources for their implementation are neither identified nor allocated. For too long education budgets have been starved of the resources necessary to make significant and sustainable inroads on increasing teacher salaries and pensions, on teacher education and deployment, on increasing and improving resources for curriculum and pedagogy renewal, and on measures that will reduce enduring disparities between social groups in educational inputs, processes and learning outcomes.

The resources available for education policy implementation in Sri Lanka need to be understood in a broader economic and political context. Earlier chapters described how the education and health sectors attracted much political attention and resource in the years leading up to independence and in the early post-independence years. This was driven by early democracy, high levels of political engagement among most social groups and a government that collected a high proportion of GDP from taxes, a sizeable proportion of which flowed from the plantation sector. However, from being a high-tax, high-spend economy in the 1940s–1960s, Sri Lanka has become an exceptionally low-tax, low-spend economy (Moore, 2017).

Limited resources for education are stretched even further as the system expands ever upwards – increasing numbers of children enrol in the highest grades of general education and move on to university and other higher education institutions. There are increased pressures for greater government involvement in pre-school education and in technical and vocational education. There are increased numbers of teachers. Part of the solution must lie in the raising of more taxes.

Concepts and theories revisited

In Chapter 2 I presented an overview of theoretical concepts of value in understanding development and education, and, by implication, learning. Concepts frame empirical analysis, but they can also be generated by it. In what ways might the empirical analyses offered in this book, grounded mainly in the Sri Lankan context, shape development and education concepts in the future?

Sri Lanka's experience of education reform in the transition to independence generated the idea that education is an investment and foreshadowed the powerful international discourse on education as human capital that emerging in the 1960s (Chapter 7). Concepts from human capital and modernisation theory on the one hand and neo-Marxist and dependency theory on the other were employed to analyse episodes of examination reform in 1972 and 1977 (Chapter 4). This application led to several conceptual refinements and additions, including the idea that in some contexts change might be better described as a series of 'punctuated equilibria' than as functional adjustment or resolution of class conflict. Seemingly radical changes in curricula and examinations in a political climate of self-reliant independence may be driven as much by individual professional interests as by group class interests. Grand theories of development do not necessarily hold their power across time and space. While the 1972 reforms appeared to have been driven by 'beneficent modernisers', the 1977 reforms appeared to have been driven more by a return to the 'old order' and by those elites whose own children stood to gain (Chapter 4). In other words, a concept drawn from one theoretical perspective might apply well at one point in time, but less well at another.

Notwithstanding the salience of the concept of education as investment in the politics of the 1940s, empirical analyses of education and job performance in public- and private sector organisations in the 1970s raised questions about it (Chapter 5). Education levels were not necessarily related to job performance, earnings were not necessarily related to job performance, and education and earnings were not necessarily correlated. Empirical analysis indicated that the skill requirements for job performance included a wide range of social and personal attributes and orientations that went beyond the cognitive. It also raised questions about the motivations for working and for learning and pointed to a range of motivations that went beyond the purely financial.

Five propositions of the 'diploma disease' thesis, which was grounded initially in the Sri Lanka of the early 1970s, were also subjected to empirical scrutiny (Chapter 6). Three, concerning the societal consensus about education as a channel of mobility, the asynchronous growth of education and of the modern sector of employment, and the raising of educational qualification levels over time for similar jobs, were broadly confirmed. However, two propositions were questioned. The first was that Sri Lanka was a 'later developer' and a 'later industrialiser' than Japan. This was questioned on the basis of Sri Lanka's early industrialisation of agriculture from the mid-nineteenth century (Chapters 6 and 10). The second was that employer behaviour in the 1960s/1970s had led to exam-dominated teaching and learning in Sri Lankan classrooms. This was questioned on the basis of documentary historical evidence which presented exam domination as an issue of concern since at least the late nineteenth century.

Sri Lanka's early achievements in fee-free education and literacy were much lauded around the world in the 1960s and 1970s (Chapter 1). That this had arisen from the application of principles of social egalitarianism in the transition to independence, combined with state intervention, political will and adequate financial resources, was promoted by the international community as a lesson for other low-income countries. However, what this lesson obscured was the relationship between the means and ends of development and social disparity in the Sri Lankan case. A large part of the government revenue that made this achievement possible was raised through the labours of the minority Tamil community in the export-oriented plantation sector. But the children of those who laboured in the plantations would have to wait many years to enjoy the same investment in education as children in the rest of the country (Chapters 1, 7, 10). The educational ends of the majority of the country appear to have been achieved by means of the profitable work of a minority.

Growth in educational opportunity does not necessarily imply social equality in education. As noted earlier, the principles of social egalitarianism that have been circulating in Sri Lanka for a century continue to face challenges in their application. Substantial growth in educational opportunities in basic education since the 1940s has not removed all divisions and social disparities in education, especially those between school type, medium of instruction, and urban/rural location. While growth led to gender parity in primary, secondary and higher education it has now been replaced by female advantage (Chapter 1). Growth in opportunities in several types of post-basic education since the wave of economic globalisation from the late 1970s has not removed all social divisions and disparities. Growth and division appear to go hand in hand (Chapter 11; Little & Hettige, 2013).

The empirical work on globalisation pointed to the need to consider what might constitute the notion of 'successful globalisation' (Chapters 11 and 12). The Sri Lankan experience of globalisation since the 1970s, alongside a civil war that lasted from the late 1970s to 2009, suggested that sustained peace and political stability should be a key ingredient in any definition of success in the future. And, reflecting contemporary ideas on *sustainable* development, future research on globalisation and education should also be framed within the ideas of sustainable growth, sustainable equality and sustainable peace (Chapter 12; Little & Green, 2009).

Finally, the empirical work on the means of learning (Chapters 5, 13, 14, 15) suggested that the broad idea of sustainable development, with its emphasis on environment, society and economy, needs to be extended to include the idea of sustainable or sustained learning through life. The achievement of SDG4 is not simply about educational provision, target-setting and indicators. It is fundamentally about the content (skills and values) of learning, the methods through which learners learn, both individually and in groups, the ways in which learning is assessed, and the motivations for learning both in the present and in the future. Sustainable development is as much about sustainable learning and personal development as it is about environment, society and economy.

Recent proposed policy reforms

The most recent education policy and strategy statements have been produced by three agencies, working separately and published as: (i) General Education Sector Development Plan (2020–2025) (Ministry of Education, 2020); (ii) Reimagining Education in Sri Lanka (Presidential Task Force on Sri Lanka's Education Affairs, 2020); and (iii) National Education Policy Framework 2020–2030 (NEC, 2022). The first covers the general education system (including non-formal and special education); the second covers general (including pre-school), technical and vocational education and higher and professional education; and the third covers early childhood care and education, general education, higher education, technical and vocational education, pirivena education (monastic colleges), special and inclusive education, non-formal education, and international school education. All three stress the aims of ensuring equitable access to education for all and improving the quality of delivery of education. All three present up-to-date information on the structure and size of the various subsectors of education. The National

Education Policy Framework departs from earlier policy documents in as much as it draws comparisons between Sri Lanka's education system and systems in the Asia region, explores the skill needs of the economy, and links National Education Goals with a National Learning Competency Framework and 12 National Learning Competencies, intended to frame curriculum design, implementation and assessment across every subsector of education. Taken together the three policy documents offer a comprehensive overview of the status of education, contemporary issues and the challenges of each subsector. They also offer myriad proposals for reform, some of which appear to be at odds with each other.

While it is beyond the scope of this chapter to offer comment on all proposals contained in these documents, I highlight just three – the classification of schools, the Grade 5 scholarship examination and skill needs for the economy.

Classification of schools

Sri Lanka's school classification system strikes many outsiders as curious, complex and, possibly, exceptional. There have been numerous proposals over the years to restructure the system. In most education systems, primary schools span between five and seven grades (years) and are self-contained institutions with a school head, a team of primary school teachers and a self-contained budget. In most systems, students then move on to secondary education which starts at Grade 6, 7 or 8. In other words, primary and secondary education are provided in separate institutions and are defined by their entry grade.

While 3,994 government schools in Sri Lanka offer primary education in Grades 1–5, conforming to the general international pattern, primary education is also offered within a *primary section* of the remaining 6,256 schools. Current school classification indicates that primary education is offered by four school types: Type 3 (Grades 1–5), Type 2 (Grades 1–11), Type 1C (Grades 1–13, arts and commerce) and Type 1AB (Grades 1–13, all streams). The majority of the popular national schools offer Grade 1–13 education across all curriculum streams. Today's classification appears to have emerged from a long history in which the earlier elementary/primary schools gradually extended themselves into 'overgrown elementary schools' in response to social demand (J. E. Jayasuriya, 1979; Little, Aturupane & Shojo, 2013).

The Ministry of Education recommends replacing the current four types with just two: Type 1 – primary schools offering Grades 1–5; and Type 2 – secondary schools offering Grades 6–13. The ministry also proposes to establish 1,000 national schools in addition to the 373 already in existence, plus 20 new trilingual national schools. The proposal to establish trilingual national schools is radical and offers the potential to transform the ethno-national schools into truly national schools, a pattern which could be scaled up over time. Students from all ethnic and linguistic groups would then be learning together, at least for major parts of the day, forming friendships, identities and social networks that would transcend ethnic-religious-linguistic boundaries. The proposal to separate primary and secondary schools has, in my view, the potential to address some of the inherent challenges posed by the Grade 5 scholarship examination.

Grade 5 scholarship examination

The Grade 5 scholarship examination was introduced in the late 1940s to admit high-achieving rural children to English-medium central schools and provide financial bursaries to low-income households (Chapter 6). The current ministry proposal explains that this exam is held at the end of Grade 5 for the purpose of 'awarding bursaries to children with outstanding performance from poor families and selection for admission to secondary education with better facilities'. This reflects the original intention.

However, as we saw in Chapters 4 and 6, the Grade 5 scholarship examination has, over time, been transformed into an exam which *all* children sit and use to gain access to the 'popular' (national) schools which offer all curriculum streams up to GCE A level and deliver better exam results. The popular schools admit students to Grade 1 on a non-competitive and supposedly catchment-area basis, and these children are guaranteed access to Grade 6 in these same popular schools. Despite their guaranteed access to Grade 6 they are still expected to sit the Grade 5 scholarship examination. These children then fill most of the Grade 6 vacancies, limiting access for others.

The Presidential Task Force's proposal is to increase the number of popular schools from the present 373 to 1,000 in order to create more opportunities and reduce pressure; to create a simpler exam designed only to award financial bursaries and to be sat only by children from low-income groups; and to create a second exam to select children into the increased number of popular schools.

The National Education Commission's proposal is to retain the Grade 5 scholarship examination as a state function and for the Ministry of Education together with the National Education Commission, National

Institute of Education and Department of Examinations to review the current Grade 5 scholarship examination and introduce appropriate reforms to eliminate its undesirable effects.

In my view, both the Presidential Task Force and National Education Commission proposals fail to confront what has become an intractable issue of long standing. The Grade 5 scholarship examination is an example of a post-colonial legacy whose terms have deviated from their original, well-thought-through and egalitarian intent. Eighty years on, is it not high time to abolish the Grade 5 scholarship? Combining the proposal to reclassify schools into primary and secondary and a new proposal that all secondary schools should admit students from defined catchment areas, there would, in principle, be no need for the Grade 5 scholarship examination.

If the broad egalitarian principles that have underpinned Sri Lankan education since independence are to continue into the future, there is no doubt that the reclassification of schools into two types would be consistent with the abolition of the Grade 5 scholarship examination, under certain conditions. One condition would be the enactment in law, on a cross-party basis, of policy changes on these and related questions. Other conditions would involve school reorganisation, detailed planning, equitable teacher deployment and equitable needs-based financing, and an increased government budget for education. Critically, there is a need for cultural change among political party leaders and politicians and the development of a consensus that once their work as policy-legislators is complete, they agree to stand aside, permit the planners, financiers and school managers to get on with the business of policy implementation, and desist from interfering in teacher appointments and transfers.

In the long term there would be several advantages. Schools would be rationalised, streamlined and simplified into just two types (something which has been suggested by successive policy committees many times over), primary and secondary schools would be allocated budgets on a needs basis, and they would be staffed by teachers and principals trained in primary subjects/methods and secondary subjects/methods, respectively. Most importantly, primary school teaching and learning would be freed from the yoke of the scholarship examination (Chapter 6), given the space to concentrate on the learning objectives of the primary curriculum, and supported by teachers trained in formative and school-based assessment (Chapter 15). Fulfilment of the learning objectives of primary education would provide a stronger foundation for learning and teaching in secondary education and on up the system.

Reducing the mismatch between education and the economy

I started my journey in Sri Lanka in the early 1970s on the coat tails of the end date of Sri Lanka's first 10-year development plan 1958–68 (National Planning Council, 1959) and the 1971 International Labour Report on *Matching employment opportunities and expectations* (ILO, 1971a). Both focussed on the need to increase productive employment, to plan the expansion of education in line with population projections, to allocate financial resources to education that were not excessive, and to gear the types of education provided to the needs of economic growth.

Many of the messages of that plan and report remain relevant today. As more young people access ever higher levels of education and skill (Chapters 6, 12), a mismatch between employment opportunities and youth qualifications and expectations remains, albeit between different stages of education and different types of employment. Politicians and employers worldwide blame many political, economic and social woes on mismatches between education and employment, on 'skill deficits' and on 'irrelevant' curricula. Sri Lanka is not exceptional in this regard. Education is an easy-to-target culprit. But there are always two sides to mismatches between education and employment.

The National Education Commission's proposals set out an ambitious framework for the improved delivery of 'value-added' skills for the domestic and international economy. For its part, the domestic economy has failed to diversify away from the pattern of low-skill plantation, textile and apparel industry exports of the 1950s–1980s (Chapters 11, 12). One must ask whether the domestic economy is ready to employ young people and use their skills in higher added value jobs. If not, this represents a colossal waste of human resources – an imbalance between education outputs and available jobs that cannot be attributed solely to the 'irrelevance' of education. Surely, more policy attention needs to be paid to the diversification of the economy and the creation of employment opportunities that can use those skills and enhance them further through job-specific training. This is primarily a task for business economists, employers and enterprises, supported – not led by – educators and trainers.

Final reflections

Throughout my career I have been keen to share ideas about education and development from around the world with others. Some innovations have often been borrowed by one country from another and re-interpreted and implemented very successfully. But the most successful borrowings appear to have occurred when those who borrow are actively seeking to borrow the idea rather than being persuaded to adopt an idea through the promise of external funding. The overriding message of the book has been that we need to understand education development in Sri Lanka, and indeed every country, in its and their own terms. Only when the exceptionalisms and specificities are understood can universal propositions and advocacies be adduced and asserted.

Learning is important for the sustainable development of economy, society and polity. It is also important for the sustainable learning of individuals across the lifespan. Learning lies at the heart of personal development throughout life. Planning for the learning of all lies at the heart of education policy situated within broader conceptions of social, cultural, political and economic purpose. The creation of education policy requires active learning of the policy lessons from the past, as well as critical engagement with selected and situated ideas and lessons from elsewhere.

My first encounters in the Sri Lanka of the 1970s left me impressed by the widespread and apparent democratic involvement of people everywhere – in towns and villages, on buses and trains – in the political discourses of the day and their belief in the power of education to drive forward self-reliant 'development' of the country and for all children. My earliest research in Sri Lanka was an exploration of the ways in which employers used educational qualifications for job recruitment, selection and promotion. I was told repeatedly that 'it is not the qualifications; it is all politics'. Initially, I refused to accept this perception of reality and would respond by suggesting that without qualifications one could not apply for a rung on the ladder of jobs of the type to which most young people aspired. Over time I came to realise that both perceptions mapped onto reality rather well. Educational qualifications were and remain a necessary condition for access to jobs. In a sense they were simply taken for granted by those who said 'it is all politics'. They did not need to be mentioned. But educational qualifications were and remain by no means a sufficient condition for recruitment and selection to the jobs to which most young people aspire. Many factors, not least political connections, smoothed and smooth the climb.

My later encounters sometimes left me wondering why so many poor parents continued to maintain such high educational aspirations for their children when their own education had done so little to change their relative position in society, when policy promises often remained unfulfilled for want of the dogged determination of education managers to see them fulfilled in every school, and when patronage politics seemed to infuse and frustrate so many daily education practices. The simple answer is that they have no choice but to maintain hope for their children through education, and to hope too that they might secure some small advantages in life for them through political patronage.

I am not without hope. I remain impressed by the daily efforts of teachers and parents to support students in their learning. When, in 2012, I listened to Tamil teachers who, with their community, had been displaced during the last years of the civil war, I was almost too moved to respond. I learned how they had fled to a safer space with as many school chairs and desks as they could transport, and about when, at a later stage, they set up a refugee camp school, they struggled to maintain their dignity, standing in front of the children when dressed only in flimsy cotton housecoats and rubber slippers. I remain impressed by the widely shared enthusiasm of students for learning – an enthusiasm and persistence that is not observed in every school system around the world. I am impressed by the efforts of many people to continue to improve their education and learning well after they graduate from school or university. I am impressed by the recent calls of people from all ethnic groups and social classes for an improved system of government and more responsible behaviour of the political classes.

Education is a rolling, recurrent investment by the state for the development of society in the future. Education is also an investment by individuals for their futures and the futures of their families. A new generation of teachers and students enrols in the institutions of learning each year. Education is an investment that requires attention year after year, day after day. Education can be a powerful force for social, political, economic and individual change, but the realisation of that potential depends on simultaneous change in many other sectors, not least in employment, health, law, taxation, and the political and government institutions that make and deliver policies for all.

References

Abeyratne, S. (2000). Policy and political issues in economic growth in Sri Lanka. In S. T. Hettige & M. Mayer (Eds.), *Sri Lanka at crossroads: Dilemmas and prospects after 50 years of independence* (pp. 19–49). Macmillan India.

Abhayadewa, C. M. (1989). *Development of multi-grade and multi-level teaching strategies: Towards qualitative development of primary education in Sri Lanka*. National Institute of Education (Sri Lanka).

Aikman, S. (1999). Alternative development and education: Economic interests and cultural practices in the Amazon. In F. E. Leach & A. W. Little (Eds.), *Education, cultures and economics* (pp. 95–110). RoutledgeFalmer.

Akila, R. (2009). *A trigger for change in primary education: An evaluation of ABL in Tamil Nadu*. Government of Tamil Nadu.

Alailima, P. (1991). *Labour force: Current situation and future prospects*. Human Resources Development Council; World Bank.

Altbach, P. G., & Kelly, C. P. (Eds.). (1978). *Education and colonialism*. Longman.

Anand, S., & Kanbur, R. (1991). Public policy and basic needs provision: Intervention and achievement in Sri Lanka. In J. Dreze & A. Sen (Eds.), *The political economy of hunger* (vol. 3). Clarendon Press.

Anderson, C. A., & Bowman, M. J. (Eds.). (1965). *Education and economic development*. Aldine Publishing Company.

Annual Census (various years). *Census reports*. Department of Census and Statistics (Sri Lanka).

Ashton, D. N., & Green, F. (1996). *Education, training and the global economy*. Edward Elgar.

Assessment Reform Group. (1999). *Assessment for learning: Beyond the black box*. University of Cambridge School of Education.

Atapattu, D. (1997). Capital formation and its financing. In W. D. Lakshman (Ed.), *Dilemmas of development: Fifty years of economic change*. Sri Lankan Association of Economists.

Attygalle, L. (2009). *The desire for trilingual education in Sri Lanka* [unpublished masters thesis]. Institute of Education, University of London.

Aturupane, H. (1993). *Is education beneficial? A microeconomic analysis of the impact of education on the economic welfare of a developing country, Sri Lanka* [unpublished doctoral thesis]. University of Cambridge.

Aturupane, H. (2009). *The pearl of great price: Achieving equitable access to primary and secondary education and enhancing learning in Sri Lanka* (Pathways to Access Research Monograph No. 29). CREATE.

Aturupane, H., Glewwe, P., & Wisniewski, S. (2011). The impact of school quality, socio-economic factors and child health on students' academic performance: Evidence from Sri Lankan primary schools, *Education Economics*, *21*(1), 2–37. https://doi.org/10.1080/09645292.2010.511852

Aturupane, H., & Little, A. W. (2020). General education in Sri Lanka. In P. M. Sarangapani & R. Pappu (Eds.), *Handbook of education systems in South Asia*. Springer.

Aturupane, H., Shojo, M., & Ebenezer, R. (2018). *Gender dimensions of education access and achievement in Sri Lanka* (South Asia Region Education Global Practice Discussion Paper No. 90). World Bank. https://openknowledge.worldbank.org/entities/publication/623f05ca-9fe5-55c8-a4d4-cab1b31c8a8d

Azubuike, O. B., Moore, R., & Vaidya, G. (2023). Using Bourdieu's theory of cultural reproduction to examine English Language learning: A multi-level study in three lower- and middle-income countries. *Social Sciences and Humanities Open*, *8*, 100578. https://doi.org/10.1016/j.ssaho.2023.100578

Bacchus, M. K. (1990). *Utilisation, misuse and development of human resources in the early West Indian colonies*. Wilfred Laurier University Press.

Bacchus, M. K. (1994). *Education as and for legitimacy: Developments in West Indian education between 1846 and 1895*. Wilfred Laurier University Press.

Bandaranayake, S. (Ed.). (1990). *Sri Lanka and the Silk Road of the sea*. Sri Lanka National Commission for UNESCO; Central Cultural Fund.

Banerjee, A., Banerji, R., Berry, J., Duflo, E., Kannan, H., Mukherji, S., Shotland, M., & Walton, M. (2017). *From proof of concept to scalable policies: Challenges and solutions, with an application* (NBER Working Paper No. 22931). National Bureau of Economic Research (USA). https://www.nber.org/papers/w22931

Batatota, L. (2020). *Becoming 'good' women: Schooling, aspirations and imagining the future among Sinhalese youth* [PhD thesis]. Brunel University, London. http://bura.brunel.ac.uk/handle/2438/21004

Becker, G. (1964). *Human capital*. Princeton University Press.

Beckford, G. L. (1983). *Persistent poverty: Underdevelopment in plantation economies of the third world*. Zed Books.

Beeby, C. E. (1966). *The quality of education in developing countries*. Harvard University Press.

Bennell, P. (1996). Using and abusing rates of return: A critique of the World Bank's 1995 education sector review. *International Journal of Educational Development, 16*(3), 235–48.

Berg, I. (1970). *Education and jobs: The great training robbery*. Penguin.

Biedermann, Z., & Strathern, A. (Eds.). (2017). *Sri Lanka at the crossroads of history*. UCL Press.

Black, P., & Wiliam, D. (1998). Inside the black box: Raising standards through classroom assessment. *Phi Delta Kappan, 80*(2), 139–48.

Bold, T., Filmer, D., Martin, G., Molina, E., Stacy, B., Rockmore, C., Svensson, J., & Wane, W. (2017). Enrollment without learning: Teacher effort, knowledge, and skill in primary schools in Africa. *Journal of Economic Perspectives, 31*(4), 185–204.

Boston, C. (2002). *The concept of formative assessment* (ERIC Digest). ERIC Clearinghouse on Assessment and Evaluation.

Bourdieu, P., & Passeron, J. C. (1977). *Reproduction in education, society and culture*. Sage.

Bowles, S., & Gintis, H. (1976). *Schooling in capitalist America: Educational reform and the contradictions of economic life*. Basic Books.

Bowles, S., Gintis, H., & Simmons, J. (1976). The impact of education and poverty: The US experience. *International Development Review, 18*(2), 6–10.

Bowman, M. J. (1966). The human investment revolution in economic thought. *Sociology of Education, 39*(2), 111–13.

Broadfoot, P., & Gipps, C. (1996). Assessment developments in England and Wales: The triumph of tradition. In A. W. Little & A. Wolf (Eds.), *Assessment in transition: Learning, monitoring and selection in international perspective* (pp. 134–53). Pergamon.

Bruns, B. (2018). *Three years after SDG adoption: It's time for action on learning data* [blog post]. https://www.riseprogramme.org/node/658

Bruns, B., & Luque, J. (2015). *Great teachers: How to raise student learning in Latin America and the Caribbean*. World Bank. https://openknowledge.worldbank.org/bitstream/handle/10986/20488/9781464801518.pdf

Cardoso, F. H. (1972). Dependent capitalist development in Latin America. *New Left Review* (First Series), *74* (July/August), 83–95.

Cardoso, F. H., & Faletto, E. (1979). *Dependency and development in Latin America*. University of California Press.

Carnoy, M. (1974). *Education as cultural imperialism*. Longman.

Carpmail, M., Burnett, L., Chapman, K., & Crowder, D. (n.d.). *Misconceptions with the key objectives* [working group paper]. https://www.google.com/search?rlz=1C1CHBF_enIM932IM932&q=Carpmail,+M.,+Burnett,+L.,+Chapman,+K.,+%26+Crowder,+D.+(a.n.d.)+Misconceptions+with+the+Key+Objectives&spell=1&sa=X&ved=2ahUKEwiE44Gn8-r_AhWrMewKHfs0CbUQBSgAegQICBAB&biw=1120&bih=492&dpr=1.5

Castells, M. (2000). *End of millennium*. Blackwell.

Cels, J., Rossetto, T., Little, A. W., & Dias, P. (2022). Tsunami preparedness within Sri Lanka's education system. *International Journal of Disaster Risk Reduction, 84*, 103473. https://doi.org/10.1016/j.ijdrr.2022.103473

Central Bank of Sri Lanka. (2003). *Annual report 2002*.

Central Bank of Sri Lanka. (2005). *Annual Report 2004*.

Central Bank of Sri Lanka. (2008). *Annual Report 2007*.

Central Bank of Sri Lanka. (2019). *Economic and social statistics of Sri Lanka, 2019.*
Centre for Poverty Analysis. (2005). *Moving out of poverty in the estate sector in Sri Lanka: Understanding growth and freedom from the bottom up.* Centre for Poverty Analysis (Sri Lanka).
Chaudhri, D. P. (1974). Rural education and agricultural development: Some empirical results from Indian agriculture. In P. Foster & J. R. Sheffield (Eds.), *World yearbook of education 1974: Education and rural development* (pp. 372–86). Evans.
Chenery, H. B., Ahluwalia, M. S., Bell, C. L. G., Duloy, J., & Jolly, R. (1974). *Redistribution with growth: Policies to improve income distribution in developing countries.* World Bank; Institute of Development Studies, University of Sussex.
Clark, B. R. (1962). *Educating the expert society.* Chandler.
Colbert, V., Chiappe, C., & Arboleda, J. (1993). The new school program: More and better primary education for children in rural areas of Colombia. In H. Levin & M. Lockheed (Eds.), *Effective schools in developing countries* (pp. 52–68). Falmer Press.
Colclough, C. L., & Manor, J. (Eds.). (1991). *States or markets? Neo-liberalism and the development policy debate.* Oxford University Press.
Coleman, J. (1988). Social capital in the formation of human capital. *American Journal of Sociology*, 94, S95–S120.
Corea, G. (1975). *The instability of an export economy.* Marga Institute.
Crossley, M., & Tikly, L. (2004). Postcolonial perspectives and comparative and international research in education: A critical introduction. *Comparative Education*, 40(2), 147–56.
Cueto, S., Leon, J., Sorto, M. A., & Miranda, A. (2017). Teachers' pedagogical content knowledge and mathematics achievement of students in Peru. *Educational Studies in Mathematics*, 94(3), 329–45.
Curriculum Development Centre. (1975). *Bulletin of the Curriculum Development Centre*, 1(1), April.
Dados, N., & Connell, R. (2012). The Global South. *Contexts*, 11(1), 12–13.
Dale, R. (1999). Specifying global effects on national policy: A focus on the mechanisms. *Journal of Education Policy*, 14, 1–17.
Dasanayaka, R. (2017). *Arabs in Serendib trade relations between Sri Lanka and West Asia from ancient time to 15th century A.D. Historical and archaeological survey.* S. Godage & Brothers.
Davis, C. P. (2020). *The struggle for a multilingual future: Youth and education in Sri Lanka.* Oxford University Press.
Davis, K., & Moore, W. E. (1945). Some principles of stratification. *American Sociological Review*, 10(2), 242–249.
Dayasiri, K., Thadchanamoorthy, V., Kankananarachchi, I., Umasankar, N., Dassanayake, S., Gunasekara, S., & Mettananda, S. (2022). 924 Impact of COVID 19 on the education and health of schooling children in Sri Lanka: A multi-provincial study. *Archives of Disease in Childhood*, 107, A330–A331. https://doi.org/10.1136/archdischild-2022-rcpch.535
De Mel, T. (2021). Education debacle: A response to *The Island* editorial 'stop brawling in a graveyard'. *Sunday Island Online.* https://island.lk/education-debacle/
De Mel, T. (2022). *Reforming education: Challenges to change.* https://www.amazon.com/Reforming-Education-Challenges-Change-Reforms-ebook/dp/B0BC5M666K (self-published).
De Silva, E. J. (2003). *Sixty years of education policy-making.* Sri Lanka Association for the Advancement of Science.
De Silva, E. J. (2004). *Management of education* (Sectoral Review of General Education Study Series 23). National Education Commission (Sri Lanka).
De Silva, E. J. (2010). *A fresh look at the Kannangara Reforms.* Published in *The Island*, 14, 15, 16, 17, 19 and 20 December.
De Silva, K. M. (1965). *Social policy and missionary organisations in Ceylon 1840–1855.* Longman.
De Silva, K. M. (1981). *A history of Sri Lanka.* University of California Press
De Silva, S. B. D. (1982). *The political economy of underdevelopment.* Routledge and Kegan Paul.
De Silva, W. A., Gunawardene, C., Jayeweera, S., Perera, L., Rupasinghe, S., & Wijetunge, S. (1991). *Extra-school instruction, social equity and educational quality in Sri Lanka* (Report to the International Development Research Centre, Singapore). International Development Research Centre.
De Silva, W. A., Gunawardene, C., & Rupasinghe, S. (1987). The case of Sri Lanka. In A. W. Little (Ed.). *Why do students learn? A six-country study of student motivation.* Institute

of Development Studies Education Research Report No. 17 (pp. 51–171). Institute of Development Studies (UK).

Deci, E. L., Koestner, R., & Ryan, R. M. (1999). A meta-analysis review of experiments examining the effects of extrinsic rewards on intrinsic motivation. *Psychological Bulletin*, *125*, 159–81.

Deci, E. L., & Ryan, R. M. (1985). *Intrinsic motivation and self-determination in human behaviour*. Plenum Press.

Del Monte, P., & Posholi, L. (2021). Decolonial perspectives on education and international development. In T. McCowan & E. Unterhalter (Eds.), *Education and international development* (pp. 79–92). Bloomsbury.

Denison, E. F. (1962). *The sources of economic growth in the United States and the alternatives before us*. Committee for Economic Development (USA).

Denison, E. F. (1964). Measuring the contribution of education (and the residual) to economic growth. In OECD Study Group in the Economics of Education, *The residual factor and economic growth* (pp. 13–55). OECD.

Department of Census and Statistics. (1990). *Sri Lanka labour force survey (third quarter)*. Government of Sri Lanka.

Department of Census and Statistics. (2021). *Education statistics*. Government of Sri Lanka.

Deraniyagala, C. P., Dore, R. P., & Little, A. W. (1978). *Qualifications and employment in Sri Lanka* (Institute of Development Studies Education Research Report No. 2). Institute of Development Studies (UK).

Dore, R. P. (1972). *The late development effect* (Institute of Development Studies Communication No. 103). Institute of Development Studies (UK).

Dore, R. P. (1976). *The diploma disease: Education, qualification and development*. George Allen & Unwin.

Dore, R. P. (1997a). The argument of the diploma disease: A summary. *Assessment in Education*, *4*(1), 23–32.

Dore, R. P. (1997b). *The diploma disease: Education, qualification and development*. George Allen & Unwin. Rev. ed. Institute of Education Publications (UK). Also a film of the same title and date, produced by the Institute of Development Studies.

Dore, R. P., Humphreys, J., & West, P. (1976). *The basic arithmetic of youth unemployment*. International Labour Organization.

Dore, R. P., & Little, A. W. (1982). *The diploma disease: An argument with pictures* (IDS Discussion Paper No. 179). Institute of Development Studies (UK). Also a film of the same title and date, produced by the Institute of Development Studies.

Dos Santos, T. (1973). The crisis of development theory and the problem of dependence in Latin America. In H. Bernstein (Ed.), *Underdevelopment and development: The third world today* (pp. 57–80). Penguin.

Dundar, H., Millot, B., Riboud, M., Shojo, M., Aturupane, H., Goyal, S., & Raju, D. (2017). *Sri Lanka education sector assessment: Achievements, challenges, and policy options*. World Bank. http://hdl.handle.net/10986/27042

Dunham, D., & Jayasuriya, S. (1998). *Equity, growth and insurrection: Liberalisation and the welfare debate in contemporary Sri Lanka* (Working Paper No. 11). La Trobe University School of Economics. https://econpapers.repec.org/paper/trbwpaper/1998.11.htm

Durkheim, E., & Bierstedt, R. (1969). *Emile Durkheim: Selections from his works together with a brief biography*. Weidenfeld and Nicolson.

Eckstein, M. A., & Noah, H. J. (1993). *Secondary school examinations*. Yale University Press.

Economic Review. (1994). Private tuition in Sri Lanka: A new style of education. *Economic Review*, May–June. People's Bank Publications (Sri Lanka).

Education Forum of Sri Lanka. (2020). *Policy Dialogues* 1, 4 and 8.
  https://educationforum.lk/2020/03/policy-dialogue-7th-march-2020/.
  https://educationforum.lk/2020/06/policy-dialogue-reforming-national-examinations-in-sri-lanka/.
  https://educationforum.lk/2020/10/policy-research-roundtable-theory-and-practice-in-assessment-in-primary-education/.

Emmerij, L. (2010). *The basic needs development strategy* [background paper]. World Economic and Social Survey. https://www.un.org/en/development/desa/policy/wess/wess_bg_papers/bp_wess2010_emmerij.pdf

Escobar, A. (2011). *Encountering development: The making and unmaking of the third world*. Princeton University Press.

Fagerlind, I., & Saha, L. J. (1989). *Education and national development: A comparative perspective*. Pergamon Press.

Fanon, F. (1961). *The wretched of the earth*. Grove Press.

Fasheh, M. (1999). Learning versus development: A Palestinian perspective. In F. E. Leach & A. W. Little (Eds.), *Education, cultures and economics* (pp. 81–94). RoutledgeFalmer.

Filmer, D., Rogers, H., Angrist, N., & Sabarwal, S. (2018). *Learning-adjusted years of schooling: Defining a new macro measure of education* (Policy Research Working Paper No. 8591). World Bank.

Foster Carter, A. (1974). Neo-Marxist approaches to development and under-development. In E. de Kadt & G. Williams (Eds.), *Sociology and development* (pp. 67–108). Routledge and Kegan Paul.

Frank, A. G. (1967). *Capitalism and under-development in Latin America*. Monthly Review Press.

Fredriksen, B. (1978). Universal primary education in developing countries: A statistical review. *Prospects: Quarterly Review of Education*, 8(3), 363–74.

Fukami, T. (2022). *Impact of COVID-19 on education: Transforming education for all post COVID-19*. UNICEF. https://educationforum.lk/wp-content/uploads/2022/03/UNICEF_26.03.2022.pdf

Fukuda-Parr, S. (2003). The human development paradigm: Operationalising Sen's ideas on capabilities. *Feminist Economics*, 9(2/3), 301–17.

Fuller, W. P. (1972). Evaluating alternative combinations of education and training for job preparation: An example from Indian industry. *Nanpoon Journal*, 8(1), 7–38.

Galtung, J. (1971). A structural theory of imperialism. *Journal of Peace Research*, 8(2), 81–117.

Ganegodage, K. R., & Rambaldi, A. (2011). The impact of education investment on Sri Lankan economic growth. *Economics of Education Review*, 30(6), 1,491–502.

Gerschenkron, A. (1952). Economic backwardness in historical perspective. In B. F. Hoselitz (Ed.), *The progress of undeveloped areas* (pp. 3–29). University of Chicago Press.

Giddens, A. (1999). *The runaway world* (Reith Lectures). BBC.

Gipps, C. (1996). Assessment for learning. In A. W. Little & A. Wolf (Eds.), *Assessment in transition: Learning, monitoring and selection in international perspective* (pp. 251–62). Pergamon.

Global Education Evidence Advisory Panel. (2020). *Cost-effective approaches to improve global learning: What does recent evidence tell us are 'smart buys' for improving learning in low- and middle-income countries?* World Bank. https://tinyurl.com/32jjbuce

Global Partnership for Education. (2023). *Sri Lanka joins the global partnership for education*. https://www.globalpartnership.org/news/sri-lanka-joins-global-partnership-education

Gnanamuttu, G. (1976). *Education and the Indian plantation worker in Sri Lanka*. Council of Churches (Sri Lanka); Christian Aid.

Goldstein, H. (1996). International comparisons of student achievement. In A. W. Little & A. Wolf (Eds.), *Assessment in transition: Learning, monitoring and selection in international perspective* (pp. 58–87). Pergamon.

Goonatilake. S. (1975). Development thinking as cultural neo-colonialism the case of Sri Lanka. *Institute of Development Studies Bulletin*, 7(1), 4–10.

Goonatilake, S. (1982). *Crippled minds: An exploration of colonial culture*. Vikas.

Government of Ceylon. (1972). *Interim report of the Committee to Inquire into a Report on Public Examinations at Secondary School Level in Ceylon*. Government Printers (Sri Lanka).

Gramsci, A. (2005). *The Southern question*. Guernica Editions.

Greaney, V., & Kellaghan, T. (2008). *Assessing national achievement levels in education*. World Bank. http://hdl.handle.net/10986/6904

Green, A. (2007). Education, globalisation and development: changing the terms of engagement. In A. Green, A. W. Little, S. G. Kamat, M. Oketch & E. Vickers, *Education and development in a global era: Strategies for 'successful globalisation'* (Researching the Issues No. 69) (pp. 7–48). Department for International Development (UK).

Green, A., Little, A. W., Kamat, S. G., Oketch, M., & Vickers, E. (2007). *Education and development in a global era: Strategies for 'successful globalisation'* (Researching the Issues No. 69). Department for International Development (UK).

Green, A., Preston, J., & Sabates, R. (2003). Education, equality and social cohesion: A distributional approach. *Compare*, 33(4), 453–70.

Gunasekara, J. (2008). Evaluating the effectiveness of Swedish International Development Authority-funded primary education projects in Sri Lanka. *SAARC Journal of Educational Research*, 6(1), 1–21.

Gunatilleke, G. (1974). Welfare and growth in Sri Lanka. *Marga Research Studies No. 2.* Marga Institute.

Gunatilleke, G. (2018). *Facets of Pluralistic Development in Sri Lanka: A collection of writings.* Marga Institute.

Gunawardana, R. A. L. H. (1979). *Robe and plough: Monasticism and economic interest in early medieval Sri Lanka.* University of Arizona Press.

Gunawardene, C. (2002). Youth and education. In S. T. Hettige & M. Mayer (Eds.), *Sri Lankan youth: Challenges and responses* (pp. 89–118). Friedrich Ebert-Stiftung Foundation.

Gunawardene, D. (2015). *Why aren't Sri Lankan women translating their educational gains into workforce advantages?* (Brookings Echidna Global Scholar Working Paper). Centre for Universal Education; UNGEI.

Gunter, B. G., & van der Hoevan, R. (2004). The social dimension of globalisation: A review of the literature. *International Labour Review, 143*(1/2), 7–43.

Haddad, W. D. (with Demsky, T.) (1995). *Education policy-planning process: An applied framework* (Fundamentals in Educational Planning Monograph No. 51). UNESCO; International Institute for Educational Planning.

Hansen, A. (Ed.). (2014). *Children's errors in mathematics: Understanding common misconceptions in primary schools* (3rd ed.). Sage.

Hanushek, E. A., & Wößmann, L. (2007). *Education quality and economic growth.* World Bank.

Harber, C. (2014). *Education and international development: Theory, practice and issues.* Symposium Books.

Hariharan, P. (2011). *Effectiveness of activity-based learning methodology for elementary school education.* Paper submitted for National Child Rights Fellowship 2010, Coimbatore, India.

Harris, J. (2014). Development theories. In B. Currie-Alder, R. Kanbur, D. M. Malone & R. Medhora (Eds.), *International development: Ideas, experience, and prospects* (pp. 35–49). Oxford University Press.

Hayes, D. (2000). Cascade training and teachers' professional development. *ELT Journal, 54* (2), 135–45.

Hayes, D. (2010). 'Education is all about opportunities, isn't it?': A biographical perspective on learning and teaching English in Sri Lanka. *Harvard Educational Review, 80*(4), 517–41.

Hayhoe, R., & Pan, J. (Eds.). (2001). *Knowledge across cultures: A contribution to dialogue among civilisations.* Comparative Education Research Centre (CERC) Studies in Comparative Education No. 11. University of Hong Kong.

Helu-Thaman, K. (1999). Different eyes: Schooling and indigenous education in Tonga. In F. E. Leach & A. W. Little (Eds.), *Education, cultures and economics* (pp. 69–80). Routledge Falmer.

Herath, H. M. J. C. (2022). *Impact of capital at school and home on educational achievement: A case study of four provinces in Sri Lanka* [unpublished doctoral thesis]. University of Colombo.

Hettige, S. T. (Ed.). (1992). *Unrest or revolt: Some aspects of youth unrest in Sri Lanka.* Goethe-Institut Colombo; American Studies Association.

Hettige, S. T. (1998). *Globalisation, social change and youth.* Goethe-Institut Colombo.

Hettige, S. T. (2000). Dilemmas of post-colonial society after 50 years of independence. In S. Hettige & M. Mayer (Eds.), *Sri Lanka at crossroads: Dilemmas and prospects after 50 years of independence* (pp. 7–18). Macmillan India.

Hettige, S. T. (2005). Shifts in the educational structure of Sri Lanka following economic liberalisation. *Globalisation, qualifications and livelihoods* (Project Research Report Series No. 3). Institute of Education; University of Colombo.

Hettige, S. T., Mayer, M., & Salih, M. (2004). *School-to-work transitions of youth in Sri Lanka.* International Labour Organization paper 2004/19.

Himaz, R. (2010). Intrahousehold allocation of education expenditure: The case of Sri Lanka. *Economic Development and Cultural Change, 58*, 231–58.

Himaz, R., & Aturupane, H. (2016). Returns to education in Sri Lanka: A pseudo-panel approach. *Education Economics, 24*(3), 300–11.

Himaz, R., & Aturupane, H. (2018). Schooling and household welfare: The case of Sri Lanka from 1990 to 2005. *Review of Development Economics, 22*(2), 459–78.

Hincapie, D. (2014). *Essays on education policy and student achievement in Colombia* [unpublished doctoral thesis]. George Washington University.

Humphrey, J. (2007). Forty years of development research: Transformations and reformations. *Institute of Development Studies Bulletin, 38*(2), 14–19. https://doi.org/10.1111/j.1759-5436.2007.tb00344.x

ILO. (1971a). *Matching employment opportunities and expectations: A programme of action for Ceylon*. ILO.
ILO. (1971b). *Matching employment opportunities and expectations: A programme of action for Ceylon. Technical Papers*. ILO.
ILO/JASPA. (1981). *First things first: Meeting the basic needs of the people of Nigeria*. International Labour Office (Nigeria).
Indrarathne, B., & McCulloch, S. (2022). *English language teaching, learning and assessment in Sri Lanka: Policies and practices in the school education system*. British Council.
Inkeles, A. (1973). The school as a context for modernisation. *International Journal of Comparative Sociology*, *14*(3/4), 163–79.
Inkeles, A., & Smith, M. (1974). *Becoming modern*. Heinemann.
Inter-Agency Commission. (1990). *World Conference on Education for All: Meeting basic learning needs. Final report*. UNDP; UNESCO; UNICEF; World Bank.
International Commission on Financing Global Education Opportunity. (2016). *The learning generation: Investing in education for a changing world*. Education Commission. https://report.educationcommission.org/wp-content/uploads/2016/09/Learning_Generation_Full_Report.pdf
International Monetary Fund. (2015). *Sri Lanka third post-program monitoring discussion. Staff report, press release and statement by the executive director for Sri Lanka*. https://www.imf.org/external/pubs/ft/scr/2015/cr15335.pdf
Isenman, P. (1980). Basic needs: The case of Sri Lanka. *World Development*, *8*(3), 237–58.
Jayasuriya, D. L. (2001). The evolution of social policy in Sri Lanka, 1833–1970: The British colonial legacy. *Journal of the Royal Asiatic Society of Sri Lanka (New Series) 46*, 1–16.
Jayasuriya, J. E. (1964). *Some issues in Ceylon education*. Associated Educational Publishers.
Jayasuriya, J. E. (1969). *Education in Ceylon: Before and after independence*. Associated Educational Publishers.
Jayasuriya, J. E. (1979). *Educational policies and progress*. Associated Educational Publishers.
Jayasuriya, S. (2005). Globalisation, equity and poverty: The South Asian experience. In N. E. Dinello & L. Squire (Eds.), *Globalization and equity: Perspective from the developing world* (pp. 137–62). Edward Elgar.
Jayatissa, R. A. (1993). *Foreign trade experience in the post-liberalisation period*. Sri Lanka Economic Association.
Jayawardena, K., & Kurian R. (2015). *Class, patriarchy and ethnicity on Sri Lankan plantations*. Orient Black Swan.
Jayaweera, S. (1986). *Educational policies and change: From the mid-nineteenth century to 1977*. National Institute of Education (Sri Lanka).
Jayaweera, S. (1989). *Extension of educational opportunity: The unfinished task*. C. W. W. Kannangara Memorial Lecture, National Institute of Education (Sri Lanka).
Jayaweera, S. (1990). *Badulla Integrated Rural Development Programme phase 1 (1984–8): Quality improvement of primary education*. Swedish International Development Authority; Ministry of Education (Sri Lanka).
Jayaweera, S. (1994). Structural adjustment policies, industrial development and women in Sri Lanka. In P. Sparr (Ed.), *Mortgaging women's lives: Feminist critiques of structural adjustment* (pp. 96–115). Zed Books.
Jayaweera, S. (2001). *Women in garment and textile industries in Sri Lanka: Gender roles and relations*. Centre for Women's Research (Sri Lanka).
Jayaweera, S. (Ed.). (2002). *Women in post-independence Sri Lanka*. Sage.
Jayaweera, S. (2003). Continuity and change in women workers in garment and textile industries in Sri Lanka. In S. Mukhopadhyay & R. M. Udarshan (Eds.), *Tracking gender equity under economic reforms: Continuity and change in South Asia* (pp. 196–226). IDRC; Kali for Women.
Jayaweera, S. (2004). *Rationalisation and closure of schools* (Sectoral Review of General Education Study Series 5). National Education Commission (Sri Lanka).
Jayaweera, S., & Rupasinghe, S. (2007). Vocational preferences of secondary school students. In S. Jayweera (Ed.), *Gender, education and socialisation*. Cenwor.
Jayaweera, S., & Sanmugam, T. (2002). *Graduate employment in Sri Lanka in the 1990s*. Centre for Women's Research (Sri Lanka).
Jayewardene, V. K. (1972). *The rise of the labour movement in Ceylon*. Duke University Press.

Johnson, C. (1982). *MITI and the Japanese miracle: The growth of industrial policy 1925–1975.* Stanford University Press.

Johnson, C. (1999). The developmental state: Odyssey of a concept. In M. Woo-Cumings (Ed.), *The developmental state* (pp. 32–60). Cornell University Press.

Jolly, R. (1974). Redistribution with growth. In A. Cairncross & M. Puri (Eds.), *Employment, income distribution and development strategy: Problems of the developing countries.* Palgrave Macmillan.

Jolly, R. (1976). The World Employment Conference: The enthronement of basic needs. *Development Policy Review, A9*(2), 31–44.

Jolly, R. (2010). Employment, basic needs and human development: Elements for a new international paradigm in response to crisis. *Journal of Human Development and Capabilities, 11*(1), 11–36.

Jolly, R., Emmerij, L., & Weiss, T. G. (2009). *UN ideas that changed the world* (United Nations Intellectual History Project). Indiana University Press.

Kariyewasam, S. (1996). Ideals and reality: Sri Lanka's attempts to resolve the roles of educational assessment. In A. W. Little & A. Wolf (Eds.), *Assessment in transition: Learning, monitoring and selection in international perspective* (pp. 219–32). Pergamon.

Kelegama, S. (2000). Development in independent Sri Lanka: What went wrong? *Economic and Political Weekly, 35*(17), 1,477–90.

Kelegama, S., & Wijayasiri, J. (2004). *Readymade garments industry in Sri Lanka: Facing the global challenges.* Institute of Policy Studies (Sri Lanka).

Kellaghan, T., Greaney, V., & Scott Murray, T. (2009). *Using the results of a national assessment of educational achievement.* World Bank.

Kelley, H. H. (1972). Causal schemata and the attribution process. In E. E. Jones, D. E. Kanouse, H. H. Kelley, R. E. Nisbett, S. Valins & B. Weiner (Eds.), *Attribution: Perceiving the causes of behaviour* (pp. 151–74). General Learning Press.

Kelley, H. H., & Michela, J. L. (1980). Attribution theory and research. *Annual Review of Psychology, 31*(1), 457–501.

Kelly, G. A. (1955). *The psychology of personal constructs.* Norton.

Kemp, C., & Little, A. W. (1987). Editorial: People in plantations: means or ends? *Institute of Development Studies Bulletin, 18*(2), 1–7.

Kiely, R. (2006). Modernisation theory. In D. A. Clark (Ed.), *The Elgar companion to development studies.* Edward Elgar.

Kotalawala, E., Peiris, K., Kuruppu, L. S., Liyanage, E. S., Edussuriya, Y., Dharmaratne, M. P., Navaratne, A., Amarakoon, A., Piayawathie, W., & Somasundaram, K. (1994). *Research on the year five scholarship examination.* National Institute of Education (Sri Lanka).

Kularatna, N. G. (2004). *An evaluation of the divisional schools development project and the programme to revamp central schools* (Sectoral Review of General Education Study Series No. 4). National Education Commission (Sri Lanka).

Kurian, R. (1982). *Women workers in the Sri Lanka plantation sector.* International Labour Organization.

Lakshman, W. D. (Ed.). (1997). *Dilemmas of development: Fifty years of economic change.* Sri Lankan Association of Economists.

Leach, F., & Little, A. W. (Eds.). (1999). *Education, cultures and economics: Dilemmas for development.* RoutledgeFalmer.

Lewin, K. M. (1981). *Science education in Malaysia and Sri Lanka: Curriculum development and course evaluation, 1970–78* [unpublished doctoral thesis]. University of Sussex.

Lewin, K. M. (1984). Selection and curriculum reform. In J. C. P. Oxenham (Ed.), *Education versus qualifications? A study of relationships between, education, selection for employment and the productivity of labour* (pp. 115–46). George Allen & Unwin.

Lewin, K. M. (1991). *Patterns of education and development* (Unit 4). International Extension College and University of London External Programme.

Lewin, K. M. (2006). Education for All and the Millennium Development Goals. In D. A. Clark (Ed.), *Elgar companion to development studies* (pp. 145–52). Edward Elgar.

Lewin, K. M. (2007). *Improving access, equity and transitions in education: Creating a research agenda* (Pathways to Access Research Monograph No. 1). CREATE.

Lewin, K. M. (2015a). *Educational access, equity and development: Planning to make rights realities.* UNESCO International Institute for Educational Planning.

Lewin, K. M. (2015b). *Goals and indicators for development: Consolidating the architectures.* Open Society Foundations. https://www.opensocietyfoundations.org/sites/default/files/lewin-goals-indicators-edu-dev-20150515.pdf

Lewin, K. M. (2023). Using a systems approach to education and development: Insights from a multi-country research programme on access and learning. In M. Faul & L. Savage (Eds.), *Systems thinking in international education and development: Unlocking learning for all?* (pp. 105–37). Edward Elgar.

Lewin, K. M., & Little, A. W. (1984). *Examination reform and educational change in Sri Lanka, 1972–1982: Modernisation or dependent underdevelopment?* Institute of Development Studies Discussion Paper D180.

Lewin, K. M., & Little, A. W. (2011). Access, equity and transitions in education in low-income countries. *International Journal of Educational Development, 31*(4), 333–7.

Lewin, K. M., Little, A. W., & Colclough, C. L. (1982). Adjusting to the 1980s: Taking stock of educational expenditure. In *Financing educational development: Proceedings of an international seminar.* Mont Saint Marie (Canada), IDRC 205E.

Lewin, K. M., Little, A. W., & Colclough, C. L. (1983a). Effects of education on development objectives (I). *Prospects: Quarterly Review of Education, 13*(3), 299–311.

Lewin, K. M., Little, A. W., & Colclough, C. L. (1983b). Effects of education on development objectives. *Prospects: Quarterly Review of Education, 13*(4), 433–47.

Lewin, K. M., Little, A. W., & Wolf, A. (2019, 14 February). The fever spreads as the diploma disease becomes a pandemic. *Times Higher Education,* 27.

Leys, C. (1975). *Underdevelopment in Kenya: The political economy of neo-colonialism.* Heinemann.

Lipton, M. (1975). Comments on Goonatilake (some notes on the dependency of 'dependency'). *Institute of Development Studies Bulletin, 7*(1), 11–14.

Little, A. W. (1980). Is education related to productivity? *Institute of Development Studies Bulletin, 11*(2), 20–27.

Little, A. W. (1982). *The development of the child's understanding of the causes of academic success and failure: Studies of English and Sri Lankan schoolchildren* [unpublished doctoral thesis]. University of Sussex.

Little, A. W. (1984). Education, earnings and productivity: the eternal triangle. In J. C. P. Oxenham (Ed.), *Education versus qualifications? A study of relationships between education, selection for employment and the productivity of labour* (pp. 87–110). George Allen & Unwin.

Little, A. W. (1985). The child's understanding of the causes of academic success and failure: A case study of British schoolchildren. *British Journal of Educational Psychology, 55,* 11–23.

Little, A. W. (1987a). Attributions in a cross-cultural context. *Genetic, Social, and General Psychology Monographs, 113*(1), 61–79.

Little, A. W. (1987b). Education and change in plantations: The case of Sri Lanka. *Institute of Development Studies Bulletin, 18*(2), 31–38.

Little, A. W. (Ed.). (1987c). *Why do students learn? A six-country study of student motivation* (Institute of Development Studies Education Research Report No. 17). Institute of Development Studies (UK).

Little, A. W. (1988). *Learning from developing countries: An inaugural lecture.* Institute of Education, University of London.

Little, A. W. (1992). *Education and development: Macro relationships and microcultures* (Institute of Development Studies Silver Jubilee Paper No. 4). Sussex.

Little, A. W. (1995a). *Insider accounts: The monitoring and evaluation of primary education projects in Sri Lanka.* Swedish International Development Authority, Education Division.

Little, A. W. (1995b). *Multigrade teaching: A review of practice and research* (Serial No. 12). Overseas Development Administration (UK).

Little, A. W. (1997). The diploma disease twenty years on: An introduction. *Assessment in Education, 4*(1), 5–22.

Little, A. W. (1999a). Development and education: Cultural and economic analysis. In F. E. Leach & A. W. Little (Eds.), *Education, cultures and economics* (pp. 3–32). RoutledgeFalmer.

Little, A. W. (1999b). *Labouring to learn: Towards a political economy of plantations, people and education in Sri Lanka.* Macmillan.

Little, A. W. (2000). Primary education in Sri Lanka: Towards a distinct identity. In A. W. Little (Ed.), *Primary education reform in Sri Lanka* (pp. 15–35). Educational Publications

Department, Ministry of Education and Higher Education (Sri Lanka). http://angelawlittle. net/wp-content/uploads/2012/07/PrimaryEdReformSriLankaFull.pdf

Little, A. W. (2003a). Clash of civilisations: threat or opportunity? An extended review of Hayhoe and Pan. *Comparative Education*, *39*(30), 391–4.

Little, A. W. (2003b). *Education for all: Policy and planning lessons from Sri Lanka*. DFID Education Research Papers 46.

Little, A. W. (2003c). Motivating learning and the development of human capital. *Compare*, *33*(4), 437–52.

Little, A. W. (2007). Paradoxes of economic and social development in Sri Lanka: The wages of civil war. In A. Green, A. W. Little, S. G. Kamat, M. Oketch & E. Vickers, *Education and development in a global era: Strategies for 'successful globalisation'* (Researching the Issues No. 69) (pp. 63–208). Department for International Development (UK).

Little, A. W. (2008a). *EFA politics, policies and progress* (Pathways to Access Research Monograph No. 13). CREATE.

Little, A. W. (2008b). Primary care. *Public Service Review* (International Development Issue 12), December.

Little, A. W. (2010). *The politics, policies and progress of basic education in Sri Lanka* (Pathways to Access Research Monograph No. 38). CREATE.

Little, A. W. (2011). Education policy reform in Sri Lanka: The double-edged sword of political will. *Journal of Education Policy*, *26*(4), 499–512.

Little, A. W. (2018). Evidence, SDG4, targets and indicators: Summative assessments of systems vs formative assessments of learners? *Journal of International Cooperation in Education*, *20*(2)/*21*(2), 85–105.

Little, A. W., Aturupane, H., & Shojo, M. (2013). *Transforming primary education in Sri Lanka: From a 'subject' of education to a 'stage' of education*. Development Sector Report No. 61. World Bank South Asia.

Little, A. W., & Evans, J. (2005). The growth of foreign qualification suppliers in Sri Lanka: De facto decentralisation? *Compare*, *35*(2), 181–92.

Little, A. W., & Green, A. (2009). Successful globalisation, education and sustainable development. *International Journal of Educational Development*, *29*(2), 166–74.

Little, A. W., Hadshar, E., Martin, K., Herath, K., Alagaratnam, E., & Mohammed, A. (2020). *Evaluation of the child-centred multi-level approach to teaching and learning in Sri Lanka*. Vol. 1: *Main report*; Vol. 2: *Appendices 1–14*; Vol. 3: *Research tools (appendix 15)*. MottMacdonald Cambridge Education.

Little, A. W., & Hettige, S. T. (2013). *Globalisation, employment and education in Sri Lanka: Opportunity and division*. Routledge.

Little, A. W., Hoppers, W., & Gardner, R. (Eds.). (1994). *Beyond Jomtien: Implementing primary education for all*. Macmillan.

Little, A. W., Indika, H. N. U., & Rolleston, C. (2009). *Access, attendance and achievement in rural schools in Sri Lanka* (Pathways to Access Research Monograph No. 73). CREATE.

Little, A. W., & Miller, E. (2000). *The international consultative forum on education for all 1990–2000: An evaluation*. World Education Forum. http://angelawlittle.net/wp-content/uploads/2012/06/TheInternationalConsultativeForumonEducationforAllanevaluation2000.pdf

Little, A. W., & Sabates, R. (2008). Economic globalisation, youth expectations and social class: The case of Sri Lanka. *International Journal of Educational Development*, *28*, 708–22.

Little, A. W., Shojo, M., Sonnadara, U., & Aturupane, H. A. C. (2019). Teaching English as a second language in Sri Lankan primary schools: Opportunity and pedagogy. *Language, Culture and Curriculum*, *32*(2), 113–27.

Little, A. W., & Singh, J. (1992). Learning and working: Elements of the diploma disease thesis examined in England and Malaysia. *Comparative Education*, *28*(2), 181–200.

Little, A. W., & Wolf, A. (Eds.). (1996). *Assessment in transition: Learning, monitoring and selection in international perspective*. Pergamon.

Lockheed, M. (1996). Assessment and management: World Bank support for educational testing'. In A. W. Little & A. Wolf (Eds.), *Assessment in transition: Learning, monitoring and selection in international perspective* (pp. 28–41). Pergamon.

Lockheed, M. (2015). *Why do countries participate in international large-scale assessments? The case of PISA* (Policy Research Working Paper No. 7447). World Bank. https://openknowledge.worldbank.org/handle/10986/22875

Madaus, G. F., & Raczek, A. F. (1996). A turning point for assessment: Reform movements in the United States. In A. W. Little & A. Wolf (Eds.), *Assessment in transition: Learning, monitoring and selection in international perspective* (pp. 101–17). Pergamon.

Manuel, G., & Posluns, M. (1974). *The Fourth World: An Indian reality*. Collier-Macmillan Canada.

Marimuthu, T. (1971). Education, social mobility and the plantation environment: A proposal for an enquiry. *Jurnal Pendidikan*, 2, 86–93.

Marshall, J. (1976). *A school in Uganda*. Gollancz.

Mayer, J. W., & Rubinson, R. (1975). Education and political development. *Review of Research in Education*, 3, 134–62.

Mazrui, A. (1975). The African university as a multinational corporation: Problems of penetration and dependency. *Harvard Educational Review*, 45(2), 191–210.

Mazrui, A. (1978). *Political values and the educated class in Africa*. Heinemann Educational Books.

McClelland, D. C. (1961). *The achieving society*. John Wiley.

McCowan, T. (2021). Theories of development. In T. McCowan & E. Unterhalter, *Education and international development*. Bloomsbury.

McCowan, T. & Unterhalter, E. (2021). *Education and international development*. Bloomsbury.

McEwan, P. (1998). The effectiveness of multigrade schools in Colombia. *International Journal of Educational Development*, 18(6), 435–52.

McGillivray, M., Carpenter, D., & Norup, S. (2012). *Evaluation study of long-term development cooperation between Sri Lanka and Sweden*. Swedish International Development Authority. https://cdn.sida.se/publications/files/sida61466en-evaluation-study-of-long-term-development-co-operation-between-sri-lanka-and-sweden.pdf

McGrath, S., & Qing Gu (2016). *Routledge handbook of international education and development*. Routledge.

McMahon, W. W. (1997). Conceptual framework for measuring the total social and private benefits of education. *International Journal of Education Research*, 27(6), 453–79.

McMahon, W. W. (1998). Conceptual framework for the analysis of the social benefits of lifelong learning. *Education Economics*, 6(3), 309–46.

McMahon, W. W. (1999). *Education and development: Measuring the social benefits*. Oxford University Press.

Mebrahtu, T. (1991). *Theories of development*. University of London External Studies Department.

Metzger, U., Stenback, T., & Athukorala, K. (1997). *Swedish support to the education sector in Sri Lanka*. Swedish International Development Authority, Department for Democracy and Social Development.

Ministry of Education. (1973). *Medium-term plan for the development of education*. Planning and Programming Division, Ministry of Education (Sri Lanka).

Ministry of Education. (2008). *School census 2008: Preliminary report*. Ministry of Education (Sri Lanka).

Ministry of Education. (2019). *School census 2019*. Ministry of Education (Sri Lanka).

Ministry of Education. (2020). *Sri Lanka: General education sector development plan (2020–2025)*. Isurupaya. https://moe.gov.lk/wp-content/uploads/2021/11/General-Education-Sector-Development-Plan-2021-2025-1.pdf

Ministry of Finance. (1955). *Economic and social development of Ceylon 1926–1954*. Ministry of Finance (Ceylon).

Ministry of Human Resource Development, Education and Cultural Affairs. (2004). *Five year national plan for the development of secondary education*. Ministry of Human Resource Development, Education and Cultural Affairs (Sri Lanka).

Ministry of Planning and Employment. (1971). *Five year plan*. Ministry of Planning and Employment (Sri Lanka).

Moeller, A. J., & Catalano, T. (2015). Foreign language teaching and learning. In J. D. Wright (Ed.), *International encyclopedia for social and behavioral sciences* (2nd ed., vol. 9, pp. 327–32). Pergamon.

Mogollon, O., & Solano, M. (2011). *Escuelas activas: Apuestas para mejorar la calidad de la educacion*. FHI 360.

Moore, M. P. (2017). *The political economy of long-term revenue decline in Sri Lanka*. International Centre for Tax and Development Working Paper 65. International Centre for Tax and Development.

Moramudali, U. (2022). Sri Lanka's story of sovereign default. *The Diplomat*, *94*. https://magazine.thediplomat.com/#/issues/-NA8bFLgsMhTx-eIrxNC/preview/-NA8bGqBaRxN46_XKKh6

Morris, P., & Sweeting, A. (1995). Education and development in East Asia: The overview. In P. Morris & A. Sweeting (Eds.), *Education and development in East Asia* (pp. 1–17). Garland.

Müller, T., Lichtinger, U., & Girg, R. (2015). *The multigrade multilevel-methodology and its global significance*. Prolog-Verlag.

Munasinghe, D. S. A., Nanayakkara, K., Fernando, D. C. V., & Jayathilake, K. K. P. M. (2021). Sri Lanka and Greco-Roman maritime trade relations. *Journal of Archaeological Studies in India*, *1*(2), 241–9.

Munasinghe, M. (1992). *Environmental economics and sustainable development*. Paper presented at the 1992 Earth Summit, Rio De Janeiro. Reproduced as *Environment paper no. 3*. World Bank.

Munasinghe, M. (Ed.). (2019a). *Sustainable Sri Lanka: 2030 vision and strategic plan*. Presidential Expert Committee. Munasinghe Development Institute.

Munasinghe, M. (2019b). *Sustainability in the 21st century: Applying Sustainomics to implement the sustainable development goals*. Cambridge University Press.

Nadesan, S. (1993). *A history of the up-country Tamil people in Sri Lanka*. Ranco.

Nakamura, H., Ratnayake, P., & Senanayake, S. M. P. (1997). Agricultural development: Past trends and policies. In W. D. Lakshman (Ed.), *Dilemmas of development: Fifty years of economic change*. Sri Lankan Association of Economists.

Nanayakkara, G. L. S. (1992). *Assessment of pupil achievement in primary mathematics with special reference to analysis of pupil errors, Sri Lanka* [unpublished doctoral thesis]. University of Sussex.

National Committee on Education. (2009). *Committee for formulating a new education act for general education*. National Committee on Education (Sri Lanka).

National Council of Educational Research and Training. (2011). *Programme evaluation report: Activity-based learning Tamil Nadu, SSA technical cooperation fund*. National Council of Educational Research and Training (India).

NEC. (1992). *First report of the National Education Commission* (Sessional Paper V). National Education Commission (Sri Lanka).

NEC. (1995). *An action-oriented strategy towards a national education policy*. National Education Commission (Sri Lanka).

NEC. (1997). *Reforms in education*. National Education Commission (Sri Lanka).

NEC. (2003). *Envisioning education for human development: Proposals for a national policy framework on general education in Sri Lanka*. National Education Commission (Sri Lanka).

NEC. (2018). *National policy on technical and vocational education*. National Education Commission (Sri Lanka).

NEC. (2022). *National education policy framework 2020–2030*. National Education Commission (Sri Lanka).

NEREC. (2004). *National assessment of achievement of grade 4 pupils in Sri Lanka*. National Education Research and Evaluation Centre, University of Colombo.

NEREC. (2009). *National assessment of grade 4 students in Sri Lanka*. National Education Research and Evaluation Centre, University of Colombo.

NEREC. (2014). *National assessment of achievement of students completing grade 4 in year 2013*. National Education Research and Evaluation Centre, University of Colombo.

NEREC. (2016). *National assessment of achievement of students completing grade 4 in year 2015*. National Education Research and Evaluation Centre, University of Colombo.

National Institute of Education. (2000). *English language syllabus for grades 3, 4, 5*. National Institute of Education (Sri Lanka).

National Institute of Education. (2002). *Let's learn English teacher guide grade 5*. National Institute of Education (Sri Lanka).

National Planning Council. (1959). *The Ten-Year Plan*. Planning Secretariat (Ceylon).

Nesiah, K. (1945). *The mother tongue in education*. Ola Book Company.

Nesiah, N. (1978). The brain drain, internal and external. Paper presented at IDS/NIM seminar *Employers, selection for employment, manpower development and education*, Colombo.

Newman, M. A. (1977). An analysis of sixth-grade pupils' errors on written mathematical tasks. *Victorian Institute for Educational Research Bulletin*, *39*, 31–43.

Newman, M. A. (1983). *The Newman language of mathematics kit*, vol. 2: *Strategies for diagnosis and remediation*. Harcourt Brace Jovanovich.

Nurske, R. (1957). *Problems of capital formation in undeveloped countries*. Oxford University Press.

Nyerere, J. K. (1967). *Education for self-reliance*. Government Printer (Tanzania).

Obeyesekere, G. (1974). Some comments on the social backgrounds of the April 1971 insurgency in Sri Lanka (Ceylon). *Journal of Asian Studies, 33*(3), 367–84.

Obeyesekere, G. (1979). The vicissitudes of the Sinhala-Buddhist identity through time and change. In M. Roberts (Ed.), *Collective identities: Nationalisms and protest in modern Sri Lanka* (pp. 279–313). Marga Institute.

OECD. (2016). *How is learning time organised in primary and secondary education?* (Education Indicators in Focus No. 38). OECD. https://doi.org/10.1787/5jm3tqsm1kq5-en

Ohmae, K. (1990). *The borderless world*. Collins.

Oketch, M. (2007). Promise unfulfilled: Educational improvement and economic decline in Kenya. In A. Green, A. W. Little, S. G. Kamat, M. Oketch & E. Vickers, *Education and development in a global era: Strategies for 'successful globalisation'* (Researching the Issues No. 69) (pp. 63–208). Department for International Development (UK).

Open University. (1997). *The Qualification Chase* (video). https://www.open.ac.uk/library/digital-archive/program/video:FOUE372P.

Oxenham, J. C. P. (Ed.). (1984). *Education versus qualifications? A study of relationships between, education, selection for employment and the productivity of labour*. George Allen & Unwin.

Parandekar, S. D., Futoshi Y., Ragatz, A. B., Sedmik, E. K., & Sawamoto, A. (2017). *Enhancing school quality in Vietnam through participative and collaborative learning: Vietnam escuela nueva impact evaluation study*. World Bank.

Paulston, R. G. (1976). *Conflicting theories of social and educational change*. Centre for International Studies, University of Pittsburgh.

Peiris, K. M. (1983). *Tiny sapling, sturdy tree: The inside story of primary education reforms of the 1970s in Sri Lanka*. Universitetsforlaget.

Peiris, K. M., & Nanayakkara, S. (2000). Curriculum and assessment. In A. W. Little (Ed.), *Primary education reform in Sri Lanka* (pp. 36–57). Educational Publications Department, Ministry of Education and Higher Education (Sri Lanka).

Perera, L., & Dharmawardana, K. (2000). The primary education reform: The Gampaha experience. In A. W. Little (Ed.), *Primary education reform in Sri Lanka* (pp. 58–74). Educational Publications Department, Ministry of Education and Higher Education (Sri Lanka).

Perera, L., Wijetunge, S., & Balasooriya, A. S. (2004). Education reform and political violence in Sri Lanka. In S. Tawil & A. Harley (Eds.), *Education, conflict and social cohesion* (pp. 375–433). UNESCO International Bureau of Education.

Perera, M. E. S. (2000). Role of attitudes in learning English in Sri Lanka: Has there been a change after independence? In *Developments in education: 25th anniversary volume* (pp. 84–95). Faculty of Education, University of Colombo.

Perera, M. E. S. (2001). *Role of classroom interaction in second language acquisition in Sri Lanka* [unpublished doctoral thesis]. University of Wollongong.

Perera, S. (2005). Education proposals for reform. Paper presented at seminar on *Globalisation and education*, Social Policy Analysis Research Centre, University of Colombo.

Pieris, M. D. D. (2002). *In the pursuit of governance: A memoir over three and a half decades in the public service of Sri Lanka*. Stanford Lake Publications.

Pieris, R. (1976). *Social development and planning in Asia*. Abhinav Publications.

Pires, E. A. (1960). Primary and compulsory education in Asia: Regional meeting of representatives of Asian member states of UNESCO, Karachi, December 1959/January 1960. *International Review of Education, 6*(2), 224–6. https://link.springer.com/content/pdf/10.1007/BF01416691.pdf

Premarathna, A., Yogaraja, S. J., Medawattegedara, V., Senarathna, C. D., & Abdullah, M. R. M. (2016). *Study on medium of instruction, national and international languages in general education in Sri Lanka*. National Education Commission (Sri Lanka).

Presidential Task Force on General Education. (1997). *General education reforms, 1997*. Presidential Task Force on General Education (Sri Lanka).

Presidential Task Force on Sri Lanka's Education Affairs. (2020). *Transforming the present system of education to a dynamic and vibrant paradigm for 21st century*. Reimagining Education in Sri Lanka Core Group Reports, vol. 11, Colombo.

Preston, R., & Dyer, C. (2003). Human capital, social capital and lifelong learning: An editorial introduction. *Compare, 33*(4), 429–36.
Psacharopoulos, G. (1973). *Returns to education: An international comparison*. Elsevier.
Psacharopoulos, G. (1994). Returns to investment in education: A global update. *World Development, 22*, 1325–43.
Psacharopoulos, G., Rojas, C., & Velez, E. (1993). Achievement evaluation of Colombia's escuela nueva: Is multigrade the answer? *Comparative Education Review, 37*(3), 263–76.
Punchi, L. (2001). Resistance towards the language of globalisation: The case of Sri Lanka. *International Review of Education / Zeitschrift für Erziehungswissenschaft, 47*(3/4), 361–78.
Radatz, H. (1979). Error analysis in mathematics education. *Journal for Research in Mathematics Education, 10*(3), 163–72.
Rahnema, M., & Bawtree, V. (Eds.). (1997). *The post-development reader*. Zed Books.
Rahula, S. (1956). *History of Buddhism in Ceylon*. M. D. Gunasena.
Ranasinghe, A., & Hartog, J. (2002). Free education in Sri Lanka: Does it eliminate the family effect? *Economics of Education Review, 21*, 623–33.
Ranaweera, M. (1975). Science at the junior secondary level. *Bulletin of the Curriculum Development Centre* No. 1. Curriculum Development Centre (Sri Lanka).
Ranugge, S. (2000). State, bureaucracy and development. In S. Hettige & M. Mayer (Eds.), *Sri Lanka at crossroads: Dilemmas and prospects after 50 years of independence* (pp. 50–73). Macmillan India.
Raudenbush, S. W., & Bryk, A. S. (2002). *Hierarchical linear models: Application and data analysis methods* (2nd ed.). Sage.
Resnick, L. B., Nesher, P., Leonard, F., Magone, M., Omanson, S., & Peled, I. (1989). Conceptual bases of arithmetic errors: The case of decimal fractions. *Journal for Research in Mathematics Education, 20*(1), 8–27.
Richards, J. (2022). Why are school systems in South Asia seriously underperforming? *International Journal of Educational Development, 95*, issue C.
Rishi Valley. (2021). *Multiple editions of the school in a box: An historical perspective*. Rishi Valley. https://www.rishivalley.org/history-of-design
Rixon, S. (2013). *British Council survey of policy and practice in primary English language teaching worldwide*. British Council.
Robeyns, I. (2005). The capability approach: A theoretical survey. *Journal of Human Development and Capabilities, 6*(1), 93–117.
Rostow, W. W. (1960). The five stages of growth: A summary. In W. W. Rostow, *The stages of economic growth: A non-communist manifesto* (pp. 4–16). Cambridge University Press.
Rotter, J., Seeman, M., & Liverant, S. (1962). Internal versus external control of reinforcement: A major variable in behaviour therapy. In N. F. Washburne (Ed.), *Decisions, values and groups* (vol. 2, pp. 473–517). Pergamon.
Ruberu, R. (1962). *Education in colonial Ceylon*. Kandy Printers.
Russell, J. (1982). *Communal politics under the Donoughmore constitution 1931–1947*. Tissara Publishers.
Ruttan, V. (1984). Integrated rural development programme: A historical perspective. *World Development, 12*(4), 393–401.
Ryan, J., & Williams, J. (2007). *Children's mathematics 4–15: Learning from errors and misconceptions*. Open University Press/McGraw-Hill Education.
Rychen, D. S., & Salganik, L. H. (2000). Definition and selection of key competencies. In *Fourth General Assembly of the OECD Education Indicators Program, the INES Compendium*, Tokyo. pp. 61–73.
Salih, R. (2002). *A review of the current labour market situation, policy and programs in Sri Lanka*. ILO.
Samaranayake, V. K. (1978). *Role of the mathematicians and mathematics education in Sri Lanka*. Presidential address, section E, 34th annual session, Sri Lanka Association for the Advancement of Science.
Samoff, J. (2003). Institutionalising international influence. In C. Torres & R. Arnove (Eds.), *Comparative education: The dialectic of the global and the local* (2nd ed., pp. 409–45). Rowman and Littlefield.
Sankar, D., & Linden, T. (2014). *How much and what kind of teaching is there in elementary education in India? Evidence from three states* (South Asia Region, Human Development

Sector Report No. 67). World Bank. https://openknowledge.worldbank.org/handle/10986/17800

Sarvi, J. (1999). Evaluation of the processes of developing a national long-term plan for primary education. *Primary Education Planning Project* (Document No. 37). Government of Sri Lanka; Cambridge Education Consultants.

Schmitz, H. (2007). The rise of the east: What does it mean for development studies? *Institute of Development Studies Bulletin*, *38*(2), 51–8.

Schultz, T. W. (1961). Investment in human capital. *American Economic Review*, *51*(1), 1–17.

Sebatane, M. (2000). International transfers of assessment: Recent trends and strategies. *Assessment in Education*, *7*(3), 401–16.

Sedere, U. M. (2019). *Education meeting knowledge economy: 21st century expectation*. White Falcon Publishing.

Seers, D. (1969). *The meaning of development* (Institute of Development Studies Communication No. 44). Institute of Development Studies (UK).

Seers, D., & Joy, L. (Eds.). (1971). *Development in a divided world*. Penguin.

Sen, A. K. (1981). Public action and the quality of life in developing countries. *Oxford Bulletin of Economics and Statistics*, *43*(4), 287–319.

Sen, A. K. (1999). *Development as freedom*. Oxford University Press.

Serpell, R. (1999). Local accountability to rural communities: A challenge to educational planning in Africa. In F. E. Leach & A. W. Little (Eds.), *Education, cultures and economics* (pp. 111–39). RoutledgeFalmer.

Sethunga, P., Wijesundara, S., Kalamy, T., & Karunanayake, S. (2014). *Study of the professional development of teachers and teacher education in Sri Lanka*. National Education Commission (Sri Lanka).

Singal, N., Pedder, D., Malathy, D., Shanmugam, M., Manickavasagam, S., & Govindarasan, M. (2018). Insights from within activity-based learning (ABL) classrooms in Tamil Nadu, India: Teachers' perspectives and practices. *International Journal of Educational Development*, *60*, 165–71.

Sklair, L. (2006). Globalisation and development. In D. A. Clark (Ed.), *Elgar companion to development studies* (pp. 200–3). Edward Elgar.

Snodgrass, D. R. (1966). *Ceylon: An export economy in transition*. Yale University Press.

Snodgrass, D. R. (1998). The economic development of Sri Lanka: A tale of missed opportunities. In I. R. Rotberg (Ed.), *Creating peace in Sri Lanka: Civil war and reconciliation* (pp. 89–107). Brookings Institution Press.

Somerset, H. C. A. (1996). Examinations and educational quality. In A. W. Little & A. Wolf (Eds.), *Assessment in transition: Learning, monitoring and selection in international perspective* (pp. 263–84). Pergamon.

Somerset, H. C. A. (1998). *The Sri Lankan general education reform programme: A report prepared for the director general education reform implementation unit*. Ministry of Education and Higher Education (Sri Lanka); UNESCO Regional Office.

Spivak, G. (1988). Can the subaltern speak? In C. Nelson and L. Grossberg (Eds.), *Marxism and the interpretation of culture* (pp. 271–313). Macmillan.

Sri Lanka Presidential Commission on Youth. (1990). *Report of the Presidential Commission on Youth*. Government of Sri Lanka.

Stallings, J. A. (1980). Allocated academic learning time revisited, or beyond time on task. *Educational Researcher*, *9*, 11–16.

Steiner-Khamsi, G. (Ed.). (2004). *The global politics of education borrowing and lending*. Teachers College Press.

Stewart, F. (1996). Globalisation and education. *International Journal of Educational Development*, *16*(4), 327–33.

Stewart, F. (2006). Basic needs approach. In D. A. Clark (Ed.), *Elgar companion to development studies* (pp. 14–18). Edward Elgar.

Sunkel, O. (1979). The development of development thinking. In J. J. Villamil (Ed.), *Transnational capitalism and national development* (pp. 19–30). Harvester Press.

Taiwo, O. O. (2022). *Against decolonisation: Taking African agency seriously*. C. Hurst and Co.

TaRL. (2023). *Teaching at the Right Level Africa*. https://teachingattherightlevel.org/

Teasdale, J. I., & Teasdale, G. R. (1999). Alternative cultures of knowledge in higher education in the Australia-Pacific region. In F. E. Leach & A. W. Little (Eds.), *Education, cultures and economics* (pp. 241–60). RoutledgeFalmer.

Tikly, L., & Bond, T. (2013). Towards a postcolonial research ethics in comparative and international education. *Compare*, *43*(4), 422–42.

Tilak, J. (2002). *Building human capital in East Asia: What others can learn*. National Institute of Educational Planning and Administration (India).

Toye, J., & Toye, R. (2003). The origin and interpretation of the Prebisch-Singer thesis. *History of Political Economy*, *35*(3), 437–67.

Trevino, E., & Ordenes, M. (2017). *Exploring commonalities and differences in regional and international assessments* (Information Paper No. 48). UNESCO Institute for Statistics.

Umar, J. (1996). Grappling with heterogeneity: Assessment in Indonesia. In A. W. Little & A. Wolf (Eds.), *Assessment in transition: Learning, monitoring and selection in international perspective* (pp. 233–47). Pergamon.

UNESCO. (2007). *The UN decade for education for sustainable development (DESD 2005–2014): The first two years*. UNESCO.

UNESCO. (2011). *Education for all global monitoring report: The hidden crisis; armed conflict and education; gender overview*. UNESCO.

UNESCO. (2014). *The global monitoring report on education: Teaching and learning*. UNESCO. https://en.unesco.org/gem-report/report/2014/teaching-and-learning-achieving-quality-all

UNESCO. (2023). *Using learning assessment data to transform literacy and learning* [blog post]. UNESCO. https://www.iiep.unesco.org/en/using-learning-assessment-data-transform-literacy-and-learning-14278

UNESCO-UNICEF. (2021). *Situation analysis on the effects of and responses to COVID-19 on the education sector in Asia: Sri Lanka case study*. UNESCO-UNICEF. https://unesdoc.unesco.org/ark:/48223/pf0000379518

UNICEF. (2009). *Children and the 2004 Indian Ocean tsunami: Evaluation of UNICEF's response in Sri Lanka* (Country Synthesis Report). UNICEF Evaluation Office.

UNICEF. (2015). *Evaluation of activity-based learning as means of child-friendly education: Final report*. UNICEF New Delhi.

United Nations. (1945). *Charter of the United Nations and the statute of the International Court of Justice*. https://treaties.un.org/doc/publication/ctc/uncharter.pdf

United Nations. (1948). *Universal declaration of human rights*. https://www.un.org/en/about-us/universal-declaration-of-human-rights#:~:text=Drafted%20by%20representatives%20with%20different,all%20peoples%20and%20all%20nations

United Nations. (1962). *The United Nations decade: Proposals for action. Report of the Secretary General*. https://documents-dds-ny.un.org/doc/UNDOC/GEN/N62/115/49/PDF/N6211549.pdf?OpenElement

United Nations. (1972). *The United Nations conference on the human environment*. https://documents-dds-ny.un.org/doc/UNDOC/GEN/NL7/300/05/IMG/NL730005.pdf?OpenElement

United Nations. (1990). *Human Development Report*. United Nations Development Programme.

United Nations. (1992). *The United Nations conference on environment and development, Rio de Janeiro, June 3–14*. https://www.un.org/en/conferences/environment/rio1992

United Nations. (2000). *United Nations Millennium Declaration, New York*. https://www.un.org/en/development/devagenda/millennium.shtml

United Nations. (2004). *Human development report: Cultural liberty in today's diverse world*. United Nations Development Programme.

United Nations (2015a). *Sustainable development goals: Targets and indicators*. https://unstats.un.org/sdgs/indicators/Global%20Indicator%20Framework%20after%20refinement_Eng.pdf

United Nations (2015b). *Transforming our world: The 2030 agenda for sustainable development*. https://documents-dds-ny.un.org/doc/UNDOC/GEN/N15/291/89/PDF/N1529189.pdf?OpenElement

Unterhalter, E. (2007). *Gender, schooling and global social justice*. Routledge.

Vijayanandan, M. R. (2008). *Access to higher education for the children of the plantation Tamil community in Sri Lanka*. Information Centre for Hindu Culture & Education of Central Province.

Vijayanandan, M. R. (2023). *The contribution of the SIDA Project in the Development of Hill Country Education* (மலையக கல்வி அபிவிருத்தியில் சீடா செயற்றிட்டத்தின் பங்களிப்பு). Kumaran Book House.

Vijayapalan, Y. (2015). *Endless inequality: The rights of plantation Tamils in Sri Lanka*. CreateSpace Independent Publishing Platform.

Vithanapathirana, M. (2006). Adapting the primary mathematics curriculum to the multigrade classroom in rural Sri Lanka. In A. W. Little (Ed.), *Education for all and multigrade teaching* (pp. 127–54). Springer.

Waage, J., Banerji, R., Campbell, O., Chirwa, E., Collender, G., Dieltiens, V., Dorward, A., Godfrey-Faussett, P., Hanvoravongchai, P., Kingdon, G. Little, A., Mills, A., Mulholland, K., Mwinga, A., North, A., Patcharanarumol, W., Poulton, C., Tangcharoensathien, V., & Unterhalter, E. (2008). *The Millennium Development Goals: A cross-sectoral analysis and principles for goal setting after 2015*. Lancet; London International Development Centre Commission.

Wade, R. (1990). *Governing the market*. Princeton University Press.

Wallerstein, E. (1976). *The modern world-system: Capitalist agriculture and the origins of the European world-economy in the sixteenth century*. Academic Press.

War and Colonial Department and Colonial Office. (1943). *Ceylon, Sessional Papers*. National Archives (UK).

Waters, M. (1995). *Globalisation*. Routledge.

Weber, M. (1963). *Sociology of religion*. Beacon Press.

Wehella, M. M. (2001). *Extending educational opportunities: A study of the causes and effects of the implications of a school restructuring programme in Sri Lanka* [unpublished master's thesis]. Institute of Education, University of London.

Wehella, M. M., & Balasooriya, B. M. J. (2014). Free education policy and its challenges: Sri Lanka. In A. Robertson & R. Parry-Jones (Eds.), *Commonwealth education partnerships 2014/15* (pp. 55–58). Commonwealth Secretariat.

Weiner, B. (1979). A theory of motivation of some classroom experiences. *Journal of Educational Psychology*, *71*(1), 3–25.

Wettewa, V. (2015). Postcolonial emotionalism in shaping education: Analysis of international school choice in Sri Lanka. *International Education Journal: Comparative Perspectives*, *15*(10), 66–83.

White, A. L. (2005). Active mathematics in classrooms: Finding out why children make mistakes – and then doing something to help them. *Square One*, *15*(4), 15–19.

White, A. L. (2009). *Counting on 2008: Final report*. Curriculum K-12 Directorate, Department of Education and Training (New South Wales).

White, A. L., & Clements, M. A. (2005). Energising upper-primary mathematics classrooms in Brunei Darussalam: The active mathematics in classrooms (AMIC) project. In H. S. Dhindsa, I. J. Kyeleve, O. Chukwu & J. S. H. Q. Perera (Eds.), *Future directions in science, mathematics and technical education: Proceedings of the tenth international conference*, pp. 151–60. University Brunei Darussalam.

Wikramanayake, D. H. (2009). *Education and economic globalisation: An analysis of national policy formation in Sri Lanka* [unpublished doctoral thesis]. University of Sydney.

Wickremaratne, L. A. (1973). Education and social change, 1832–c. 1900. In K. M. de Silva (Ed.). *History of Ceylon*, vol. 3, pt. 2. University of Ceylon.

Wijemanne, E. L. (1978). *Education reform in Sri Lanka* (Report Studies C 70). UNESCO Division of Education Policy and Planning.

Wilson, A. J. (1972). *The People's Liberation Front and the revolution that failed* (Report Series No. 23). McGill University Centre for Developing Area Studies.

Winkler, D. R. (1987). Screening models and education. In G. Psacharopoulos (Ed.), *Economics of education, research and studies*. Pergamon.

Wolf, A. (2002). *Does education matter? Myths about education and economic growth*. Penguin.

Wolf-Phillips, L. (1979). Forum: Why third world? *Third World Quarterly*, *1*(1), 105–15.

Wood A. (1995). *North–South trade employment and inequality: Changing fortunes in a skill-driven world*. Clarendon.

Woodhall, M. (2001). Human capital: Educational aspects. In N. J. Smelser & P. B. Baltes (Eds.), *International encyclopaedia of the social & behavioural sciences* (vol. 10, pp. 6,951–5). Elsevier.

World Bank. (1993). *The East Asian miracle: Economic growth and public policy*. Oxford University Press.

World Bank. (2004). *Sri Lanka data profile*. Colombo.

World Bank. (2005). *Treasures of the education system in Sri Lanka: Restoring performance, expanding opportunities and enhancing prospects*. World Bank South Asia Region.

World Bank. (2007). *Sri Lanka. Poverty assessment, engendering growth with equity: Opportunities and challenges.* World Bank South Asia Region.

World Bank. (2018). *World development report: Learning to realise education's promise.* http://www.worldbank.org/en/publication/wdr2018

World Bank. (2021). *Realizing the promise and potential of human capital in Sri Lanka.* World Bank.

World Bank. (2023). *New World Bank country classifications by income level: 2022–2023* [blog post]. https://blogs.worldbank.org/opendata/new-world-bank-country-classifications-income-level-2022-2023#:~:text=The%20World%20Bank%20assigns%20the,the%20previous%20year%20(2021)

World Commission on Education and Development. (1987). *Our common future.* Oxford University Press.

World Conference on Education for All. (1990). *Meeting basic learning needs: A vision for the 1990s.* WCEFA Inter-Agency Commission.

Wurgaft, L. D. (1985). Review of 'Crippled Minds' by S. Goonatilake. *Association for Asian Studies, 44*(2), 434–6.

Wyatt-Smith, C., & Cumming, J. (Eds.). (2009). *Educational assessment in the 21st century: Connecting theory and practice.* Springer.

Yates, C., & Little, A. W. (2005). *Learning, education and development: Concepts and theories.* University of London External Studies Department MA in Open, Distance and Flexible Learning, Module 1.

Yew, L. K. (2000). *From third world to first: The Singapore story 1965–2000.* HarperCollins.

Zhou, Y., & Ng, M. L. (2016). English as a foreign language (EFL) and English medium instruction (EMI) for three to seven year old children in East Asian contexts. In V. A. Murphy & M. Evangelou (Eds.), *Early childhood education in English for speakers of other languages* (pp. 137–58). British Council.

Index

Page references to figures, tables and boxes are in *italic*.

Abhayadewa, C. M. 290, 295
academic selection points 12
access, to education 14, 98–9, 129, 130, 224–6, 251–2
accountability 310
accountancy courses 241, 243
activity-based learning (ABL) 236, 305, 307
Acts of Parliament (1960s) 146–7
adaptation, fidelity and (MGML and ML) 295–6
advanced colleges 243
Advanced Level (A level)
  cross-generational shift 251
  diploma disease 131
  employment 235, 238
  English at 278
  enrolment 241
  girls 87, 247
  introduction 85
  pass rates 88, 264, 344
  plantation education 224–5, 227
  practical assessment 155
  qualification escalation 127, 133–4
  reforms 77–8
  reinstated 94–5, 98, 131, 154, 236, 328
  replaced 89, 153
  results as influence 12, 244
  skill requirements 239
  system 67
  unemployment 237, 247
Advanced School Certificate 85
advertised courses 240–2
Africa 59, 330
Agenda 21 (Earth Summit, 1992) 47
Agenda for 'Sustainable Development' (2030) 33
agricultural industrialisation 123, 132, 341
An inquiry into the nature and causes of the wealth of nations (Smith) 29, 103
Annual Status of Education Report (ASER) *313*, 314
anti-colonial and egalitarian policy reforms 23, 144–6
apprenticeships 241, 243
Argentina 34
Ashton, D. N. 105
Asian countries 62, 255–70, 289, 330
Asian Development Bank 334
Asian Tigers 233, 255, 256, 257, 258, 262, 264
assessment
  continuous 67, 131, 154–5
  criterion-based 317
  design 312–13, *313*, 314
  errors in learning 310, 318–22, 322–5, *322–5*
  formative 316–20, 320–2, 322–5, *322–5*
  individualised 306
  national English language 279, 286
  norm-based 317
  political economy of 315–16
  regional *313*
  surveys – international, regional and foundational skills 312–14, *313*
  teacher-assessed exam components 91

assessment for sustainable learning and development 309–26
large-scale international/national surveys of learning outcomes 310–12
prospects for formative assessment 322–5
purposes of learning assessment 310
summative vs formative assessment 316–20
technical challenges of learning assessment 312–14, 315–16
training in formative assessment for learning 320–2
assets, social and cultural 115–16
assisted schools, nationalisation of 144, 146, 235
Athulathmudali, Lalith 156
attendance, school 20
attribution theory 54–61
Australia 319–20, 321

Bacchus, M. K. 210–11
Badulla district 219, 227
Bailey, Revd J. B. H. 129–30
Bandaranaike, S. W. R. D. 23, 51, 146
Bandaranayake, Sirimavo 151
basic needs approach (BNA) 42–3
basic needs, welfare and (1931–91) 141–60
anti-colonial and egalitarian policy reforms 22, 144–6
constitutional change (1970s) 150–2
education policies and international development ideas 158–9
education policy stakeholders (early 1990s) 156–8
'national' project and ethnicity 148–9
political patronage and the implementation of education policy 150
post-independence: the nationalist project 146–7
transition from colonial education 141–4
waves of political unrest and education reforms 152–6
welfare state 217
Becker, G. 104
Beckford, G. L. 210
Beeby, Clarence E. 36, *37*, 69, 134
Beijing Declaration and Platform for Action (1995) 46–7
Berg, I. 106
Bilingual Education Programme 278
birth rates 246, 262
Blair, Tony 171
Board of Education 143
Board of Investment 242, 244
borrowing and lending, education 65–9
Bourdieu, P. 115
Bowles, S. 80, 112
boys
compulsory education 141
enrolment 21, 213
gender gap 13, 33, 47, 125, 337–8
'brain drain' 85–6, 93
Brazil 34, 44
Bretton Woods Institutions 31, 34
British Council 279–80
Brownrigg, Sir Robert 20
Brundtland Commission (1987) 47, 270
Bruns, B. 311
Buddhism 16, 18, 19, 86, 149
Buddhist schools 21, 22
Burgher people 16–17, 23, 83
Burma 148

Calcutta, University of 84, 130
Cambridge, Examinations Syndicate of the University of 84, 92–3
Cape Coast, University of (Ghana) 107
capitalist countries 46, 80
capitals, range of 115–16
Caribbean Examinations Council 69
Carpmail, M. 319

Castells, M. 257, 258, 262
casual employment 238
Catalano, T. 280
census (1901) 214
Center for Educational Studies (Mexico) 107
Central Bank 261, 338
Central Province 281, 296, 298, 303, 306, 307
'central schools', rural 131, 145, 175, 176, 344
Centre for Development Studies and the Department of Sociology (Ghana) 107
certification of competency or legitimation of economic inequality (educational change and conflict) 81–2
Ceylon 17–18, 142–3, 150
Ceylon Administrative Service 263–4
Ceylon Civil Service (CCS) 83, 263
Ceylon Daily News 88, 89, 93, 95
Ceylon Indian Congress Labour Union 216
Ceylon Tamils *see* Tamil people
Ceylon Workers' Congress (CWC) 216, 222
challenges
  continuing challenges into the 2020s 227–8
  ML implementation challenges 303–4
  technical challenges of learning assessment 312–14, 315–16
  training strategy implementation 191–2
change, continuity and 328–9
change, drivers of twenty-first century
  COVID-19 pandemic 333–4
  economic and political crisis (2022) 334–5
  Tsunami 2004 332–3
Chaudhri, D. P. 106
child labour 210, 213, 215

China
  attribution theory 59
  British teacher post-grad studies in 60–1
  developmental patterns 66
  education system 61, 120, 330
  eyesight tests 60
  fulfilling basic needs 42–3
  loans from 334
  rise of economy 48
  'successful globalisation' 268
  trade with Sri Lanka 18
Chinese, Singaporean 265
Christianity 16, 19, 83, 148–9, 226
Christian schools 21, 23
civil service 21, 83, 150, 151, 263–4
civil strife, and internal security 198–9
civil war 24, 131, 180, 198, 262–3, 265, 267–9, 342, 348
classification of schools 343–4
Class, patriarchy and ethnicity on Sri Lankan plantations (Jayawardena and Kurian) 209
closures, school 177–8
'clothing technology' courses 241
'clusters', school 154
Cockcroft, Sir Wilfred 68
coffee plantations 16, 17, 209, 212, 213, 232
Cold War 30, 40
Colebrooke-Cameron Commission (1833) 21, 83
Coleman, J. 115
collegiate education 12
Colombia 305
Colombo Academy 20, 85, 130, 170
Colombo district 247–8
Colombo Plan for Cooperative Economic and Social Development in Asia and the Pacific 27, 51
Colombo, University of 86, 241
  National Institute of Management 107

INDEX 369

colonial governments
  British 17, 20–2, 83–5, 123, 212–16, 235, 330
  Dutch 20, 22
  Portuguese 20, 22
commerce streams 241, 248, 278
Commonwealth, British 11, 18
Communism 87
complementarities, building on (PEPP) 192–3
compulsory education 21, 32, 141
Compulsory Education Regulations (1997) 171
concepts and theories revisited 340–2
conferences, educational 32, 193–5
conflict, consensus or (educational change and conflict) 81, 97
conflict, educational change and 80–3
constitutional change (1970s) 150–2
controllability (attribution theory) 56, *56*, 58
Corea, Gamini 123
courses, advertised 240–2
COVID-19 pandemic (2020–2) 333–4
craft/trade apprenticeships 241, 243
creation of knowledge about education, collective 61–5
crèches 220, 223
criterion-based assessment 317
cross-cultural attribution studies 57–9
cross-generational shifts (youth expectations) 251–3
Cuba 42, 120
cultural alienation, dependency and 38–40, 79
cultural capital 115–16
culture, globalisation of 46
Curriculum Development Centre 90, 91, 93, 129
curriculum renewal, quality and relevance in primary education 178–80

daily teaching and learning practices, integration of ML into 300–2, *301*
Dakar Framework for Action: Education for all (WEF) 32
dame school (Beeby) 36, *37*
Davis, K. 79
Decade of Education for Sustainable Development (2005–14) 48
Deci, E. L. 111
demographers 35
demographic transition (politics and the state) 262–4
denominational schools 21, 23, 24, 125, 146
dependency, and cultural alienation 38–40
dependency theory 40, 48–9, 70, 340
De Silva, Eric J. 153, 170, 175
developing countries
  attribution theory 54–61
  collective creation of knowledge about education 61–5
  'early developer' 66, 76, 119, 132
  education borrowing and lending 65–9
  education programmes 310
  'late developer' 41, 66, 76, 119
  'later developer' 66, 76, 119, 120–1, 122
  learning from 53–71
  lessons 69–71
  'much later developer' 41, 76, 119
  structural adjustment 41–2
  trade and 46
developmental state (politics and the state) 263
development and education
  basic needs and redistribution with growth 42–3
  development as 'human development' and human capability 44–5
  globalisation 45–6
  how does development come about? 33–8
  international discourse 27–51

locating Sri Lankan ideas, policies and practices on an international map 50–1
MDGs 46–7
meaning of 'development' 28–9
neo-liberalism and structural adjustment 41–2
post-development and post-colonial perspectives 48–50
'sustainable development' 47–8
terminology 30–1
underdevelopment 38–41
development as freedom 44
Development Assistance Committee (DAC) 47
Development in a divided world (Seers and Joy) 66
'development', meaning of 28–9
Development Programme, UN 117
development, stages of 35–6, *37*
'development' thinking, theoretical perspectives 78–80
deviation, norm or (educational change and conflict) 81
'diploma disease' 119–35
  exploring the validity of the propositions 122–30
  forecast intensification of the 130–2
  a pathology of societies or individuals? 120
  pattern of educational development in Sri Lanka compared with England and Japan 122
  propositions re-assessed 132–5
  'qualification chase' 135
  Sri Lanka: a 'later developer'? 120–1
  thesis 61, 105, 119–20
Diploma disease: An argument with pictures (Dore and Little) 105
Diploma disease: Education, qualification and development, The (Dore) 41, 61, 119, 120, 132–3
disadvantaged districts 227
disparities, socio-economic 246–9

Divisional Schools Development (DSD) project 175, 176
Donoughmore Commission (1928) 22, 142, 143
Dore, Ronald
  developing countries 66
  economic modernisation 123
  on examinations 128
  forecasts intensification of the diploma disease 130
  'genuine' education 135
  ILO 'employment mission' 126
  'qualification escalation' 127
  social mobility 124
  The diploma disease: An argument with pictures 105
  The diploma disease: Education, qualification and development 41, 61, 119, 120, 132–3
drama festivals, music and 195–6
Dravidian languages 16
dropout, early school 177–8, 207, 290, 292, 300
'dualities' (education system) 142, 216
Durkheim, Emile 80
Dutch language 20
Dutch Reformed churches 19–20

early childhood education programmes 12
'early developer' countries 66, 76, 119, 132
Early Grade Mathematics Assessment (EGMA) *313*, 314
Early Grade Reading Assessment (EGRA) *313*, 314
earnings, job performance and 109–10
Earth Summit (1992) 47
East Asia 15, 34, 48
'East Asian miracle' 256
East Asian Tiger economies 233
Eastern Province 296, 303, 306
economic and political crisis (2022) 334–5

economic changes and crises, political and 23–4
economic growth 232–4
  agricultural 87
  Asian countries 255, 262
  encouraging 41
  export-led 209–29, 234
  human capital and 36–8
  modern sector 87
  through import substitution 34
Economic Review 131
economics, development 29
economic strategies
  availability of foreign exchange 260
  income inequality 261
  investment and savings rates 260–1
  manufactured exports 259–60
  rural landowners and rural productivity 261
  transition to higher value-added activity 260
economists 115
economy, capitalist 46
economy, global 45–6
economy, reducing the mismatch between education and the 346
educational change, and conflict 80–3
educational development, pattern of
  drive for modernisation after independence 123–4
  'educated unemployment' 126
  employers raising qualifications required 127–30
  social mobility channels 124–5
  validity of propositions 122–30
educational opportunities
  equitable distribution of 175–6
  export-led plantation economy 209–29
  growth in (1950–2021) 24–5, *26*
educational progress, phases of (plantation economy) 211–26
  Phase 1 – 1840–69: diffuse inception of line and mission schools 212–13
  Phase 2 – 1869–1900: slow growth of line and mission schools 213–14
  Phase 3 – 1900–48: widespread establishment of plantation schools 214–16
  Phase 4 – 1948–77: stagnation of low-quality schooling in plantations 217–19
  Phase 5 – 1977–2000: state takeover and widespread increases in enrolment 219
  broader underlying drivers 222–4
  views and voices on the ground 219–22
  Phase 6 – 2000–20: continued expansion of opportunity and disparities 224–6
educational provision, changes in public and private 242–4
Educational Publications, Department of 12, 22
Education and Cultural Affairs, Ministry of 150
education and skills, globalisation comparing Sri Lanka with elsewhere 255–70
education and social disparities, late twentieth-century globalisation 231–53
education and the economy, reducing the mismatch between 346
education and training
  characteristics of successful Asian countries (common/uncommon) 258–9
education and training provision, changes in 240–2
education borrowing and lending 65–9
education, colleges of 12
Education, Department of 141
Education Executive Committee 142
education finance revisited 338–9

'education for all' (EFA) 31, 135, 141–60
  technical work of planning for 183–202
Education in Developing Countries, Department of 69
education, measuring returns to learning 'quality' 115
  non-monetary benefits 114–15
  research within a human capital framework 116–17
  specification of time 115
Education Ordinances 22, 141, 144, 215
education policy 87–8, 158–9
  British colonial 20–2
  political patronage and the implementation of 150
education reforms (1997) 161–82
  change of government, continuation of policy formulation 164–6
  drivers and inhibitors of policy formulation and implementation 180–2
  drivers of policy formulation 170–4
  evaluations of implementation 174–80
  National Education Commission 161–2
  origins 24, 161
  outline 167–70
  political will 162–4
  Presidential Task Force 166–7
Education Reforms Implementation Unit (ERIU) 171, 172–3, 192, 195, 196
Education Reforms Policy 193
Education Review Committee 88, 89, 152–3
education strategies and characteristics 264–6
Eelam Tamils *see* Tamil people
EFA-Fast Track Initiative 311
effectiveness of ML in practice 299–305
  implementation challenges 303–4
  integration into daily teaching and learning practices 300–2, *301*
  parent perceptions of 302–3
  system barriers 304–5
'efficiency bar' (pay grades) 110
egalitarianism 23, 125, 345
Egypt 40
eighth-grade school exam, 'local' 83–4
elections, general
  1930s 13, 142
  1960s 23, 149
  1970s 93, 151, 235, 237
  2000 199
  post-independence 217
elections, presidential 199
elections, provincial council 199
elementary education 21, 22, 32, 53, 141, 214, 215, 343
Elementary School Leaving Certificate 85
elite group interests 100
employers 104–5, 157, 238–40, 250
employment
  agricultural 237
  casual 238
  educated 86, 119
  education–employment sector 248–9
  exams for 12
  foreign 238, 246
  government schemes 238, 240
  opportunities 40, 235
  self- 238
  sectors 149, 237–8
  women 238, 240, 246
  See also unemployment
'employment missions' (ILO) 42, 126
endogenous or exogenous conditions (educational change and conflict) 28, 39, 82, 99
energy crisis (1979) 41
Engels, Friedrich, *Das Kapital* 29

England
  attribution theory comparison with Sri Lanka 57–8
  Blair's views on education 171
  compulsory education 330
  'an early developer' 119, 120–1
  educational development comparison with Sri Lanka 122
  industrialisation 61, 66, 69, 124
  learning assessment 310
  linking motives for learning with motives for working 112–13
  primary education 120
  SLOG group 61
  students' learning motivation 62, 63, 64, *64*
  trainee teachers 320
  Victorian values 143
English language
  comparisons with elsewhere 285–6
  current policy on teaching methods 279–80
  early twenty-first century teaching of 277–87
  growth in role 241–2
  guidelines on learning time and activities 280
  guidelines vs practice 281
  language of planning 197–8
  lesson activities 283
  as medium of instruction 14, 20–1, 23, 84–5, 125, 143, 145, 147, 247–8
  relegation of 144–5, 235
  skill requirement 250
  subject of study 20, 83, 277, 278
  teaching intensification of 236
  teaching policy past and present 278
  time for learning English: opportunity and loss of opportunity 281–3
  variations in learning outcomes 279
  variations in time spent on student-centred learning 283–5
enrolment
  boys 21, 213
  England 120, 121
  girls 21, 33, 213, 215
  government schools 246
  growth in 24, 86, 131, 227, 233
  low birth rates 246
  NER 33
  university 265
  widespread increases in 219
entry age, raising/reducing school 90, 94, 95
environmental flux 198–201
  civil strife and internal security 198–9
  political flux 199–201
equality of access 98–9
equality of opportunity in education revisited 336–7
equitable distribution of educational opportunities 175–6
error diagnosis 321, *322–5*
errors in learning (assessment) 310, 318–22, 322–5, *322–5*
Escuela Nueva (EN) (New School) programme, Colombia 305–7
Estate Infrastructure and Livestock Development, Ministry of 225–6
ethnicity 97, 162, 168, 224, 265, 269, 344
  conflict 24, 155, 223–4, 262–3, 267–8
  national project and 148–9
Evaluation of Educational Achievement, International Association for the 59, 310
evaluations of implementation (1997 reforms) 174–80
  curriculum renewal, quality and relevance in primary education 178–80
  equitable distribution of educational opportunities 175–6

school restructuring and
	rationalisation 177–8, 181
examination reforms, school
	(1970s) 77–101, 131
	educational change and conflict
		80–3
	increased participation in
		school examinations in
		the post-independence
		period 85–7
	school examinations during the
		British colonial period 83–5
	theoretical perspectives 78–80
	reconsidered 95–100
examination reforms, school (1987)
	131
examinations
	centralised system 78
	Dore on 128
	fees 95
	foreign 69, 83–4, 92–3, 94–5,
		242
	Grade 5 scholarship exam 12, 14,
		157, 179, 181, 304, 344–5
	integrated science 129
	local 83–4
	-oriented teaching 128–30
	pre-vocational studies 92, 93
	public 12, 77, 84, 101, 129, 135
	Senior School Certificate 85
	trial 91
	university entrance 130
		See also General Certificate of
			Education (GCE)
Examinations Department 12, 93,
	245, 345
Examinations Syndicate of the
	University of Cambridge 84
exam-oriented teaching 128–30
exceptionalisms in education 13–15
exceptionalisms revisited 335–42
	concepts and theories 340–2
	education finance 338–9
	equality of opportunity in
		education 336–7
	gender parity 337–8
exclusion from learning zones,
	inclusion in and 292, 293

Executive Committee for Education
	143–4
exogenous conditions, endogenous
	or (educational change and
	conflict) 28, 39, 82, 99
expansion, educational 224–6, 264
exports
	export-led growth 209–29, 234,
		255
	manufactured 259–60
	plantation economy 211–28

factory sector, Indian 106–7
failure, success and 55–6, 56, 60
farmers, education and 106
Federated Malay states 255
'feeder' schools, preparatory 20
fees, school 14, 23, 247
fidelity and adaptation (MGML and
	ML) 295–6
final reflections 347–8
finance
	education finance revisited 338–9
	financial capital 116, 215
	financial support from World
		Bank 260
	'grant-in-aid' system 21, 22, 214
	non-government schools 21
	and policy formulation 172–4, 187
Finance and Planning, Ministry of
	184, 195
Finance Commission 184, 195, 201
Financing Global Education
	Opportunity, International
	Commission on (2016) 311
First Development Decade, UN 79
First World 30
foreign
	aid 223, 234
	employment 238, 246
	exams 69, 83–4, 92–3, 94–5, 242
	exchange 244, 260, 266, 334
	investment 235, 244, 260
	qualifications 244–5, 247
	universities 14, 244
formal education 14, 18–19, 24, 70,
	246
formalism stage (Beeby) 36, 37

INDEX   375

formative assessment
  prospects for 322–5, *322–5*
  vs summative assessment 316–20
  training in for learning 320–2
Foundational Skills, Assessments of *313*
Four Asian Tigers 255, 256, 257, 258, 262, 264
Fourth World 30
France 285, 330
free education 145–6
  access to 131, 134, 144, 328, 341
  Declaration of Human Rights 32
  fee-charging vs 22, 142, 149
  government institutions 14
  remaining in 86
Free Education Act (1945) 28, 158, 217
free trade zones 235, 238
Fuller, W. P. 106–7

Gampaha district 171, 172, 173, 178, 188, 192
garment manufacturing sector 240
gender
  gap 33, 46–7, 125, 237
  parity 13, 46–7
    revisited 337–8
  record on education and 13
  US differences 55–6
General Certificate of Education (GCE) *see* Advanced Level (A level); Ordinary level (O level)
General Certificate of Secondary Education, British (GCSE) 67
General Education Programmes 190, 196
General Education Reforms (1997) 161–82, 185, 280
  policy texts: tensions and resolutions 168–70
General Education Sector Development Plan (2020–5) 308, 342
general education system 11–12, 12, 22, 142
General Treasury 201

Germany 319, 330
Gerschenkron, A. 41, 66
Ghana 40, 61, 107
Gini Index coefficient 159, 233
Gintis, H. 80, 112
girls
  Advanced level examinations 87, 247
  aspirations 250
  compulsory education 141
  enrolment 21, 33, 213, 215
  gender gap 13, 33, 47, 125, 337–8
  Sinhala-Buddhist 243
Global Education Partnership 311
globalisation 45–6
globalisation and education, interface between late twentieth-century 231–2
globalisation, education and skills
  common and uncommon education and training characteristics of successful Asian countries 258–9
  common political and economic characteristics of successful Asian countries 256–8
  comparing Sri Lanka with elsewhere 255–70
  demographic transition 262–4
  education strategies and characteristics 264–6
  Sri Lanka compared 259–61
  technology 261–2
globalisation, late twentieth-century 231–53
  changes in
    education and training provision 240–2
    education policy 235–7
    public and private educational provision 242–4
    skill requirements 238–40
    labour market 237–8
  interface between late twentieth-century globalisation and education 231–2
  internationalisation of education and training 244–5

reintegration and export-led growth post-1977 234
retreat from nineteenth-century globalisation 232–3
socio-economic disparities 246–9
socio-economic transformation 235
youth expectations and social class 249–53
globalisation, retreat from nineteenth-century 232–3
Global North 30
Global Partnership for Education 337
Global South 30
Goonatilake. S. 39
Gordon Estate (Nuwara-Eliya district) 219
government-aided schools 21, 125, 215, 242
government schools 20–2
1950–2021 24–5, 26
English language teaching policy 278
enrolment 12, 156
free education 14, 343
funds 141
growth of 125, 246
vernacular-language instruction 23
government service jobs 83–4, 249–50
Grade 5 scholarship exam 12, 14, 157, 179, 181, 304, 344–5
graduate programmes, government 238, 240
Gramsci, A. 30
Greek language 20
Green, Andy 45, 258
Green, F. 105
Gross National Income 117
Gross National Product (GDP)
call for increase in spending 339
development and education 36
'development' thinking 79
educational spend as a proportion of all 14–15, 41, 158–9, 233, 234, 338

growth rate 262
investment as a percentage of 260–1
non-concessionary debt 334
per capita 44, 66
Seers and 42
US variance 37–8
group or individual interests (educational change and conflict) 81, 98
guidelines, English language teaching 280–1
Gunatilleke, Godfrey 17–18, 24, 43, 124, 143, 148, 158–9
Gunawardene, Chandra 250

Hambantota 18
health improvements 24
Hebrew language 20
Hettige, Siri T. 235, 250
higher education 12, 144–5
Higher National Certificate of Education (HNCE) 77, 89–93, 98
High Performing Asian Economies (HPAEs) 255–6, 257, 260
Hill Country New Villages, Infrastructure and Community Development, Ministry of 226
Hinduism 16, 18, 86, 226
Hindu schools 19, 21, 22
historical practices 99–100, 330
Hong Kong 255, 257, 258, 262, 268
household welfare 116
human capability approach (HCA) 44–5
human capital, and economic growth 36–8
human capital and modernisation (HCM) 79
NAM differences between 80–3
reconsidered 95–100
human capital, education and development 103–18
concept of human capital 103–4
do earnings reflect job performance? 109–10
human capital and its critics 104–6

human capital, education and development (*cont.*)
   human capital theory extensions 114–16
   Is education related to productivity? 106–9
   linking motives for learning with motives for working 112–14
   motivations for education and learning 110–11
   Sri Lankan research within a human capital framework 116–17
Human Capital Index (HCI) 117
human development 13, 44–5, 255
Human Development Index (HDI) 117
Human Development Report (UN, 1990) 44
Human Environment, UN Conference on the (1972) 47

ICT sector 240, 241, 243
illiteracy 70, 170, 212
implementation challenges, ML 303–4
implementation, origins, political will and (education reforms, 1997) 161–82
import substitution industrialisation (ISI) 34, 147, 232–3, 257, 266
Improvement of Schools by Division (ISD) 175
inclusion in and exclusion from learning zones 292, *293*
income inequality 261
independence 18, 124, 142–4, 211, 217, 262, 266
India
   activity-based learning 305
   attribution theory 59
   colonial 262
   economy 17
   education and productivity 106–7
   literacy rates 13
   MGML model 295
   migrate to plantations 213
   NAM and 40
   partition 148
   poverty reduction 42
   repatriation scheme 217
   RIVER-MGML model 295–6, 305–8
   school year 285
   SLOG group 61
   'successful globalisation' 268
   Tamil Nadu 16
   Teaching at the Right Level 305
Indian Residents (Citizenship) Act (1948) 217
Indian Tamils 16, 149, 211, 217, 228
indigenous
   development resources 87–8
   elites 38, 79, 80
   population 15, 83
   schools 20
individual interests, group or (educational change and conflict) 81, 98
Indonesia 16, 40, 255, 256, 258
industrialisation 66–9, 256–8
   agricultural 123, 132, 341
   Ashton & Green on 105
   'developed' 41
   England 61, 66, 69, 120–4
   Japan 66, 120–4, 258
   See also import substitution industrialisation (ISI)
industrialised countries 41, 57, 61, 66–7, 68, 105, 206, 207, 266
inequality, income 261
information and communications technology (ICT) 240, 241, 243, 247, 248, 261–2, 278
Inkeles, A. 58
innumeracy 70
Institute of Development Studies (Sussex) 107
institutions, educational 12
integrated science exam 129
internalised control (trait) 112
internal security, civil strife and 198–9
international assessments *313*

International Development,
    Department for 185, 187
international development ideas,
    education policies and 158–9
International Development Targets
    (1996) 47
International Development, UK
    Department for 279
internationalisation of education
    and training 244–5
International Labour Organization
    (ILO) 42–3, 90, 233, 346
    Employment Mission 126, 260
international legitimacy,
    maintaining 98–9
international literature
    (development and
    education) 27–51
International Monetary Fund (IMF)
    31, 41, 234
international qualifications 135
international schools 12, 242,
    244–5
internships 248–9
investment, and savings rates
    260–1, 266
Iriyagolle, I. M. R. A. 150
Islam 16, 18
Islamic schools 19, 22
Israel 285

Janatha Vimukthi Peramuna
    (People's Liberation Front)
    (JVP) 126, 153, 161, 171
Japan
    compulsory education 330
    economic modernisation 124–5
    educational development
        comparison with Sri Lanka
        122
    HPAE country 256
    industrialisation 66, 124, 258
    'a late developer' 119, 120–1
    loans to Sri Lanka 334
    primary education 32, 121
    SLOG group 61
    students' learning motivation
        62–3, *64*

Jathika Sangamaya (main teachers'
    union) 88
Jayasuriya, J. E. 20, 22, 24, 84, 106,
    142–3, 145
Jayawardena, Kumari, *Class,
    patriarchy and ethnicity on
    Sri Lankan plantations* 209
Jayaweera, S. 147
Job Bank Scheme 157
job performance, earnings and
    109–10
Jobs and Skills Programme for
    Africa (ILO) 43
Johnson, C. 257–8
Joy, Leonard, *Development in a
    divided world* 66
Junior School Certificates 85
junior secondary education 12, 125,
    175, 177

Kalutara district 219
kanganies (plantation labour
    supervisors) 212, 214–15,
    215
Kannangara, Dr C. W. W. 22, 125,
    142, 144, 145, 158
Karma 57, 58–9
Kelegama, S. 260
Kelley, Harold 54, 56–7
Kelly, G. A. 107
Kenya 119, 268
Kerala, India 42
Korea, Republic of 262, 268
Kotalawala, Elsie, *The Year 5
    scholarship examination and
    the implementation of the
    primary school curriculum*
    131
Kumaratunga, Chandrika 163, 164,
    170
Kumaratunge, Vijaya 171
Kurian, Rachel, *Class, patriarchy
    and ethnicity on Sri Lankan
    plantations* 209

labour market changes 237–8
land reforms 257, 261
language courses 241

language mediums 14, 125, 144–6, 226–7, 241, 263, 267, 312, 321
  See also English language
language of planning 197–8
languages, official 23, 146, 148, 197, 263, 265–6, 277
language subjects 19, 20, 84–5
large-scale international and national surveys, large-scale (learning outcomes) 310–12
'late developer' countries 41, 66, 76, 119, 132
'later developer' countries 66, 76, 119, 120–1, 122
Latin America 34, 70, 289
Latin American Laboratory for Assessment of the Quality of Education (LLECE:) *313*, 314
Latin language 19, 20
Lawton, Prof Denis 53, 60, 68
'learning-adjusted years of schooling' measure 115, 117
learning deficits 115
learning, improvement of 310
learning, linking motives for working with motives for 112–14
Learning Metrics Task Force 311
learning motivation 61–3
learning outcomes 273–4, 306–7
  assessment and 309, 320
  enhancing 292
  equality and 337
  Grade 8 students 116
  large-scale international and national surveys of 310–12
  ML and 297, 299–300
  'National Learning Competency Domains' 135
  'quality' 115, 339
  social group disparities 227, 247
  United Nations and 33
  variations in 279, 290
  'years of schooling adjusted for 117
learning time and activities, English language 280

Lee Kwan Yew 11, 255, 258
left-leaning parties 23, 146, 152
legitimation of economic inequality, certification of competency or (educational change and conflict) 81–2
Lenin, Vladimir 38
lesson activities (English language) 283, *284*
lessons and reflections 327–48
  continuity and change 328–9
  exceptionalisms revisited 335–42
  final reflections 347–8
  myriad conditions for and drivers of education reform 329–35
  recent proposed policy reforms 342–5
  reducing the mismatch between education and the economy 346
lessons (developing countries) 70
Lewin, K. M. 129
Liberation Tigers 199
life expectancy 44
'line schools' 212–13, 214–15
Literacy and Numeracy Assessment (LANA) *313*
literacy rates
  adult 24, *26*, 235, 246
  gaps in 214
  gender gap 13
  growth in 125, 170, 219
  historically high performance in 13, 57
  illiteracy 70, 170, 212
  plantations 211–12
  youth 33
Little A.W., *The diploma disease: An argument with pictures* 105
Liverant, S 58
London, University of 84, 85, 92–3, 94
long-term planning (primary education) 189, 190, 193, 198, 200, 201–2

McMahon, W. W. 114–15
madrasa schools 12

Madras, University of 84
Mahajana Eksath Peramuna
 (People's United Front) 23,
 146
mainstream education 'system' 22
Malay language 16
Malaysia
 education of plantation children
  210
 HPAE country 255, 256, 258
 linking motives for learning
  with motives for working
  112–13
 public expenditure on education
  15, 338
 SLOG group 61
 students' learning motivation 63,
  64
Malays, Sri Lanka 16
management courses 241, 243
manpower supply 79, 129, 264
 educated 85–6, 94, 99, 265
Manuel, George 30
manufactured exports 259–60
manufacturing sector 123–4, 132,
 235, 240, 250, 252, 259–60,
 263
Marimuthu, T. 210
maritime trade 17–18, 46, 205–6
marriage 16–17, 86–7
Marxism 38
Marx, Karl, *Das Kapital* 29, 66
Master Plan for Primary Education
 project (MPPE) 183, 185,
 187–9
*Matching employment opportunities
 and expectations* (ILO) 42,
 346
materials, ML teaching and learning
 299
mathematics education research
 318–19
Mazrui, Ali, *Political values and the
 educated class in Africa* 70
meaning stage (Beeby) 36, *37*
measuring returns to education
 learning 'quality' 115
 non-monetary benefits 114–15

research within a human capital
 framework 116–17
specification of time 115
Mexico 41, 61, 107
Mexico, National University of 107
Michela, J. L. 57
Middle East 238, 246
migration 15, 16–17, 211–13, 216,
 235, 238, 245, 289
Millennium Development Goals
 (MDGs) 31, 32–3, 46–7, 226
missionaries 212–13
mission schools 20, 21, 84, 212–14
modalities, ML training 298
modernisation
 beneficent modernisers 82–3, 100
 development as 35
 Dore on 123
 educational development post-
  independence 123–4
 theorists 35, 48–50, 79
modernisation, human capital and
 (HCM) 79
 NAM differences between 80–3
 reconsidered 95–100
modern sector jobs 17, 40, 78, 86,
 87, 93–4, 107, 119, 126
Moeller, A. J. 280
Mohan (1992) 47
Moneragala district 227, 247–8
monks, Buddhist 19
Moore, W. E. 79
Moors, Indian 16
Moors, Sri Lankan 16
Morgan Committee (1867) 21,
 129–30
mortality rate, infant 13
mother-tongue education 14,
 144–5
motivations
 for education and learning
  110–11
 linking learning–working 112–14
 school exam reforms 99
 students' learning motivation
  61–4, *64*, 111
'much later developer' countries 41,
 76, 119

multi-grade and multi-level learning (MGML) 295–6
multi-level teaching in practice, relevance of 294–9
  MGML and ML: fidelity and adaptation 295–6
  need, policies and priorities 295
  and primary curriculum delivery 297
  teacher training 297–8
  teaching and learning materials 299
  training modalities 298
multi-level teaching method (ML) 289–308
  compared with similar programmes elsewhere 305–7
  effectiveness of ML in practice 299–305
  multi-level teaching method (ML) 290–4
  relevance of ML in practice 294–9
  sustainable development 307–8
  zones of exclusion and transitions from child to adult *293*
Munasinghe, Mohan 47, 270
music and drama festivals 195–6
Muslim Religious and Cultural Affairs, Department of 12
Muslim schools 21, 23, 226, 227
Myanmar 15

NALO-NEREC surveys 311–12
Nanayakkara, G. L. S. 321
national assessments of learning outcomes (NALOs) 311–12
National Certificate of General Education (NCGE) 77, 89–93, 98
National Colleges of Education 243–4
national curriculums 57, 68, 184, 292, 308, 315
National Development Plan (1958–68) 40

National Educational Research and Evaluation Centre (NEREC) 174
National Education Commission (NEC) 157–8, 164–5, 194–5
  evaluations of implementation 174, 176, 177–9
  on formative assessment 322
  Grade 5 scholarship exam 344–5
  'National Learning Competency Domains' 135
  policy formulation and implementation 180, 184, 188, 191, 339
  political will and 170
  teaching English 279
  'value-added' skills 346
National Education Goals 343
National Education Policy 156, 164, 185
National Education Policy Framework (2020–2030) 342–3
National Education Research and Evaluation (2017 survey) 117, 147, 156, 161–2
National Education Research and Evaluation Centre (NEREC) 311
national elites (beneficent modernisers or conspiratorial hegemonists) 82–3
National Front 147
National Institute for Labor Studies (Mexico) 107
National Institute of Education (NIE)
  Essential and Desirable Learning Competencies 295, 299–300
  Grade 5 scholarship exam 344–5
  policy implementation 12, 172, 181, 184, 192–3
  Primary English Language Programme 279–80
National Institute of Management (Colombo) 107
nationalisation 24–5, 146, 147, 218, 219, 233, 242, 278, 331

nationalist project
  and ethnicity 148–9
  post-independence 146–7
'National Learning Competency Domains' 135
National Learning Competency Framework 343
national level 165, 185, 190, 194
National Planning Council
  10-year development plan (1959–68) 42, 152, 346
National Planning Division 195
National Policy on Education (1995) 183
National Primary Education Programme 196
national schools *see* 'popular' schools
National Vocational Qualification System 13
Nation, The 129
Nayapane Estate (Kandy district) 219–20
'need for achievement' tests 59
need, policies and priorities, ML 295–6
neo-liberalism, and structural adjustment 41–2
neo-Marxist and dependency (NMD) theory 75, 79, 340
net enrolment ratio (NER) 33
networks, deepening education 193–7
  communicating with multiple stakeholders 195–6
  extending beyond education 195
  listening to the provinces and the teachers 194–5
  multiple roles 196–7
New Zealand 36
Nigeria 43, 59, 61, 63, *64*
Njabili, Dr Agnes 68
non-agricultural occupations 121, 123–4
Non-Aligned Movement (NAM) 30, 40, 51
  HCM differences between 80–3
  reconsidered 95–100

normative consensus 81, 97
norm-based assessment 317
norm or deviation (educational change and conflict) 81
North Atlantic Treaty Organization (NATO) 30, 40
North Eastern Province 198–9
Northern Province 296, 303, 304, 306
North Korea 258
'no schooling' 224, 246
Nuttall, Desmond 69
Nuwara-Eliya district 219, 227, 248

Obeyesekere, Gananath 57, 89
Official Languages Act (1956) 148
oil crisis (1973) 41
open-access nature 14
opportunity in education revisited, equality of 336–7
opportunity/loss of opportunity (teaching English language) 281–3
Ordenes, M. 312
Ordinary level (O level)
  cross-generational shift 251
  employment 126, 235
  English at 278
  enrolment 241
  introduction 85
  papers 91–2
  pass rates 88, 264, 344
  plantation education 222, 224, 227
  qualification escalation 127, 133–4
  reforms 77–8, 88
  reinstated 94–5, 98, 131, 154, 236
  replaced 89, 153
  results as influence 12
  skill requirements 239
  system 67
Organisation for Economic Co-operation and Development (OECD) countries 285, 311, 315

Organisation of Professional Associations of Sri Lanka 12–13
origins, political will and implementation (education reforms, 1997) 161–82
Ormsby-Gore, William 130
Overseas Children's School 242
overseas universities 244

Pacific countries 15, 36
Pacific Islands Literacy and Numeracy Assessments (PILNA) *313*
Paddy Lands Act (1958) 261
Pakistani Residents (Citizenship) Act (1949) 217
Pali language 16
parents
  cross-generational shifts (youth expectations) 251–3
  educational progress and 157, 222
  exam entry fees 95
  and family 156
  interests on education 156–7
  Nayapane Estate (Kandy district) 219
  parental 'interference' 132
  parental pressure 63
  perceptions of ML effectiveness 302–3
  personal effort 86
  plantation community 223
  rural 93
  school choice 106
  as 'significant others' 62, 63–4
  teachers and 55, 284
  value of education 220
parish schools 20, 21
Park Chung Hee 258
Parliamentary Consultative Committee on Education 170
Passeron, J. C. 115
past and present
  building a unified system of education 22–3
  exceptionalisms in education 13–15
  growth in educational opportunity (1950–2021) 24–5
  an island's people 15–17
  maritime trade 17–18
  political and economic changes and crises 23–4
  settler and colonial roots of education 18–22
  today's system of education 11–13
Pathirana, Richard 166–7
patronage, political 150, 151
Peiris, Kamala 166, 179
People's Alliance 175, 224
Perera, Marie 283
Perera, Stirling 236
personality traits 112
physical capital 103–4, 116
physical science courses 86
Piaget's Conservation Task 59
Pieris, M. D. D. 163–4
pirivenas (monastic colleges) 12
planners, education 183–202
Planning and Employment, Ministry of 88
planning-cum-training strategy (PEPP) 189–93
  building on complementarities 192–3
  unanticipated challenges 191–2
planning for 'education for all', technical work of 183–202
  deepening education networks 193–7
  development of national and provincial plans for primary education 185
  environmental flux 198–201
  interface between policy formulation and planning 185–9
  language of planning 197–8
  planning-cum-training strategy 189–93
  who are the planners? 184–5

plantation economy, export-led
  continuing challenges into the
    2020s 227–8
  and educational opportunity
    209–29
  phases of educational progress
    211–26
plantation sector
  no schooling 224
  phases of educational progress
    232
  poverty headcount index 225
  provinces 226
  schools 214–16, 217–18, 225,
    227
  success of 17
  superintendents 220–1, 222
  teachers of plantation community
    origin 222–3
  university education 224
  See also coffee; rubber; tea
Plantation Sector Teachers
  Programme 222–3
Planters' Association 213, 214
planters, prominent 212
policy formulation and planning
  change of government and
    continuation of 164–6
  duplication and competition? 188
  interface between 185–9, 186
  MPPE or PEPP 189
  post-independence 146–50
policy formulation, drivers of 170–4
  drivers and inhibitors of
    policy formulation and
    implementation 180–2
  finance 172–3
  political will 170–2
policy reforms
  anti-colonial and egalitarian
    policy reforms 23, 144–6
  changes in education policy
    235–7
political and economic
  characteristics, common
  (Asian countries) 256–8
political and technical elites 263–4
political crises 23–4, 334–5

political economy of assessment
  315–16
political flux 199–201
political franchise 142, 216, 228
political patronage, and the
  implementation of education
  policy 150, 151
political scientists 35
political unrest
  and education reforms 152–6
  first wave 152–3
  second wave 155
  third wave 155–6
  See also youth insurrection
political will 140, 151
  and implementation, origins
    (education reforms, 1997)
    161–82
politics and the state (demographic
  transition) 262–4
  developmental state 263
  initial political conditions 262–3
  political and technical elites
    263–4
polity and society, global 46
'popular' schools 12, 14, 157, 227,
    343, 344
population 26
Portuguese language 19–20
post-development, and post-colonial
  perspectives 48–50
post-preparatory schools 83
poverty 42–3, 225, 261, 337
practice, English language
  guidelines vs 281
practice, ML teaching in 299–305
  implementation challenges 303–4
  integration into daily teaching
    and learning practices
    300–2, 301
  MGML and ML: fidelity and
    adaptation 295–6
  need, policies and priorities 295
  parent perceptions of 302–3
  and primary curriculum delivery
    297
  relevance of ML in practice 294–9
  system barriers 304–5

practice, ML teaching in (*cont.*)
  teacher training 297–8
  teaching and learning materials 299
  training modalities 298
Prebisch–Singer hypothesis 30
Premadasa, Ranasinghe 163
preparatory schools 20, 83
Presidential Commission on Youth 156, 161, 175
Presidential Task Force (PTF) 166–7
  communicating with multiple stakeholders 195
  policy texts: tensions and resolutions 168
  political will 170
  'popular' schools 344–5
  school restructuring and rationalisation 177, 191, 192
  sub-committees 196
  technical committee 167, 171, 172, 174, 179, 180, 187, 188
Presidential Youth Commission 180
prestigious national schools 14, 157
pre-vocational studies (NCGE exam) 92, 93, 94
primary curriculum delivery, ML and 297
primary education 183–202
  activity learning 236
  Beeby and 36, *37*
  development of national and provincial plans for 185
  English language learning 280, 281–3
  enrolment 120, 292
  expansion 264
  fee-free 145
  Kotalawala study 131–2
  long-term planning (primary education) 189, 190, 193, 198, 200, 201–2
  ML and primary curriculum delivery 297
  MPPE 183, 185
  NER 33
  reforms 178–80, 181, 236
  relegation of English 144
  school numbers 343
  stages of development *37*
  UNESCO and 32
  vernacular as medium of instruction 125
  See also Grade 5 scholarship exam
Primary Education Branch 196
Primary Education Planning Project (PEPP) 191–3, 197–8, 200–1
  extending the network beyond education 195
  Five-Year Plan 189, 197, 198–9
  goal, purpose and activities *186*
  MPPE renamed as 183, 189
  PPTs 190
  steering committee 196
Primary Education Reforms Policy 193, 194
Primary English Learning Programme 284
private institutes/colleges 12, 13
private schools 12, 14, 20, 21, 23, 24, 265
  See also international schools
private sector 247–9, 252–3
  assessment in 108, 316, 340
  education in 12, 14, 242–4, 245, 248
  education levels in 107, 127
  engine of growth 235
  foreign qualifications 245
  growth in 265
  incentives for 232
  investment in 234
  PEPP and 198
  policy texts: tensions and resolutions 168–9
  skill requirements 127, 238–40, 250
  small size 14
private tuition 12, 86, 131, 242–3, 338–9
privatisation 42, 234, 235, 245, 261
productivity, education and 106–9
professional education 12, 99–100, 239, 243

Programme for International Student Assessment for Development (PISA D) *313*
Programme for International Student Assessment (PISA) 311, *313*, 314, 315
Programme for the Analysis of Education Systems (PASEC) *313*, 314
Progress in International Literacy Study (online reading) (ePIRLS) *313*
Progress in International Literacy Study (PIRLS) *313*
Protestantism 19, 20, 21
provincial devolution 155, 161, 166, 174, 194, 201–2
provincial level 12, 160, 180, 184–5, 189, 279, 281, 294, 295, 303–4, 320
provincial planning teams (PPTs) 190–1, 194–5
provision, changes in public and private educational 242–4
Prussia 330
Psacharopoulos, G. 104
psychologists 54, 111
public education 242–4
public examinations 12, 77, 84, 101, 129, 135
public expenditure
   educational spend as a proportion of all 14–15, 41, 158–9, 233, 234, 338
Public Instruction in Sri Lanka, Department of 84
   Committee on Oriental Studies 85
public sector
   access to jobs in 149, 240
   clerk grades 109–10
   courses offered 243
   decline in 245
   inefficient 266, 268
   labour market changes 237
   post-independence 149
   skill requirements 106, 127, 238–40
   socio-economic transformation 235

Public Service Commission 150, 160, 264
public training institutions 13
pupil profiles 67

'qualification escalation' 127–8, 239, 240–2
qualifications, foreign 244–5, 247
quality and relevance in primary education, curriculum renewal 178–80, 236

Radatz, H. 319
Rajapakse, Gotabaya 334
Rajapakse, Mahinda 334
Ranaweera, M. 127–8
rationalisation, school restructuring and 177–8, 181
Ratnapura district 227
Reaganomics 41, 207
Realizing the promise and potential of human capital (World Bank report, 2021) 312
redistribution with growth, BNA and 42–3
reflections, final 347–8
reflections, lessons and 327–48
reform, Myriad conditions for and drivers of education 329–35
   drivers of change in the twenty-first century 332–5
reforms, education (1943–2005) 236–7
reforms, school examination (1972) 87–94, 153–4
   dilution of 96
   growing disillusionment 92–4
   implementation 91–2, 100
   motivation 99
   overturned 95, 236
   precursors and proposals 87–90
reforms, school examination (1977) 94–5, 97, 98–100, 154, 236
regional assessments *313*
Reimagining Education in Sri Lanka (PTF, 2020) 342
reintegration' strategies 234

religion 16, 18–19, 86, 146, 226, 330
remedial teaching 284, 285, 325
remediation plan *324–5*
residential workshops 320–2
restructuring and rationalisation, school 177–8, 181
Rishi Valley Institute for Educational Resources (RIVER) 295–6
RIVER-MGML model 295–6, 305–7
Robeyns, I. 45
roles, multiple (PEPP) 196–7
Roman Catholic schools 19, 20, 21, 23
Rostow, W. W. 35–6
Rotter, J. 58
rubber plantations 16, 17, 148, 149, 209, 211, 232, 243
rural sector
  exams and assessments 227
  integrated development programmes 43
  A levels 225
  multi-level teaching in 289–308
  no schooling 224
  poverty headcount index 225
  private tuition 243
  rural landowners and rural productivity 261
  youth expectations 249
  See also plantation sector
Russia 40, 319, 330
Ryan, R. M. 111

Sabaragamuwa Province 227
Sabates, Ricardo 250
Sanskrit language 16
Sauvy, Alfred 30
savings rates, investment and 260–1, 266
School Curriculum Development Committee, British 68
school year comparisons 285–6
Schultz, Theodore W. 36–7, 103–4, 158
science streams 227–8, 241, 248
Scotland 330

screening theory 104–5, 114, 128
scripts 16
secondary education 90, 129, 144–5, 241, 264
  See also General Certificate of Education (GCE)
Secondary Examinations Council, British 67–8
secondary schools
  enrolment 86
  gender parity 13
  ISD and 175
  junior secondary education 12, 125, 175, 177
  senior secondary education 12, 90, 175, 177, 227
  types 147, 343
  vernacular as medium of instruction 125, 146
  See also examinations
Second World 30
Seeman, M. 58
Seers, Dudley 42, 43,
  Development in a divided world, 66
segregation 168, 235, 265, 267–8
selection systems 67, 99, 146
self-employment 238
self-rule, limited 22
semi-skilled labour 93, 237, 238, 252
Sen, Amartya 44–5
Senanayake, Dudley S. 146, 147, 148
Senior School Certificate Examination 85
senior secondary education 12, 175, 177, 227
service sector 123, 132, 237–8, 240, 245, 250, 252, 263
service suppliers 158
settlers
  early 18–19
  European 19–20
Singapore 11, 255, 257, 258, 259, 262, 265, 268
Singh, Jasbir Sarjit 112–13
Sinhala language 84–5, 197–8
  ethnic segregation and 168
  majority language 14, 23, 143

as medium of instruction 19, 20, 95, 125, 146, 226, 227, 263
plantation schools 218
written form 16
'Sinhala-only' Act 23, 148
Sinhalese-Buddhism 57, 148, 149, 243
Sinhalese people 15–16, 84, 212
  youth insurrection (1971) 24, 41, 88–9, 97, 98, 106, 126, 153, 233
skilled labour 93, 237, 238, 252, 316
  requirements for 127, 238–40, 250
  shortages 239
Sklair, L. 45
slavery 46, 209
Smith, Adam, *An inquiry into the nature and causes of the wealth of nations* 29, 103
Smith, M. 58
social and economic development, concept of 65–6
social capital 115–16
social class 21, 67, 149, 246, 249–53
social disparities, late twentieth-century globalisation, education and 231–53
social group disparities (learning outcomes) 227, 247
social mobility 24, 124–5, 134, 246
social status 20
social stratification 235
socio-economic disparities 246–9
socio-economic transformation 235
sociologists 35, 79
South Africa 44
South Asia 117, 255
South-East Asia 255
Southeast Asia Primary Learning Metrics (SEA-PLM) *313*
Southern and Eastern Africa Consortium for Monitoring Educational Quality (SACMEQ) *313*, 314

South Korea 15, 255, 257, 258, 259, 265, 338
Special Committee on Education 144
special needs 45
special schools 12
Sri Lanka
  economic strategies compared with Asian countries 259–61
  an island's people 15–17
  maritime trade 17–18
  past and present 11–25
  population 15, *26*
Sri Lanka Freedom Party (SLFP) 23, 87, 94, 146, 151, 152, 232, 262–3
Sri Lankan Tamils 16, 211, 217, 224
Sri Pada teacher education college, Kotagala 226
stakeholders
  assessment systems 315
  communicating with multiple 195–6
  education policy (early 1990s) 156–8
  national conferences 193–4
Stallings, J. A. 283
standard of living 18, 255, 261
standard setting, student assessment surveys 313
State Council 142, 143, 145
state sector *see* public sector
statistical characteristics, student assessment surveys 313
Stewart, F. 43
strategies and characteristics, education 264–6
structural adjustment 41–2, 234
student-centred learning 277–8, 280, 281, 283–5, *284*, 286–7
Student Learning Orientations Group (SLOG) 61
students
  assessment surveys 312–14, *313*
  attribution theory 54–61
  cross-generational shifts (youth expectations) 251–3
  definitions of why they learn 61–3

students (*cont.*)
  English comprehensive school 62
  personal effort 86
  self-evaluation 291, 306
  students' learning motivation 111, 112–13, 221
  student-teacher ratios 24, 25, *26*, 191, 246
submission to authority (trait) 112
subsidies 14, 24, 34, 143, 217, 221, 234, 335, 336
success and failure 55–6, *56*, 60, 86
suffrage, universal 13, 22
Sumathipala, K. H. M. 151
summative vs formative assessment 316–20
Sunday Observer 86–7
superior education 18–19
Sussex, University of
  Institute of Development Studies 107
sustainable development 47–8, 270
  EN, RIVER-MGML and ABL programmes 307–8
Sustainable Development Goals (SDGs) 31, 33, 48, 135, 290, 309, 313, 326
sustainable learning and development, assessment for 309–26
  large-scale international/national surveys of learning outcomes 310–12
  prospects for formative assessment 322–5
  purposes of learning assessment 310
  summative vs formative assessment 316–20
  technical challenges of learning assessment 312–14, 315–16
  training in formative assessment for learning 320–2
Swedish International Development Authority 223, 225
system barriers, ML 304–5
system of education, current 11–13

system performance, monitoring of 310

Taiwan 255, 257, 258, 259, 265, 268
Tamil Eelam 24, 155, 161, 199
Tamil language 84–5, 197–8
  discrimination 263
  ethnic segregation and 168
  Indian Moors 16
  as medium of instruction 19, 20, 95, 125, 143, 146, 226, 227
  minority language 14
  plantation schools 218
  'Sinhala-only' Act and 23, 148–9
Tamil Nadu 16
Tamil people 15–16, 24, 84, 223–4
  See also Indian Tamils; Sri Lankan Tamils
Tanzania 66, 67–8, 120
tasks, on–off (English language teaching) 283, *284*
tax revenue 217, 334–5, 339
teacher-assessed exam components 91
teacher-centred learning 179, 277–8, 283–5, *284*, 285, 286–7
teachers
  absences 282, 284
  constraints and 221
  continuous assessment 154–5
  educational progress and 222
  government employees 156–7
  growth in numbers 246
  lesson planning 284
  'master teachers' 173, 181
  ML training 297–8
  morale 179–80
  multi-level teaching method (ML) 289–308
  Muslim 226
  needs 181
  and parents 55
  parents and 55, 284
  planning 184–5
  of plantation community origin 222–3

post grad studies in China 60–1
'punishment transfers' 151
recruitment and education 226
salary 338
school principals 190, 219–20, 297
 in-service training 179, 184, 284, 285, 298, 320–2
 shortage of 176
 stages of development of primary education 37
 students' learning motivation and 113, 114
 student-teacher ratios 24, 25, 26, 191, 246
 trainee 319–20
 training 12, 284
 training modalities 298
 unions 88, 169, 180
 See also English language
teacher training colleges 12, 145, 226, 244
teaching methods, current policy on 279–80
teaching policy past and present, English language 278
tea plantations 16–17, 148–9, 207, 209–11, 213–15, 222, 232, 243
technical colleges 166, 237, 243
technical education and vocational training (TEVT) 237
technical elites, political and 263–4
technical training 12, 13
technical work of planning for 'education for all' 183–202
 deepening education networks 193–7
 development of national and provincial plans for primary education 185
 environmental flux 198–201
 interface between policy formulation and planning 185–9
 language of planning 197–8

planning-cum-training strategy 189–93
 who are the planners? 184–5
technology 236, 261–2
 ICT 240, 241, 243, 247, 248, 261–2, 278
telephones 262
temperament (trait) 112
temple schools, Buddhist 19
tensions and resolutions (1997 reforms) 167–70
10-year development plan (1959–68) 42, 152, 346
terminology (countries/groups of countries) 30–1
tertiary education 12–13
 enrolment 86, 122, 265
 expansion 237, 242, 259, 264
 fee-free 145
 numbers 339
 private 14
 social class discrepancies 246
 task forces 166
Thailand 15, 32, 255, 256, 258, 338
Thatcherism 41, 207
theories revisited, concepts and 340–2
Third World 30, 39
Thondaman, Arumugan 226
Thondaman, Savumiamoorthy 218, 224, 226
time loss, teaching 281–3
trade/craft apprenticeships 241, 243
training provision, changes in education and 240–2
transition from colonial education 141–4
transition stage (Beeby) 36, 37
transition to higher value-added activity (economic strategy) 260
Trends in International Mathematics and Science Study (TIMSS) 117, 313, 314
Trevino, E. 312
trial exams 91
trilingual national schools 344

Trincomalee 17
Trotsky, Leon, *History of the Russian Revolution* 66, 87
tsunami (2004) 332–3

Udagama, Premadasa 151
Uganda 55
unanticipated challenges (training strategy implementation) 191–2
underdevelopment
  definitions 29, 79
  dependency and cultural alienation 38–40
  development and education 38–41
  diploma disease 40–1
unemployment
  educated 86, 119, 126
  education levels and 238
  graduates and 248–9
  National Development Plan 40
  rates 24, 87, 88, 222, 233, 237
  reductions 238
unified system, building a 22–3
unions, labour trade 215, 216, 222, 228
unions, teaching 88, 169, 180
United Front 126, 218
United National Party (UNP)
  in government 94, 146, 150, 154, 157, 224, 233, 234
  opposition 23, 149
  reintroduces GCE level exams 236
United Nations
  country, regional and world goals for education 31–3
  How does development come about? 33
  specialist organisations 27
  Universal Declaration of Human Rights 32, 51
United Nations Children's Fund (UNICEF) 294, 304, 311
United Nations Educational, Scientific and Cultural Organization (UNESCO) 32, 48, 51, 90, 311, 315, 325

United Nations Millennium Summit (2000) 32, 47
United States Agency for International Development (USAID) 311
United States (US)
  Cold War 40
  education and productivity 106
  errors in arithmetic 319
  fostering unity 330
  gender differences 55–6
  GNP variance 37–8
  system performance monitoring 310
Universal Primary Education 31
university education 88–9
  access 23, 129, 130, 227
  admissions criteria 91
  courses offered 241
  enrolment 265
  fee-free 145
  international league tables 135
  international marketplace 71
  numbers 339
  plantation children 224
  private 243
  relegation of English 145
  types 12
  vernacular as medium of instruction 125, 146
University Entrance Examination 130
University Grants Commission 12
unrest, political *see* political unrest
unskilled labour 213, 237, 238, 240
urban sector
  exams and assessments 227
  learning outcomes 246
  A levels 225
  no schooling 224
  poverty headcount index 225
  private tuition 243
Uttar Pradesh, India 106
Uva Province 227, 296, 303–4, 306, 307

Uwezo Annual Learning Assessment (UWEZO) *313*, 314

Vedda people 15
Vernacular School Leaving Certificate 85
vernacular schools 14, 21, 23, 84, 125, 145
Vietnam 15, 338
Vietnam Escuela Nueva Programme (VNEN) 305–7
Vijayapalan, Y. 209
Vijaya, Prince 15
Vithanapathirana, M. 307
vocational training 12, 13, 166, 237, 243

Wales 69, 171, 310
Wallerstein, Immanuel 30
Wang Cheng Xu, Professor 60
Warsaw Pact 30, 40
Weber, M. 58
Weiner, Bernard 54
welfare and basic needs (1931–91) 141–60
  anti-colonial and egalitarian policy reforms 22, 144–6
  constitutional change in the 1970s 150–2
  education policies and international development ideas 158–9
  education policy stakeholders in the early 1990s 156–8
  'national' project and ethnicity 148–9
  political patronage and the implementation of education policy 150
  post-independence: the nationalist project 146–7
  transition from colonial education 141–4
  waves of political unrest and education reforms 152–6
welfare measures 24, 217
West Asia 93
Western Province 247–8

West Indian colonies 20–11
White Papers on Education
  1948 146
  1964 147
  1981 154–5, 171
Wickramasinghe, Ranil 334
women
  employment 238, 240, 246
  equal rights 31
  family abuse/violence 246
  freedom of choice 44–5
  literacy rates 33
  marriage 16–17, 86–7
  success and 56
  suffrage 142
  tea pickers 210, 213
Woodhall, M. 104
working, linking motives for learning with motives for 112–14
World Bank
  creation of knowledge about education, collective 31
  financial support from 181, 191, 234, 256–7, 260, 334
  Four Asian Tigers 258
  General Education Programme 190, 196
  'Human Capital Project' 116
  Learning Metrics Task Force, 311
  lending to 'developing countries' 41, 310
  reports 312, 315–16
  TEVT sector 237
World Conference on Education for All: Meeting basic learning needs (1990) 32, 134–5
World Education Forum (WEF) 32
World Summit on Sustainable Development (2002) 47–8
'world systems' approach (globalisation) 46

Year 5 scholarship examination and the implementation of the primary school curriculum, The (Kotalawala et al) 131–2

youth expectations and social class 249–53
youth insurrection (1971) 24, 41, 88–9, 97, 98, 106, 126, 153, 233

youth insurrection (1987) 156
Yugoslavia 40

zonal level 157, 177, 184, 189, 190

Milton Keynes UK
Ingram Content Group UK Ltd.
UKHW020930051224
452138UK00025B/374